DATE DUE

MY 21 '95			
DE 17 '95			
OC 20 '97			
AP 23 '99			
MY 26 '99			
MY 21 03			

DEMCO 38-296

SPACE
THE NEXT 100 YEARS

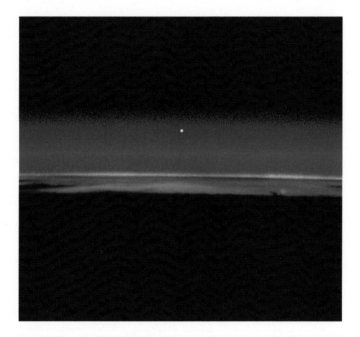

Nicholas Booth

SPACE
THE NEXT 100 YEARS

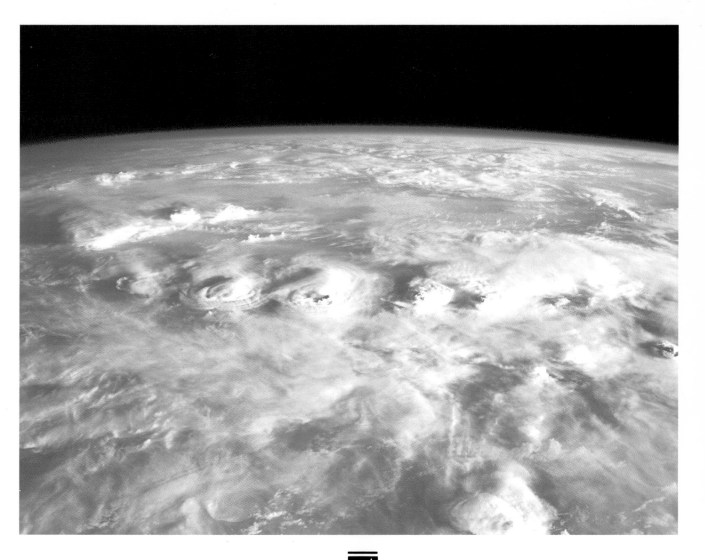

ORION
BOOKS

...ears' consideration, ...of deepfelt gratitude ...bearance, help and advice during the gestation period of this book. In particular, I'd like to thank Robin Rees who "believed" in the project throughout, despite the gnashing of teeth and exasperation that his most recalcitrant author caused him. He was also on hand to provide inspiration, halves of lager at The Coach and Horses and unbridled threats to keep on schedule when entirely appropriate.

Marek Walisiewicz had the unenviable task of turning my *non-sequiturs*, split infinitives and ungrammatical sentences into some semblance of imaginative expression. Similarly, Jacky Palmer turned what could have been a sow's ear into a veritable silk purse of a design. Brigitte Arora also put up with my constant entreaties to "get hold of the picture I saw seven years ago in a German magazine at Schiphol Airport" with the fortitude of a saint. I also owe a great deal of thanks to the others at MB who had to tolerate my constant hectoring and ribald badinage: Ute, Frances, Siân, Iona and Marilyn.

Al and Marka Hibbs in Pasadena have been something of mentors throughout my career. Drawing on his experience at the Jet Propulsion Laboratory, Al has been a source of great advice and amusing anecdotes. My visit to California during the writing of this book would not have been possible without them. I'd also like to thank Robin McKie of the *Observer* and Nigel Williams of the *Guardian* for allowing me to travel to cover space stories. Similarly, Peter Beer (Editor of *Business In Space*) and Frank Miles gave me consistently good advice. Frank, in particular, cured me of a curious affliction to purposefully split infinitives.

And finally, to my friends and flatmates who provided advice and read through nascent manuscripts: Claire D'Albertanson, Andy Bartram, Christine Bödder, Stephanie Brouder, Bea Gonzalez, Alev Hussein, Sabina Pusch, Anita Woodhull and in particular, Meera Chawla. To you all, many, many thanks.

NICHOLAS BOOTH   May 1990.

Space: The Next 100 Years

Published in the United States by Orion Books, a division of Crown Publishers, Inc., 201 East 50th Street, New York, New York 10022.
Member of the Crown Publishing Group

ORION and colophon are trademarks of Crown Publishers, Inc.

Published in Great Britain by Mitchell Beazley International Limited, Artists House, 14-15 Manette Street, London W1V 5LB

Typeset in Garamond by Bookworm Typesetting, Manchester
Printed and bound in Portugal by Printer Portuguesa, Sintra

Library of Congress Cataloging-in-Publication Data

Booth, Nicholas. Space: the next one hundred years/Nicholas Booth –

p. cm.

ISBN 0–517–57764–X

1. Astronautics – Popular works. I. Title. II Title: Space: the next one hundred years.

TL793.8633199090–31246
629.4—dc20CIP

10 9 8 7 6 5 4 3 2 1

First American Edition

Editorial consultants

Dr Peter Muller, University College, London, UK

Dr Gordon Oswald, Cambridge Consultants, Cambridge, UK

Advisors

The publishers wish to thank the following scientists for their generous help in providing information for the project and reading the manuscripts. The views expressed in the book do not necessarily reflect their own opinions.

Dr Alan Bond, Culham Laboratory, Atomic Energy Authority, Culham, UK

Dr Jim Burke, The Planetary Society, Pasadena, USA

Dr William V. Boynton, University of Arizona, Tucson, USA

Dr Jim Garvin, NASA Goddard Space Flight Centre, Washington, D.C., USA

Dr Douglas A. O'Handley, NASA Office of Exploration, Washington, D.C., USA

Dr G.K.C. Pardoe, General Technology Systems Ltd, Uxbridge, UK

Dr R.C. Parkinson, British Aerospace, Stevenage, UK

Dr Charles Pellerin, NASA Headquarters, Washington, D.C., USA

Mr Theo Pirard, Space Information Centre, Pepinster, Belgium

Dr Donna Pivirotto, Jet Propulsion Laboratory, Pasadena, USA

Mr Romano Barbera, ESA Headquarters, Paris, France

Dr Cordula Robinson, University of London Observatory, London, UK

Dr B.G. Taylor, ESA Astrophysics Division, Noordwijk, The Netherlands

Dr John Zarnecki, University of Kent at Canterbury, Canterbury, UK

The affiliations cited above are for identification purposes only.

CONTENTS

INTRODUCTION

We have been privileged to live in one of the most challenging and exciting eras in human history. With the opening of the space frontier more than three decades ago, we have advanced our knowledge of ourselves and of our place in the universe further than in all previous history.

As the 21st century approaches, I believe the opportunity has never been greater for humanity to chart an even more exciting and productive path for the future. We have built a solid foundation to bring the benefits of space to all peoples, not only for the next century, but for centuries to come. Mark Twain said "Predictions are difficult to make, especially when they deal with the future." But if the past is any guide, we have a pretty good idea of how the next few decades in space will evolve.

We have explored space with increasingly sophisticated spacecraft. We have visited the Moon. Our spacecraft have observed at close range all of the planets of our Solar System except Pluto, and have landed on Mars and Venus. Spacecraft have looked out to study the universe and down to benefit life on Earth in ways that our ancestors could never have imagined. With the Space Shuttle, we are advancing our knowledge about how people can live and work safely and productively in space. With space station Freedom, to be operating in the mid-1990s, the United States will build on that knowledge and work to fulfil our long-term goal to expand the human presence beyond Earth orbit into the Solar System.

President Bush embraced this goal on July 20, 1989, the 20th anniversary of the Apollo 11 lunar landing. The president called for a long-term national commitment to human exploration of the Solar System, beginning with the completion of Freedom, which the United States is building with our partners in Europe, Canada and Japan; and continuing with a return to the Moon to stay; to be followed by a manned mission to Mars.

Much work remains to be done before that vision can be realized. I have no doubt, however, that it will be realized, and not by the United States alone, but by the United States working with other nations who share our vision and our goals.

No one can predict the future with confidence. Even so, with the exploration of Mars, I believe our rendezvous with the cosmos will just be beginning. The next century could be half over before the first baby is born at the lunar base. By that time we could be working on expanding our lunar and Mars settlements, beginning to mine the asteroids and starting to think of how best to terraform Mars to make it as habitable as the Earth.

Space has an infinite potential to astonish. Looking back at our achievements in space, it is clear that what has happened has been more exciting than anyone could have predicted.

Looking ahead, we know there is much more to know. That is why our voyages of discovery will continue far longer than we can imagine, and why our most important discoveries will be ones we have not yet dreamed of.

ADMIRAL RICHARD H. TRULY   ADMINISTRATOR, NASA

Space exploration has come of age. More than thirty years have passed since Sputnik 1 ushered in a new era in human affairs. We have long since become accustomed to the sight of astronauts working in space or the latest pictures of a planet never seen in detail before. We take for granted telephone calls to the other side of the globe at the touch of a button and television weather forecasts using images taken only minutes before. Without satellites both would be unthinkable.

The achievements of space exploration are already considerable. Twelve men have walked on the surface of the Moon. All the planets known to the ancients have been explored directly, including landings on Venus and Mars, where probes have revealed eerie, yet aesthetically compelling, landscapes. And there is now a permanent presence of humans in space aboard the Soviet Mir space station. Ours is truly the space age generation.

It is clear that activities in space will become – and indeed are becoming – increasingly diverse. The 1990s, the fourth decade of the space age, promises to see the rise of space exploitation as opposed to exploration or pure research. Within the next decade, permanently manned stations carrying astronauts from all over

the world will become a reality. Robotic probes will be sifting the soils of Mars for signs of life and returning samples from the hearts of comets to see if they contain valuable minerals, reserves of which are rapidly dwindling on Earth.

More and more people will become directly engaged in space activities. Revolutionary reusable launch systems will come into being, making space ever more accessible. During the next century, many human beings will spend their lives away from the Earth, some never to return. A whole new world will come into its own beyond the atmosphere with vast factories in space, bases on the Moon and Mars and eventually flights to the stars.

If these predictions seem fantastic, just think that a generation ago flights to the Moon seemed equally preposterous. The timespan of the twentieth century separates the Wright Brothers' Flyer and a permanently manned space station. What changes will occur during the next century? This important question provides the central theme for this book but may be very difficult to answer correctly. Predicting the future in any field is an exercise fraught with danger. Even the most realistic and erudite predictions have a way of catching up with their authors.

▼ **Laika** on Sputnik 2 in 1957

1957 *"The sky had always been so friendly and brought us beautiful stars and moonlight and comfort; all at once it seemed to have some question marks written all over it. I guess for the first time I started to realize that this country of mine might perhaps not be ahead in everything."*
Lyndon Johnson on Sputnik 1.

1961 *"I saw with my own eyes the spherical shape of the Earth . . . the horizon is unusual and very beautiful. The Sun in space is tens of times brighter than here on Earth. The stars are easily visible, bright and distinct. The entire picture of the firmament has much more contrast than when seen from the Earth."*
Yuri Gagarin's recollections of his flight.

▲ **Yuri Alexeyich Gagarin.**

◀ **Sputnik 1.**

◀ **A NASA mission controller** prays for the deliverance of Friendship 7.

▼ **Valentina Tereshkova,** the first woman in space, 1963.

1963 *"A brilliant star has flared up in the cosmic firmament that outshines all the film stars in the world. Never and in no country did women ever attain such height."*
TASS, on the launch of Valentina Tereshkova.

1957-1959	1960	1961	1962	1963
• 1957 Sputnik 1 launched • 1958 NASA formed • 1959 Lunik 3 views Moon's farside	• First weather satellite, TIROS • First Communications Relay, ECHO	• Gagarin launched • Kennedy unveils Apollo	• John Glenn launched • First Venus fly-by, Mariner 2	• Tereshkova laun

Past predictions have been too optimistic in the short term and overly pessimistic in the long term. It is a common thread in the art of prophecy that major scientific breakthroughs are expected to circumvent particularly thorny problems which threaten mankind's future well-being. History tells us that this seldom happens: nuclear power hasn't brought about "free" energy: computer technology hasn't produced intelligent household robots: nor has interstellar travel taken place with antimatter ramjets. Yet.

Looking back to looking forward

Before contemplating the future in space, we must consider the past. History provides some telling precedents in space exploration. If future activity is to be predicted with any degree of accuracy, then the lessons thus far must be heeded.

The early years of the space age were dominated by the race to the Moon. Space became an arena in which the competing systems of superpower government tried to demonstrate their superiority. Indeed, it all started with a shock: on Saturday, October 5th, 1957, the Western world awoke to staggering news.

A football-sized sphere named Sputnik – the world's first artificial satellite – had been launched. That the Russians had beaten the United States into space was an embarrassment: the fact that Sputnik had been launched by a converted missile was perhaps more worrying. American commentators began talking of a "missile gap" – a perceived imbalance in defence capability – which served to deepen the political Cold War of the late 1950s.

The early success of the Soviet space programme reverberated around the world with the radio transmissions of the Sputnik satellite. As Walter Cronkite remarked, Sputnik's beeps became as much a part of the twentieth century as the whirr of a domestic vacuum cleaner. Within five years, the Soviets had launched the first animal, the first Moon probe and in April 1961, Yuri Gagarin, into space. It was this last event which prompted a dynamic new president to throw down the technological gauntlet. John F. Kennedy had come to power promising to establish American pre-eminence in all things. Space was to be no exception. After Gagarin's flight, he decided to play for double or quits. Addressing a joint session of Congress, Kennedy announced the goal of a manned Moon landing before the decade was over.

1965 *"Please Ed, please get back in!"*
Mission control to Ed White, on performing the first EVA by a US astronaut.

1967 *"How the hell can we get to the Moon if we can't talk between two buildings?"*
Ten minutes before the fatal fire which killed his crew, Gus Grissom loses his temper in a communications test.

◄ **Apollo 1 crew patch**: the crew perished on the pad.

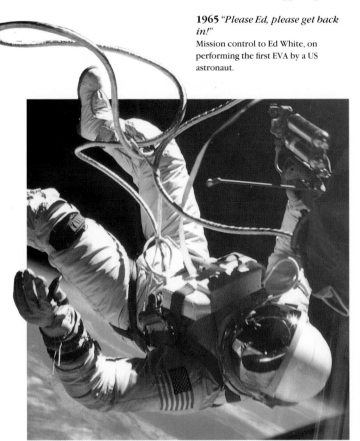

1968 *"From the crew of Apollo 8, we close with goodnight, good luck, a Merry Christmas and God bless all of you – all of you on the good Earth."*
Frank Borman, commander of Apollo 8, concluding a live telecast from lunar orbit on Christmas day.

▼ **The crescent Earth**, as seen from Apollo 8 at Christmas 1968.

1969 *"That may have been a small step for Neil, but it's one hell of a leap for a little guy like me!"*
Pete Conrad, commander of Apollo 12.

▲ **Buzz Aldrin** makes a small step onto the Sea of Tranquility.

▲ **Ed White** spends 21 minutes outside his Gemini 4 capsule in June 1965. "In deference to the President, I didn't step on Texas," he later recalled.

	1965	1966	1967	1968	1969	1970
iner 4, first Mars aunched ee men in orbit, od 1	• Alexei Leonov, first spacewalk • Gemini 6 and 7 rendezvous in orbit	• First successful lunar landing, Luna 9 • Korolev dies	• Apollo 1 fire • Komarov killed, Soyuz 1	• Apollo 8 rounds the Moon	• Apollo 11: One Small Step • Nixon rejects manned Mars Mission	

Twenty years after Neil Armstrong's tentative footsteps in the Sea of Tranquillity, it would be easy to overestimate the certainty and alacrity with which Apollo was executed. In 1961, NASA had neither the technology nor the experience to know whether it would be possible to land a man on the Moon, let alone return him safely. In just eight years, NASA amassed the necessary experience and succeeded in pulling off the greatest organizational feat of this century – winning the race to the Moon.

Political interference

Development of the Soviet space programme was also directed by political expediency. Prime Minister Nikita Khrushchev was astute enough to realize the immense propaganda value of space, but the whim of the Soviet leader was to have serious repercussions on Russia's contribution to the Moon race. Throughout the early 1960s, he demanded of the chief Soviet space official, Sergei Korolev, ever more spectacular "stunts" to amaze the world. Space became Khrushchev's personal fiefdom, the kudos from which was to be reflected in the canny politician's public image.

To add to the mystique, Korolev was referred to as the "Chief Designer", the cloak of anonymity only being removed after his untimely death in 1966. Khrushchev's continual demands interfered with Korolev's work and more or less hounded him into the grave, as he tried to accommodate ever more pointless spectaculars into an otherwise coherent space programme. The best example of this is the launch of Voskhod 1 in October 1964. As NASA was about to launch the two-man Gemini spacecraft, Khrushchev demanded a three-man mission. So Korolev converted the same capsule which had carried Gagarin aloft to take a crew of three. Only by removing emergency equipment and spacesuits could they be accommodated. Whilst Voskhod 1's crew miraculously survived, their patron didn't. Khrushchev was deposed during the flight and banished into isolation.

Korolev's death and the loss of purpose resulting from Khrushchev's interference lost the Soviets the edge in the Moon race. Only now has *glasnost* revealed arguments which raged within the Soviet space administration in the mid-1960s. There was disagreement about which sort of booster was to be used, which cosmonauts were to be assigned to Moon flights and the

1970 *"Houston, we've had a problem!"*
Apollo 13's pilot, Jack Swigert reports an onboard explosion.

▼ **Jack Swigert** (left). Luckily he had written the emergency procedures which saved the Apollo 13 crew after an explosion.

▲ **Apollo 15's Jim Irwin** salutes at the foot of Mt Hadley, July 1971.

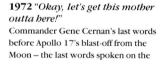

1972 *"Okay, let's get this mother outta here!"*
Commander Gene Cernan's last words before Apollo 17's blast-off from the Moon – the last words spoken on the Moon.

▲ **Apollo 17s Gene Cernan** bids farewell to the Moon.

▶ **Splashdown** for the Apollo 17 capsule.

1970	1971	1972	1973	1974
• Apollo 13 crew survive	• Salyut 1, first orbital space station • Mariner 9, first Mars orbiter	• Apollo 17 draws project to a close • Pioneer 10, first probe to leave Solar System	• Skylab salvaged in orbit • Mariner 10, first Mercury fly-by	• Soviets launch Salyu • Pioneer 11 reaches

sort of missions in which they should participate. Ultimately, the Soviets may have decided in favour of caution, preferring not to risk the lives of their crews.

Backlash

Project Apollo cost the US taxpayer $25 billion and dominated America's space research in the sixties. Other projects, such as the first phase of planetary exploration, rode high on the financial floodwave which accompanied NASA at that time. But by the early 1970s, things had changed: the euphoria generated by the Apollo project was dampened by the harsh realities of a new decade.

One thing which even the most prescient had failed to account for was a "backlash" against space. The war in Vietnam, escalating inflation and civil unrest compounded to reduce the political appeal of ambitious space exploration. If Apollo was a visionary enterprise, that vision certainly was not shared by a general populus increasingly bored by the latest news from the Moon. In turn this boredom was picked up by their political representatives who controlled the financial faucets. Apollo became a mere shadow of what NASA had intended.

Indeed, space as a whole failed to become the self-fulfilling endeavour that many of its protagonists had blithely predicted. Typical of the new attitude was a politician's response to NASA's pleas for securing funds for the unmanned Viking mission to Mars: "I don't care about microbes on Mars so long as I know there are rats in Harlem apartments."

The only large, long-term project which Congress would sanction was the Space Shuttle, touted as a reusable transportation system for the '80s and '90s. Its genesis during the economic recession of the early seventies led Congress to cut the proposed vehicle's budget in half. Trying to build the Shuttle "on the cheap" led to cost overruns as planners tried to reconcile the immutable laws of aerodynamics with ever decreasing funds. Worse still, the Shuttle consumed funds allocated to other projects. Such financial haemorrhages often resulted in their cancellation.

The legacy of the Shuttle's budgetary problems was catastrophically revealed one cold January morning in 1986. Design changes, resulting from decisions taken fifteen years earlier on Capitol Hill, ultimately compromised the vehicle's safety margins. It may be said that *Challenger's* destruction had its origins in the

▼ **After a launch mishap**, one of Skylab's solar panels failed to deploy. Astronauts repaired the station, though its final occupants, Carr and Pogue, grew "revolutionary" beards in protest against increased workloads.

1973 *"You do have a sense of up and down, and you can change it in seconds whenever it's convenient to you. If you go from one deck to the other and you're upside down, you say to your brain: 'I want that way to be up' and your brain says 'OK, then that way is up'. It's strictly eyeballs and brain."*
Dr Joe Kerwin, NASA's first doctor in space, describing orientation aboard Skylab.

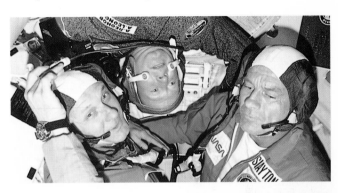

1975 *"Man that was worth waiting sixteen years for!"*
Deke Slayton, getting his first flight aboard Apollo-Soyuz.

▲ **Handshake in space**: Stafford, Leonov (upside down) and Slayton during Apollo-Soyuz.

▼ **Jupiter**, the largest planet, as seen by Voyager 1, March 1979.

1979 *"Our sense of novelty couldn't have been greater had we come across a new solar system."*
Voyager scientist's reaction to exploring Jupiter and its moons.

▲ **The Viking 2 lander** captures an eerie sunrise from the surface of Mars in 1976.

	1976	1977	1978	1979	1980
ollo Soyuz Test Project eras 9 and 10 graph surface of Venus	• Vikings 1 and 2 land on Mars • Luna 24 returns lunar samples	• Voyagers launched • Shuttle flight tests in California	• Pioneer Venus launched • Veneras 11 and 12 reach Venus	• Voyagers reach Jupiter • Pioneer 11 reaches Saturn	

cost-cutting decision to use solid rocket boosters, rather than developing liquid fuelled rockets, to augment the Shuttle's main engines. Like fireworks, they could not be switched off once ignited and many deemed them fundamentally unsafe for manned flight. Originally, NASA had promised "a flight a week" by the mid-1980s, producing calculations which proved that the Shuttle would take the astronomical costs out of astronautics. Those calculations might best be described as over-optimistic: at its peak the Shuttle was managing less than one flight per month.

The Soviet space programme seemed to fare better over the same period. After losing the race to the Moon, the main thrust of the Russian space effort went into developing the Salyut series of space stations, later followed by an improved version called Mir. Largely unnoticed in the West, Soviet cosmonauts learned to live in the strange conditions of zero gravity and make their home in low Earth orbit. By December 1988, two cosmonauts had spent a total of a year in orbit, returning in fine health and talking gamely of tackling a flight to Mars.

To western observers, Soviet space research presented a paradox. Achievements in space were glorified with a national fervour similar to that which acclaims the Bolshoi, yet their exact details were shrouded with that peculiar Soviet secrecy which until recent times made it impossible to obtain street maps of Moscow. In 1985, the changes wrought by Mikhail Gorbachov gave rise to a new space agency – Glavkosmos – which quickly started hawking its wares in the West. The Proton booster, the mainstay of the Russian launch vehicle fleet, was actively being touted to Western customers. In July 1988, the Soviets co-ordinated an international project in which two of the most sophisticated probes ever built were despatched to Mars and its largest moon, Phobos.

Sadly both Phobos probes failed. The newly-elected People's Council of Deputies, acutely aware of the country's ailing economy, looked aghast at space expenditure and promptly lopped 25 percent off the budget. As happened nearly twenty years earlier in the United States, Soviet space officials are now learning to live with economic realities. Like the American Shuttle before it, the Soviet Buran programme has been held back. Test flown unmanned at the end of 1988, its first manned flight has been irrevocably delayed until the early 1990s. And financial

▲ **Voyager 2** encounters Saturn.

▼ **Astronauts** Young (left) and Crippen fly *Columbia* on its maiden voyage, April 1981.

1981 "*Anybody who's not apprehensive about climbing on top of the first-time flight of a liquid-fuelled rocket ship just really doesn't understand the problem!*"
John Young, commander of maiden shuttle flight, recalling the launch.

▼ **In February 1984**, Bruce McCandless became the first human satellite when he tested the Manned Manoeuvring Unit.

▲ **Shuttle launches** were almost mundane events until 1986.

1980	1981	1982	1983	1984
• Voyager 1 reaches Saturn • Space Endurance Record to 184 days (Popov and Ryumin)	• Shuttle flown in Earth orbit • Voyager 2 reaches Saturn	• Colour Pictures from surface of Venus (Venera 13 and 14) • Salyut 7 launched	• Infra Red Astronomical Satellite (IRAS) launched • Pioneer 10 crosses orbit of Pluto	• First human satellite Bruce McCandless • Space Endurance Rec to 237 days (Kizim, Sol and Atkov)

cutbacks have meant that the larger projects have eaten into the budgets of the smaller.

To support their space effort, the Soviets are now planning a number of rouble-generating ruses. Spacesuits and hoardings aboard Mir will carry advertisements from anyone who wants them. Places aboard the craft are being offered like airline seats to anyone who wants to buy them. French and Austrian cosmonauts will fly to Mir in 1992, following in the footsteps of candidates proffered by both the Tokyo Broadcasting System and the British organizers of Project Juno.

Alone in the emptiness
If nothing else, the lesson to be learned thus far is that activities in space depend very much on the political climate of the time. While at the start of the nineties our progress into space appears to be limited by economics, it is economic necessity that will ultimately return space to its former prominence on the political agenda. I believe that the next hundred years will see human expansion into space being recognized as the key to the long-term survival of our species.

In the short-term the greatest motivation for space exploration chimes with perhaps the most pressing concern about our world today: the environment. One of space exploration's most significant accomplishments has been to raise our awareness of the Earth's fragility. It is no coincidence that the worldwide ecology movement gained momentum after the Apollo missions to the Moon in the late 1960s sent back the first flickering images of our planet, poetically described by one Apollo astronaut as "a round and bounded globe that is utterly alone in the emptiness". Nobel laureate Norman Cousins summarized this by remarking that "on the way to the Moon, mankind discovered the Earth".

The future of space exploration will become supremely important to further studies of the environment. Consider three terms which have become part of everyday language: greenhouse effect, ozone hole and global warming. All three owe their genesis to observations from space. The very phrase "greenhouse effect" came from studies of the atmosphere of Venus, a vast broiling envelope resembling Dante's vision of hell. Potentially catastrophic depletion of the ozone layer above Antarctica and the attendant rise in global temperatures were first detected in the

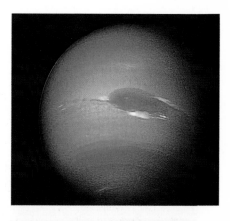

▶ **Neptune:** Voyager 2's final planetary destination, 1989.

▲ **Jean-Loup Chretien** – the first West European spacewalk.

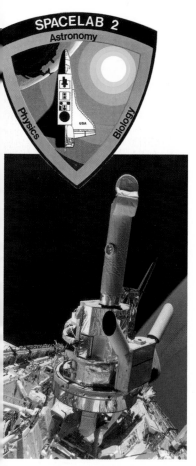

▲ *Challenger's* **destruction** – the human cost of space travel.

◀ **Spacelab 2** – carrying instruments to investigate the Sun – aboard the Shuttle, 1985.

▶ **Crew patch** for Chretien's flight aboard Mir.

▲ **The failed** Soviet Phobos craft.

1989 *"We didn't use stupid computers. It's just that they didn't work very well."*
Alec Galeev, now director of the Soviet Space Research Institute, commenting on press questions about the failure of Phobos 1 and 2.

	1986	1987		1989	1990
…as deploy balloons in …ian atmosphere …ut 7 rescued in orbit	• Voyager 2 reaches Uranus • *Challenger* lost • Mir launched • Probes reach Halley	• Space Endurance Record to 326 days (Yuri Romanenko) • ESA approves Ariane 5, Columbus and Hermes	• Space Endurance Record to 365 days (Munarov and Titov) • Soviet shuttle tested • Phobos probes launched	• Voyager 2 reaches Neptune • Galileo and Magellan launched from Shuttle	

1980s by instruments in space, particularly those aboard NASA's Nimbus 7 satellite. Space agencies the world over have detailed plans to continue and increase such global monitoring through the 1990s.

A question of survival

In the longer term, space exploration will take on a greater urgency. Traditional reasons for venturing into space, such as the early pioneering spirit and ill-conceived political concerns, will be succeeded by a new imperative – survival. If mankind does not extend its presence beyond the shackles of Earth's gravitational field during the next century, then humanity may be doomed forever to the surface of our planet and suffer an untimely decline and demise.

Such notions of "the end of civilization as we know it" have been a recurrent theme in future predictions. Today, of course, we have a veritable panoply of technological tools at our disposal with which to look into the future. Demographers agree that the world's population will probably grow to between eight and ten billion by 2050, a number so large that meeting its energy needs alone would be impossible. But our precise understanding of this demographic "time bomb" depends on the type of predictive model used. The most widely cited are those based on the observations of an eighteenth century English clergyman, Thomas Malthus, who observed that populations tend to grow exponentially while the availability of resources increases only linearly. Various soothsayers over the years have taken his basic premise as the starting point for doom and gloom portraits of the future, none so effectively as the Club of Rome, a group of scientific dignitaries, in the early 1970s.

Using the first numerically powerful computers, the Club of Rome extended the Malthusian model taking into account the interrelationships between population, pollution, food production, industrialization and availability of resources. Their results, published in February 1972 as *The Limits To Growth*, foresaw a depletion of the planet's resources – probably involving an ecological disaster – causing crisis in industry. The resulting reduction in economic prosperity would be accompanied by an inexorably soaring population. Within 100 years, civilization would collapse as standards of living plummeted, and widespread social upheaval caused chaos across the globe.

Many critics of *The Limits To Growth* point out its sloppy methodology and accuse it of irresponsible panic-mongering. Its most obvious deficiency is that it failed to take into account technological advances, mainly because The Club Of Rome was trying to show that limits to development were needed. So a number of researchers rejigged the basic Malthusian model to accommodate new technology which they supposed would eliminate waste more effectively, make agriculture more efficient and so on. Technological advances would increase standards of living and thus lower the birth rate, which could also be held in check by "social engineering". This revised model foresaw a population that would reach an equilibrium level by the middle of the next century.

But would new technology play such a pivotal role? A painful lesson of the closing years of the twentieth century is that technological advance is not a panacea: its environmental side effects are potentially catastrophic. We have seen that ozone depletion, global warming, desertification and pollution of both land and sea are the inevitable conditions of change.

Now or never

Given the pessimism of the predictive models, you could be forgiven for thinking that mankind is doomed. But all the models

◄ *Columbia* in the foreground as *Discovery* lifts Hubble into orbit, April 1990.

1990	1991	1992	1993	1994
• Hubble Space Telescope launched • Ulysses launched	• ERS-1 returns first data • First manned test of Buran	• International Space Year • Ulysses flys by Jupiter	• Infra-Red Space Observatory launched • Mars Observer arrives at Mars	• Soviet Mars '94 orbiter launched • Topex/Poseidon launc

assume that the Earth is a closed system, limited by finite, dwindling resources. Humanity is assumed to spend its life on the Earth, redistributing those resources with increasing futility. Space provides the way out of the dilemma. Solar energy is effectively inexhaustible: raw materials are available in the asteroid belt and on the surfaces of the other planets: toxic and radioactive by-products can be dumped harmlessly in space. By industrializing space, we can open up the closed systems on which predictions of our demise are based

But again economic reality casts its shadow over the optimism offered by space: if mankind does not industrialize space and expand outward within the next century, it may simply be too late. Earth's natural resources will become so depleted that the cost of producing power will be prohibitively high. The vehicles needed to transport human beings into space cannot miraculously be fashioned out of the ether. There will come a time when it will be impossible for mankind to migrate into space. Given current rates of resource depletion, this will happen in the twenty-first century.

If we are to survive, the rationale behind space exploration will have to become "when?" rather than "why?"

Key to the future
In mankind's colonization of space, certain paths of development are more likely than others. Certainly the major breakthroughs will be brought about by simple extensions to existing technology – a fact which is central to the predictions in this book. For example, by modifying the Mir space station, the Soviet Union could establish a tentative base on Mars by the start of the next century. By adapting the main engines and solid rocket boosters of the Space Shuttle, the United States could mass-produce a cost-effective booster capable of lifting heavy payloads into orbit.

By upgrading its Ariane launcher, the European Space Agency plans to launch its own astronauts to NASA's space station on a mini-Shuttle called Hermes, which is already being built.

The key to space is transportation. Nearly all the spacefaring nations are now designing a new generation of spaceplanes and cargo vehicles which will make access into orbit routine. The goal is a cost effective, totally reusable, single-stage-to-orbit vehicle. New engine technology will allow hypersonic planes to use oxygen from the atmosphere, switching to liquid oxygen only at very high altitudes. As a result, less fuel – and a greater cargo payload – will be carried, thus reducing launch costs to a fraction of their present level. Only when this happens will a true revolution in space transportation be possible.

Beyond that, there is literally a universe of possibilities. The future will see human colonization of worlds beyond our own. This has been envisaged by generations of science fiction writers who supposed that once mankind broke free of the shackles of our planet's gravity, "commuting" to space would become commonplace. But long-duration missions have shown that the human body re-adapts poorly to Earth conditions following a lengthy period in space. Yet these problems are not insurmountable because they are only of concern if the travellers return to Earth. Many spacefarers of the future will have little cause – or desire – to return to the planet of their birth.

We stand on the verge of an even greater breakthrough – human evolution in space. This will be as significant a watershed as the development of primordial life on Earth, the migration of lifeforms onto the land, the development of simple tools and communication by the early man, or indeed the opening up of new lands by the sixteenth century explorers.

So long as we endeavour to reach beyond our technological grasp, then our future will be assured.

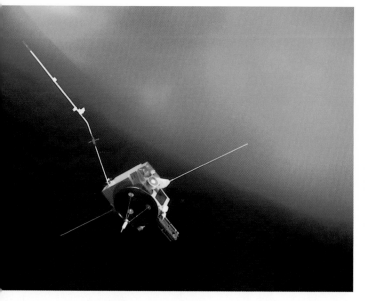

◀ **Ulysses**, like its mythological inspiration, will aim to investigate "the uninhabited world behind the Sun".

▼ **The Hermes spaceplane** will take Europe into the arena of manned spaceflight in the course of the next decade.

	1996	1997	1998	1999	2000
eo reaches Jupiter nd Mir complex ction begins launched	• Cassini launched to Saturn • Hubble instrument replaced • Aster-1 launched	• Galileo mission ends • Main elements of Freedom launched	• Cassini Earth fly-by • First Mars Rovers launched • Freedom: man-tended	• Hermes test flown by astronauts in space • Freedom construction complete	

"When a distinguished, but elderly scientist says that something is possible, he is almost certainly right. When he says it is impossible, he is very probably wrong."

"The only way of finding the limits of the possible is by going beyond them into the impossible."

Arthur C. Clarke's First and Second Laws.

Any book that attempts to predict the future is haunted by the past. Prediction has been one of mankind's most enduring activities, particularly concerning so futuristic an activity as space exploration. Looking over past predictions is healthily reassuring: some were uncannily correct and others right for the wrong reasons. The vast majority were totally and completely wrong.

The earliest known writings on the subject are from second century Greece. These fanciful tales are the charming folklore of space: fleets of swans and demonic spirits were conjured up by their authors to account for space travel. By the 19th century,

"Men might as well project a voyage to the Moon as attempt to employ steam navigation across the stormy North Atlantic Ocean."

Dionysus Lander, address to the British Association, 1838.

however, writers began to put science into the fiction: Jules Verne's *From the Earth to The Moon* (1865) correctly foresaw a three-man trip around the Moon followed by a splashdown landing. In *The First Men in the Moon* (1901), H.G. Wells described a Moon landing by two men propelled into space by "cavorite", a fanciful gravity-insulator.

Konstantin Tsiolkovskii was born in Russia in 1857 – a century before the launch of Sputnik 1. His pioneering work on the theory of rocket propulsion gave him a good vantage point from which to view the distant horizons of astronautics. Amongst his visions were multi-stage rockets, space stations, solar sails and even nuclear-powered interstellar flight. But even Tsiolkovskii did not believe that manned flight into space would occur until 2017.

"That Professor Goddard, with his chair in Clark College and the countenancing of the Smithsonian Institution, does not know the relation of action to reaction, and of the need to have something better than a vacuum against which to react – to say that would be absurd. Of course he only seems to lack the knowledge ladled out daily in high schools."

"A Severe Strain on Credulity", *New York Times* editorial on Robert Goddard, 1920.

"A spaceship would be able to escape from the Earth with a plentiful supply of fuel. The ship would arrive at the outward station with its fuel supply all but gone. But after refuelling, it would be in a position to proceed spacewards with the expenditure of comparatively little fuel."

Theo von Pirquet, *Rockets Through Space – The Dawn of Interplanetary Travel*, 1934.

Early public perceptions of rockets and space travel were shaped by the work of Hermann Oberth, whose book *Rocket into Interplanetary Space* (1923) independently predicted space stations and satellites. In 1928, as a consultant to Fritz Lang on the movie *Frau Im Mond* (Woman In The Moon), he designed the bulbous, aerodynamically streamlined vehicle that became the quintessential "rocket". This design was used by Hergé in the Tintin books and adapted for the cinema serials Flash Gordon and Buck Rogers in the 'thirties.

◄ **H.G. Wells** was a writer of impeccable scientific pedigree. In 1932, Robert Goddard wrote to him that "aiming at the stars is a problem to occupy generations".

▼ In *The Shape Of Things To Come*, Wells envisaged a war to end all wars. The film version of his book starred a curiously-attired Raymond Massey.

▼ In *Frau Im Mond*, director Fritz Lang used a rocket prototype designed by the VFR, the German rocket society.

► **In the 1930s**, space rockets featured in Hergé's Tintin adventures. In July 1989, a scale model of the Tintin rocket was test fired to commemorate the cartoon character's sixtieth anniversary.

The 1950s are considered by many to be the "golden age of science fiction". It became obvious that space travel was imminent and the almost tangible allure of space exploration fuelled considerable speculation. Yet seminal sci-fi movies like *When Worlds Collide* (1951) and *Destination Moon* (1950) owe their existence less to the popularization of space than to the paranoia inspired by McCarthyism and the cold war. Much of the science fiction of the time is clearly political allegory: typically, an extraterrestrial force – read communism – threatens the physical and spiritual well-being of the American people.

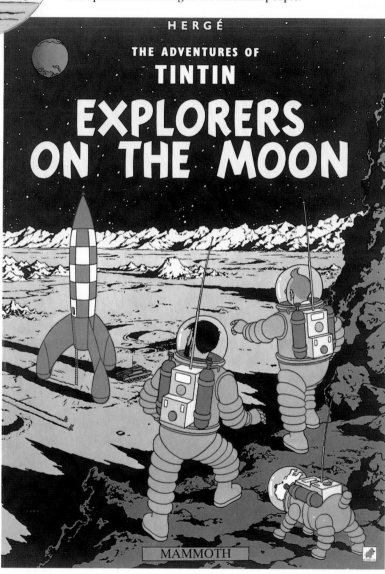

"Rest enough for the individual man. Too much of it and too soon, and we call it death. But for Man no rest and no ending. He must go on . . . at last out across immensity to the stars. And when he has conquered all the deeps of space and all the mysteries of time – still he will be beginning."

H.G. Wells, *The Shape of Things to Come*, 1933.

"There has been a great deal said about a 3,000 miles high-angle rocket. In my opinion such a thing is impossible for many years . . . I say technically that I don't think anyone in the world knows how to do such a thing . . . it will not be done for a very long period of time to come."

Vannevar Bush, Director of the Office of Scientific Research and Development, 1945

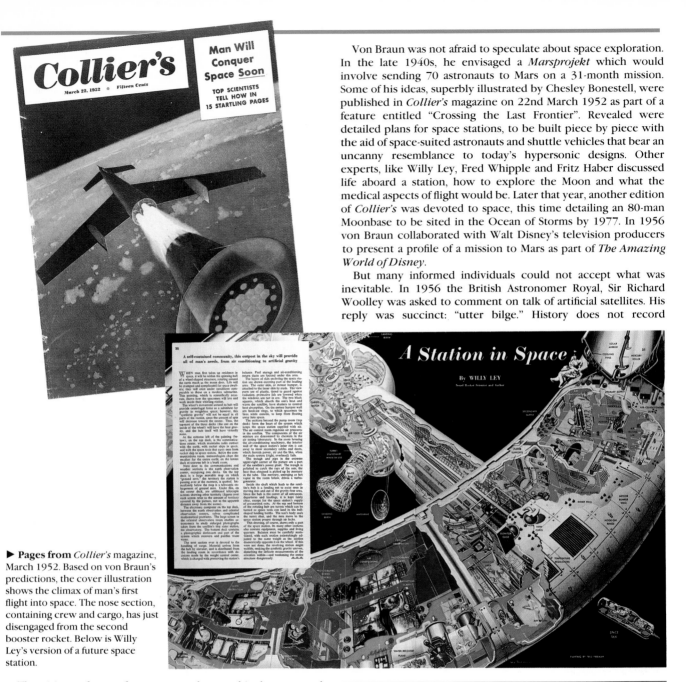

Von Braun was not afraid to speculate about space exploration. In the late 1940s, he envisaged a *Marsprojekt* which would involve sending 70 astronauts to Mars on a 31-month mission. Some of his ideas, superbly illustrated by Chesley Bonestell, were published in *Collier's* magazine on 22nd March 1952 as part of a feature entitled "Crossing the Last Frontier". Revealed were detailed plans for space stations, to be built piece by piece with the aid of space-suited astronauts and shuttle vehicles that bear an uncanny resemblance to today's hypersonic designs. Other experts, like Willy Ley, Fred Whipple and Fritz Haber discussed life aboard a station, how to explore the Moon and what the medical aspects of flight would be. Later that year, another edition of *Collier's* was devoted to space, this time detailing an 80-man Moonbase to be sited in the Ocean of Storms by 1977. In 1956 von Braun collaborated with Walt Disney's television producers to present a profile of a mission to Mars as part of *The Amazing World of Disney*.

But many informed individuals could not accept what was inevitable. In 1956 the British Astronomer Royal, Sir Richard Woolley was asked to comment on talk of artificial satellites. His reply was succinct: "utter bilge." History does not record

A Station in Space

By WILLY LEY

► Pages from *Collier's* magazine, March 1952. Based on von Braun's predictions, the cover illustration shows the climax of man's first flight into space. The nose section, containing crew and cargo, has just disengaged from the second booster rocket. Below is Willy Ley's version of a future space station.

The visions of some forecasters endure to this day: one such man was the *Wunderkind* of German rocketry, Wernher von Braun. His work on liquid fuelled rocket propulsion culminated in the development of the V-2 missile. After the Second World War, von Braun and key members of his team were spirited away by US Army Intelligence to continue their research in the United States. In his adopted country von Braun seamlessly resumed his pre-war career, being appointed Technical Director of the US Army ballistic weapon programme in 1952 and Deputy Associate Administrator of NASA in 1970.

"Our candid opinion is that all talk of going to the Moon, and all talk of signals from the Moon is balderdash – in fact just moonshine."

Daily Mirror editorial, 1948.

"Within the next 10 or 15 years, the Earth will have a new companion in the skies, a man-made satellite that could be either the greatest force for peace ever devised, or one of the most terrible weapons of war – depending on who makes and controls it. Inhabited by humans, and visible from the ground as a fast-moving star, it will sweep around the Earth at an incredible rate of speed in that dark void beyond the atmosphere which is known as 'space'."

Wernher von Braun, *Collier's* magazine, 1952.

Woolley's reaction to the launch of Sputnik 1 the following year.

Another pioneer whose visions have endured the test of time is Arthur C. Clarke. Among his most notable predictions is an accurate description of the communications satellite in the

November 1945 issue of *Practical Wireless*. Clarke wrote science fiction and science fact throughout the fifties, but perhaps his finest work was *Profiles Of The Future*. Published in 1958, the book considered space developments over the next 200 years. He predicted landings on the planets by 1980, interstellar probes by 2025, near-light velocity by 2075 and manned flight to the stars by the close of the 21st century. Clarke also predicted weather control by 2015, human-like robots by 2025 and gravity control by 2050. In 1964, Clarke began work with Stanley Kubrick on what would eventually become *2001: A Space Odyssey*. By the time the movie and the book appeared, fact had overtaken the fiction with Apollo 8's flight around the Moon during Christmas 1968.

"The NASA-supported reviews carried out [all] indicate that space colony construction is technically feasible, and a vigorous program could lead to a functioning space colony, constructing solar power satellites with a value of many billions of dollars each year, well within this century."

G. K. O'Neill, *2081: A Hopeful View of the Human Future, 1981.*

"Was that gigantic leap really heroic or just an act of self-deception? As we ourselves look back on the Moonshot nearly twenty years later, we wonder what it really achieved for the human race? Did it bring us any closer to some ultimate truth or to any greater sense of humanity. In many ways it seems to have been one of the greatest and most baffling dead-ends humanity has ever reached in our long emergence from an unconscious state of nature."

Christopher Booker, *Daily Telegraph*, 1987.

There is never a dearth of exciting new projects, but as astronaut Gus Grissom once remarked, "No Bucks, no Buck Rogers". So, space stations that waltz to the music of Richard Strauss, space factories producing wonder drugs, utopian colonies in space, bases on the planets and travel to the stars remain in the realm of fiction. Yet these very concepts are as valid as ever. If political and public interest is forthcoming, as I believe it will be, then they will become a reality in the 21st century. In space, at least, the old

▲ "Open the pod bay doors HAL." A scene from Kubrick's *2001: A Space Odyssey.*

▲ **Blade Runner**, Ridley Scott's rendering of Philip K. Dick's book *Do Android's Dream of Electric Sheep,* foresaw gravity-free transport across a rain-soaked urban landscape.

As the last chapter showed, the political and economic realities of the early 1970s caught up with prediction. In an early draft of *2001,* Clarke wrote that "Apollo dominated the 1970s like a bloodless war": indeed, NASA had planned at least three landings beyond Apollo 17 which were cancelled by Congress, as was the ambitious Apollo Applications Programme. This would have seen Moonbases established by the late 1970s and flights up to around Apollo 50. In 1971, Clarke acceded that "Apollo was dominated by the 1970s".

Despite the harsh reality of public disinterest, many new ambitious plans for space continued to be proposed. The 1970s saw the concept of self-contained colonies become fashionable, whilst the 1980s saw much interest in Moon and Mars bases.

adage that "today's dreams will become tomorrow's realities" will undoubtedly come into its own.

"President Bush's 'masterplan' for revitalizing America's space hopes, outlined [on the] twentieth anniversary ceremony of Apollo 11's lunar landing has been received with deserved lack of enthusiasm. His plan – to complete the orbiting US space station Freedom, construct a Moon base and then send an expedition to Mars – was high in rhetoric and low in budgetary detail. Many experts had heard it all before."

The Observer editorial, 1989.

ROBOT EXPLORERS

"My thoughts? Today I say to astronomers everywhere have a holiday and celebrate. This is the last holiday you'll have: when Hubble starts working you're going to need all the rest you can get."

Ed Weiler, NASA Hubble Manager, at the launch of STS-31

"We set sail on this new ocean because there is new knowledge to be gained, and new rights to be won, and they must be won and used for the progress of all people."

President Kennedy, addressing Rice University, September 1962

"We shall not cease from exploration and the end of all our exploring will be to arrive where we started and know the place for the first time."

T.S. Eliot, *Four Quarters*

◀ **Into orbit:** With a precision entirely typical of the enterprise, Shuttle *Discovery* lifts off at 8.33.51:0492 EDT on Tuesday, April 24th 1990. Mission commentator George Diller announced the launch of "a new window on the universe" as the Hubble Space Telescope was finally hoisted into space.

It was billed as the most important scientific instrument ever built, as significant a step forward as the invention of the telescope itself. The Hubble Space Telescope – named after Edwin Hubble, the doyen of American astronomy – was finally launched in April 1990 after nearly twenty years of planning and the expenditure of an estimated US$2 billion. But the euphoria surrounding Hubble's launch was soon soured by the detection of a fundamental flaw in its optical system.

Throughout its development period, Hubble was plagued by problems that resulted from its being oversold and underfunded. Indeed the aberration within its optical system remained undetected partly because NASA couldn't afford to test the telescope's two mirrors together. But the most formidable hurdle faced by Hubble was the 1986 *Challenger* accident, after which the launch of the joint NASA-European Space Agency (ESA) project was pushed back into the new decade. Scientists at the Space Telescope Science Institute (STScI) in Baltimore were thankful for the enforced delay as it gave them time to upgrade the telescope's control programs. A network of three communications satellites in low Earth orbit – NASA's Tracking Data Relay Satellite System (TDRSS) – now allows astronomers at STScI to maintain radio contact with Hubble.

In very simple terms, Hubble is suffering from myopia: although the 2.4-metre (8-foot) main mirror and the smaller secondary mirror are optically perfect, they are not correctly aligned, and aberration has therefore crept into the system. In time, astronomers at STScI may learn to compensate for these optical distortions by developing new programming techniques, but the hoped-for tenfold increase in resolution over ground-based telescopes will now not be possible.

Hubble's great asset is its position: 595 kilometres (370 miles) above the Earth, the instrument's gaze is free from the turbulence of our atmosphere and mirror distortions caused by gravity. Perhaps more significantly, those wavelengths – such as the ultraviolet – which are absorbed by our atmosphere will be opened up for study.

Light from the mirror can be focussed on to any of five instruments. There are two imaging cameras, two spectrographs and a photometer. The Wide Field Planetary Camera has a "retina" made up of eight arrays of charge-coupled devices (CCDs) – highly sensitive electronic imaging detectors. The focussing problems mean that the resolution will be only as good as – or slightly better than – the best Earth-based telescopes. ESA's Faint Object Camera (FOC) will also be limited, and will not be capable of detecting distant planets as originally intended.

The FOC and both spectrographs will scan the ultraviolet part of the electromagnetic spectrum: ultraviolet radiation is emitted in many common atomic transitions, so by scrutinizing these wavelengths, astronomers will be able to build up a clearer picture of the chemical composition and physical properties of the universe.

Hubble will be serviced by replenishment flights when space-suited astronauts (shown here) will perform necessary maintenance work such as the routine replacement of the British-built solar arrays. The telescope's optical problems mean that a suitable lens system will be added as soon as possible to correct Hubble's myopia. In 1996, one of the five instruments will be replaced by the Near Infrared Camera and Multi-Object Spectrometer which will extend Hubble's vision beyond the red part of the spectrum. Towards the 21st century, a second generation ultraviolet imaging spectrograph will be installed, further upgrading the telescope's capabilities. The combination of man and machine will ensure that Hubble remains a state-of-the-art observatory well into the twenty-first century.

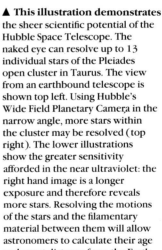

▲ **This illustration demonstrates** the sheer scientific potential of the Hubble Space Telescope. The naked eye can resolve up to 13 individual stars of the Pleiades open cluster in Taurus. The view from an earthbound telescope is shown top left. Using Hubble's Wide Field Planetary Camera in the narrow angle, more stars within the cluster may be resolved (top right). The lower illustrations show the greater sensitivity afforded in the near ultraviolet: the right hand image is a longer exposure and therefore reveals more stars. Resolving the motions of the stars and the filamentary material between them will allow astronomers to calculate their age and exact distance from the Earth.

▶ **Astronauts will be able** to carry out repairs and replace scientific instruments relatively easily *in situ*, since Hubble's modular design allows for the rapid disconnection of cables and supports. Replenishment flights are expected every three years, with major overhauls every five years or so. In an emergency, Hubble could be returned to Earth for more extensive repair.

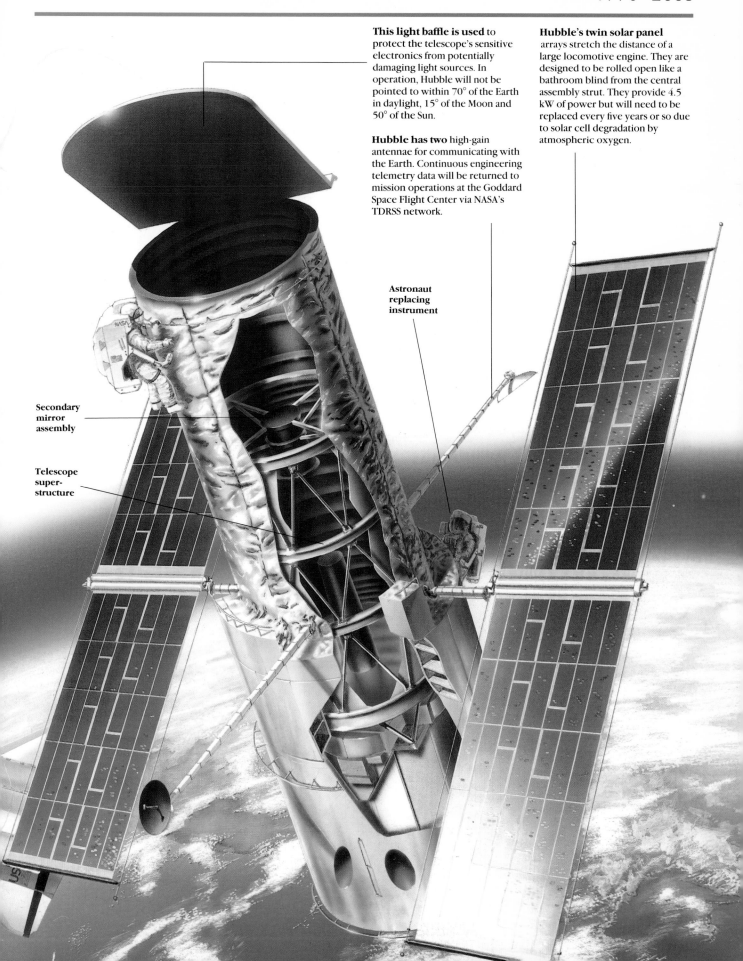

This light baffle is used to protect the telescope's sensitive electronics from potentially damaging light sources. In operation, Hubble will not be pointed to within 70° of the Earth in daylight, 15° of the Moon and 50° of the Sun.

Hubble has two high-gain antennae for communicating with the Earth. Continuous engineering telemetry data will be returned to mission operations at the Goddard Space Flight Center via NASA's TDRSS network.

Hubble's twin solar panel arrays stretch the distance of a large locomotive engine. They are designed to be rolled open like a bathroom blind from the central assembly strut. They provide 4.5 kW of power but will need to be replaced every five years or so due to solar cell degradation by atmospheric oxygen.

Astronaut replacing instrument

Secondary mirror assembly

Telescope super-structure

To astronomers, our atmosphere represents a frustrating barrier to observing the universe. This gaseous envelope stops much of the radiation emitted by objects in space from reaching the ground, allowing through only certain wavelengths – specifically visible light, part of the infra-red and some radio frequencies. From the Earth, our view of the heavens is akin to that from the bottom of the sea – hampered by the vast ocean above.

Astronomy from orbit has been one of the great triumphs of the space age. Instruments aboard satellites have opened up our view of the universe right across the electromagnetic spectrum. Monitoring of the most energetic radiation to be generated by stars and galaxies – gamma and X-rays – has revealed the most cataclysmic processes occurring in the universe. Ultraviolet telescopes have enabled astronomers to investigate the chemical processes at work in stars and planetary atmospheres, while infra-red analysis has revealed interstellar dust and elucidated the mechanisms of star formation. These observations have transformed the universe into a vast laboratory in which scientists strive to reconcile observation with theory. Astronomers sometimes talk of the cosmic zoo to describe the range of new objects and phenomena that have been revealed.

◀ **Virgo A**, a black hole, is depicted in this illustration. To the radio astronomer, it is a bright or "noisy" source in the sky. Greater sensitivity at other wavelengths may reveal unknown details.

▼ **Radiation from space** occurs across the whole electromagnetic spectrum, from radio waves to gamma rays. The optical waveband is a narrow region of the spectrum to which our eyes are sensitive. As shown below, our atmosphere absorbs most of this radiation (dark areas). Even those signals that do get through can be affected by atmospheric phenomena such as the aurora borealis.

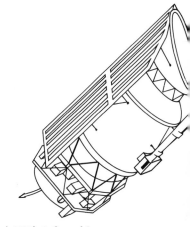

▲ **ESA's Infrared Space Observatory** will give greater resolution in the infra-red (1993).

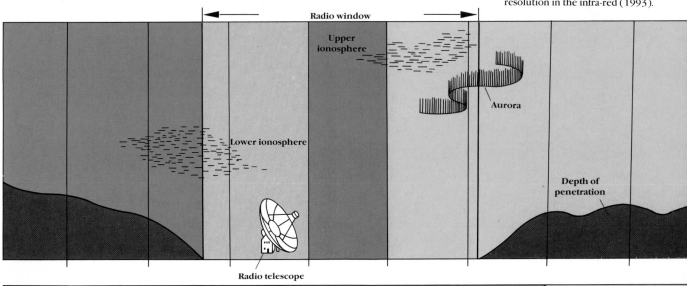

Radio window

Upper ionosphere

Aurora

Lower ionosphere

Depth of penetration

Radio telescope

RADIO WAVELENGTHS

INFRA-RED

During the 1990s, a new generation of orbital observatories will put these strange objects under closer scrutiny. The world's space agencies are planning a number of missions which are ultimately complementary. The main thrust of NASA's research is focussed on what it calls its Great Observatories: four large satellites with multiple functions. The Hubble Space Telescope is the first (see page 22), the Gamma Ray Observatory, scheduled for launch from the Shuttle in November 1990 is the second. The Advanced X-Ray Astrophysics Facility is now under development, while the Space Infra-Red Telescope Facility still awaits congressional approval.

Experience has shown that large projects like Hubble often suffer from budgetary and scheduling problems. The space agencies have incorporated this lesson into a new philosophy: low key missions are planned in parallel with more ambitious projects, in an atmosphere of close international cooperation. During the late 1980s, NASA and ESA considered a joint mission, called Lyman/FUSE (Far Ultraviolet Spectroscopic Explorer), which was a natural follow on from the highly successful International Ultraviolet Explorer. In 1988, ESA decided to pursue the Cassini project instead (see page 46), while NASA

went ahead with its part of the joint project – FUSE. The final spacecraft, however, will retain some features devised by European scientists in the original studies. Similarly, the data returned by ESA's Hipparcos astrometry satellite – which failed to achieve its intended orbit due to the failure of its onboard apogee boost motor – encouraged the Soviets to plan a similar mission called Lomonosov.

Predicting what the new orbiting observatories will reveal, let alone how the synthesis of their data will enable astronomers to redraw our portrait of the universe, is well-nigh impossible. They may yield some evidence of astronomy's holy grail – cold dark matter. This ubiquitous stuff has been postulated to resolve the apparent dilemma that 90 percent of the mass of the universe seems to be missing. Theorists have waxed lyrical on exotic particles like photinos to explain this mathematical discrepancy: observers have suggested brown dwarfs and unexpected concentrations of interstellar gas clouds may hold the key. But what is needed is empirical evidence. It is probably true to say that the facts, when they finally emerge, will bear witness to J.B.S. Haldane's remark: "the universe is not only queerer than we suppose, it is queerer than we can suppose".

▼ **NASA's Extreme Ultraviolet Explorer** will work in the 10-100nm range (1991).

▼ **The Soviet X-ray mission,** Spectrum X, will carry nine advanced instruments (1992).

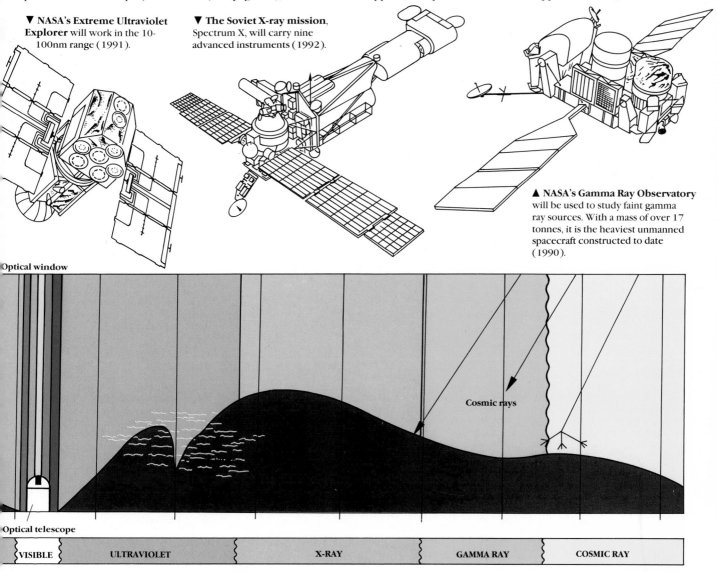

▲ **NASA's Gamma Ray Observatory** will be used to study faint gamma ray sources. With a mass of over 17 tonnes, it is the heaviest unmanned spacecraft constructed to date (1990).

Optical window

Cosmic rays

Optical telescope

| VISIBLE | ULTRAVIOLET | X-RAY | GAMMA RAY | COSMIC RAY |

The 1990s will see the construction of a telescope the size of the Earth. Although the instrument will not be physically as large as our planet, this statement is no exaggeration. Using a powerful technique called Very Long Baseline Interferometry (VLBI), this revolutionary radio telescope will have a working aperture greater than the Earth's diameter.

Radio astronomy was born in 1931, after Karl Jansky accidentally discovered radio signals emitted by the Milky Way. The science matured rapidly, fed by radar technology developed during the Second World War. Since then, ever larger radio dishes, often doubling as satellite tracking stations, have peppered landscapes from Chile to Tasmania. But even the world's largest steerable dish at Effelsburg in Germany, an impressive 100 metres (330 feet) in diameter, can only resolve about one minute of arc – roughly the same as the unaided human eye.

A telescope's resolving power depends on the ratio of the frequency of incident radiation to the aperture of the instrument. So, for a given aperture, the longer the wavelength, the poorer the resolving power. As radio telescopes often pick up wavelengths a million times greater than optical telescopes, the limits to their resolution are immediately apparent.

In recent years, the technique of interferometry has enabled astronomers to see more clearly in the radio part of the spectrum. The hardware needed consists of two or more antennae whose separations are accurately known. Radio waves from an object arrive at different times at each antenna, sometimes in step, sometimes out of step. The information is recorded by both on a magnetic tape on which an accurate time code – generated by a standard atomic clock – is superimposed. When the data received at the two stations are combined, the radio signals interfere with each other, either constructively or destructively. Analysis of the interference patterns across an object reveals detailed information about its structure.

The greater the distance between antennae – or baseline – the better the resolution. By making use of the Earth's rotation, a number of dishes can be used to synthesize a telescope with an aperture equivalent to the extent of the dishes. So, for example, the 27 dishes of the Very Large Array in New Mexico have an aperture equivalent to 27 kilometres (16.7 miles).

Individual dishes and arrays of dishes have been linked across the globe to synthesize telescopes of enormous size. At a frequency of 22 GHz, a global, ground-based VLBI network has a resolution of 0.003 arcseconds – already a hundred times that of the best Earth-bound optical telescopes. VLBI observations from Earth have already led to many discoveries – for example, objects that appear to move faster than the speed of light, plasma jets that extend hundreds of times further than the outer limits of their parent galaxies, and the possibility of "central engines" which power galactic nuclei.

The obvious next step is to extend the baseline into space. This idea was put to the test after the *Challenger* accident when the satellites of the Tracking Data Relay System became available. Although these satellites were not designed for radio astronomy, they performed well in VLBI experiments.

There are three projects in the offing for VLBI from space. The Soviet Union and Japan plan to launch spacecraft carrying movable ten-metre (33-foot) dishes in 1993 and 1995 respectively. The satellite in orbit is only part of the network: VLBI arrays on the ground will observe with the orbiting antenna and telemetry stations will receive the signals from the satellite and relay stable reference frequency signals to it. ESA has proposed a second-generation VLBI mission, known as the International VLBI Satellite (IVS), which will give a tenfold increase in maximum angular resolution over the Japanese and Soviet probes. If suitable collaborators are found, ESA plans to launch IVS somewhere around the turn of the century.

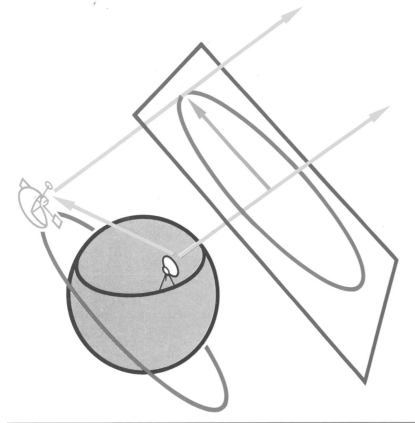

Aperture synthesis in space: By launching radio astronomy satellites into space, it will be possible to increase the effective size of the receiver to the size of the Earth. Known as aperture synthesis or Very Long Baseline Interferometry (VLBI), the technique has already been successfully employed by radio astronomers on the ground. As shown here, the effective aperture of the ground- and satellite-based dishes is the radius of Earth. As the planet rotates and the space-based telescope follows suit – not necessarily at geostationary, but its orbit is well known – they both "sweep" across the sky. It will be possible to perform astrometric measurements at radio weavelengths as resolution will increase beyond the milliarcsecond mark.

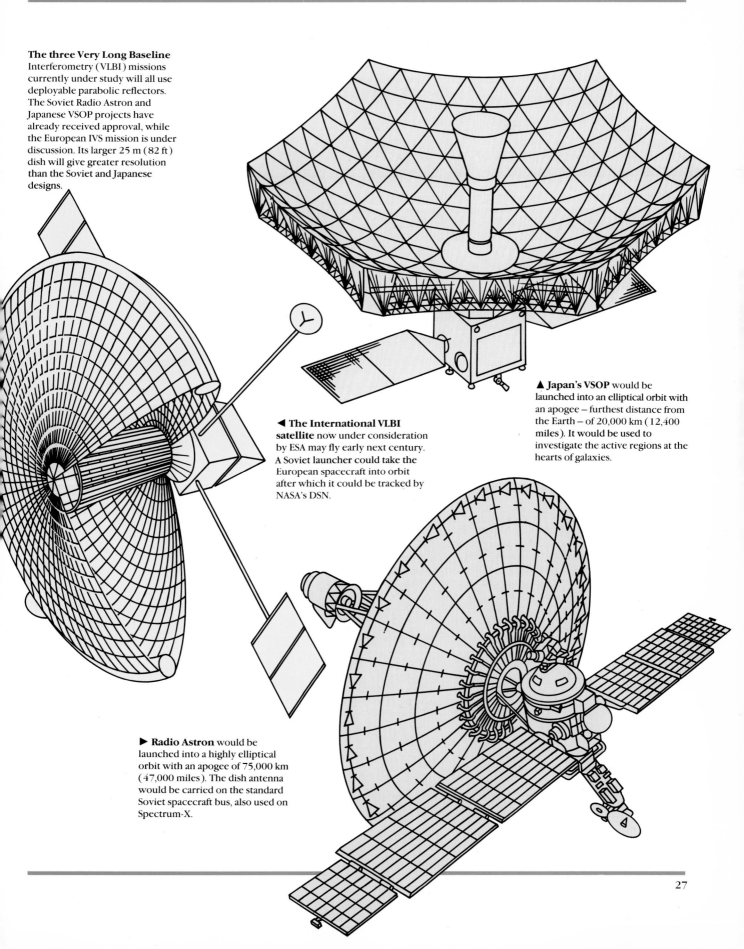

The three Very Long Baseline Interferometry (VLBI) missions currently under study will all use deployable parabolic reflectors. The Soviet Radio Astron and Japanese VSOP projects have already received approval, while the European IVS mission is under discussion. Its larger 25 m (82 ft) dish will give greater resolution than the Soviet and Japanese designs.

◀ **The International VLBI satellite** now under consideration by ESA may fly early next century. A Soviet launcher could take the European spacecraft into orbit after which it could be tracked by NASA's DSN.

▲ **Japan's VSOP** would be launched into an elliptical orbit with an apogee – furthest distance from the Earth – of 20,000 km (12,400 miles). It would be used to investigate the active regions at the hearts of galaxies.

▶ **Radio Astron** would be launched into a highly elliptical orbit with an apogee of 75,000 km (47,000 miles). The dish antenna would be carried on the standard Soviet spacecraft bus, also used on Spectrum-X.

Space exploration has transformed the planets of our solar system from distant blurs on photographic plates into familiar landscapes. In many ways, our own planet was left behind in this process, with earth science missions tending to be small, low key affairs. But today's concern for the environment is likely to make monitoring the Earth from orbit our most significant enterprise in space during the 1990s. Though a shade dramatic for some people, NASA's description of a "Mission to Planet Earth" best encapsulates this new thinking.

One of the first probes to be launched as part of this international initiative is the European Remote Sensing Satellite, ERS-1, the most sophisticated satellite ever built by the European Space Agency. Land, sea and ice will be the objects of its attention. The craft's five sensors include microwave detectors, able to "see" through dense cloud and operate at night. In 1994, ERS-1 will be replaced by a second craft, by which time a joint US/French probe called Topex/Poseidon will be in orbit. Topex/Poseidon is specifically tailored to monitor the oceans: its data and those returned by ERS will make a crucial contribution to the World Ocean Circulation Experiment (see page 30).

More than three-quarters of the Earth's surface is covered by ocean, yet we are largely ignorant of how that vast body of water affects our climate. It is known that oceans play a fundamental role in modifying climatic patterns: without the Gulf Stream, Iceland would be too cold for habitation. But the exact mechanisms of how solar energy affects ocean currents, which in turn exchange heat with the atmosphere and ultimately drive weather patterns, remain enigmatic. More heat is exchanged between the upper millimetres of the ocean and the atmosphere than is exchanged within the whole of our atmosphere itself. Studies of ocean dynamics have obvious applications: for example, it has been established that hurricanes form in tropical waters when the sea surface temperature rises above 26°C (79°F). Monitoring from space will allow more accurate predictions to be made and more expedient countermeasures to be taken.

Ice has a fundamental influence over climate. Ten percent of the Earth's surface is covered by an ice blanket which limits the exchange of heat between atmosphere and ocean. Quite suddenly, cracks the size of small countries can appear in the ice which suddenly alter the thermal balance and dramatically change weather patterns, ultimately affecting global circulation patterns. The long polar nights (in both hemispheres) have impeded our monitoring of these changes. ERS instruments will be able to measure the extent and age of polar ice sheets and determine whether ice cover is increasing or decreasing. Melting sea ice causes the sea level to rise, while increased cover leads to global cooling. Both are potentially catastrophic.

Radar measurements of winds and waves will also be invaluable to our understanding of climate. The wind can literally cause the sea to well up: if freak weather conditions and high tides coincide, then storm surges result. In the past they have often flooded coastal towns and devastated the low countries' sea defences. Satellites like ERS-1 will help to predict the onset of such storms.

In the late 1990s, the polar platforms (see page 74) of the international space station, Freedom, will continue the work of ERS-1 and Topex/Poseidon. NASA has allocated over US$15 billion for its Mission to Planet Earth programme, which includes funding for the various observation platforms. With this enormous injection of resources, it is hoped that by the turn of the century, scientists will have amassed all the pieces of the important jigsaw that is the Earth's climate. And with the advances in numerical modelling made possible by the advent of supercomputers, we should be able to assemble them into a coherent picture.

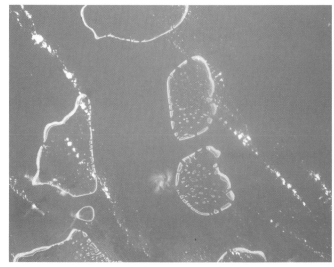

▼ **Pacific Atolls**, naturally occurring barriers of coral, were photographed by Skylab astronauts in 1973. However, visual images are limited in the information they carry: repeated measurements in the infrared and microwave regions of the spectrum are needed to monitor the "healthiness" of the planet.

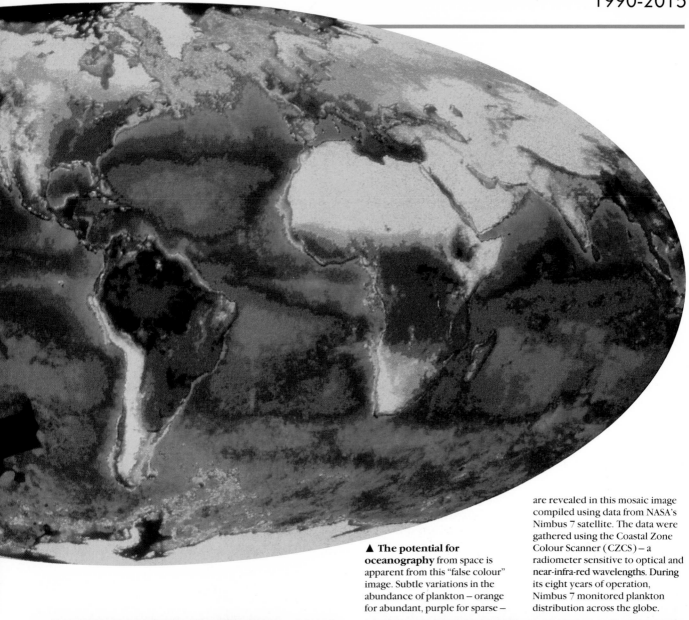

▲ The potential for oceanography from space is apparent from this "false colour" image. Subtle variations in the abundance of plankton – orange for abundant, purple for sparse – are revealed in this mosaic image compiled using data from NASA's Nimbus 7 satellite. The data were gathered using the Coastal Zone Colour Scanner (CZCS) – a radiometer sensitive to optical and near-infra-red wavelengths. During its eight years of operation, Nimbus 7 monitored plankton distribution across the globe.

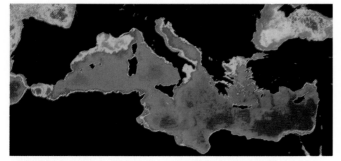

▲ The Mediterranean as seen by the CZCS instruments. Because marine food chains ultimately depend on plankton, these data are invaluable to fishermen as well as academics. Similarly, ERS-1 data will be distributed throughout the world for a nominal access fee.

▶ The Amazon basin as photographed from the Shuttle *Discovery* in 1988. The "milky haziness" is caused by the deliberate burning of trees. Only fifteen years earlier, this area appeared crystal clear when viewed from space.

Changes in the face of our planet cannot be detected at a glance. Repetitive observations over as broad an area as possible are needed to track dynamic environmental processes through time and space: the European Remote Sensing Satellite (ERS-1) will perform precisely these tasks.

The probe is planned to lift off from French Guiana atop an Ariane 4 launcher early in 1991. In its near-polar orbit, inclined at 82° to the equator, ERS-1 will cross roughly the same part of the globe every three days and repeat its measurements over exactly the same areas every 35 days. To achieve this three-day "repeat cycle", ERS-1 will orbit at an altitude of 780 kilometres (480 miles), though height and thus cycle length can be altered as scientific requirements dictate. The orbit is Sun-synchronous which means that whenever it crosses a particular point on the Earth, the Sun will be in the same position in the sky as at the time of the previous pass: so objects on the ground will be "lit" consistently, enabling changes to be monitored.

The spacecraft "bus" is based on an existing design – the French SPOT remote sensing satellite – but the difference is that ERS-1 carries microwave rather than optical imaging devices. The use of these five sensitive and sophisticated instruments is expected to revolutionize the earth sciences.

A ten-metre (33-foot) antenna – part of the satellite's Active Microwave Instrument (AMI) will direct a radar beam downwards onto the Earth's surface, cutting a swath 100 kilometres (62 miles) wide. The reflected signals will be synthesized into high resolution images, enabling subtle changes in vegetation, crops and forestry to be monitored. The AMI will also be used to track wave and wind motions over the oceans, providing vital information for managers of oil rigs and ships' navigation officers, as well as entirely new data for climatologists.

The AMI produces 100 million bits of information per second. Such a large volume of data cannot be stored on the spacecraft and must be relayed to Earth in real time. Use of the AMI will therefore be restricted to parts of the ERS orbit within "sight" of the mission's receiving stations. ESA's prime receiving station is Kiruna in Sweden, which sees ERS-1 on 9 out of 14 of its daily orbits. Other stations are located in Italy, Canada, the Canary Islands, Alaska and the Antarctic.

ERS-1 will carry a radar altimeter which, by measuring the time taken for a microwave pulse to bounce back from the Earth, will produce a surface sea map accurate to within ten centimetres (four inches). As the sea surface mimics the shape of the underlying land, the altimeter will reveal the structure of the seabed. The probe's Along-Track Scanning Radiometer (ATSR) will monitor the sea-surface and cloud-top temperature down to 0.25°C (0.45°F), allowing accurate computation of heat transfer between the oceans and the atmosphere.

The precision with which ERS-1 is capable of monitoring our planet would be wasted without very accurate geographical reference – that means we must know exactly where the satellite is in its orbit at any given time. The Precise Range and Range Rate Equipment (PRARE) and Laser Retro Reflector (LRR) will perform this crucial function. Over time, the ranging data will enable the true shape of the Earth – the so-called geoid – to be determined. This "reference-shape" is far more fundamental than the arbitrary height assigned to "mean sea level".

As the probe's instruments begin to degrade, ESA's Earth monitoring programme will be continued by a new satellite, ERS-2, to be launched in 1994. ERS-2 will be built as the first data from ERS-1 are being returned, so it will benefit from improvements in design and instrumentation. The second craft may carry an advanced ATSR, capable of even more accurate temperature measurement and assessment of vegetational change, as well as a spectrometer which will be used to map ozone abundances across the globe.

▶ **The world below the oceans** is perhaps more staggering than the features above it. Satellite techniques have revolutionized the science of bathymetry – measuring the shape and structure of the ocean floor. This mosaic image maps the relief of the ocean bed. Blue indicates deep areas while yellow indicates shallows. The mid-atlantic ridge (1) rises to within 2,000 m (6,600 feet) of the ocean surface. Deep ocean trenches (2,3), 10,000 m (33,000 feet) lower than the surrounding sea bed, can be seen in the Pacific basin. As these features were caused by the motion of tectonic plates, a greater knowledge of their structure and how they change over time will enable geologists to build up a better picture of how the ocean floor affects the geology of land masses. Advanced altimeters carried on satellites like ERS-1 and Topex/Poseidon will greatly increase the accuracy of bathymetric maps, allowing variations in sea level caused by global tides and ocean currents to be monitored.

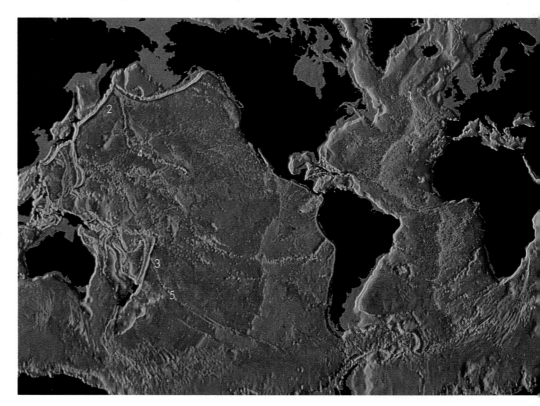

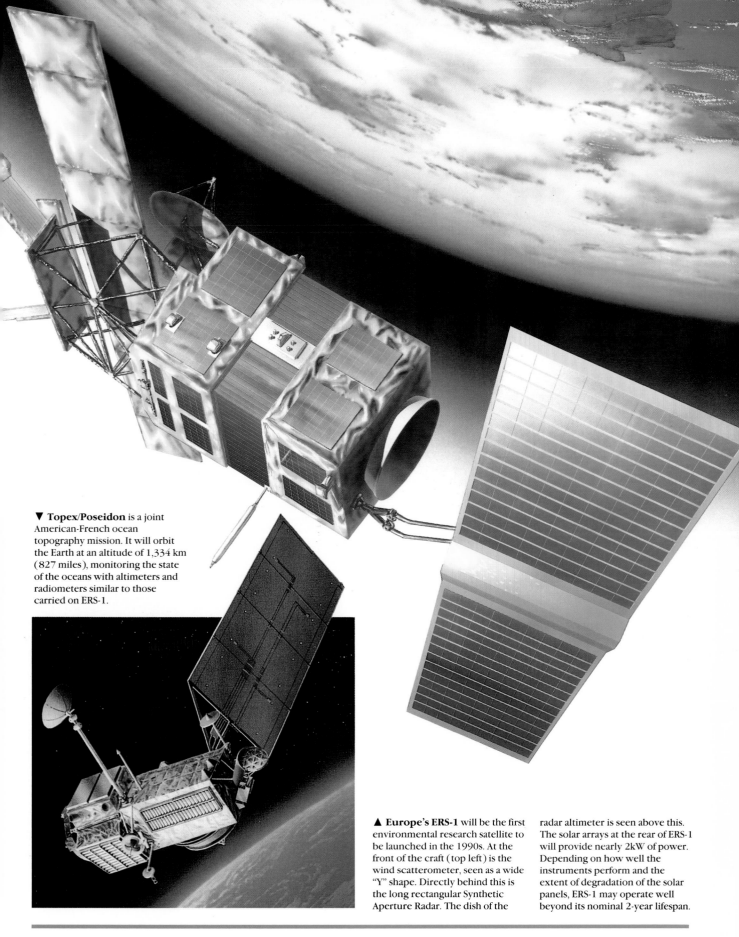

▼ **Topex/Poseidon** is a joint American-French ocean topography mission. It will orbit the Earth at an altitude of 1,334 km (827 miles), monitoring the state of the oceans with altimeters and radiometers similar to those carried on ERS-1.

▲ **Europe's ERS-1** will be the first environmental research satellite to be launched in the 1990s. At the front of the craft (top left) is the wind scatterometer, seen as a wide "Y" shape. Directly behind this is the long rectangular Synthetic Aperture Radar. The dish of the radar altimeter is seen above this. The solar arrays at the rear of ERS-1 will provide nearly 2kW of power. Depending on how well the instruments perform and the extent of degradation of the solar panels, ERS-1 may operate well beyond its nominal 2-year lifespan.

31

Throughout history, Venus has been surrounded by folklore, reflecting both its prominence – it is the brightest planet in the sky – and its veiled mystery. To the ancients it represented the goddess of beauty, so pleasing was its appearance in the twilight sky. Science fiction writers saw the planet's cloud-enshrouded surface populated by dinosaurs in swamp-like vegetation. To today's space scientists, Venus represents a missing link in our knowledge of planetary evolution and offers important information on what can result from a runaway greenhouse effect.

Of the inner planets, Venus has come under the most detailed scrutiny: more than 20 space probes have been sent there, showing the planet's atmospheric composition and surface conditions to be quite different from their terrestrial equivalents. Because Earth and Venus have roughly the same dimensions and density, they have been described as sisters. Perhaps step-sisters is more appropriate: on Venus a dense, acidic cloud deck extends from 25 to 70 kilometres (15 to 44 miles) above the surface, virtually blotting out the Sun. Beneath this is a suffocating carbon dioxide atmosphere which exerts a surface pressure 90 times that on Earth and maintains temperatures of up to 470°C (880°F). Venus has no magnetic field, despite its apparently substantial nickel-iron core. This is due to the planet's sluggish rotation: it takes 243 Earth days to complete one revolution, and this in retrograde motion – the "wrong" way round compared to the other planets.

To the naked eye, Venus appears bland: but in the ultraviolet, some features become apparent such as a gigantic dark "Y"-shaped cloud pattern. The planet's mask of cloud can effectively be penetrated using radar: this was first carried out from Earth in the 1950s and from space in the early 1980s by NASA's Pioneer Venus Orbiter. These studies revealed a landscape of mountains, plains and valleys far more dramatic than on Earth. Many of the mountains are believed to be volcanic in origin, as Venus once had – and may still have – sufficient internal energy to generate geological features. The largest are the Maxwell Montes, which rise six kilometres (3.7 miles) above the surface of Ishtar Terra – an elevated "continent" the size of Australia – and 11 kilometres (6.8 miles) above the nearby plains.

Some of the volcanoes may still be active. Soviet landers recorded much radio noise that could have been generated by volcanic discharge. Similarly, Pioneer Venus measurements of radio discharges seemed to occur over volcanic regions.

Current maps of Venus are on a scale similar to a school atlas of the Earth, though Pioneer Venus and Venera probes made more detailed observations in certain areas. Geologists believe that Venus does not display Earth-style plate tectonics, but that its crust has been broken up into distinct regions by internal activity such as volcanism. The Magellan spacecraft, which arrived at Venus in August 1990, will usher in a tenfold increase in the resolution of its geological features. The mission will spend at least one year using its large radar dish antenna to produce a global landform map showing height variations as small as 30 metres (98 feet). The Magellan synthetic aperture radar system can also be used as a radiometer to observe thermal emissions from the planet's surface and thus enable scientists to determine its density and texture.

Venus and Earth evolved from roughly the same part of the nebula which surrounded the nascent Sun 4.7 billion years ago. They probably formed with roughly the same inventory of materials, and indeed there is evidence that Venus was once covered by expanses of water. Magellan's radar may even reveal the ancient shorelines of long-evaporated oceans. By finding out what happened to the oceans on Venus, we may be able to prevent a similar catastrophe on Earth.

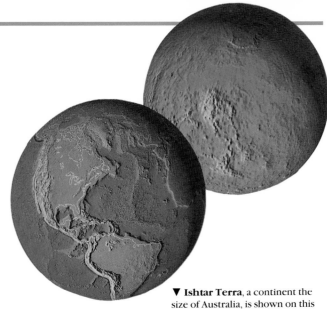

▲ **Strange siblings**. Computer-generated topographic maps of Venus and Earth show that our knowledge of our sister planet's surface is vague. Magellan's high resolution images should answer many questions.

▼ **Ishtar Terra**, a continent the size of Australia, is shown on this computer-generated map. The ridge on the right-hand side is the Maxwell Montes – over a mile higher than Mount Everest. To their left is a high plateau called Lakshmi. The obvious depressions are believed to be collapsed volcanic craters.

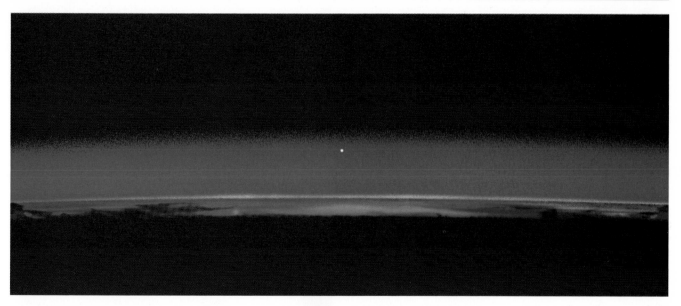

◄ **On Shuttle mission STS-30**, Magellan was successfully deployed from the payload bay of *Atlantis*. The Inertial Upper Stage booster was successfully fired a few days later to send Magellan on its 15-month journey to Venus. Magellan's main antenna, seen at the top of the picture is a "spare" from the Voyager project.

Similarly, the spacecraft's ten-sided electronics bus was originally developed for the Galileo craft.

▲ **Appearing above the Earth's atmosphere**, Venus was photographed by the crew of Space Shuttle *Atlantis* a few days after Magellan's departure.

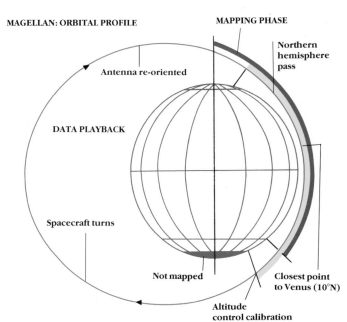

MAGELLAN: ORBITAL PROFILE

MAPPING PHASE

Northern hemisphere pass

Antenna re-oriented

DATA PLAYBACK

Spacecraft turns

Not mapped

Closest point to Venus (10°N)

Altitude control calibration

▲ **Magellan's elliptical orbit** will be divided into distinct phases. When the spacecraft is closest to Venus, the antenna will point at the planet and the radar will map the surface. After radar operations are completed, the spacecraft will turn to point its antenna toward Earth so that data can be transmitted. After calibration of the spacecraft's attitude control subsystem and another data playback, Magellan will turn its attention once again to the surface.

We take the Sun for granted. Yet without our daytime star, we would literally be powerless: it is the generator upon which all biological processes on Earth ultimately depend. Despite its proximity, we are wholly ignorant of many aspects of the Sun, paradoxically, because we have a limited view of it. Most observations have been made within plus or minus ten degrees of the ecliptic plane – the plane in which the planets orbit the star. It's been likened to making a weather forecast with readings only available from the Earth's equator. Space missions for the 1990s will help extend and refine this incomplete picture and will include the first ever views of the Sun's poles.

The Sun's influence permeates the whole of the Solar System – a region known as the heliosphere, which extends as far as a hundred times the distance from the Earth to the Sun. That influence takes the form of the solar wind, the vast stream of electrons, protons, heavier ions and nuclei which are constantly radiated from the Sun's upper atmosphere. This exotic cocktail of high-energy particles, superhot ions and magnetic fields has been described as "the greatest astrophysical laboratory in the universe". These particles travel at speeds of between 200 and 900 kilometres per second (125 to 560 miles per second), such that the faster ones overtake the slower, resulting in collisions which generate distinct waves in the plasma. Reaching the Earth's magnetic field, the particles decelerate to subsonic speeds and become trapped in belts first detected by James van Allen. Solar flares are "gusts" in the solar wind during which particles stream out from the Sun and slam into the Earth's magnetosphere. The auroral displays which result can be accompanied by the shorting out of satellite electronics and corrosive cracks induced in Alaskan oil pipelines.

Modern instruments permit the observation of the Sun's three outermost layers – the photosphere, chromosphere and corona. But further in toward the core, the greater opacity of the Sun's constituent gases hinders any real examination. And though the heliosphere has been studied out beyond Pluto (by Pioneer 10), we need more information on its small-scale structure near to the Sun and the turbulent events within it. Part of the problem is that our view of the solar wind is complicated by our position. In the ecliptic plane, the Sun's extensive magnetic field causes the solar wind to co-rotate, so the particles are emitted spirally, like water from a garden sprinkler. The electrically conducting wind traps the Sun's magnetic field, forcing the field lines into a similarly-spiralling pattern.

The joint NASA/ESA Ulysses mission (see page 36), scheduled for launch in October 1990, will give us our first views of the Sun from above and below its poles. It is expected that the flow of the solar wind will be simpler there and measurements at higher latitudes will reveal more about the Sun's internal structure. For example, holes in the corona, the outermost atmosphere of the Sun, result in surges of particles flowing along open magnetic field lines which stretch out into space. Holes at higher latitudes, seen as dark patches in X-ray and ultraviolet images, may be easier to observe away from the complicated and turbulent magnetic regions in the ecliptic.

At around the same time, the Sun's properties will be investigated by a flotilla of spacecraft forming part of an international scientific programme called the Solar Terrestrial Science Programme. A number of small craft will chart the interaction between the solar wind and the Earth's magnetosphere in far greater detail than previously possible. The Solar and Heliospheric Observatory (SOHO) will also be stationed outside the Earth's magnetosphere at a Lagrangian point – a stable orbit between the Earth and the Sun – from where it will monitor the violent processes that occur in the Sun's atmosphere.

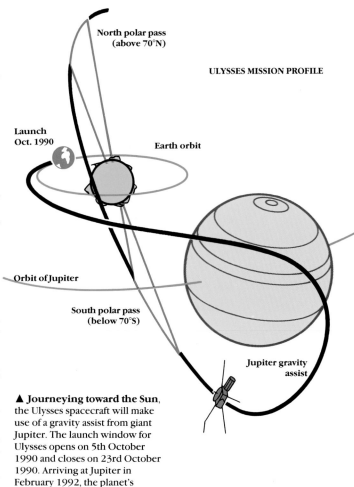

ULYSSES MISSION PROFILE

North polar pass
(above 70°N)

Launch
Oct. 1990

Earth orbit

Orbit of Jupiter

South polar pass
(below 70°S)

Jupiter gravity
assist

▲ **Journeying toward the Sun**, the Ulysses spacecraft will make use of a gravity assist from giant Jupiter. The launch window for Ulysses opens on 5th October 1990 and closes on 23rd October 1990. Arriving at Jupiter in February 1992, the planet's gravitational field will deflect Ulysses southwards. The spacecraft's elliptical orbit, totally out of the ecliptic, is such that in August 1994, it will pass over the south pole of the Sun at a distance of 2.3 AU. Between May and September 1995, Ulysses will pass over the Sun's north pole.

▼ **The Solar corona**, viewed in false colour from Skylab, is shown here. Ulysses will investigate the properties of the Sun from its unique polar perspective.

▶ **Ulysses** will use the combined power of the Payload Assist Module (front) and the Inertial Upper Stage (rear) to reach Jupiter in a record-breaking 16 months. Prominent features on the spacecraft are its high gain antenna and the Radio-Isotope Thermonuclear Generator (RTG). The support mechanism carries cooling lines for the RTG.

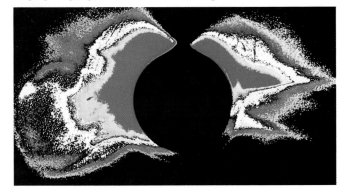

ULYSSES: FASTEST AND FURTHEST

The Ulysses spacecraft is the mortal remains of a project that started out as the International Solar Polar Mission. In 1977, NASA and ESA jointly planned the launch of two identical vehicles which would have simultaneously flown over the Sun's north and south poles in 1985. But NASA's budgetary problems reduced US participation in the project: building of their craft was cancelled in 1981 and the launch of the European vehicle was delayed to 1986. Ulysses is due to be launched from Space Shuttle *Discovery* in October 1990. In 1984, ESA renamed the "Solar Polar" (which some felt was better suited to an ice lolly) after the hero of the *Odyssey*, Homer's epic poem.

No launch vehicle has sufficient energy to carry Ulysses directly over the poles of the Sun. So Ulysses will first head out towards Jupiter to be accelerated by the largest planet's gravitational field, picking up the velocity needed to head over the solar poles. After deployment from the Shuttle, a combination of upper stages will shoot the craft towards Jupiter. A two-stage IUS booster will fire first, carrying Ulysses away from the Earth: it will then be spun at 50 rpm for stability – crucially important for highly critical navigation. The PAM-S booster will then fire and the vehicle's onboard propulsion systems will target it on Jupiter. This adjustment in course will require Ulysses to reduce its rate of spin. To do this, the spacecraft will extend its instrument booms, like a spinning ice-skater stretching out his arms.

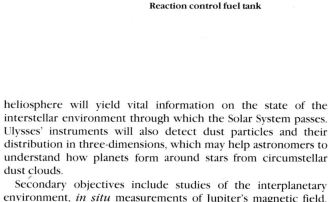

ULYSSES SPACECRAFT

High-gain ante[nna]

Wire boom

Reaction control fuel tank

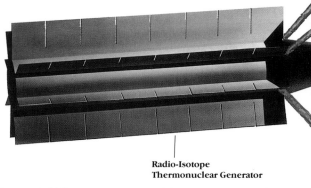

Radio-Isotope Thermonuclear Generator

Travelling at 11.4 kilometres per second (7 miles per second), Ulysses will be the fastest man-made object to date. Its aim point is slightly north of Jupiter's equator, which it will reach after 16 months and then head down, towards the south pole of the Sun. By the time it has come "half circle" over the north pole, five years will have elapsed. Because of the mission's duration, power is at a premium. Close to the Sun, solar panels would be the obvious source of energy, but the rendezvous with distant Jupiter means that Ulysses will be equipped with a radio-isotope thermonuclear generator. The probe will not remain in constant contact with Earth, so data will have to be stored on board for later transmission. Bearing this in mind, the spacecraft control systems are as autonomous as possible, so that Ulysses will automatically check its course every other day or so.

Ulysses' main scientific objective is to investigate the Sun's surface properties – particularly the extent and structure of its magnetic field – at higher latitudes than previously possible. Ulysses will also investigate solar radiations such as X-rays, radio bursts and plasma waves, as well as cosmic rays. These charged particles from beyond the Solar System tend to get swept away or mixed up with the solar wind, so observations from Earth reveal little information about their origin. But it is believed that cosmic rays detected near the solar poles will be relatively unperturbed, making it far easier to trace their sources.

The probe's direct measurements of neutral helium in the heliosphere will yield vital information on the state of the interstellar environment through which the Solar System passes. Ulysses' instruments will also detect dust particles and their distribution in three-dimensions, which may help astronomers to understand how planets form around stars from circumstellar dust clouds.

Secondary objectives include studies of the interplanetary environment, *in situ* measurements of Jupiter's magnetic field, the monitoring of high-energy gamma ray bursts from elsewhere in the galaxy and the search for gravitational waves. These are predicted by Einstein's Theory of General Relativity, but have not yet been detected since gravitation is by far the weakest of the forces of nature. By analysing Ulysses' radio signal, tiny movements of the spacecraft may be measured: these could reveal the presence of passing gravity waves.

◄ **Sunward-bound**: The Ulysses spacecraft is essentially a honeycombed aluminium box containing an array of sensors. Magnetic and gamma ray sensors are located on a radial boom, well away from the spacecraft's own electronics. Three wire booms carry radio and plasma wave experiments which will monitor changes in the solar environment. The main feature of the craft is its large, high gain radio dish (1.65 m/5.4 feet in diameter) which is needed to communicate with

Earth. On the left-hand side is its power source, a Radio-Isotope Thermonuclear Generator (RTG) which can deliver 300 watts of power. The Ulysses RTG was configured for flight in preparation for the 1986 launch opportunity, and a major concern arising from the four-year launch delay is the loss of power due to the radioactive decay of the fuel source. The problem is exacerbated to a certain extent by the long mission duration (almost 5 years), and could result in the

need for power sharing among the scientific instruments towards the end of the mission. The spacecraft telemetry system will operate in the X band (8 GHz). A low-power S-band (2 GHz) transmitter will also be carried for dual-frequency radio-science investigations and early orbit manoeuvres. Uplink communication will be at S-band frequencies. The spacecraft will nominally be tracked for 8 hours per day throughout the mission by NASA's Deep Space Network.

▼ **Empire of the Sun:** Lines of magnetic force, both outwards from and inwards to the Sun, follow a spiral pattern in interplanetary space. Solar wind particles flow around the Earth's magnetic field. High-speed particles form violent outbursts in the Sun's upper atmosphere, sometimes producing amazing auroral displays. ESA and NASA are collaborating within the International Solar Terrestrial Science Project on SOHO (left) and the various spacecraft within the Cluster project (right).

Experiment locations

Equipment platform

Radial boom

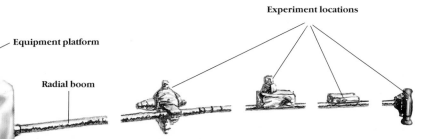

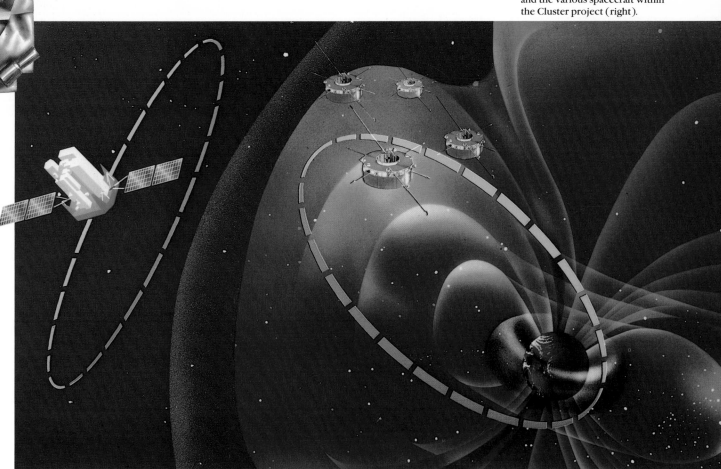

ROCKS FROM A RED PLANET

Mars has always been the subject of a very special human fascination. The tantalizing possibility that life exists – or once existed – there has exercised an all-pervasive influence on studies of the Red Planet. A procession of increasingly sophisticated probes has been dispatched to the planet, beginning with Mariner 4 in 1964 and culminating in the landings of the Viking mission in 1976. To date, no sign of life has been detected: the Viking landers, equipped with an impressive array of biological sensors, found no evidence of the organic compounds on which terrestrial life depends. However, the surface was sampled at only two sites, so these results cannot be taken as the last word, and the question of life on Mars remains open.

During the 1990s, the world's space agencies will once again focus their attention on the Red Planet. The first mission will be NASA's Mars Observer, scheduled for a 1992 lift-off atop a Titan III booster. On reaching Mars just over a year later, it will be placed into a polar, Sun-synchronous orbit, just 380 kilometres (247 miles) high, to facilitate accurate and consistent observation of the entire planet. Mars Observer is expected to operate for a year (687 Earth days) during which time it will pass over the same point on the surface once every 26 Martian days, mapping the entire planet at least a dozen times.

The Mars Observer mission aims to survey the whole planet's chemical composition, as well as monitoring its climate and atmospheric chemistry. Its eight instruments include a magnetometer and a digital camera which will be able to resolve objects a mere four metres (13 feet) across on the Martian surface. A ranging laser altimeter will provide extremely detailed profiles of relief down to a scale of two metres (6.5 feet).

By the time it completes its mission, Mars Observer will be joined in orbit by two spacecraft of the Soviet Mars '94 mission. Their scope is broadly similar to that of Mars Observer, but there are many operational differences. Once they have achieved orbit in September 1995, the two Soviet craft will deploy balloons, laden with remote sensing equipment, into the Martian atmosphere (see page 40). In addition, shell-like devices carrying meteorological and analytical instruments will be fired into and onto the planet's surface. Below the surface, the presence of permafrost will be mapped by long-wave radar sounders aboard the orbiters.

Past missions to Mars have amassed a considerable volume of information, but there are still significant gaps in our knowledge of the planet. The most puzzling questions about Mars concern its interior – particularly whether the core is molten and if it is large enough to generate a magnetic field. In early 1989, the Soviet Phobos 2 craft returned evidence to suggest that Mars did have a weak magnetic field, but more data are needed. Both the Mars '94 craft and the Mars Observer will carry magnetic and particle detectors to accurately monitor trapped radiation belts and signatures associated with a magnetic field.

Perhaps even more important is the question of water on Mars. Although the planet is now dry, the ubiquity of channel systems, thought to have been carved out by ancient rivers, and an analysis of the planet's past axial tilt both suggest that the Martian climate may once have allowed liquid water to flow. The next phase of Mars exploration may tell us why that water was lost, how much remains and what caused the climatic changes that led to its disappearance. Important clues are locked up in the planet's surface: towards the end of the decade both the Soviet Union and the United States plan to send rovers to traverse the Martian terrain and selectively sample rocks (see page 42). The ultimate goal is the return of rock samples to Earth, for no amount of miniaturization can compare with the analytical facilties available on our planet. Such detailed studies may finally reveal the secrets of the Red Planet and set the stage for future human visitation and exploration.

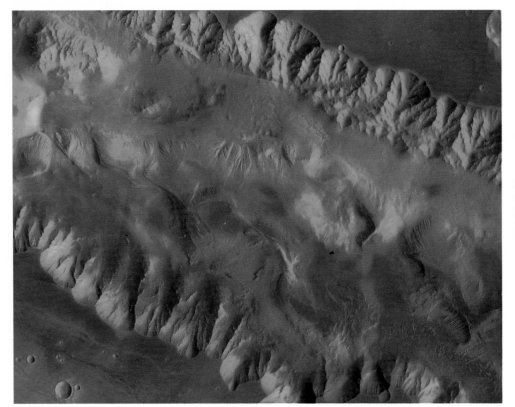

▲ **Sunset on Mars** as witnessed by Viking. Dust in the Martian atmosphere scatters red light by day, so the skies have a pinkish hue. A whitish tinge appears on the horizon after the Sun disappears.

◀ **A Viking view** of the Valles Marineris (Mariner Valley) which scars the Martian equator. This enhanced image reveals the wind and ice erosion which has taken place in the valley walls. In certain areas, hanging valleys are seen – these may have been formed by glacial flows in earlier epochs. The floor of the canyon may once have been covered by shallow seas in which primitive life evolved.

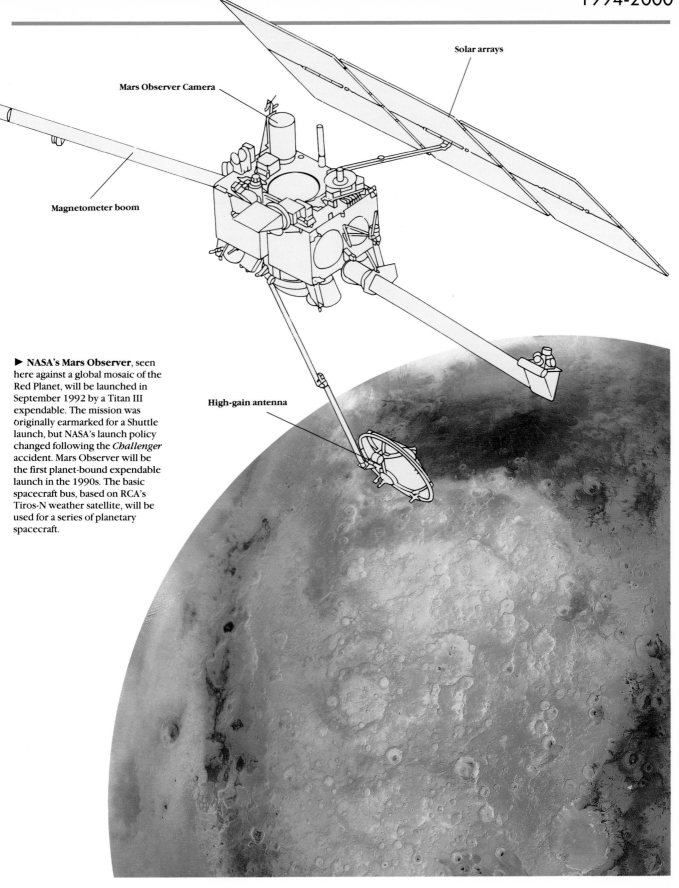

Solar arrays

Mars Observer Camera

Magnetometer boom

High-gain antenna

► **NASA's Mars Observer**, seen here against a global mosaic of the Red Planet, will be launched in September 1992 by a Titan III expendable. The mission was originally earmarked for a Shuttle launch, but NASA's launch policy changed following the *Challenger* accident. Mars Observer will be the first planet-bound expendable launch in the 1990s. The basic spacecraft bus, based on RCA's Tiros-N weather satellite, will be used for a series of planetary spacecraft.

Mankind's next step in exploring Mars began two centuries ago with a sheep, a duck and a rooster on the outskirts of Paris. History recalls that in 1783 the Montgolfier brothers sent this strange payload to the dizzy height of three kilometres (1.9 miles) in a hot-air balloon. Many advances have been made since then and scientific balloons are now a common tool in terrestrial meteorology. Under the auspices of the Montgolfiers' fellow countrymen, balloons will be dropped into the atmosphere of Mars in the 1990s, providing a new way of studying the planet.

The surface of Mars is a rock-strewn desertscape that presents many hazards for any roving vehicle. Balloons can avoid many of these problems, though aviating on Mars presents its own challenges. The surface atmospheric pressure on Mars corresponds to that 30 kilometres (19 miles) above the Earth, where even the most advanced aeroplanes cannot sustain flight. While the thinness of the atmosphere allows for greater freedom of movement, it also means that far more atmospheric gas must be displaced to generate sufficient aerostatic lift. The pull of gravity on Mars is 40 percent of that on Earth which helps to offset the problem of buoyancy and reduces the size of balloon needed.

Two balloons will be deployed on Mars: their exact flightpaths will be determined by the vagaries of atmospheric circulation. During the day, the balloon will expand due to heating from the Sun and rise to its operating altitude from where its scientific instruments will be afforded a unique vantage point over the surface of the planet. At night, the balloon will cool and descend, allowing an instrument "snake" to make contact with the ground.

Mars balloons were first postulated by the chief scientist of the Centre National D'Etudes Spatiales, Dr Jacques Blamont, a well known advocate of international cooperation. He originally planned a balloon composed of two separate envelopes – one open to the atmosphere and the other, with a smaller diameter, filled with helium to keep the whole buoyant. Tests showed that this design was too complex, so a far simpler, but less controllable, vehicle – the "aerostat" – was developed.

When fully inflated, the balloon part of the aerostat is 15 metres (49 feet) in diameter and about 40 metres (130 feet) long. Halfway down a 100-metre (330-foot) guiderope is the instrument gondola, provided by the Soviet Union. At the business end of the rope is a ten metre-long (33-foot) snake, three centimetres (1.2 inches) in diameter. Its instruments, designed to make contact with the surface, are powered by lithium batteries. The snake is clad in titanium to help it survive the battering it will receive as it is dragged along the rocky terrain.

The snake will be segmented to prevent it snagging on surface obstacles. It will house several instruments including a gamma-ray spectrometer to perform *in situ* analyses of surface chemistry and a radar probe to map sub-surface permafrost. The snake will be entirely separate from the instrument gondola, but will transmit data to it via a "walkie-talkie" radio.

The gondola will carry a small power source to ensure it does not freeze during the Martian night, when temperatures can fall to −50°C (−58°F). Its instruments will include a high resolution television camera system capable of viewing the surface down to ten centimetres (four inches) resolution. An infra-red spectrometer will map the chemical characteristics of the surface and an electromagnetic sounder will be used to probe sub-surface structure. An altimeter and a solar sensor will monitor the aerostat's aerodynamic profile. All data will be stored in an onboard processor and relayed back to Earth via both the Soviet Mars 94 orbiters and NASA's Mars Observer. Each aerostat has a life expectancy of ten days and the second will be released after the first has "died". The balloons will be dropped before November 1995 when the next global dust storm is expected.

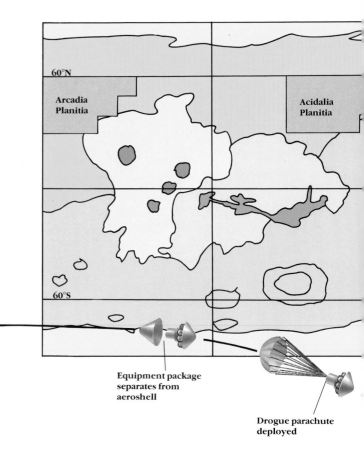

Equipment package separates from aeroshell

Drogue parachute deployed

▶ **Flight profile**. Both Mars 94 orbiters carry one aerostat housed inside a descent module. This makes an aerodynamic entry into the Martian atmosphere, protected by a conical heatshield: its further descent is slowed by three parachutes. The balloon – a helium pressurized polyester mylar envelope, five to ten microns thick – is deployed at an altitude of 8-9 km (5-5.5 miles) once the parachutes have stabilized. The envelope unfurls and is inflated over a four-minute period, after which it is jettisoned from the module, carrying a cone-shaped ballast to lower it onto the surface. Nominal landing sites are in three regions at a latitude of 45°N: Utopia Planitia, Arcadia Planitia

and Acidalia Planitia.

The balloon takes off at around 8am local time and reaches its operating altitude of 2-4 km (1.2-2.5 miles) within one hour. During the late afternoon (4-5pm), it descends to around 50-100 m (160-330 feet), allowing the instrument snake to "trawl" the planet's surface at an estimated 7m/s (23 feet/s).

At 5pm local time, data gathered by the aerostat are relayed to Earth via the Mars 94 orbiter. In addition, French-built instruments on board the NASA Mars Observer collect information at 2am and 2pm. In the few minutes available for information transfer, data are dumped at 100 kbits per second and real-time TV images relayed.

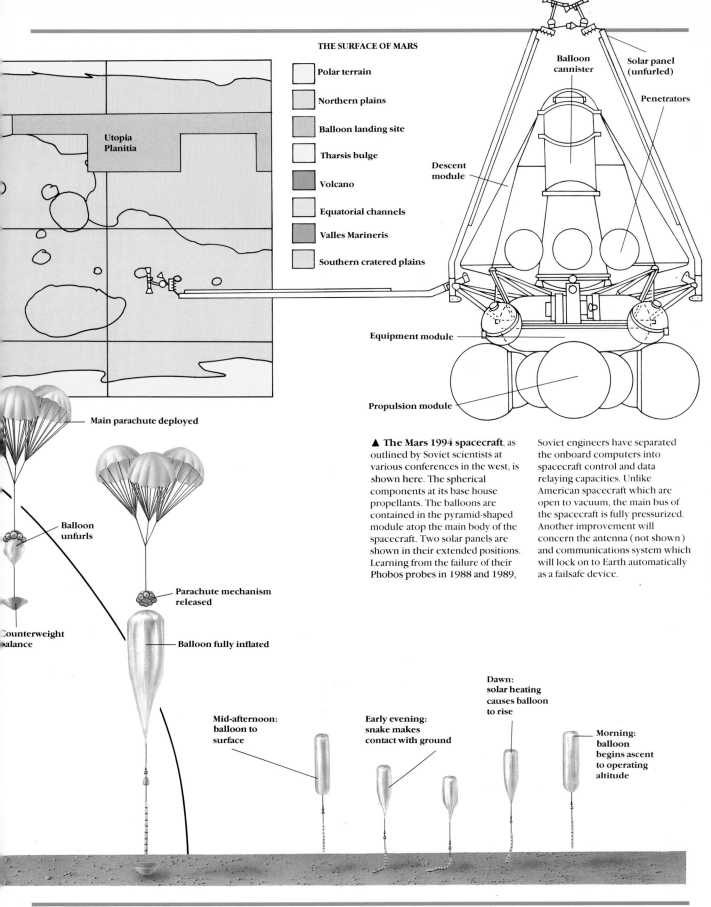

THE SURFACE OF MARS

Balloon
cannister

Solar panel
(unfurled)

- Polar terrain
- Northern plains
- Balloon landing site
- Tharsis bulge
- Volcano
- Equatorial channels
- Valles Marineris
- Southern cratered plains

Utopia
Planitia

Penetrators

Descent
module

Equipment module

Propulsion module

Main parachute deployed

Balloon
unfurls

Parachute mechanism
released

Counterweight
balance

Balloon fully inflated

Mid-afternoon:
balloon to
surface

Early evening:
snake makes
contact with ground

Dawn:
solar heating
causes balloon
to rise

Morning:
balloon
begins ascent
to operating
altitude

▲ The Mars 1994 spacecraft, as outlined by Soviet scientists at various conferences in the west, is shown here. The spherical components at its base house propellants. The balloons are contained in the pyramid-shaped module atop the main body of the spacecraft. Two solar panels are shown in their extended positions. Learning from the failure of their Phobos probes in 1988 and 1989, Soviet engineers have separated the onboard computers into spacecraft control and data relaying capacities. Unlike American spacecraft which are open to vacuum, the main bus of the spacecraft is fully pressurized. Another improvement will concern the antenna (not shown) and communications system which will lock on to Earth automatically as a failsafe device.

Across the tundra of the Kamchatka peninsula in Siberia and the dry river beds of the San Gabriel foothills north of Los Angeles, something stirs. Clumsy-looking vehicles, equipped with a perplexing battery of ungainly instruments and moving on six outsize wheels made of aluminium mesh, can surprise the unwary visitor. These vehicles are the next generation of Mars explorers.

We have seen how atmospheric balloons neatly circumvent the difficulties of traversing the Martian surface: but in other ways they are not ideal. Helium slowly escapes from the balloon envelope, limiting its working life to about ten days. More significantly, they are passive, non-steerable objects: for optimum scientific return over a long period, roving vehicles present a more satisfactory solution. Over at least the last ten years, Soviet and American space agencies have been developing their own designs for Mars rovers. Although they differ in detail, their basic approaches are similar, having been dictated by the immutable laws of mechanics and the demands of the Martian landscape.

By the end of the century, NASA and the Soviet Academy of Science plan to deploy rovers on Mars. Each rover will enter the Martian atmosphere in a protective "aeroshell": in the case of missions where samples are to be collected for analysis on Earth, the rover will be carried with an ascent stage which will later undertake the return journey. Orbiting above the planet will be a craft equipped with cameras capable of resolving features as small as one metre (3.3 feet) on the surface. Its orbit will be such that it passes over the rover's original landing site at roughly the same time every day.

The dilemma central to the idea of Mars roving is that of vehicle control. Given that a signal takes up to 20 minutes to reach Mars from the Earth, a remotely-steered vehicle would be far too cumbersome – to avoid disastrous collisions it would have to move agonizingly slowly. On the other hand, a totally autonomous vehicle, capable of making its own decisions independently, would require enormous – and enormously costly – advances in computing. The compromise solution arrived at by both the Soviet and the American design teams is "semi-autonomous navigation".

Each day, the orbiter will take stereo images of the terrain around the rover which will later be stereo-matched on Earth to create a three-dimensional map. Mission scientists will use this information to plan a detailed route for the vehicle. However, atmospheric opacity and shadow effects mean that small, but potentially treacherous, boulders and obstacles may be missed. So once the rover loads its instructions from Earth, it will use its own onboard stereoscopic imaging system to point out these unforseen hazards, accurately locating them with its forward-mounted ranging laser. After synthesizing these data, the vehicle's sophisticated computer will "choose" the best path.

It is hoped that a rover will be capable of travelling one kilometre (0.62 miles) a day: its daily range will be dictated by the time spent collecting samples as well as the obvious mechanical constraints. The vehicle will have to avoid steep inclines – though work at the Jet Propulsion Laboratory has shown that rovers can scale 35 percent inclines in dunefields at a pinch. The Viking landers showed the surface cohesiveness on Mars to be similar to that found on terrestrial lava flows: theoretically rovers should be able to tackle 60 percent inclines in Viking-like dune fields, but this will have to be verified by simulations and field tests on Earth. Ultimately, if the vehicle experiences "local difficulties it may have to reverse and execute a better route.

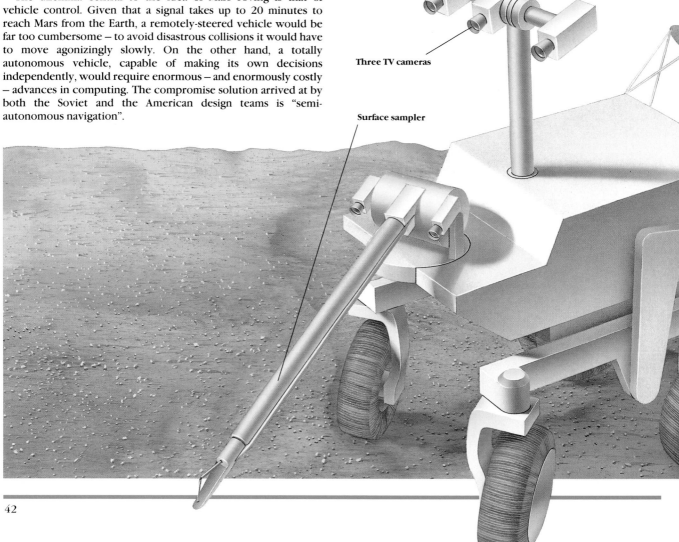

Three TV cameras

Surface sampler

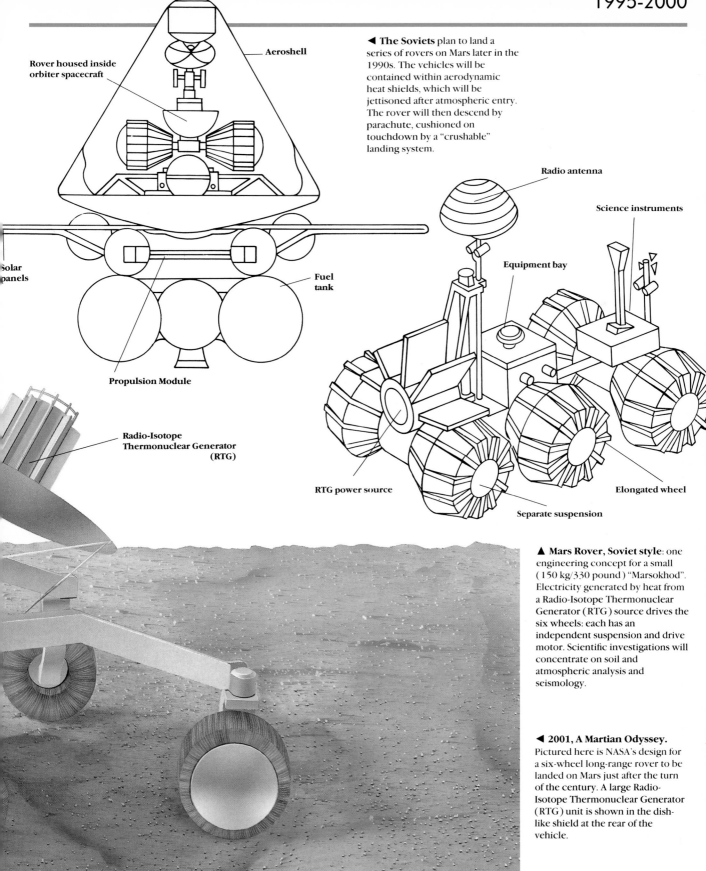

Aeroshell

Rover housed inside orbiter spacecraft

◄ **The Soviets** plan to land a series of rovers on Mars later in the 1990s. The vehicles will be contained within aerodynamic heat shields, which will be jettisoned after atmospheric entry. The rover will then descend by parachute, cushioned on touchdown by a "crushable" landing system.

Radio antenna

Science instruments

Equipment bay

Solar panels

Fuel tank

Propulsion Module

Radio-Isotope Thermonuclear Generator (RTG)

RTG power source

Elongated wheel

Separate suspension

▲ **Mars Rover, Soviet style**: one engineering concept for a small (150 kg/330 pound) "Marsokhod". Electricity generated by heat from a Radio-Isotope Thermonuclear Generator (RTG) source drives the six wheels: each has an independent suspension and drive motor. Scientific investigations will concentrate on soil and atmospheric analysis and seismology.

◄ **2001, A Martian Odyssey.** Pictured here is NASA's design for a six-wheel long-range rover to be landed on Mars just after the turn of the century. A large Radio-Isotope Thermonuclear Generator (RTG) unit is shown in the dish-like shield at the rear of the vehicle.

Until comparatively recently, the outer planets were the *terra incognita* of the Solar System. During the 1960s and 1970s, flotillas of robotic probes visited Mars and Venus like so many interplanetary package tourists, but not until the late 1970s did the giant planets – Jupiter and Saturn – come under similar scrutiny. On their odyssey through the outer solar system, NASA's Voyager spacecraft revealed these planets to be far stranger than ever imagined, with vast retinues of curious moons. But the Voyagers sent back only the barest snapshots of the outer planets. Over the next decade, our first detailed, long-term views of them will be provided by a new generation of spacecraft.

The first is already under way: in October 1989, the Galileo probe was launched towards Jupiter from the Space Shuttle after a series of altogether too familiar difficulties. Arguments over which booster to use, cost overruns with the Shuttle, the *Challenger* accident and even a controversy about Galileo's onboard nuclear power system all conspired to delay the start of the mission.

Galileo's trajectory to Jupiter is, to say the least, circuitous, as the diagram opposite highlights. The immense distances involved, together with the limited capacity of its solid-fuelled Inertial Upper Stage (IUS) booster mean that Galileo will chart a course known as the Venus-Earth-Earth Gravity Assist. The spacecraft will pass each planet in turn and pick up speed by stealing some

volcanically active, with at least eight plumes spewing sulphurous material over its surface. During the 21 months it will spend in orbit around Jupiter, Galileo will make a close pass of each Galilean moon. Again, Galileo's trajectory has been so designed that each moon encounter will accelerate the craft to its next destination without needless expenditure of its own fuel supply.

Many astronomers prefer to consider Jupiter as a failed star since its interior is hotter than the surface of the Sun. Heat wells up from it into the atmosphere, driving ferocious storms such as the Great Red Spot which has been observed for over 350 years. Thanks to Voyager, meteorologists have a basic understanding of the planet's atmosphere, but there is still much more to learn. To

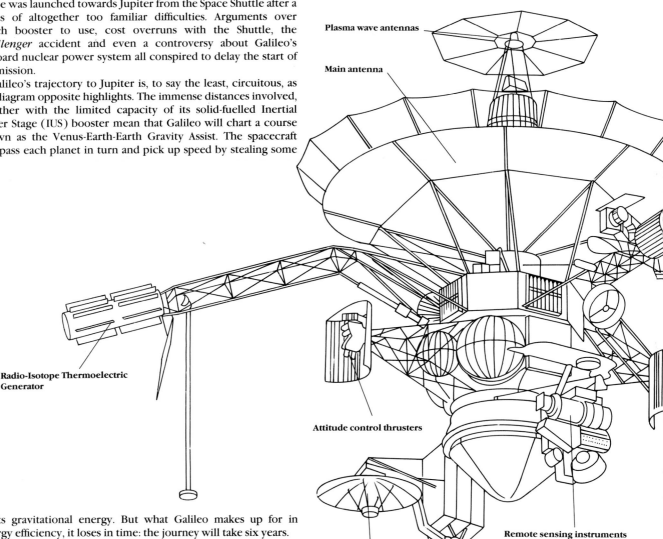

Plasma wave antennas

Main antenna

Radio-Isotope Thermoelectric Generator

Attitude control thrusters

Low gain antenna

Remote sensing instruments

of its gravitational energy. But what Galileo makes up for in energy efficiency, it loses in time: the journey will take six years.

The mission is well named after the Italian scientist who developed the first astronomical telescope: among his many discoveries were four of Jupiter's moons. Though a further twelve have since been identified, none are as interesting as the original quartet, which now bear his name. The Voyager craft showed the Galilean moons to be incredibly diverse in their properties and appearance: Callisto was found to be the most heavily-cratered body ever seen – a stark contrast to Europa's smooth, icy surface; Ganymede appeared to be covered by a network of vast icy furrows; and Io, the innermost Galilean satellite, showed a huge range of surface features and colours. Voyager found Io to be

this end, Galileo will drop an entry probe, whose instruments will reveal the atmosphere's structure, cloud composition and wind fields. In its descent just north of Jupiter's equator, the probe will experience rapid and violent deceleration: its delicate instruments will be protected by a large heat-shield. At a height of 40 kilometres (25 miles) above the planet's surface, a mortar device will spring open, releasing a parachute which will allow the probe to sample Jupiter's gaseous envelope for up to an hour before it is consumed by the extremes of temperature and pressure.

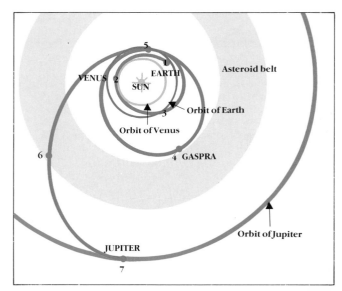

◀ **"The most sophisticated**
planetary spacecraft ever
launched" is how some NASA
managers describe the Galileo
orbiter. Because it will bob in and
out of Jupiter's hazardous radiation
belts, the craft's components have
been "hardened" against radiation.
The craft does not have a single
master computer: each scientific
instrument has its own
microprocessor so that if one
system fails, it will not crash the
whole network. A novel element in
its design is a so-called "spin-
despin" mechanism, which allows
the centrally located particle and
magnetic field-detectors to take
almost continual measurements
about the axis of the orbiter.

Magnetometer

1. **Launch: Oct. 1989.**

2. **Venus encounter: Feb. 1990.**

3. **1st Earth pass: Dec. 1990.**

4. **Gaspra encounter: Oct. 1991.**

5. **2nd Earth pass: Dec. 1992.**

6. **Ida encounter: Aug. 1993.**

7. **Jupiter arrival: Dec. 1995.**

▶ **The circuitous route** that
Galileo will take on its 6-year
odyssey is shown here. Known as
the Venus-Earth-Earth-Gravity-
Assist, it will allow Galileo to reach
Jupiter without the need for
additional rocket stages.

▼ **"We're on our way!"** Galileo is
finally dispatched from the payload bay of the Shuttle. This wide
angle picture – taken by the IMAX
camera used for the *Dream Is Alive*
movie – shows Galileo attached to
its booster. It was taken from the
rear flight deck of the Orbiter.

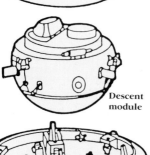

Descent
module

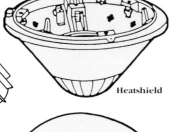

Heatshield

Aeroshell

◀ **Just before Galileo reaches
Jupiter**, it will dispatch a probe
into the Jovian atmosphere. During
descent the probe will decelerate
from 180,000 km/h (112,000
mph) down to 150 km/h (93 mph)
when a parachute will open. Two-
thirds of the probe's mass is
devoted to a heat-shield. The heat-
shield and aeroshell (bottom two
diagrams) will be deployed 2 mins
after atmospheric entry.

When Galileo first observed Saturn in 1610, he was mystified: "Saturn is not one alone, but is composed of three which almost touch each other", he recorded. Two years later, the mystery deepened – two of the planets seemed to have vanished. We now know that Galileo was not looking at a triple planet as he supposed, but at the rings of Saturn. In 1655, the Dutch astronomer Christiaan Huygens used a more powerful telescope to resolve Galileo's conundrum. He also identified Saturn's largest moon, Titan, and in common with Galileo, declared that he felt "no small rapture" at his discoveries. Twenty years later, further development of the optical telescope enabled Giovanni Cassini, the Italian-born director of the Paris Observatory, to identify divisions within the rings.

This brief history provides a telling metaphor for the future exploration of Saturn. In a sense, we have much in common with Galileo: for despite the information returned by the Voyager missions, we still do not have detailed, systematic observations on the make-up Saturn's rings, its atmosphere and its myriad moons. The next step in exploring the planet is the launch of an ambitious joint European/American project, appropriately named Huygens/Cassini.

After its launch in 1996 by a Titan IV/Centaur expendable, NASA's Cassini orbiter will carry ESA's Huygens probe to Saturn, eventually deploying it into Titan's atmosphere. The probe will have to operate for a few hours after "cold storage" in space for many years: its electronic components and materials will have to be extensively tested before launch. As with Galileo's journey to Jupiter (see page 44), Cassini's route to Saturn will be dictated by orbital mechanics. Its circuitous trajectory will involve a close fly-by of asteroid 66 Maja, a pass by Earth in June 1998 and then an encounter with Jupiter in February 2000. Huygens/Cassini will pass behind the giant planet, investigating its magnetotail – the "shadow" cast by the planet in the solar wind. In October 2002, Huygens/Cassini will arrive at Saturn, entering the first of 36 elongated orbits which it will describe over the next four years. Using gravitational assistance from the individual Saturnian moons, it will make a close pass of each one in turn. Cassini will also observe the rings from a variety of different geometries, paying particular attention to occultations – those configurations in which stars and the Sun pass behind the rings.

Without doubt, the focus of the mission is Titan. This massive moon is covered by a dense, orange-coloured haze which hides its surface from view. The Voyagers showed that 90 to 95 percent of its atmosphere is nitrogen, with smaller quantities of methane, ethane and even hydrogen cyanide. The presence of organic compounds has led to Titan being described as a "pre-terrestrial life environment" – like a primitive Earth in deep freeze. Huygens will return valuable data for biologists which may reveal clues about how life formed on Earth.

The probe will be dispatched into the daylit hemisphere of the moon, entering the atmosphere hypersonically, protected by an aeroshell which will be jettisoned at an altitude of around 200 kilometres (124 miles). Slowed by a parachute, the probe's further descent to Titan's surface will take between two and three hours. During this time it will take direct measurements of cloud structure and composition, assess wind conditions and determine whether there is lightning in the atmosphere. From measurements made by the Voyager probes, we know the temperature on Titan's surface to be around −180°C (−290°F) and the pressure to be 1.6 times that on Earth. Under such conditions, methane may exist as either a solid, liquid or gas. So the surface of Titan may prove to be a frozen sea with towering ice cliffs and icebergs. Only time and the probe's instruments will tell. We can, of course, expect no small rapture.

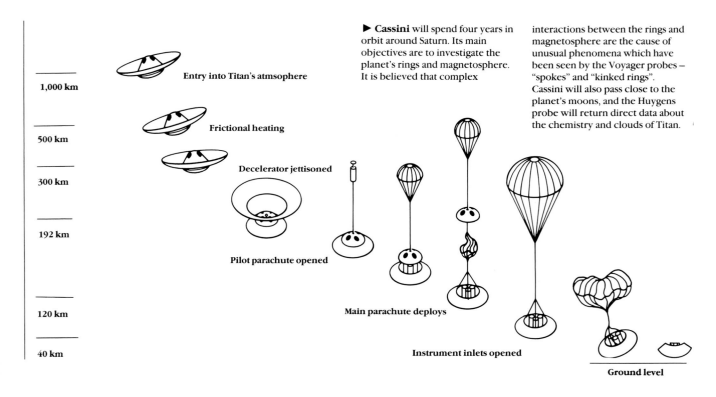

► **Cassini** will spend four years in orbit around Saturn. Its main objectives are to investigate the planet's rings and magnetosphere. It is believed that complex interactions between the rings and magnetosphere are the cause of unusual phenomena which have been seen by the Voyager probes – "spokes" and "kinked rings". Cassini will also pass close to the planet's moons, and the Huygens probe will return direct data about the chemistry and clouds of Titan.

1,000 km

Entry into Titan's atmsophere

500 km

Frictional heating

300 km

Decelerator jettisoned

192 km

Pilot parachute opened

Main parachute deploys

120 km

Instrument inlets opened

40 km

Ground level

▶ **The Huygens probe** (lower) will separate from the Cassini orbiter on arrival in the Saturn system. Cassini's design is common to the Comet Rendezvous Asteroid Fly-By, though the latter's antenna will be slightly smaller. Both craft will have instrument platforms at the ends of long booms: Cassini has a turntable upon which fields and particles instruments rotate. Remote sensing instruments, including the imaging cameras, are carried on the right-hand boom.

▲ **High-altitude haze** in the atmosphere of Titan, is visible in this Voyager 1 view taken in 1980.

Asteroids and comets have had a chequered history. In ancient times, the sight of a comet in the night sky was interpreted as a portent of doom, a sure sign that evil would descend upon the Earth. In a similar (though less frightening) vein, asteroids were viewed with heart-sinking suspicion by observers of the heavens in the early 19th century. So many were discovered with telescopes of the day that astronomers referred to them as the "vermin of the skies".

Today, however, our perception of these "small bodies" has come full circle. They are believed to hold vitally important clues about the primordial Solar System which will help reveal the way in which the planets were formed. For this reason, comets and asteroids have been termed the rosetta stones of the solar system (the Rosetta stone was an Egyptian tablet whose deciphering led to the understanding of hieroglyphics). To decipher the way in which the planets formed from interstellar material, we will need to land on comets and asteroids and eventually return samples to Earth for analysis. These endeavours are planned by the world's space agencies over the next ten years.

To date, planetary exploration has given us a relatively coherent picture of how the Solar System formed. Between 4 and 5 billion years ago the planets formed out of a giant expanse of dust and gas. This material contracted under its own gravitational influence: it coalesced at its centre and the accompanying thermonuclear fusion "ignited" the Sun. But unmanned missions have so far revealed little about the composition and extent of the primordial dust and gas. It is as though vital pieces of the chemical jigsaw are missing. That information is locked up in the comets and asteroids.

Asteroids are thought to be fragments of the material from which the planets formed. Astronomers believe that the original dust and gas clumped together into "planetismals" which then further aggregated to form the inner planets and the cores of the much more massive outer planets. This pristine material was then physically altered by the intense temperatures and pressures inside the cores of the planets.

There was enough planetismal material between Mars and Jupiter to form a planet-sized body, but the all-pervading influence of Jupiter's gravity ensured that this did not happen. The variously sized and differentiated bodies that remained in orbit around the Sun between the orbits of Mars and Jupiter, collectively make up the asteroid belt.

Our picture of the chemistry of the asteroids comes in part from meteorites which periodically land on the Earth's surface and are believed to originate in the asteroid belt. Some are predominantly stony, perhaps derived from the bedrock of the planetismals, while others have a greater metallic content, so are perhaps from their cores.

Unlike asteroids, which remain rather enigmatic, comets have already been scrutinized from space. In 1986, the Soviet VeGa and European Giotto spacecraft returned invaluable information about the most famous of the comet fraternity – Halley. The icy nucleus at Halley's heart was found to be an irregular object which reflected only four percent of the incident sunlight, making it darker than soot. But by far the greatest surprise was the direct detection of organic compounds carried by the comet. Halley's nucleus seems to be rich in silicates containing carbon, hydrogen, oxygen and nitrogen – the very building blocks of terrestrial life. One unresolved question concerns the origin of comets: some astronomers believe that they formed out of interstellar grains outside our Solar System, others that they crystallized within the outer depths of the Solar System. Until we analyse cometary material in detail we will not be able to determine which is true.

▶ **The icy nucleus** of Comet Kopff will be the quarry for the penetrator fired from CRAF in July 2001. The nozzle and spherical propellant tank of the rocket motor used to fire the instrument are seen at the top of this artist's impression. The probe's electronics and batteries are housed between the lattice-like structures immediately below that. The ball-shaped device directly below that is an accelerometer to measure the strength of the cometary material. Needle-like temperature probes can be seen down the length of the penetrator. The instrument nearest the tip is a gamma ray spectrometer used to analyse the comet's chemical composition.

▶ **Aster-1**, the Soviet asteroid mission planned for the late 1990s will carry a pair of surface penetrators. The schematic diagram (far right) shows how they could be fired. The penetrators would be deployed on an independent approach module which would "spin up" to reduce the speed of the penetrators relative to the asteroid. An onboard braking rocket would fire before impact with the asteroid.

▲ **Phobos** is the larger of the two Martian moons. It is believed by some astronomers to be a captured asteroid. Its irregular shape is apparent from the superimposed co-ordinate grid (right) used by Soviet scientists to plan the Phobos missions in 1988. Before a penetrator can be fired in to any asteroidal surface, its aim point will have to be precisely defined, taking into account both *in situ* data and global position.

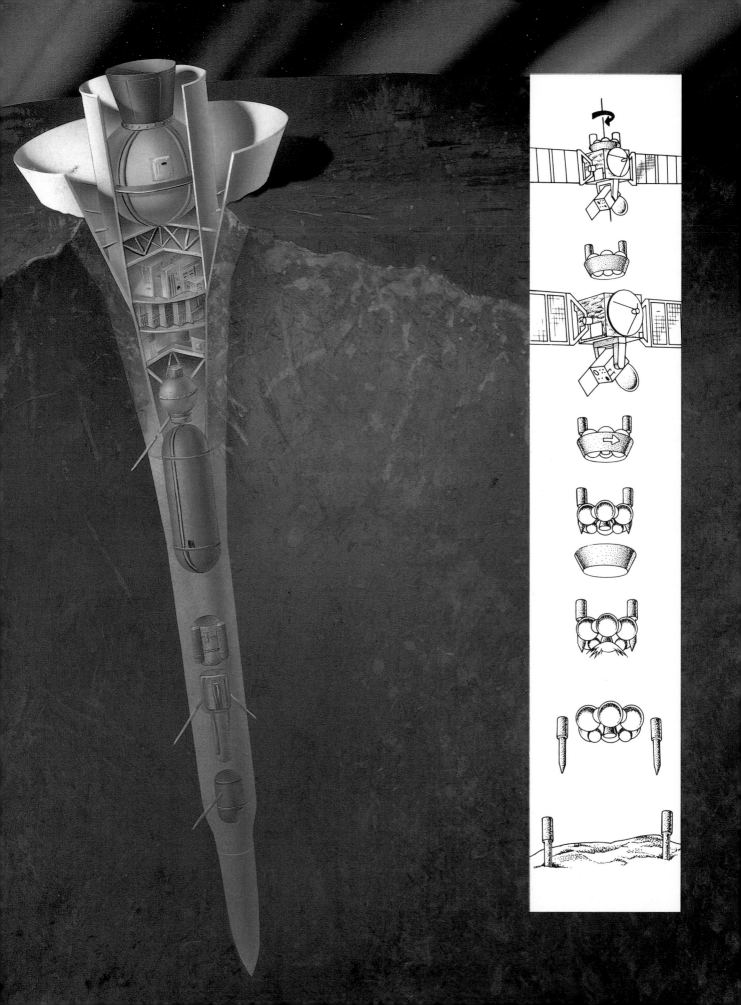

ON THE TRAIL OF A COMET

Chasing a comet is no longer a quixotic preserve of the imagination. When Halley's comet returned to the inner solar system in February 1986 after about 70 years in deep space, no less than five spacecraft passed through its dusty coma – and survived. ESA's Giotto craft – which shot toward the comet as it was leaving the inner solar system with a relative speed of 70 kilometres per second (43 miles per second) – remained intact after the battering it received from Halley's dust and has now been directed on towards another comet, Grigg-Skjellerup, which it will encounter in July 1992.

The first of the new missions to the small bodies (the comets and asteroids) is NASA's Comet Rendezvous/Asteroid Fly-By, known as CRAF for short. After launch in August 1995, the spacecraft – the same generic design as Cassini, and known in NASA parlance as a Mariner Mark II vehicle – will harness the Earth's gravitational energy to reach the speed required to keep its 1998 appointment with asteroid Hamburga, and finally rendezvous with Comet Kopff in August 2000. CRAF will then trail Kopff from a distance of 50-100 kilometres (31-62 miles) as it heads in towards the Sun and becomes warmer and increasingly active, emitting ever-greater quantities of dust and gas.

Astronomers will get their clearest picture yet of how a comet behaves as it "warms up" before its closest pass of the Sun, for as CRAF moves around Kopff, it will examine its surface at a resolution of one metre. Spectroscopic techniques will identify minerals and ices on the comet's surface, while thermal mapping will reveal its energy balance, and thus allow scientists to predict which parts of the nucleus surface will become active as the Sun is approached. Precise tracking of CRAF will enable the mass of the nucleus to be calculated, which in turn will allow its density to be computed.

About a year after CRAF starts tagging Kopff, it will fire a penetrator into the comet nucleus. For about a week, the penetrator will transmit direct measurements of the comet's thermal properties, surface strength and composition back to the parent craft. The assertion of some astronomers that prebiotic organic molecules delivered to the Earth by comets formed the basis of terrestrial life, will come under close scrutiny. The penetrator data will also reveal the conditions under which the cometary material accumulated: this may help us understand how the Solar System formed.

In late 1989, Soviet space scientists unveiled plans for Aster-1 –

▼ **NASA's Comet Rendezvous Asteroid Fly-By** (CRAF) mission will play tag with Comet Kopff for two and a half years. The firing of its penetrator will allow the first *in situ* measurements of a comet to be taken. When the comet makes its closest pass of the Sun, CRAF will use its instruments to investigate the interaction between cometary gas and the solar wind. This may reveal how cometary tails form and subsequently change.

▶ **CRAF's penetrator** will be targeted using the main spacecraft's imaging system. CRAF's instruments, located on the ends of two booms, will scan the comet's surface. High resolution CCD cameras will help determine the volume of the cometary nucleus, surface structure and features as well as its rotation rate. A spectrometer, sensitive to both optical and infrared wavelengths, will map changes in the surface of the nucleus over time.

CRAF MISSION PROFILE

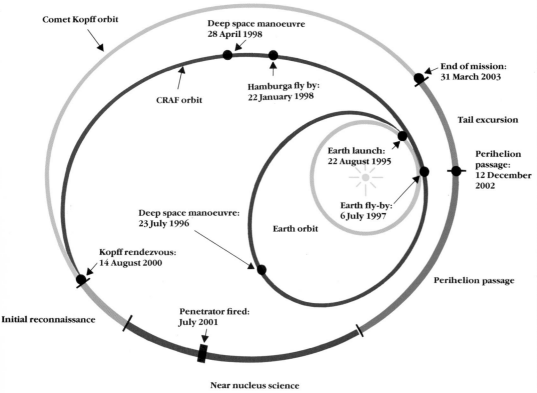

Comet Kopff orbit

Deep space manoeuvre 28 April 1998

CRAF orbit

Hamburga fly by: 22 January 1998

End of mission: 31 March 2003

Tail excursion

Earth launch: 22 August 1995

Perihelion passage: 12 December 2002

Deep space manoeuvre: 23 July 1996

Earth orbit

Earth fly-by: 6 July 1997

Kopff rendezvous: 14 August 2000

Perihelion passage

Initial reconnaissance

Penetrator fired: July 2001

Near nucleus science

a mission to the asteroid belt, which is essentially an updated version of an aborted joint French/Soviet project called Vesta. Though plans are vague at the moment, it is expected that France and possibly other European nations will participate in Aster-1. Ten months after its December 1996 launch, the spacecraft will reach Mars. Accelerated by the Red Planet's gravitational field, it will head into the asteroid belt, where encounters with asteroids Fortuna, Harmonia, Haldej, Juewa and Vesta are planned at roughly six-monthly intervals. Aster-1's instruments will allow the physical differences between the asteroids to be determined as a function of their position. But the mission's primary target is Vesta, the most prominent asteroid in the night sky, into which Aster-1 will fire surface penetrators.

For the turn of the century, ESA is planning a comet nucleus sample return mission, provisionally named Rosetta. Detailed studies are now under way to choose the most suitable comet candidate and to devise experiments which will give the greatest scientific return. Rosetta will home in on its target comet and return samples of core and surface material to Earth. The samples will be kept below 160K to avoid contamination or loss of the more volatile compounds.

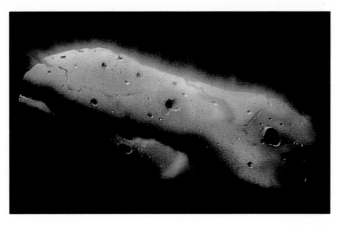

▲ **A cometary nucleus** is a dark, icy body that forms a tail when its surface molecules are vapourized. CRAF's first images of Kopff may look like this artist's impression.

THE HIGH FRONTIER

"America has always been greatest when we dared to be great. We can reach for greatness again. We can follow our dreams to distant stars, living and working in space for peaceful, economic and scientific gain."

Ronald Reagan, announcing the Space Station, January 1984

"NASA continues to believe in Freedom's potential as a spaceport for planetary exploration, but the agency is faced with a by now familiar dilemma. Without bold leadership from the White House and Congress, our space policy is being shaped by the short-term, often conflicting goals of the disparate aerospace community. Despite promises that Freedom will be all things to all members of this group, it will actually satisfy very few of them well."

Astronaut Buzz Aldrin, *Men from Earth*, 1989

◀ **International skyport:** By the start of the new millennium, the western nations will have their own space station in low Earth orbit. A Shuttle carrying vital supplies is seen here docking at a forward port.

Every ninety minutes or so, the world's first truly operational space station completes another orbit of the Earth. Looking like a motley collection of modules attached to a truncated telescope, Mir's curious appearance belies its significance: the station is the latest stage in a long-term programme in which the Soviets have developed the techniques to support crews in low Earth orbit for periods of up to one year.

At the time of writing, Soviet cosmonauts have spent a total of 15 man-years aloft, compared to the 7.5 years for US astronauts. Although Mir is the direct descendant of the Salyut stations, it is much more versatile and flexible: its launch in February 1986 was heralded as marking "the transition from research to full-scale production in space". Apart from a five-month period of abandonment, the station has been permanently occupied since February 1987.

It is immediately apparent from the slightly ghostly television pictures relayed to Earth that Mir has benefited from the Soviet experience with Salyut: unlike its predecessors, Mir is not cluttered with equipment, and its environmental control system is far more efficient. The forward control section houses a computer which automatically monitors onboard systems. The central living section is split into two – the curtained-off sleeping quarters, plus a toilet and wash-basin with push-button faucets, and a dining area with a pull-down table in which a heating ring warms meals. A choice of 60 meals is maintained by regular, monthly visits of Progress re-supply vehicles – the same craft used to service the Salyut stations in the 1970s.

The Progress vehicles normally dock at the rear of the station to allow easy access to Mir's fuel lines during the refuelling of its attitude control system. Recent advances in navigational capacity mean that Mir no longer has to be aligned for docking with Progress, as was previously the case.

The main illustration shows how Mir will appear by 1992 if all goes to plan. The original module will become the central hub of an even larger station, assembled by launching new elements from the ground. Mir's inherent flexibility stems from its six docking ports, five located at the front of the station and one at the rear. The forward port will be used to dock and ferry crews from Soyuz vehicles: when not used, additional modules can be docked there temporarily, and later moved to the required lateral port. A remote robotic arm, similar to that used on the US Space Shuttle, will carry out these "shunting" operations.

In March 1987, Kvant 1 (Quantum) became the first module to join Mir, docking at the rear of the station. It contains astrophysical instruments, including a battery of X-ray telescopes with which Supernova 1987A was fortuitously observed. In early December 1989, Kvant 2 was docked at the axial front port, then transferred to the upper port at the front of the station. This module carries a large German remote sensing camera, and an airlock which allows extra-vehicular activities without having to evacuate the front part of Mir – a cumbersome procedure at the best of times.

Over the next two years, Mir will continue its growth, supplied by an improved version of the Progress vehicle – Progress M – which will carry a return capsule with a capacity of 150 kilogrammes/330 pounds. The Korund 1-M metallurgical furnace currently aboard Mir produces about this mass of metallic composite material per month, so the capsule may be used to return samples to Earth. In 1990, a module called Krystal docked to the lower port of Mir to continue Soviet materials science research (see page 72). In 1991 and 1992, two further modules will be docked either side of Mir – one will carry astronomical instruments, while the other will be used for Earth resources and global monitoring.

◀ **Mir's versatility** stems from its forward docking port (left), which allows up to six modules to dock. As shown in this engineering mock up, a Soyuz TM craft is docked with Mir. The Soyuz TM benefits from advanced thruster units and a more versatile docking system which can "lock onto" Mir from a great distance.

▶ *Glasnost* has even brought about openness in the the Soviet space programme. The Houston-based Space Commerce Corporation (SCC) offers its services as agent for the Soviet space agency, Glavkosmos. This SCC poster advertizes space on Mir for hire. The price of training and flying a guest cosmonaut is about US$10 million. To fly a microgravity experiment of your choice would cost roughly half that. The Soviets are also actively marketing launchers like the Proton and Zenit, which may be launched from Cape York in Northern Australia. By launching from a non-Eastern bloc country, it is hoped that the traditional reluctance to share space technology can be overcome.

MIR 2: HOME FROM HOME

Musa Munarov and Vladimir Titov are by no means household names. As joint holders of the endurance record for a spaceflight – exactly a year – their anonymity is a curious quirk in a world where the biggest, furthest and longest are revered, and particularly so since their achievement is not likely to be surpassed in the immediate future. This is symptomatic of the world's indifference to the successes of the Soviet manned space programme, which persists even now in the age of *glasnost*.

Manned flights to Soviet space stations are now routine: twenty years of experience has fine-tuned the day-to-day operation of these missions. Long-stay crews are launched to Mir aboard a Soyuz TM capsule, which then docks with the station a day later. These crews are usually accompanied by cosmonauts who stay aboard Mir for about a week, then returning in the Soyuz TM which has been in space for the duration of the previous long-term stay. Traditionally, these short flights have carried "guest" cosmonauts, a term which now includes anyone with a large enough bank balance. For a price of US$10 million, a week-long flight aboard Mir can be bought. The Tokyo Broadcasting System has already raised this considerable sum, and a Japanese cosmonaut will fly to Mir at the end of 1990. However, Project Juno – which was to have sent a Briton to the station in 1991 – was unable to generate sufficient funds. Over the following two years, Austrian, French and West German cosmonauts are scheduled to visit the station.

Changes in the funding of the Soviet manned programme have shifted its emphasis away from scientific endeavour in favour of commercial return. Long-term flights, like those of Munarov and Titov, can no longer be justified, and the optimum time period for a crew in space is now considered to be between four and six months. But through the earlier long-stay missions, Soviet space planners have gained an important understanding of the psychology of living in space. Unlike NASA, the Soviets employ a team of psychologists – known as The Group for Psychological Support – to monitor the progress of flights and improve the well-being of the cosmonauts. The station has been made as "homely" as possible by the use of soft lighting and pastel shades, and to minimize disorientation, "ceilings" have been painted darker than "floors". On replenishment flights, the crew receive individual food parcels (officially no alcohol), videotapes, cassettes and novels. Two-way TV links with friends and family, as well as regular newscasts and broadcasts by famous entertainers all help to alleviate their sense of isolation. The standard of the food in space may be discerned from the Salyut 6 cosmonauts who grew onions as part of a life sciences experiment. They became increasingly cagey about the results as the weeks went by and it became obvious they had eaten the experimental evidence.

On first arriving aboard Mir, cosmonauts have typically wanted to work continuously and ignore rest periods: later, fatigue and listlessness have set in. To prevent this effect, psychologists have devised a strict timetable – tied to Moscow time for the sake of convenience – in which the 15-hour "day" is split into four work periods interspersed with physical exercise and free time. Two hours of exercise a day are necessary to mitigate the medical effects of long term weightlessness, the most worrying of which are muscle wastage and bone demineralization. To this end, Mir is equipped with a "mini-gymnasium" made up of isometric bars and an exercise machine on which Soviet cosmonauts have to cycle the equivalent of four kilometres (2.5 miles) a day to prevent muscular decay. Crew members can also use a spring-loaded suit called Chibis, which provides tension against which their muscles can work. To minimize calcium loss, cosmonauts are treated with a variety of drugs: Munarov and Titov only lost five percent by mass of bone during their year in space.

▲ **Soviet crews**, it is rumoured, particularly relish the arrival of guest cosmonauts because food supplies are generally "improved". Soviet authorities banned garlic on the grounds that the air purifiers couldn't handle it and French wines because the crews couldn't handle them! In the central living section of Mir there are fold-down tables with heaters to warm up the meals on offer. Soviet statements boast of meat, dairy products, breads, cakes, fruits and fruit juice, drinks and seasoning. But one cosmonaut reportedly told an American colleague: "Our food is slop and your food is slop". Shown here is a typical meal for one served aboard Mir.

▲ **Just before Christmas 1988**, the crew aboard Mir pose for an informal portrait (top). From left to right: Jean-Loup Chretien, Musa Munarov, Valeri Polyakov, Sergei Krikalev, Vladimir Titov and Aleksander Volkov. Munarov and Titov had spent nearly a year aboard the station by this point.

▶ **At the front end of Mir** is the control compartment, shown here in this mock-up of the station. The forward docking port is seen beneath the extended hatch cover. The computer terminals are used to check that Mir is "behaving" properly. Temperatures are maintained between 18 and 28°C, and air humidity between 30 and 70%.

Advanced technology is at a premium in the USSR. By force of circumstance, Soviet engineers have often adapted the work of others to suit their own needs. So, for example, the Soviet Shuttle Buran bears an uncanny resemblance to NASA's own Space Transportation System. And though its chief designer Yuri Semyenov has said "Anyone who thinks Buran is a copy of the American Shuttle is a fool", western engineers noted the clever way in which the Soviets avoided the problems which plagued NASA's Shuttle. Buran's thermal protection system is more resilient than the Shuttle's, but requires more frequent replacement – a sensible compromise.

The theme underlying Soviet attitudes to space hardware is: "If it works, keep on using it." So the standard launcher used in the Soviet space programme bears the same basic design of that introduced by Sergei Korolev for Sputnik 1. The Soyuz capsule itself first flew in the 1960s, but has since been upgraded by incorporating improved technology, resulting in the latest Soyuz-TM (Modernised Transport) vehicle. When the French cosmonaut Jean-Loup Chretien spent nearly a month aboard Mir, he was amazed to see that the onboard television was a Sony Stratocruiser. Similarly, the Korund metallurgical furnace aboard

Mir is so technologically antiquated that the Soviets are eager to buy a commercial design off the shelf.

In the past, Soviet access to western technology has been restricted: for example, in 1984, American scientists were careful to avoid the use of microprocessors on their experiments flown on the VeGa probes to Halley's Comet. It is hard to predict how the thaw in superpower relations may affect the transfer of space technology, but this issue will certainly influence the development of the Soviet space programme.

Many Soviet missions have been dogged by technical deficiencies: Salyut 6 started to degrade after four years, and after only three years, Salyut 7 was totally without power and lifeless, though it was later salvaged. In September 1988, two returning cosmonauts were forced to spend an extra day in orbit when the automatic re-entry system on their Soyuz TM malfunctioned. The landing navigation system had been programmed with two sets of (conflicting) data, which caused the retro-engines to misfire. It was later revealed that the computer used for orbital changes and navigation had a capacity similar to that used by Gemini astronauts in the 1960s. When Mir was left temporarily uninhabited in early 1989, the head of training, Vladimir Shatalov

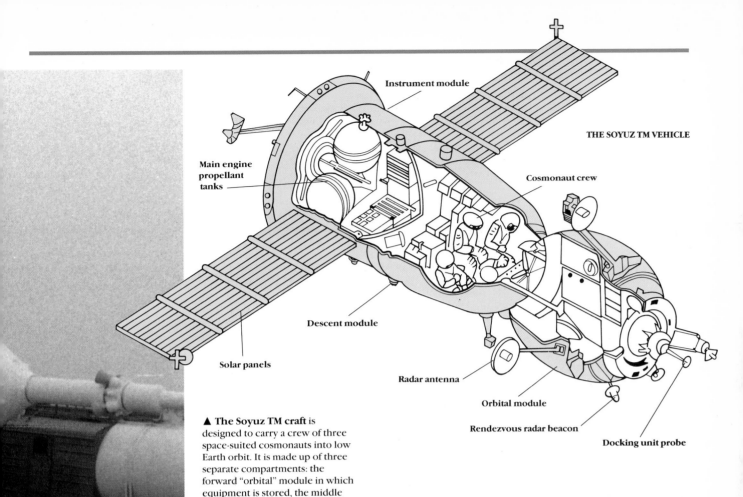

Instrument module

THE SOYUZ TM VEHICLE

Cosmonaut crew

Main engine
propellant
tanks

Descent module

Solar panels

Radar antenna

Orbital module

Rendezvous radar beacon

Docking unit probe

▲ **The Soyuz TM craft** is designed to carry a crew of three space-suited cosmonauts into low Earth orbit. It is made up of three separate compartments: the forward "orbital" module in which equipment is stored, the middle "descent" module in which the cosmonauts are housed, and the aft "instrument" module which contains the propulsion system. Though the TM is a great improvement on earlier Soyuz vehicles, it is still relatively unsophisticated by western engineering standards.

(himself a former cosmonaut) railed against the unreliability of its equipment – up to half of Mir's experiments were not operating at any one time and cosmonauts were spending most of their time carrying out repairs. Some observers of the Soviet programme now doubt whether Mir will survive well into the nineties.

The economic restrictions forced by *perestroika* mean that the next flight of Buran will not take place until 1991. It will be launched unmanned and dock with Mir, where a crew of three led by chief test pilot Igor Volk will transfer and bring the vehicle home. The first manned launch in 1992 will be followed by one Buran mission per year until the mid-1990s – assuming that technical problems do not interfere. The Soviets had talked about returning Salyut 7 back to Earth, piece by piece, and refurbishing it. This now seems unlikely for economic reasons. It is a measure of their need for funds that the Soviets have sold a back-up of Mir to a Japanese entrepreneur to make into a star exhibit in a futuristic theme park.

Whatever the current economic situation dictates, the Soviets have risen remarkably well to the challenges of space engineering. Soviet engineers can be consoled by the thought that the tortoise, not the hare, passed the winning post first.

◄ **A Soyuz launcher** (main picture) en route to the pad at Tyuratam. This particular vehicle was used in the Franco-Soviet Mission which launched Jean-Loup Chretien in November 1988. The three-stage vehicle can launch over 7 tonnes into low Earth orbit.

▲ **Soyuz launches** were once secretive events, but are now announced well in advance. In 1974, a Soyuz capsule failed to separate from its upper stage, causing it to tumble back to Earth. In 1983, an engine fire led to an explosion on the pad.

In the Soviet Union, Konstantin Tsiolkovskii is known as the "father of astronautics", a label not tritely applied in a country so acutely aware of its past. Since his death in 1935, the great man's scientific legacy has continued to provide a bright guiding light for the Soviet space programme. His visionary writings are replete with far-reaching goals, many of which already feature in the catalogue of Soviet space successes. While many of his ideas have come to fruition far sooner than he envisaged, perhaps the most ambitious remains unfulfilled, for towards the end of his life, Tsiolkovskii earnestly discussed the concept of "Kosmograd" – the city in the sky. But with their extensive experience aboard Mir, the Soviets have the basic building blocks for such a city in place now.

Sometime in the mid-1990s, the first Mir complex will be handed over totally to biomedical research. By that time, a replacement for Mir-1 – a station generally known as Mir-2 – will be in construction. As ever, Soviet plans are vague, but those designs which have surfaced in the west show gantry-like structures similar to Freedom. At 300 tonnes, Mir-2 will dwarf its 140-tonne predecessor. Between nine and twelve crew members will live aboard a "base unit" which will be supplied with around 100 kilowatts of power. This orbital complex will be serviced by – and indeed service – orbital tugs and manipulators. Soviet planners also talk of using Mir-2 as a testing ground for elements of new space systems being developed for eventual use on manned flights to the Moon and Mars.

Just how advanced the Soviet plans are may be discerned from a presentation given at the 1985 International Astronautical Federation, held in Stockholm. Under the umbrella of the Orwellian title "Socio-Economic Benefits Connected With The Use of Space Power and Energy Systems", Sergei Sarkisjan and his colleagues set out a grand plan for space industrialization. His team of economists discussed the lighting of Earth from space, specifically mentioning geostationary mirrors to reflect sunlight toward darkness-enshrouded Siberia. Other concepts included the generation and retransmission of energy through space – at first between space stations, but eventually from space to the Earth (see page 86).

The proposed timescale for these developments was set at thirty years, a figure so optimistic that it caused almost apoplectic mirth in certain quarters at the time. With the economic cutbacks forced by *perestroika,* the programme has already been delayed. But such criticisms miss the point: fanciful or not, these ideas reflect the commitment of Soviet planners to finding alternative energy sources. The scope of their thinking is quite unparalleled in the west.

Effective space transportation is the *sine qua non* of these ambitious Soviet plans. The Soviets already have a heavy lifting (greater than 100 tonnes) vehicle in the shape of their Energia "superbooster", which was first tested in May 1987. Western observers fall into two camps when considering the intended role of Energia. One school of thought believes it to be the socialist solution to minimizing launch costs: build enough of them, using tried and tested technology and you can hardly fail to keep launch costs down. Other authorities believe Energia to be primarily a military system: it is so powerful that it could launch a laser-toting satellite into a slightly retrograde geostationary orbit. The world's communications and geostationary satellites would coast pass this invidious weapon like so many sitting ducks – an obvious strategic advantage in the event of war.

Whatever the precise facts, no-one disputes Energia's capacity to shunt the central elements of Mir-2 into orbit very quickly. The only question is whether the Soviet space authorities will be given the necessary funding in the new era of cost-consciousness.

▲ **In September 1988**, Tass revealed the existence of a Soviet "shuttle". Buran was flight-tested unmanned two months later: it made three orbits of the Earth before making a successful landing at the Tyuratam Space Centre.

▶ **Salyut 7** was developed through fifteen years of experience with earlier Salyuts. After its launch in 1982, it was occupied by the crews of ten separate Soyuz missions. In 1986 – after Mir had been launched – it was "mothballed" by cosmonauts Solovyov and Kizim. Subsequently, Soviet authorities have talked of using Buran to bring Salyut 7 back to Earth piece by piece. In this artists's impression, Salyut 7 is shown with a Soyuz crew carrier at the top and a Progress supply vehicle below.

Total mass:	33 tonnes
Research equipment:	2 tonnes
Crew:	2-6
Power:	4 kW

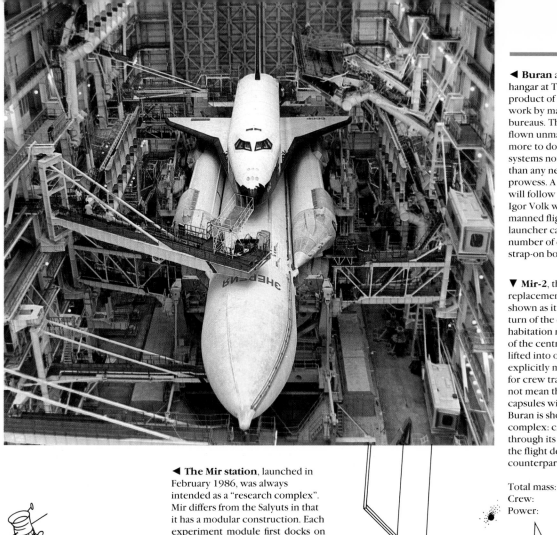

◄ **Buran** atop Energia in the hangar at Tyuratam: the craft is the product of more than 15 years' work by many individual design bureaus. The fact that it was test flown unmanned probably had more to do with its life support systems not being ready rather than any new-found technological prowess. A further unmanned test will follow in 1991, and cosmonaut Igor Volk will command the first manned flight in 1992. The Energia launcher can be flown in any number of configurations of its strap-on boosters.

▼ **Mir-2**, the large-scale replacement to the first Mir is shown as it might appear by the turn of the century. The large habitation modules in the middle of the central gantry would be lifted into orbit by Buran. Buran is explicitly mentioned as the vehicle for crew transfer, though this does not mean that "old faithful" Soyuz capsules will not be used. Here Buran is shown docking with the complex: crews will transfer through its airlock, located behind the flight deck like its NASA counterpart.

Total mass:	200-300 tonnes
Crew:	9-12
Power:	Up to 200 kW

◄ **The Mir station**, launched in February 1986, was always intended as a "research complex". Mir differs from the Salyuts in that it has a modular construction. Each experiment module first docks on temporarily to the single aft docking port; a remote manipulator then positions it on a temporary "socket" on the main module. The arm then swings through a right angle to re-dock the module with a side docking port.

Total mass:	Up to 140 tonnes
Research equipment:	4 tonnes per 19 tonne module
Crew:	3-6
Power:	Up to 18 kW

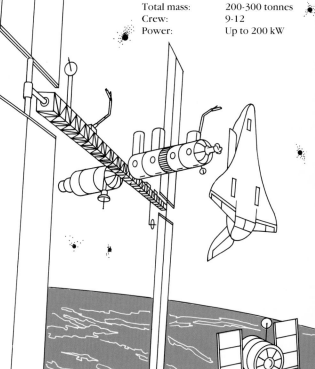

FREEDOM 1: MAN NOT MACHINE

400 kilometres (250 miles) above the Earth, a spidery framework, bedecked by numerous radio dishes and solar panels, extends for hundreds of metres around four cylindrical modules, each the size of a railway carriage. This curious object is Freedom, the western world's first long term space station. The project is truly international in nature: NASA supplied two of the modules and shunted all the elements into orbit on individual Shuttle flights, while Japan developed a sophisticated research module which carries experiments both in a pressurized environment and open to space. Canada provided a "mobile repair facility", akin to a travelling crane in a factory roof, which allowed great flexibility in building the station, and the European Space Agency (ESA) furnished the last of the four main modules, as well as one autonomous, free-flying module on which experiments are carried. Visiting supply craft, including NASA's Shuttle, ESA's Hermes and the Japanese Hope spaceplane, allow crew and equipment changes every 90 days or so.

This vision of the future is expected to become reality by the year 2000. Since it was announced by President Reagan in January 1984, Freedom has come to occupy centre stage in the west's plans for space well into the next century, but typically for projects of its size, it has been plagued by financial problems. Political indifference in the United States and the *Challenger* accident have not helped to smooth its passage. The original budget estimate of US$8 billion is now acknowledged to be wildly inaccurate, and the most pessimistic predictions now suggest that Freedom could cost as much as US$30 billion – a figure which has horrified certain elements in the space community. Estimating the true cost of Freedom is hampered by the difficulty of putting a figure to the station's true operating costs and by the uncertainty of whether the proposed assembly sequence can be maintained.

As currently envisaged, eighteen dedicated Shuttle flights, starting in March 1995 and finishing by July 1999, will be required to complete construction of the station. Astronauts will not have to wait until then to board Freedom, since a habitable laboratory module, with its own power supply, should be in place by flight seven in June 1996. By the twelfth Shuttle flight in July 1997, enough elements of the vast orbital Lego kit will have been assembled to allow the first crew of eight astronauts to move in. The original sequence of construction flights has been adjusted to minimize disruptions caused by failures in the Shuttle programme. The station's propulsion systems will now be carried aloft on an early flight, so that Freedom would not have to suffer the ignominy of re-entry.

Before discussing the station in detail, it is important to re-examine the traditional "manned vs unmanned" space research arguments. They are at the very heart of discussions of Freedom. Manned spaceflight has always been viewed with suspicion by certain sections of the scientific community. As far as performing specific scientific experiments is concerned, unmanned probes are undoubtedly cheaper and more cost effective than manned missions. The latter are financed by large industrial contracts involving intense lobbying in the corridors of power, and these big projects often eat up space agency budgets for the smaller ventures which produce more scientific results. But if the aims of space exploration are considered more broadly, then extending human experience beyond the Earth can be seen as a justifiable goal in itself and manned spaceflight is highly necessary. That is why the western nations have been – and still are – devoting resources to building a space station despite its enormous problems to date. Freedom is seen as the key to a permanent future in space.

FREEDOM
Pink: Habitation modules
Blue: Central gantry
Yellow: Solar panels

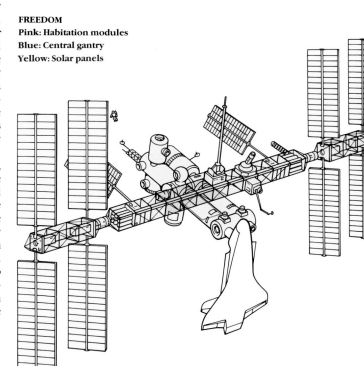

▼ **Freedom's elements** will be ferried into orbit by NASA's Space Shuttle fleet. The Canadian-built remote manipulator will jockey the modules into position. In the event of non-deployment of solar panels, space-suited astronauts could resolve the problems. In the worst scenario, elements of the station could be returned to Earth.

CONSTRUCTION SEQUENCE
1. Remote manipulator retrieves module from payload bay
2. Module deployed in space
3. Next Shuttle docks next module in place

▲ **Building the station**: NASA estimates that it will take at least 18 separate flights of the Space Shuttle over a four year period to assemble the fully-fledged station. The materials and modules will be carried in the payload bay of the Shuttle and assembled piece by piece, overseen by space-suited astronauts. By the eleventh flight, the outline of the station will be in place, allowing the first crews to arrive. A full complement of astronauts will be possible by 1999. The area outlined in red is shown in detail opposite.

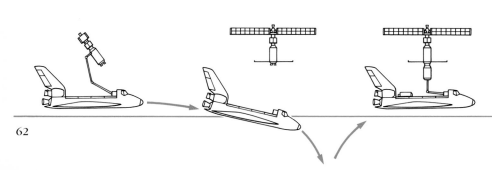

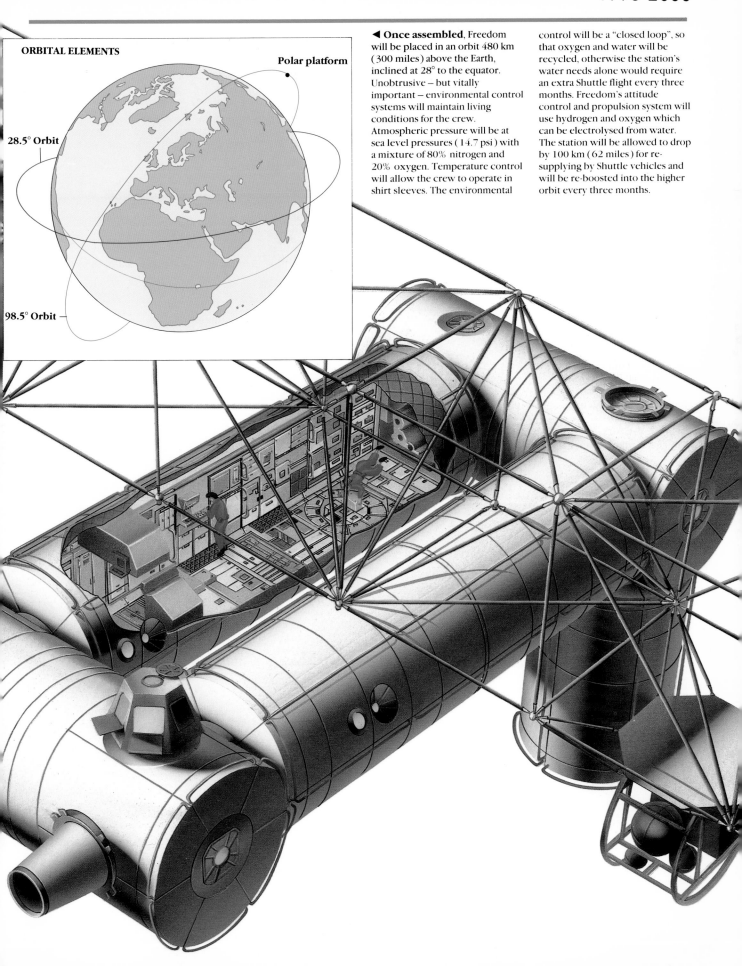

ORBITAL ELEMENTS

Polar platform

28.5° Orbit

98.5° Orbit

◄ **Once assembled**, Freedom will be placed in an orbit 480 km (300 miles) above the Earth, inclined at 28° to the equator. Unobtrusive – but vitally important – environmental control systems will maintain living conditions for the crew. Atmospheric pressure will be at sea level pressures (14.7 psi) with a mixture of 80% nitrogen and 20% oxygen. Temperature control will allow the crew to operate in shirt sleeves. The environmental control will be a "closed loop", so that oxygen and water will be recycled, otherwise the station's water needs alone would require an extra Shuttle flight every three months. Freedom's attitude control and propulsion system will use hydrogen and oxygen which can be electrolysed from water. The station will be allowed to drop by 100 km (62 miles) for re-supplying by Shuttle vehicles and will be re-boosted into the higher orbit every three months.

At the heart of Freedom are the four modules in which up to eight astronauts will live and work in a relatively comfortable, shirt-sleeve environment. "Home" will be the US Habitation Module, which is split into three separate sections: wardroom, central buffer area and a personal sleeper compartment. The wardroom will be large enough to permit the whole crew to eat and relax together: its galley will be equipped with two ovens, drinks dispensers and, for the first time, a refrigerator which will contain a selection of "TV dinner" style meals. Although space on replenishment flights will be at a premium, each crew member will be allowed to bring his or her own supply of clothes, to be "recycled" with the unprecedented luxury of an automatic washer and drier.

The central "buffer zone" between the rest and sleeping areas contains the euphemistically termed "personal hygiene" facilities including a shower unit, enclosed in a cubicle with a special hydraulic system adapted for weightlessness. Another shower located in the US Experiment Module will provide cover in case of toxic spillage. In their personal sleeping compartments, the astronauts will be able to choose between audio and video entertainment. Noise will be minimized so that the crew members can be assured a good night's rest which they will

certainly need, as they will be expected to work for six days a week on 12-hour shifts.

Crew members working in different parts of the station will be able to communicate with each other through an extensive fibre-optic network made up of a digital audio system, plus automatic video cameras located at the ends of each module. From workstations throughout Freedom, it will be possible to "punch up" views from any camera, and tilt and zoom to focus in on anything of interest. The video system will also be able to transmit back to Earth on a high-definition channel reserved for special experiments that require monitoring from the ground.

Although they are tailored for specific uses, Freedom's four modules are basically similar in internal layout. Equipment and materials will be stowed away in standard racks which will not hinder movement through the station. Each new crew member will bring up his or her own experiments, carried in these replaceable racks.

A number of onboard computer systems will relieve the astronauts' workload. The day-to-day running of the space station will be simplified by a computerized "instruction manual" system: instead of carrying vast technical documents, information on how to operate Freedom's instruments will be archived on laser discs

which will be almost instantaneously accessible. A system which detects, and automatically corrects, changes in cabin pressure is under development by ESA: and by the time Freedom flies, interactive computers capable of responding to human speech may be used.

The greatest worries aboard a manned space station are accidents and medical problems. Freedom's crew will be able to exercise and carry out routine health checks in the Habitation Module. There will be facilities to monitor vital signs and take X-rays and blood samples. Given that some of the experiments on Freedom will be run at very high temperatures, fire is an omnipresent risk. Should a fire break out, the crew could evacuate the module, sealing it off automatically, and "flood" the area with a fire suppressant to minimize the damage. Enough food and raw material is contained in each of the areas designated as a "safe haven", to support the crew for up to three weeks, and since the station's orbit regularly takes it over Cape Canaveral, this should buy enough time to launch a Shuttle mission to return the crew – assuming one is being readied on the pad. But as a back-up, Freedom will carry Crew Emergency Return Vehicles (CERVs) – basically recoverable capsules – just in case the crew have to leave in a hurry.

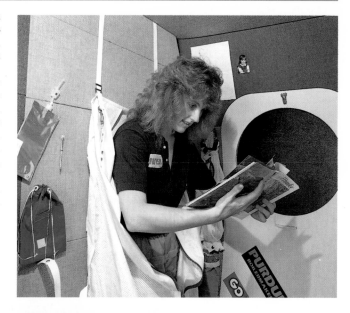

◀ **When fully operational**, Freedom will look like this dramatic artist's impression (far left). The lattice-like framework of the station spans 155 m (508 feet). The mobile transporter provided by Canada will be used for transport and assembly of the four modules during their integration.

▲ **Each crewmember** will have his or her own sleeping "compartment" about the size of a telephone box. Personal belongings will be kept in "duffel bags" that can easily be removed when the crewmember leaves for home. Individual fabric sheets will be used to decorate the compartment as paint would be impossible to use in zero gravity. Crew members will also be able to work in their personal compartments using a portable workstation linked to the space station data management system.

◀ **Corridors of power**: The four pressurized modules at the heart of the station will be the very acme of "functional" packaging. Equipment and stores will be kept in racks hidden from view. The decor may leave something to be desired as fluorescent lighting and lightweight alloys will predominate. The lower half of each module will be shaded darker to indicate it is a "floor".

The financial problems which have dogged the American side of the Freedom project are not the only obstacles to be overcome before the international space station becomes a reality. A number of technical difficulties which can be anticipated – and many more which cannot – present hidden dangers which may seriously affect Freedom's future.

The tragic events of January 28th 1986 when *Challenger* was lost still cast a shadow over the American space programme. In the aftermath, Shuttle operations and safety margins were reviewed and improvements were made: for example, emergency egress equipment which could have saved *Challenger's* crew was installed, booster seals were vastly improved and the orbiter's airframe was overhauled. NASA's own Quality and Safety Division now estimates the probability of losing an orbiter during any one mission to be between 1 in 36 and 1 in 168. Before January 1986, the figure of 1 in 10,000 was quoted.

The probability of Shuttle loss has also been addressed by the Office of Technology Assessment (OTA) in the US Congress. Their report "Round Trip to Orbit: Human Spaceflight Alternatives", published in August 1989, was even less hopeful. NASA's expectation that each Shuttle orbiter would last for 97 out of a possible 100 missions was criticized as being an optimistic target. Even though *Challenger's* replacement, the fourth orbiter, *Endeavour*, will be introduced in 1992 to aid space station construction, the OTA analysis remains pessimistic. It states that "Even if reliability is 98 percent, launching Shuttles at the rates now planned would make it unlikely that space station assembly could begin before another orbiter is lost." Although predictions of reliability inevitably vary, the message is clear. Problems with the Shuttle programme will undoubtedly occur, causing delays in the delivery of Freedom's components into orbit.

In recent years, space scientists have become increasingly conscious of another very real danger which can only be assessed in terms of statistics – space junk. Thirty years of space exploration have left a potentially lethal legacy of orbiting detritus made up of exploded rocket stages, flakes of paint and even lens caps dropped by astronauts. At present, US Space Command tracks nearly 8,000 objects larger than ten centimetres (four inches), but this is just the tip of the iceberg. A telescope operated by the Massachusetts Institute of Technology has tracked some 40,000 objects with a diameter of around one centimetre (0.4 inches), and in total there may be as many as three million objects, the majority between 1 and 50 microns (thousandths of a millimetre) in diameter, forming a hazardous cloud of debris. Some estimates suggest that up to three percent of all commercial, scientific and military satellites could be destroyed through collisions with space junk by the end of the century. This debris represents an enormous threat to Freedom, since the likelihood of impact is proportional to the square of the area of the object in question. The massive space station is thus little more than a sitting target.

The final problem for the space station is power: when "permanent manned capability" is reached, Freedom's onboard systems will require 75 kilowatts of electrical power: this demand will be met by an array of eight solar panels. In time, more experiments will be added to the station, and its demand for power will double. The shortfall will be made up by solar dynamic generators which operate by focussing sunlight onto a receiver which heats up a thermocouple. Conventional solar panels are at best only 30 percent efficient, and can seriously be eroded by atomic oxygen in the upper reaches of the atmosphere. Their repair will depend on regular Shuttle flights: if these are interrupted, serious power shortages may result and experiments, or even habitation modules, may have to be abandoned.

▲ **Early morning lift-off** for *Columbia* on January 9th 1990 on mission STS-32. Though safety margins have been increased since the loss of *Challenger*, there are still many dangers involved in spaceflight, and Shuttle launches are far from routine. Once touted as an "airliner for space", the Shuttle is now flown at roughly 1.5 month intervals. Operating a system as complex as the Space Transportation System means that delays and launch scrubs will inevitably be a feature of future Shuttle missions.

▶ **Mankind's profligate pollution** endangers life on the surface of our planet and has now extended to the skies: in November 1986, the upper stages of a European Ariane rocket exploded over Africa. The way in which the debris from this accident spread over a period of four years is shown in this sequence of graphics. The gravitational effects of the Sun and Moon, the pressure of solar radiation and the effects of atmospheric drag all serve to spread the debris.

STATISTICAL PROBABILITY OF SHUTTLE LOSS

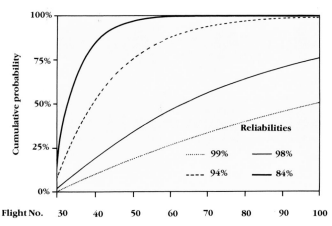

◄ These graphs show the cumulative probability that at least one of NASA's Shuttle fleet will not be recovered after a flight. Starting with the 30th flight of the Shuttle fleet (early 1990), it shows that sometime during the 1990s a shuttle may be lost. The values assigned here to orbiter recovery reliability come from a variety of sources compiled by the Office of Technology Assessment. Reducing the flight rate would slow the growth of the cumulative probability of losing an orbiter. If only five flights per year (instead of the normal seven) took place from 1990 onwards, then the chance of an orbiter being lost (assuming recovery reliability of 98%) falls from 70 to 44%.

◄ Orbital debris has the appearance of a swarm of bees in this computer-generated ESA image. Based on tracking data provided by US Space Command in mid-1988, it shows concentrations of objects larger than 10 cm (4 inches). With today's launch rates and the expected rate of decay of current debris clouds, it is estimated that a hazardous collision between any two space objects may occur once every 1-4 years. The industrialization of space will inevitably increase the concentration of "space junk" in low Earth orbit.

AFTER EFFECTS OF UPPER STAGE EXPLOSION

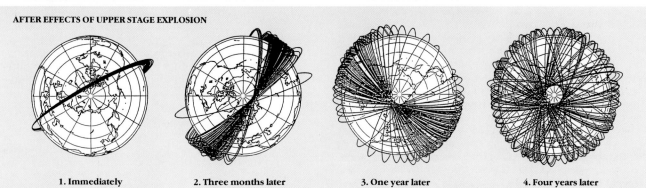

1. Immediately   2. Three months later   3. One year later   4. Four years later

TROIS, DEUX, UN . . . ALLUMAGE!

Over the last decade, the inhabitants of French Guiana have become used to their coastal road being closed for a few hours every month or so. For the location of France's overseas department – just north of the equator – makes it an ideal launch site for the European Space Agency's Ariane programme. But the citizens of French Guiana ain't seen nothin' yet – for by the end of the century, an advanced version of Ariane, carrying a mini-spaceplane called Hermes, will take Europe into the arena of manned spaceflight. Hermes will allow ESA's own corps of astronauts to visit the international space station regularly and service the Agency's free-flying experiments. In May 1990, ESA announced the establishment of a European Astronauts' Centre in Cologne to train the pilots and mission specialists who will fly Hermes into low Earth orbit. Astronauts will be recruited from all member states leading to a full complement of twenty.

Hermes started life as a French proposal which was later adopted by the European Space Agency. The French connection has been maintained, as CNES, the French space agency, may fly its own spationautes to the Soviet station Mir in the late 1990s. Throughout its development, the spaceplane has been beset by so many problems that some engineers have taken to calling it lead-footed Hermes. Many of the project's difficulties stem from the fact that the European space programme has virtually no experience in vitally important areas of space technology, such as winged re-entry, thermodynamic profiles and avionic controls. ESA's experience with Hermes has truly been a baptism of fire.

When the original plans for Hermes were drafted in 1985, a true "mini-Shuttle" was envisaged, with space for a crew of six, a payload bay, clam-shell doors similar to those on board the Space Shuttle, and a remote robot arm. The reality at the start of the 1990s is quite different: ESA's ambitious design had its wings clipped by prudence and the resulting Hermes is less versatile and will carry only a crew of three. The earlier Hermes carried no crew escape system, but after the *Challenger* accident of 1986, this omission could not be ignored. Only after two further years of research was an escape system (inspired by the ejector seats on the Soviet Buran vehicle) finalized for Hermes.

The introduction of the escape system cost not only time, but also weight: Hermes swelled from its original 17 tonnes to over 24 tonnes. The laws of aerodynamics dictate that a heavier craft needs a greater wing area to keep it airborne: but wing size had to be kept below a certain threshold or else the existing Ariane 5 booster would not have been able to lift Hermes into orbit. A solution was found: on its return into the atmosphere, Hermes will weigh less than 15 tonnes, losing its excess weight by ejecting a resource module before re-entry. Two other sections of the spaceplane are the crew and payload compartments, the latter containing spacesuits for EVA activities, rudimentary kitchen, toilet and sleeping facilities.

In the mid-1990s, Hermes will be test flown on the back of a transport aircraft to qualify its aerodynamics: its first flight into space will occur in 1998. On its third flight, Hermes will be used to service the free-flying Columbus platform (see page 70). Thereafter service flights to the free-flyer will take place every six months. Hermes' other role will be to ferry crew, and up to three tonnes of cargo, to the space station itself.

Many people have criticized Hermes for relying on 'sixties technology and not advancing the techniques needed for totally reusable spaceplanes. Yet one cannot run before walking: Hermes will allow Europe to develop the technical expertise and operational experience to move towards this goal. And whatever form the vehicle finally takes, the experience gained will go some way towards guaranteeing European autonomy in manned spaceflight for the 21st century.

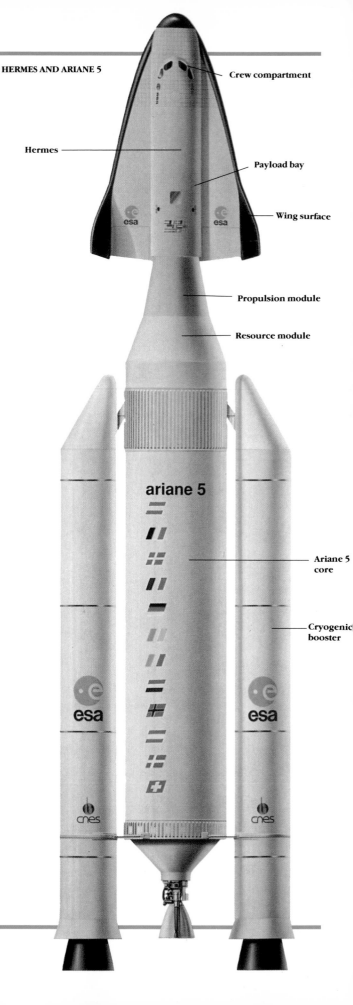

HERMES AND ARIANE 5

Crew compartment

Hermes

Payload bay

Wing surface

Propulsion module

Resource module

ariane 5

Ariane 5 core

Cryogenic booster

esa

esa

cnes

cnes

◀ **Ariane 5** will be the European workhorse in the commercial launch market of the late 1990s. Marketed by Arianespace, it will have the capacity to launch 5,900 kg (13,000 pounds) of payload into geostationary orbit. Adapted to carry the Hermes spaceplane, it will be operated by ESA from a dedicated launch pad in French Guiana. Note the absence of the Union Jack on the booster, as Britain is not participating in either Ariane 5 or Hermes.

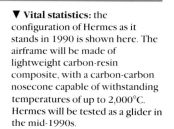

▼ **Vital statistics:** the configuration of Hermes as it stands in 1990 is shown here. The airframe will be made of lightweight carbon-resin composite, with a carbon-carbon nosecone capable of withstanding temperatures of up to 2,000°C. Hermes will be tested as a glider in the mid-1990s.

HERMES SPACEPLANE

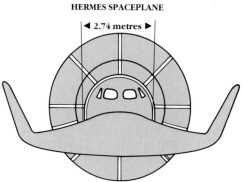

◀ 2.74 metres ▶

▲ **Return to Earth for Hermes** after a mission to the Columbus free-flyer will occur roughly ten days after launch. It will glide back to Earth in roughly the same manner as the US Shuttle, landing at 300 km/h (186 mph) on a runway 3,000 m (3,280 yards) long. The French space agency, CNES, is discussing with the Soviet Union the possibility of flying Hermes to dock with Mir. With a financial contribution of 43%, France has the largest stake in Hermes, followed by West Germany (27%), Italy (12.1%) and Belgium (5.8%).

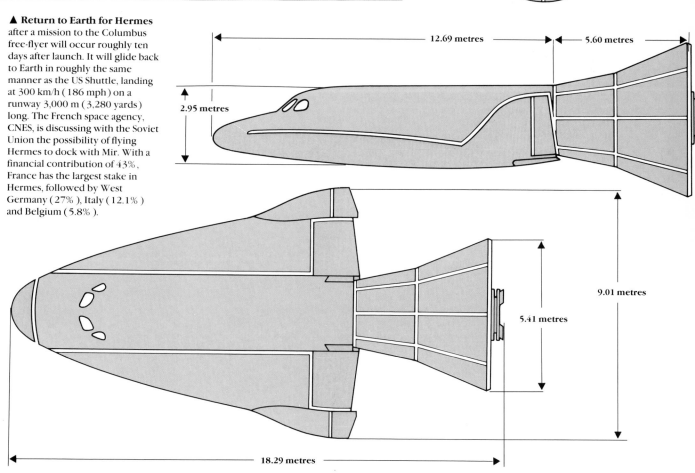

12.69 metres

5.60 metres

2.95 metres

9.01 metres

5.41 metres

18.29 metres

The international space station Freedom will have at least one companion in orbit: the Columbus Free-Flying Laboratory, will "trail" the main station and occasionally dock with it. The free-flyer will be built, launched and operated by the European Space Agency, whose astronauts will also visit the laboratory and service its experiments.

The free-flyer's design is based on units common to the main Columbus Habitation Module, and the power systems of the two elements are compatible so that they can be linked if necessary. The free-flyer will be 12 metres (39 feet) long by 4 metres (13 feet) wide and will be made up of two sections – an unpressurized part which will carry utilities and service equipment required for docking operations and servicing missions, and a larger pressurized section which will house a range of materials science and biological experiments.

Performing such experiments under undisturbed microgravity conditions is the *raison d'être* for the free-flyer (see page 72). On board the laboratory, gravity levels will be one hundred thousand times lower than on Earth. And because the free-flyer will be physically separate from the main Freedom space station, it will be fully insulated from all gravitational disruptions. On the main station, even the smallest vibrations caused, for example, by the footsteps of an astronaut, could disturb the most sensitive scientific experiments.

A variety of materials science experiments will be conducted on board the laboratory: one objective is to grow protein crystals large enough to be studied by conventional crystallography methods back on Earth. The microgravity environment is also ideal for growing purer crystals, such as those of gallium arsenide for use in semiconductors. There are many other materials science applications, for example, the manufacture of perfectly spherical ball bearings. Studies of tissue cultures aboard the free-flyer will determine how gravity affects cell reproduction, development and maturation.

The free-flyer will be "parked" in orbit behind the space station: by firing its onboard thrusters, Columbus will be able to catch up with, or move away from, Freedom. However, such manoeuvres will be kept to a minimum since use of the flyer's attitude control system would interfere with onboard experiments. Columbus will initially be placed in a higher orbit than the main complex so that as it descends – due to friction with the Earth's atmosphere – it will be travelling faster, thereby allowing it to catch up with the Freedom space station.

Roughly every six months, a manned Hermes vehicle (see page 68) will dock with the free-flyer. These replenishment flights will allow astronauts to check up on experiments and replace faulty hardware. Every two years or so, Columbus will be totally refurbished by docking with Freedom. Hermes itself does not have the capacity to act as a tug for this, so approaching unmanned vehicles will be guided into their docking positions by Orbital Manoeuvering Vehicles controlled from onboard the station. Originally, NASA was none too keen to have any craft other than their own Shuttles docking with Freedom, but since it now seems likely that Freedom will be used as a staging post to planetary destinations (see page 76), this restriction has been lifted. Freedom's new role as an interplanetary service station means that more than one vehicle will need to be docked to it at any one time. In the meantime, docking the free-flyer and Hermes itself to Freedom will allow the space agencies to practice these complex docking procedures.

To coordinate the movement of vehicles around Freedom, a "space traffic control zone" extending in three-dimensions around the station will be imposed, with approach rules similar to those used at airports around the world.

Columbus aloft: The European Space Agency will operate the first free-flyer in the whole Freedom programme. The Hermes spaceplane will be launched by an Ariane 5 booster from French Guiana. European astronauts will service the microgravity experiments aboard every six months or so.

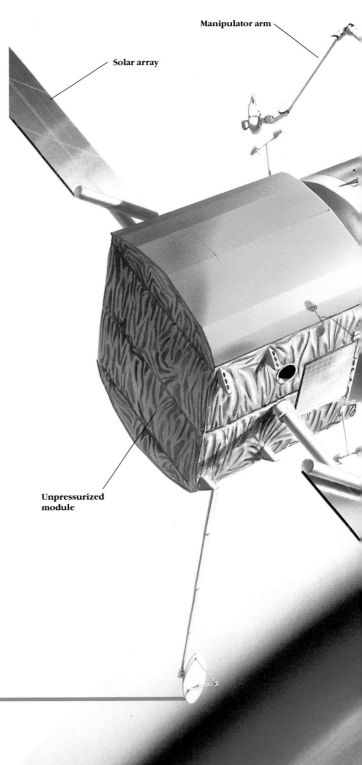

Manipulator arm

Solar array

Unpressurized module

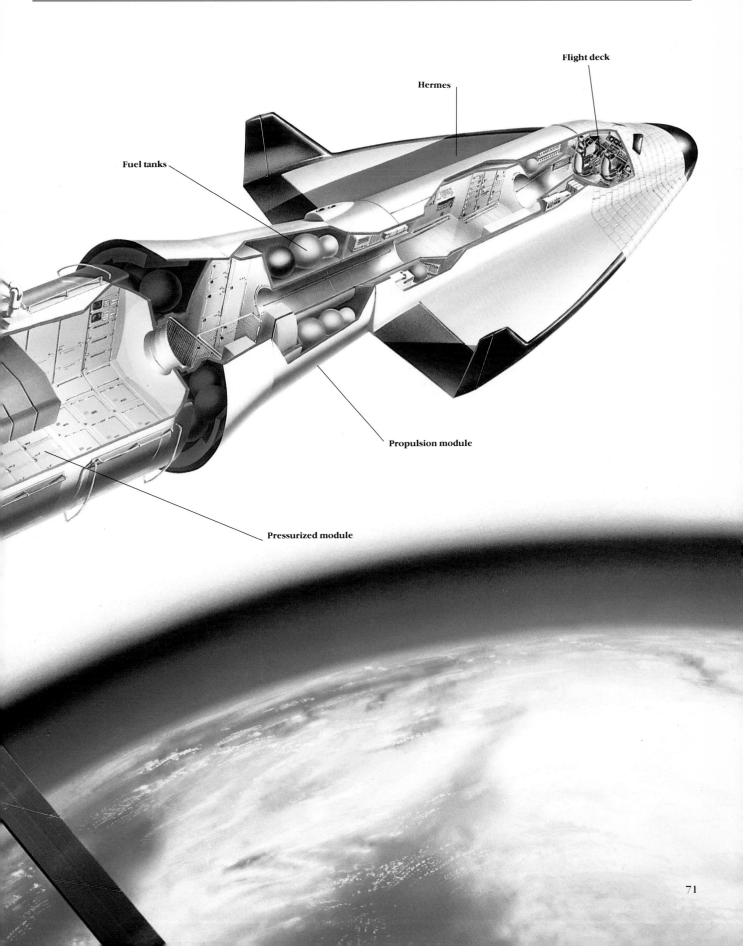

Flight deck

Hermes

Fuel tanks

Propulsion module

Pressurized module

One of the most enduring images of the space age is that of astronauts and cosmonauts floating in the eerie world of weightlessness. The absence of Earth gravity is immediately apparent as a novelty which provides a humorous distraction from the serious business of work in orbit. But research under the conditions of weightlessness – or more correctly, microgravity – has manifold commercial applications, and although microgravity research does not evoke the same level of excitement as other space endeavours, it offers the most promise in harnessing the unique environment of space for human benefit.

On Earth, gravity interferes in many industrial processes: for example, it induces faults and stresses in crystals grown for use in semiconductors or for their magnetic or optical qualities. Under microgravity, this interference is lifted and perfect, ultra-efficient crystals – worth several hundred times their weight in gold – can be manufactured. Already, the Korund 1M furnace aboard Mir has

been used to produce gallium arsenide for microchips, and with the operation of Krystal – a materials science experiment module – from the early 1990s onwards (see page 54), the Soviets may well corner the market.

Similarly, faults appear in objects cast from metal or plastic when gravity induces convection currents during cooling. This is a particular problem in composite materials where a liquid is solidified around a matrix of carbon or plastic fibres: faults in the structure spoil the strengthening effect. Gravity can also result in some substances not mixing at all. In space, scientists would be free to mix novel cocktails which could result in revolutionary alloys and compounds with many industrial uses. For example, new combinations of metals would allow the construction of smaller, lighter and therefore more efficient electric motors.

While the influence of gravity prevents some substances from mixing, it also stops others from separating. On Earth, the process

of electrophoresis – the use of an electric field to separate charged components of a mixture – is slow and often uneconomic, but in the microgravity environment of space, it is far more rapid. The manufacture of many pharmaceuticals, including the anti-cancer drug Interferon, growth hormones, urokinase for treating blood clots, and erythroprotein for kidney failure, depends on electrophoretic techniques, and could be carried out far more efficiently in orbit. Encouraging results in this field of research were reported by McDonnell Douglas engineer Charlie Walker, who flew three times aboard the Shuttle with his electrophoresis experiment before the *Challenger* accident.

To date, materials research in space has been a low-key affair. The experiments performed have been rudimentary and, on manned missions, often complicated by the relative proximity of crew members which has disturbed the most subtle chemical reactions. The many months of isolation afforded by the free-flying elements of the space station Freedom will provide exciting opportunities for new research in orbit.

With the launch of the first satellites, telecommunications became the first space-related arena to be commercially exploited: remote sensing – spurred on by environmental research – promises to be the next, and materials science is likely to follow. In 1985, the US Center for Space Policy predicted that profits from microgravity research in the first years of the 21st Century could reach a staggering US$20 billion, a figure which was immediately criticized as being wildly optimistic. But even taking into account the long lag time required for the development and application of materials science research in space, it is likely to become economically significant within the next ten to twenty years. Unlike the alchemists of days gone by, we have the scientific basis to turn many materials into their equivalent weight in gold.

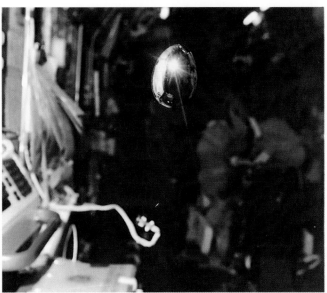

◀ **A golden egg** may be an apt metaphor for the riches to be gained from microgravity research. This gold-plated metallic egg was photographed aboard Spacelab in November 1985.

◀ **Designs for "free-flyers"** have been proposed by a number of American aerospace companies. The importance of microgravity research is indicated by the fact that US Congress has insisted that the US Experiment Module aboard Freedom be in place before the European and Japanese ones. The illustration (far left) shows a free-flyer design from McDonnell Douglas, a company which has flown electrophoresis experiments aboard the US Shuttle, yielding valuable pharmaceutical products.

▲ **The Columbus free-flyer** will provide a quiet laboratory in which a variety of microgravity experiments can be performed without human interference. Every six months or so, Hermes will be docked to replace the materials and life science experiments carried aboard.

▲ **Interferon crystals** were prepared aboard the Space Shuttle *Discovery* in September 1988. Pure crystals can be grown more easily in microgravity. Though industrial manufacture of this cancer-reducing drug is perhaps a decade away, the potential of the process is abundantly clear.

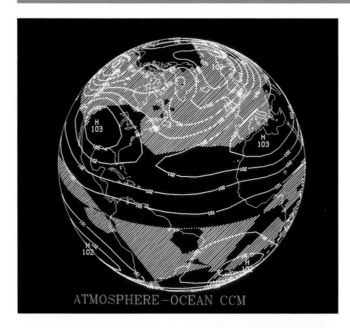

ATMOSPHERE-OCEAN CCM

▲ **Climate circulation models** using supercomputers like the Cray Y-MP, attempt to predict weather conditions across the globe up to ten days in advance (top). Ultimately, their accuracy depends on the frequency and volume of data gathered. Platforms in low Earth orbit will allow continuous readings to be taken.

▲ **This Shuttle photograph** of the coast of Mozambique shows silt deposited into the sea by a river, smoke trails from forest clearance and subtle differences in soil colour caused by agricultural activity. Remote sensing from space will allow climatologists to assess how these processes affect each other and local climate.

Sultan Salman Al-Saud, the Saudi Arabian astronaut who flew on board the Shuttle in 1985, made a poignant observation on life in orbit: "The first day or so we all pointed to our own countries. The third or fourth day we were pointing to our continents. By the fifth day we were aware of only one Earth." His words summarize the ethos driving the third, final and possibly most significant element of the whole Freedom project – that of addressing the problems of environmental change in a truly international light. For by the end of the century, three enormous platforms – one each provided by NASA, Europe and Japan – will be in orbit over the poles, scrutinizing the Earth as never before.

These first three platforms have a life expectancy of around five years, after which they will be replaced by improved structures. NASA plans to launch a further six platforms through to the year 2015 as part of its Earth Observing System (EOS): three separate pairs of platforms will be put into orbit, with each successive pair replacing its predecessor as and when deemed necessary. Planners at ESA envisage launching another two platforms in the early part of the next century.

The word "platform" is used to distinguish these large orbiting Earth observatories from smaller satellites. The first NASA platforms will weigh 3.2 tonnes on the launch pad, while ESA's structures will weigh in at around two tonnes (their design has not yet been finalized). This means that many dozens of complementary experiments can be flown, allowing a unique synthesis of the disparate studies of our planet.

NASA's first platform will be launched from the Vandenburg Air Force Base in California in December 1996 at the earliest: three months later, an Ariane 5 vehicle will take ESA's first platform into orbit. The Japanese platform is not expected to depart until 1998, the year which should also see the launch of NASA's second platform. Later generations of American platforms may be placed into geostationary orbit, and could then focus their attentions on specific areas of the globe, but before this is possible, new technology will be required to accurately point the platform's instruments onto the Earth's surface.

The first three platforms will be placed in Sun-synchronous orbits roughly 700 kilometres (435 miles) above the Earth, such that each satellite completes its cycle of orbits every three to five days, passing over any particular point on the globe at the same local time. The orbits of the different platforms will be closely coordinated with each other: for example, the first NASA platform, EOS-1, will already cross the equator from south to north at 2.30 pm local time. ESA's platform will have crossed the equator at roughly the same point, but from north to south, at 10.30 am. This orbital intertwining allows novel measurements of immense scientific value to be made. For example, on morning passes, surface rocks are cooling down from the heat they absorbed the previous day, while in the afternoon, they are absorbing radiant energy and warming up. If their temperatures at different times of day can be correlated, the capacity of these rocks to absorb heat can be determined, revealing a great deal about their natural state.

In the past, satellite studies have tended to focus only on single aspects of Earth science, yet it is clear that the Earth is a dynamic system in which oceans, atmosphere and crust all interact with each other, causing marked changes in the planet's appearance even within the course of one year. The instruments to be flown on the EOS will address these interactions; atmospheric soundings will be related to sea surface temperature measurements; vegetation monitoring will be related to local hydrology. By the second decade of the next century, we should have the most complete picture of how mankind is affecting the climate of the planet on which we live.

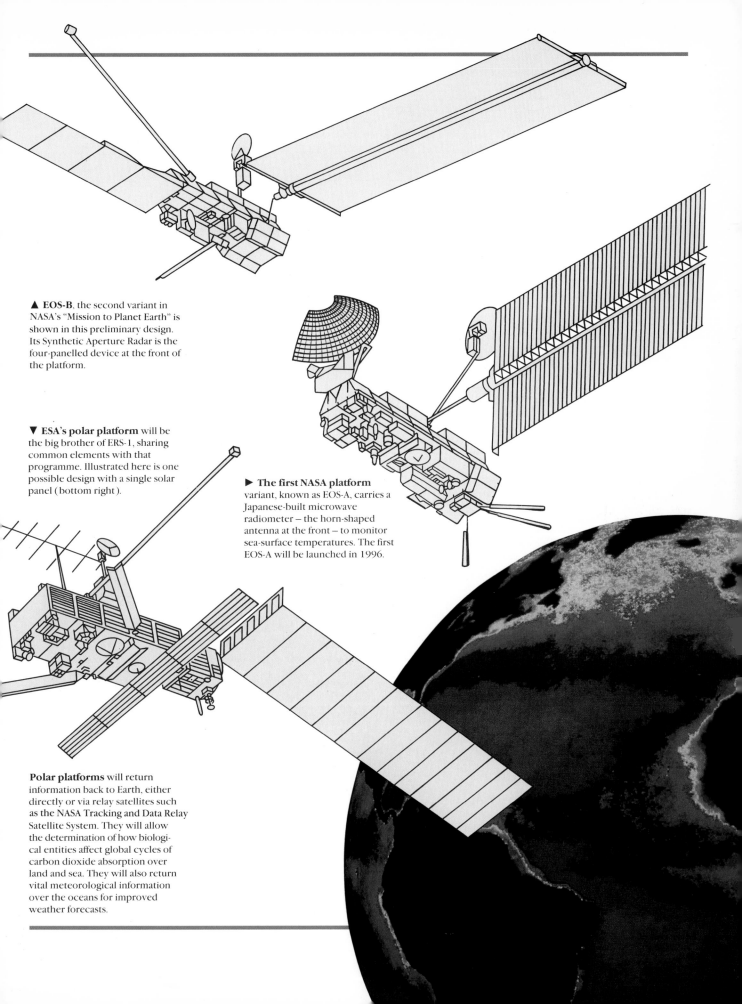

▲ **EOS-B**, the second variant in NASA's "Mission to Planet Earth" is shown in this preliminary design. Its Synthetic Aperture Radar is the four-panelled device at the front of the platform.

▼ **ESA's polar platform** will be the big brother of ERS-1, sharing common elements with that programme. Illustrated here is one possible design with a single solar panel (bottom right).

► **The first NASA platform** variant, known as EOS-A, carries a Japanese-built microwave radiometer – the horn-shaped antenna at the front – to monitor sea-surface temperatures. The first EOS-A will be launched in 1996.

Polar platforms will return information back to Earth, either directly or via relay satellites such as the NASA Tracking and Data Relay Satellite System. They will allow the determination of how biological entities affect global cycles of carbon dioxide absorption over land and sea. They will also return vital meteorological information over the oceans for improved weather forecasts.

On the twentieth anniversary of Apollo 11's landing on the Moon, George Bush addressed an expectant crowd at the Smithsonian Institution. Flanked by astronauts Armstrong, Aldrin and Collins, NASA Administrator Richard Truly and J. Danforth Quayle (Chairman of the Interagency National Space Council – a role which curiously led the Vice-President to address Armstrong *et al.* as "my fellow astronauts"), Bush declared that America would first return to the Moon and then focus its attention on the next target – Mars. The President was anxious to avoid an Apollo-like programme, declaring that "In 1961, it took a crisis – the Space Race – to speed things up. Today we do not have a crisis: we have an opportunity."

Somewhat overlooked in all this excitement was the new role that had been defined for Freedom. As the illustrations on this page show, the space station will be expanded to become a "transportation node" for missions to Mars and the Moon. Some sections of the scientific community are concerned that Freedom, originally designed as a research station, will become little more than a servicing and refuelling depot, and that in trying to be all things to all people, it may end up satisfying nobody. But despite these disagreements, all parties agree that a space station in Earth orbit is crucial to the exploitation and colonization of the Moon and Mars.

Freedom's pivotal role comes from the surprising realities of celestial mechanics: it requires only a marginally greater expenditure of energy to reach the lunar surface than it does to achieve geostationary orbit. Certain elements of the space station programme could be readily adapted to fit Freedom's new role of service station in the sky. The Orbital Transfer Vehicle (OTV) is being developed as a kind of space tug. Powered by the most efficient cryogenic propellants known – liquid oxygen and hydrogen – it will be capable of shunting heavy payloads up to geostationary orbit, 22,000 kilometres (13,600 miles) above the equator. In its new guise, the OTV will become a cargo carrier used to ferry materials to and from lunar bases. The Orbital Manoeuvring Vehicle (OMV), likened to a space taxi, will be powered by more conventional fuels. Its role will be to jockey free-flying platforms toward the station and to carry material to and from Shuttles in lower orbits.

To transform the space station into a true "gateway to the planets", many changes in its design are called for. The additional gantries envisaged in the early plans for Freedom will have to be built up. The lower keels and boom will be used for flights to the Moon, and within a decade, upper ones will be furnished for flights to Mars. To facilitate this, eight more personnel will be required, four to refit and refurbish the crew and cargo modules and another four to inhabit the nascent lunar base. At least one additional habitation module will be needed to house these new astronauts. More people means higher energy consumption, so eventually Freedom's solar dynamic power units will have to be upgraded to provide up to 175 kilowatts of power.

Ninety days after Bush's announcement, NASA's Office of Exploration released its report on how the Presidential directive could best be achieved. NASA pointed out that for a permanent manned presence on the Moon and Mars, entirely new hardware and expertise would have to be developed. "Closed loop" life support systems, aerobraking techniques, advanced propulsion systems and radiation protection would have to be perfected. NASA's euphemism for these is "technology drivers" – but they may well turn out to be formidable hurdles. The National Space Council criticized NASA's report for its lack of innovation without really saying what was meant by innovative. But no matter how the challenges of colonizing the planets are tackled, Freedom will be the crux upon which they will depend.

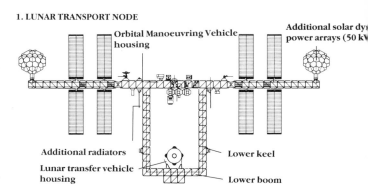

1. LUNAR TRANSPORT NODE

Orbital Manoeuvring Vehicle housing

Additional solar dyn power arrays (50 kW

Additional radiators

Lunar transfer vehicle housing

Lower keel

Lower boom

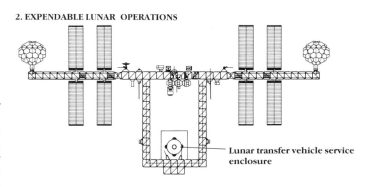

2. EXPENDABLE LUNAR OPERATIONS

Lunar transfer vehicle service enclosure

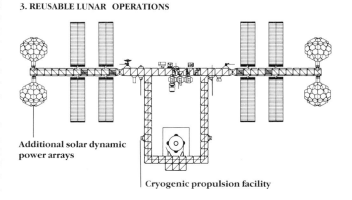

3. REUSABLE LUNAR OPERATIONS

Additional solar dynamic power arrays

Cryogenic propulsion facility

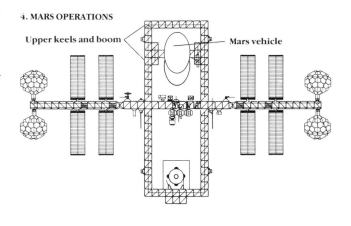

4. MARS OPERATIONS

Upper keels and boom

Mars vehicle

◄ **From laboratory to garage**: To service a lunar base, lower keels and a lower boom will be added to Freedom's assembly truss. The second stage will see routine furnishing of habitation and cargo vehicles. To house the four astronauts who will set up the lunar base, an additional habitation module will be added to Freedom. The third step will be to refurbish crew and cargo modules heading to and from the Moon: up till now, all the vehicles will have been left on the Moon. For this refuelling and refitting, two more crew members will be required, as will further solar dynamic power units to increase Freedom's power to 175 kW. To service Mars-bound vehicles, an upper boom will be added later.

◄ **It was twenty years go today**: The Apollo 11 astronauts watch George Bush sign his declaration for the "Space Exploration Initiative". Astronauts Neil Armstrong (centre), Buzz Aldrin (right) and Michael Collins (left) share a joke with NASA administrator Admiral Richard Truly and Vice President Dan Quayle.

▼ **Lunar colonists** will have to cope with the demands of a lunar night lasting 14 terrestrial days. Shown here are the collectors of a photovoltaic power system on the surface of the moon. Photovoltaic systems use semi-conductor devices to convert sunlight directly into electricity. This power will be stored in batteries and used during the lunar night.

EXTENDING THE FRONTIER

"I am proposing a long-range, continuing commitment. For the coming decade, space station Freedom – our critical next step in all our space endeavours. And next for the new century, back to the Moon. Back to the future. And this time, back to stay. And then, a journey into tomorrow, a journey to another planet, a manned mission to Mars."

President George Bush

"The British! First they have a fighter plane that takes off vertically, now a spaceplane that takes off horizontally"

French Minister of Technology, Herbert Curien's reaction to British plans for the HOTOL spaceplane

"Oh, I have slipped the surly bonds of Earth
And danced the skies on laughter-silvered wings;
Sunward I've climbed, and joined the tumbling mirth
Of Sun-split clouds – and done a hundred things
You have not dreamed of . . .
And, while with silent, lifting mind I've trod
The high untrespassed sanctity of space,
Put out my hand, and touched the face of God."

John Gillespie Magee Jr, *High Flight*

◄ **Sailing to Mars**: In this stunning artwork by Carter Emmart, a vast, sprawling solar sail is shown en route to Mars. The Red Planet is reflected in the thin mylar film of the sail.

The space-faring nations stand at the threshold of a new revolution. At its heart is the development of technology which will make journeying into space as accessible an experience as flying by Concorde is today. For the first time, routine access to and from Earth orbit will become an economic reality, allowing regular flights to space stations and scheduled intercontinental passenger services.

At present, launching satellites into space using throwaway boosters (or "expendables") is a scarcely-affordable luxury. Even the much-vaunted "reusable" Space Shuttle has failed to cut launch costs significantly. With this in mind, a number of countries are developing wholly reusable aerospaceplanes which will take off and land like conventional jet aircraft but generate enough power to leave the atmosphere altogether. The United States, Britain, France, West Germany, Japan, the Soviet Union and India are all planning hypersonic spaceplanes – the race towards economically-viable space travel is on.

All the planes share common features: they use a single booster stage to reach orbit: they are totally reusable and are propelled to hypersonic speeds by revolutionary engines that "breathe" both atmospheric and liquid oxygen. At present, launch vehicles require five tonnes of fuel to put one tonne of payload into orbit. Burdensome quantities of even the most efficient fuels such as liquid oxygen and hydrogen must be carried – for the US Space Shuttle, 610 tonnes of liquid oxygen (LOX) at lift-off. But if engines could extract oxygen from the atmosphere, LOX would only be needed when the air became too rarefied at altitude.

Extracting sufficient oxygen from the atmosphere requires the development of highly efficient engines which can cope with the switch-over to LOX from atmospheric oxygen. British engineer Alan Bond was the first to tackle the practicalities of air-breathing technology in 1982. His work gave birth to the HOTOL concept – the HOrizontal Take-Off and Landing vehicle, the first aerospaceplane to be revealed to the public.

HOTOL was designed as a communications satellite launcher for the twenty-first century. As such it was unmanned. Later, rival designs, such as the National Aerospaceplane in the United States and the West German Sanger, have crew cabins. The HOTOL variant shown here in commercial livery could well become a standard hypersonic plane for civil transportation purposes. It is interesting to note that most trans-Atlantic aeroplanes fly most of the journey on automatic pilot: but perhaps for psychological reasons, inter-continental commuters would need the reassurance of a pilot on board.

There will also be military versions. Air-breathing engine technology has immense military applications: a handful of hypersonic vehicles could replace fleets of conventional bombers almost overnight. As a result, the development of aerospaceplanes has taken place under the strictest security.

New materials will be used to cover the vehicles, to protect them from the fierce heat encountered at hypersonic speeds. These materials will need to have very high strength and very low density – seemingly contradictory properties. Considerable advances in automated flight control systems and in computing power are also required before these aerospaceplanes become a reality. The typical flight profile for all hypersonic vehicles envisages an acceleration of roughly one Mach per minute up to a speed of Mach 25. Since speeds greater than Mach 8 cannot be simulated in wind tunnels, aerodynamic designs have to be tested in purely numerical models run on supercomputers.

Despite these herculean hurdles, within a few short years, prototype test vehicles will take to the skies. Aeronautical development of hypersonic flight is analogous to that of super-sonics in the 1940s. Even the most conservative estimates suggest that launch costs of hypersonic vehicles will be reduced by a factor of five – others predict a hundredfold reduction. But for the man in the street, the most exciting development will be in civil transportation. It will be possible to fly halfway across the world in under an hour. Sub-orbital aerospaceplanes would literally allow commuting across continents.

In the 1930s, flying the Atlantic was the province of a handful of aviating dare-devils: who then would have thought that only fifty years later more than 25 million people would fly across the Atlantic every year. Very little imagination is needed to predict what may result forty years hence thanks to a new generation of remarkable vehicles.

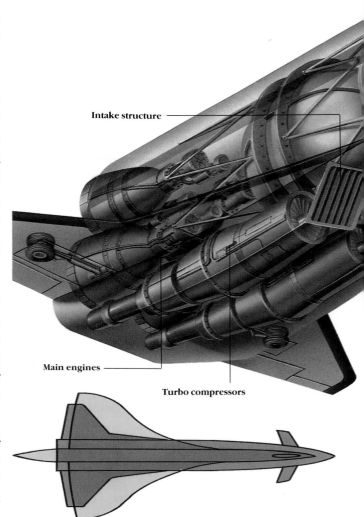

Intake structure

Main engines

Turbo compressors

A comparison between a supersonic airliner like Concorde and the hypersonic HOTOL that could be in passenger service by 2020 exemplifies aviation's unwritten creed: "higher, faster, cheaper!". Both vehicles are roughly the same size, though HOTOL's fuselage is wider – it needs to accommodate large satellites and bulky fuel tanks. HOTOL is heavier but, surprisingly, each of its four RB545 engines weighs less than Concorde's Olympus engines. Improvements in materials science have made modern engines lighter and more efficient. Because of the extremes of temperature in hypersonic flight (up to 2,000°C), the craft requires flexible thermal insulation. HOTOL is totally automated and needs no cockpit. It will carry about the same number of passengers as Concorde in a wider but shorter cabin.

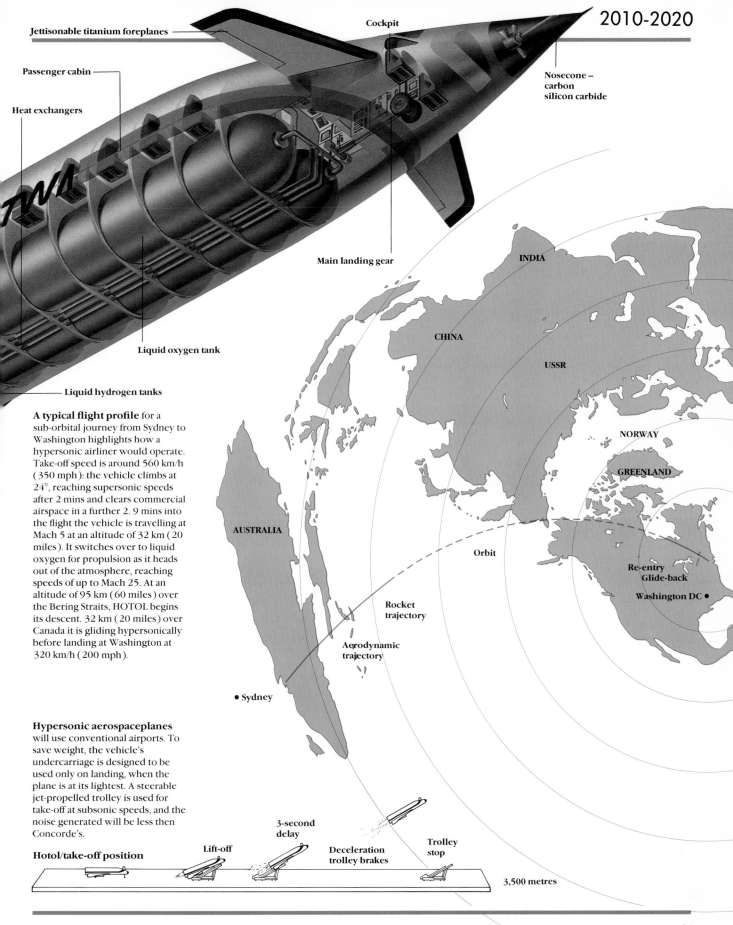

Jettisonable titanium foreplanes

Cockpit

Nosecone – carbon silicon carbide

Passenger cabin

Heat exchangers

Main landing gear

Liquid oxygen tank

Liquid hydrogen tanks

A typical flight profile for a sub-orbital journey from Sydney to Washington highlights how a hypersonic airliner would operate. Take-off speed is around 560 km/h (350 mph): the vehicle climbs at 24°, reaching supersonic speeds after 2 mins and clears commercial airspace in a further 2. 9 mins into the flight the vehicle is travelling at Mach 5 at an altitude of 32 km (20 miles). It switches over to liquid oxygen for propulsion as it heads out of the atmosphere, reaching speeds of up to Mach 25. At an altitude of 95 km (60 miles) over the Bering Straits, HOTOL begins its descent. 32 km (20 miles) over Canada it is gliding hypersonically before landing at Washington at 320 km/h (200 mph).

INDIA

CHINA

USSR

NORWAY

GREENLAND

AUSTRALIA

Orbit

Re-entry Glide-back

Washington DC •

Rocket trajectory

Aerodynamic trajectory

• **Sydney**

Hypersonic aerospaceplanes will use conventional airports. To save weight, the vehicle's undercarriage is designed to be used only on landing, when the plane is at its lightest. A steerable jet-propelled trolley is used for take-off at subsonic speeds, and the noise generated will be less then Concorde's.

Hotol/take-off position

Lift-off

3-second delay

Deceleration trolley brakes

Trolley stop

3,500 metres

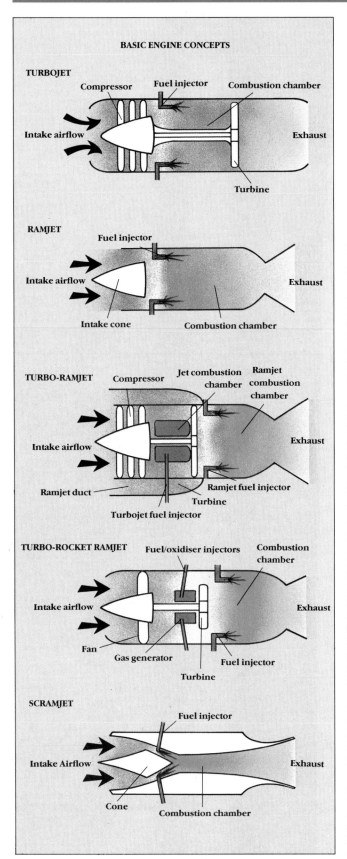

BASIC ENGINE CONCEPTS

TURBOJET
Compressor
Fuel injector
Combustion chamber
Intake airflow
Exhaust
Turbine

RAMJET
Fuel injector
Intake airflow
Exhaust
Intake cone
Combustion chamber

TURBO-RAMJET
Compressor
Jet combustion chamber
Ramjet combustion chamber
Intake airflow
Exhaust
Ramjet duct
Ramjet fuel injector
Turbine
Turbojet fuel injector

TURBO-ROCKET RAMJET
Fuel/oxidiser injectors
Combustion chamber
Intake airflow
Exhaust
Fan
Gas generator
Fuel injector
Turbine

SCRAMJET
Fuel injector
Intake Airflow
Exhaust
Cone
Combustion chamber

In laboratories all over the world, the race is on to develop the technology to fly hypersonically into orbit. At present, most of the aerospaceplane projects are deemed "technology demonstrators", a bureaucratic form of bet-hedging whereby funds are committed only to the development of the technology, without the promise of further backing. Britain was first to announce plans for an aerospaceplane, HOTOL. It has since languished due to governmental and industrial indifference, even though its chief engineer, Alan Bond, had such faith in the project that he himself tried to raise the necessary £120 million from financiers in the City of London. Bond has now proposed an improved propulsion system called SATAN which he refuses to patent so that he can be free to do with it as he chooses. Similarly, despite President Reagan's enthusiasm, financial backing for America's NASP aerospaceplane has not been forthcoming. The vehicle's first demonstration flight has been delayed until 1997.

The various aerospaceplane propulsion systems will use engines known as ramjets and scramjets. Ramjets are essentially "flying drainpipes", consisting of a long conduit into which fuel is fed. Combustion is effectively dictated by the compression caused by forward velocity of the plane, though they only work efficiently at high speed. Conventional turbojets or conventional rocket thrusters will be used to launch the vehicles into the atmosphere. Ramjets become most efficient at around Mach 2 (twice the speed of sound), but work with subsonic air: the incoming flow has to be reduced or else it becomes too hot for the engine to use. The engine is cooled using the cryogenic propellants from the onboard fuel tanks.

At around Mach 6, air enters the ramjet at such a rate that there is little time for it to burn, and shock waves are set up inside the combustion chamber. Beyond Mach 5, supersonic ramjets — known as scramjets — must be used. However, the development of scramjets presents many technological problems. So at these speeds most of the European aerospaceplane designs switch over to liquid oxygen or, in the case of HOTOL's RB 545 engine, pre-cooled liquefied air. But America's NASP aerospaceplane will use scramjets at Mach 6, and airbreathe oxygen up to Mach 16 or "as fast as possible". As a result, NASP's air-intakes will be actively cooled to reduce temperatures. Once in orbit, all the aerospaceplanes will use onboard supplies of their cryogenic fuels.

The use of ramjets and scramjets requires the manufacture of materials which can resist the very high temperatures generated by friction with the Earth's atmosphere. It's not just a case of keeping the occupants cool, as the way in which the air intakes are designed can alter the vehicle's aerodynamic profile. Heat-shields for the aerospaceplanes will require new technological advances, since a thermal protection system similar to the US Shuttle's silica tiles would simply fall off. The airframes of the new planes will have to be coated with such luxuries as carbon fibre-reinforced ceramics, silicon carbide and titanium aluminides to deal with the extremes of temperature.

The nose cone and leading edge of the wings will be heated up to around 1,600°C (2,900°F), so still more resistant compounds such as carbon-carbon and carbon silicon-carbide will have to be used. Because NASP airbreathes right up to Mach 16, its airframe will have to be coated with rapidly-solidified titanium and metal matrix composites.

Throughout the next decade, research will hopefully pinpoint some of the technological difficulties involved in hypersonic travel. One problem in particular — though perhaps not on the cutting edge of technological research — will doubtless have to be considered before aerospaceplanes become a reality: how can baggage handling be improved to cope with the increased volume of intercontinental traffic?

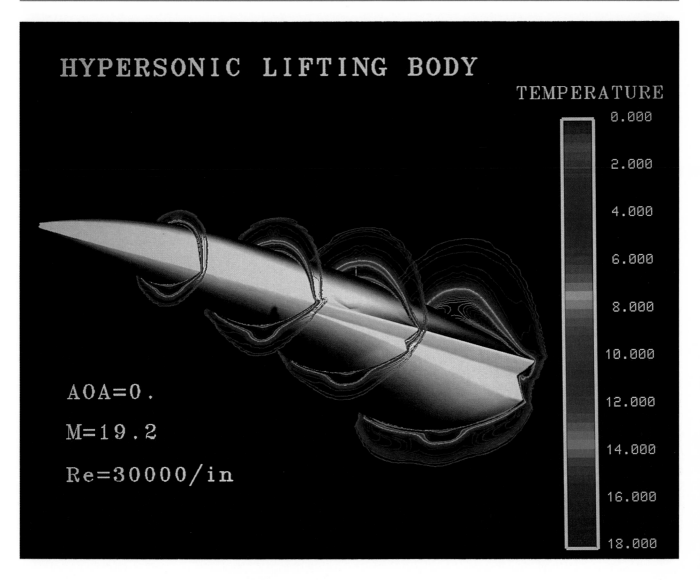

HYPERSONIC LIFTING BODY

TEMPERATURE

0.000

2.000

4.000

6.000

8.000

10.000

12.000

14.000

16.000

18.000

AOA=0.

M=19.2

Re=30000/in

▲ **Computational fluid dynamics** codes are being developed to help design aerospaceplane airframes. These computer codes will help engineers predict the behaviour of the aerospaceplanes during their ascent. The above NASA photograph shows a simulation of shock waves around a model of the NASP aerospaceplane as it travels at Mach 12.

◄ **Engine concepts** (far left): the plans for propulsion systems for the first generation of aerospaceplanes. Ramjets can only operate at high speed and so must be used in conjunction with more conventional engine designs. The development of scramjets will require new advances in technology.

▶ **A flight profile** from Europe to Freedom. After accelerating to nearly Mach 7, the vehicle would match the orbital inclination of Freedom (28.5°). It would then take another 45 minutes or so to reach Freedom's orbital altitude of 450 km (280 miles). This scheme has been proposed by West German engineers for their Sanger aerospaceplane.

Second stage separation and flyback

Transfer orbit

28.5° orbit plane

Apogee

Space station orbit

Since the earliest days of space exploration, the public has been tantalized by the possibility of pleasure trips into orbit and beyond. In 1967, the founder of the Hilton hotel chain, Barron Hilton, declared to the American Astronautical Society (AAS) that "we are going to have Hiltons in outer space, perhaps even soon enough for me to officiate at the formal opening of the first". After the Apollo 11 Moon landing in July 1969 Pan Am rather optimistically took bookings for the first commercial trips into orbit: on the passenger list was one Ronald Reagan, then the Governor of California.

However, given today's exorbitant launch costs and the dangers associated with chemical rockets, leisure trips into space are unlikely to be sanctioned by civilian authorities. The loss of *Challenger* in 1986 was a bitter reminder of the risks involved. But the advent of commercial aerospaceplanes (see page 80) will bring the concept of a space hotel into the realms of reality.

Outlined on these pages is the design for an orbiting hotel proposed by Japan's Shimizu Corporation, the world's largest construction company. At a cost of US $28 billion, the hotel could be in orbit by 2020 as the first element in a chain that may also include a hotel on the Moon. The hotel is bounded by a ring of guest rooms attached to a central elevator shaft that ends in a pyramid-shaped observation platform. The Shimizu corporation is touting six-day visits to space, including a two and a half-day stay aboard the hotel, for up to 64 guests at a time.

The Shimizu Corporation's ambitious plans to corner the market in space leisure travel are all the more surprising since Japan entered the space age very recently, with the launch of a weather satellite in 1970. But since then, Japanese interest in space has snowballed. Towards the end of the 1980s, the country's space budget more than doubled, and Japan's contribution to the Freedom project has overtaken that of the 13 member states of ESA combined. In early 1990, the Tokyo Broadcasting System bought the US $10 million seat aboard Mir outright (see page 54), whilst Britain's Project Juno suffered an ignominious demise for lack of money.

Aboard the Tokyo Orbital International, the space tourist will have no shortage of pastimes. Shimizu talks of space walks, theatre activities and even the possibility of performing wedding ceremonies in orbit! Observing and photographing the Earth would doubtlessly occupy endless hours, and curious derivatives of terrestrial sports, such as squash and handball, could develop in the hotel's low-gravity environment. Unusual forms of jacuzzis and swimming pools could provide endless hours of fun.

Tourists in distant lands have often suffered from exotic diseases and ailments. In this respect, space presents its own hazards, for waiting to vex the short-term visitor to the orbiting hotel is "space adaptation syndrome" or nausea induced by the sudden alteration of the balance mechanism in the inner ear. Around half the travellers in space have suffered from this unpleasant side-effect, and as yet there seems to be no way of screening potential sufferers before the flight. Sedative drugs such as scopolamine-dexedrine have been prescribed to counteract the nausea, though they tend to make the user drowsy.

Eating in orbit could prove entertaining, but possibly for the wrong reasons: Skylab astronauts found that drinking fluids under low gravity conditions often resulted in chronic flatulence! The Shimizu plans do not mention a bar, but as Barron Hilton told the AAS "If you think we're not going to have a cocktail lounge you don't know travellers."

▶ **Shimizu Corporation's** "hotel in the sky" would have a mass of around 7,500 tonnes, and would require at least 300 visits by supply craft to complete its construction. The hotel rooms are mounted on the wheel shaped frame (top) some 140 m (460 feet) in diameter. The whole structure will rotate three times per minute. Though Japanese businessmen are used to the privations of "capsule hotels" (insert), the rooms on the Shimizu Hotel will have such luxuries as sofa beds, toilets, showers, windows, desks and liquid-screen TV monitors. Shimizu Corporation believes its investment of US $28 million could be recouped by charging around US $45,000 per ticket. At least the prospective guest has thirty years to start saving.

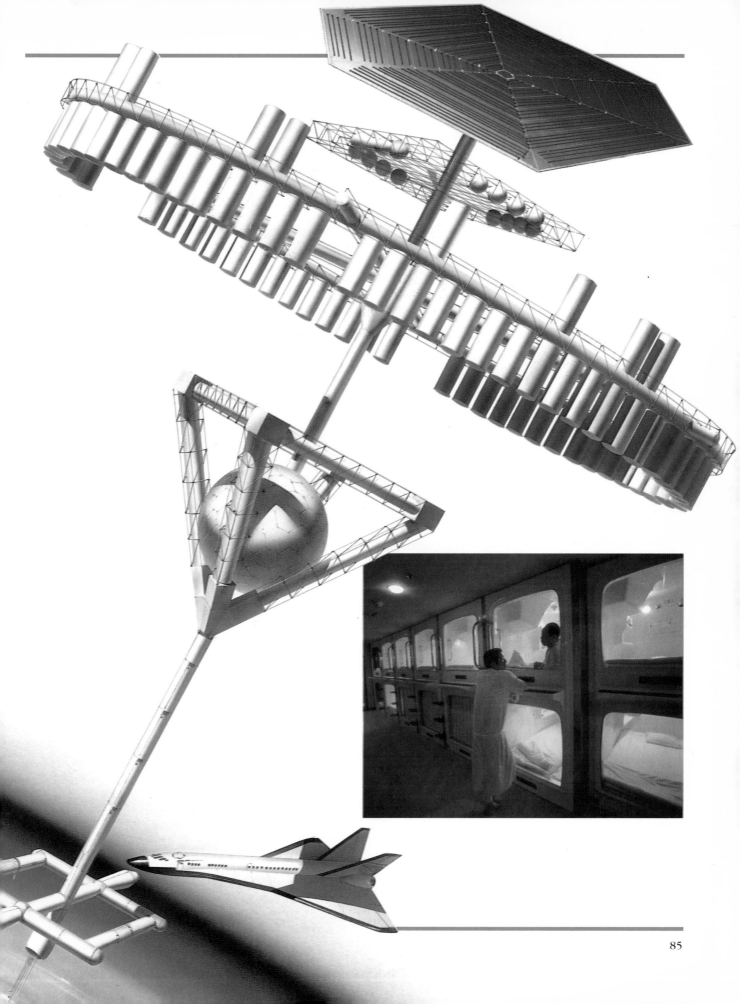

Perhaps the most pressing dilemma for mankind during the next century will be that of energy production. Today the world demand for energy is around 1,500 gigawatts, of which roughly a third is consumed in the United States. By the year 2030, it is estimated that this consumption will increase by a factor of five. Even with self-imposed restraints, the rapid depletion of fossil fuels means that alternative energy sources will have to be found. Wind and wave power, plus ocean and geothermal sources offer some hope, but they may not be enough to head off an energy shortfall. Politically, of course, fission and fusion sources commend themselves. Yet cheap, unending power from "our friend the atom" has proved not to be the miracle solution to our energy needs. The prospect of building an additional 6,000 nuclear reactors, each with a capacity of one gigawatt, is not something to be taken lightly.

Yet above our heads is a virtually inexhaustible supply of solar energy, an untapped reserve waiting to be harnessed. A network of solar power satellites could conceivably solve the industrialized world's power shortages. This concept was first proposed by Peter Glaser of the Arthur D. Little company in 1968. He envisaged a network of Solar Power satellites in geosynchronous orbit that would "transmit" power down to Earth, where it would be converted into electricity and fed directly into the national grid of the country in question. During the 1970s, various NASA-led studies concluded that around fifty city-sized solar power satellites could satisfy the current demand for electrical power in the United States.

To say that "thinking big" is the rationale behind solar power satellites is perhaps an understatement. To produce 5 gigawatts of power, a satellite 10 kilometres (6.2 miles) long and around 5 kilometres (3.1 miles) wide, and weighing nearly 60,000 tonnes would be needed. The receiving antenna or "rectenna" on the ground would also be of behemoth-like proportions. The vastness of the solar panels required for the systems in orbit would pose little problem as advances in material science would enable lightweight, film-like panels to be manufactured. Similarly, advances in technology would allow highly efficient photovoltaic convertors to be used on the ground.

Super high-frequency microwaves or lasers would be used to transmit the energy down to Earth. A laser has the advantage that light photons have higher energies than radio photons, and can be transmitted in a narrower beam, thereby reducing the size of the receiver. However, the efficiency of energy conversion is less than that at radio frequencies and light has the disadvantage of being absorbed by clouds. Microwaves pass quite freely through cloud and could be converted into electricity with up to 80 percent efficiency. The biggest problem with microwaves is "spill-out" into space and the atmosphere. The leakage of microwaves into the atmosphere could drown out natural radio transmissions, and thus put certain radio astronomers out of business. The environmental side-effects of beaming high-energy microwaves down to our planet would obviously have to be investigated before such a scheme could go ahead.

The Soviet Union has devoted a great deal of research time to the concept of solar power satellites. The Soviet designs for microwave transmitters use higher frequencies than the western variants, which means that the receivers on the ground can be smaller. The Soviet Space Agencies have formulated many ambitious and far reaching plans – such as space-based reflectors which could "light-up" enormous areas of agricultural land during winter, with obvious economic benefits. Writing in 1987, Yuri Zaitsev of Moscow's Space Research Institute concluded that "Even today, the development of an engineering design of a space-borne electric power station seems quite feasible."

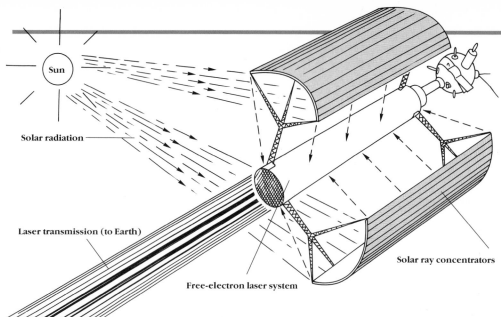

Solar radiation

Laser transmission (to Earth)

Free-electron laser system

Solar ray concentrators

▲ **Endless supply**: Shown here is a schematic design for a Soviet solar power laser, which directly converts sunlight into radiation energy by concentrating solar rays onto a free-electron laser. The radiation could then be beamed directly down to Earth. The Soviets talk of using infra-red wavelengths to transmit up to 500 megawatts of power. Solar power satellites could also be used to send energy between satellites in low Earth orbit.

◀ **Proof of concept**: Direct conversion of sunlight into power has been achieved at this solar power station in Alberquerque, New Mexico. The mirrors focus the solar radiation onto a receiver atop the tower seen in the distance. It then heats a water supply which is vapourized into steam to run a turbine. Receiving stations for solar power satellites would extend as far as the eye can see in this particular view.

▲ **Save it**: Wind farms near Palm Springs, California are a familiar sight to local residents. Even if energy conservation measures reduce the five-fold increase in demand for power expected by the year 2030, there will still be an energy shortfall unless technologically advanced nations grow to depend more heavily on nuclear power. What price – environmentally and socially – solar power satellites?

January 26th 1990 saw the launch of the first Moon-bound probe for fourteen years. The spacecraft was put into a highly-elliptical cigar shaped orbit around the Earth, such that it made a close pass of the moon on March 18th, when a tiny probe was deployed into lunar orbit. Normally a straightforward engineering test of type kind would not merit much attention. But the fact the MUSES-A probe was launched from the Uchinoura Space Centre in south-east Japan atop a booster built by the Nissan car company, meant that many people sat up and took note. Japan had become the third nation to launch a probe to the Moon.

Modest it may be, but MUSES-A marks the start of the Japanese lunar initiative. The spacecraft was the first engineering test of a lunar probe and will be followed by still more advanced Moon probes. Japan's Institute for Space and Astronautical Science has also proposed a similar technology demonstrator mission to fly to

Venus in the mid-1990s. Emboldened by their participation in Freedom, the Ministry of International Trade and Industry (Miti) is steering Japan's manned space programme efforts towards the Moon. Miti sees Japan's space programme as a "driver" – a force which will accelerate developments in high technology. It was with this in mind that a Soviet delegate at an international conference in 1987 quipped that the superpowers ought to send humans to Mars quickly or else the Japanese would get there first with one of their robots!

The Japanese have set their sights squarely on the Moon: since 1987, a team of 25 engineers at the Shimizu Corporation has been looking into the feasibility of lunar bases. The all-important area of lunar architecture is just one in which the Japanese are achieving pre-eminence. It is easy to see the rationale behind Japan's interest: a country with few natural resources can look to

the Moon as a bountiful source of metals and minerals. And with unit costs roughly half those in the West, the extraction of these riches is likely to become economically viable in Japan far sooner than anywhere else.

The lunar samples returned by past American and Soviet missions showed lunar soil to have many potential uses: for example, it makes excellent concrete. By powdering the soil and binding it with epoxy resin, a durable building material can be made: moreover the ingredients are ubiquitous across the lunar surface. The lunar soil appears to be totally desiccated – both water and chemically-bound hydrogen are absent. But oxygen, bound up in the rocks as metallic oxides, is readily available: chemical engineers have devised a process of heating Moonrock with methane to produce water and carbon dioxide and electrolysing it to produce oxygen. The oxygen thus liberated could be liquefied and used as a propellant, or fed into the lunar base to sustain human life.

The metallic oxides in the lunar soil could be profitably mined. The seas of the Moon are rich in titanium and iron, while the highlands contain deposits of aluminium. Experiments suggest that spin-casting methods would allow the manufacture of metallic fibres from the basaltic material – these would be ideal for use in fibre-composite materials. The titanium could also be worked upon to produce high-strength metallic foam composites. Glass-like crystals in the lunar soil could also be drawn into fibres by relatively simple mechanical extension processes.

For a country starved of natural resources, facing a world that is polluting itself to death, the Moon does not appear to be a barren place at all. Centuries ago, Japanese emperors built special pavilions from which they and their minions could view the Moon. Some time in the next century this form of celestial voyeurism may well come full circle when Japanese engineers build viewing ports from which they can observe the Earth from the vantage point of the Moon.

Moon City: A Japanese Moonbase designed by engineers from the Shimizu Corporation. In 1989 alone, the giant Corporation made a profit of US $9 billion and is now looking to invest in major space projects. The Moonbase is its ultimate goal for the first half of the 21st century. To the left of the picture are solar dynamic arrays, partly obscured by the base's main communication antenna. The eight main housing "nodes" which protrude above the surface are linked by a series of tunnels. To the right of the picture is a service road and lunar vehicle.

A base on the Moon will pose many design problems for future lunar settlers. And the way in which those problems are solved will be of great significance, since NASA sees its "lunar outpost" as a testing ground in which the technology and experience needed before human beings can venture further out into the Solar System will be developed. The first excursions to the Moon – in which a crew of four and a variety of cargo will spend a month on the lunar surface – will put into place the barest bones of a lunar base, most probably by linking habitation modules from the Freedom space station. However, this is likely to prove unsatisfactory in the long term, since the Moon boasts 1/6th Earth gravity, while Freedom's modules were designed with weightless conditions in mind. On the lunar surface, the absence of gangways and the vertically-mounted sleeping quarters will be more than just a slight inconvenience!

What would turn this motley collection of habitat and laboratory modules into a true lunar base would be the construction of an inflatable dome – what NASA describes as a "Constructable Habitat Concept Design". At just under nine metres (30 feet) in diameter, the dome could house a dozen astronauts on four levels. The dome's skin, made of Beta cloth (used in spacesuits) or Kevlar (used in bulletproof vests), would be inflated from the inside, and the whole structure strengthened from within by self-deploying columns. A spiral stairwell running through the centre of the dome would give access to the four different levels: exit would be via a habitation module attached to one side of the dome and adapted for use as an airlock.

The 14-day cycle of lunar day and night presents its own challenges: temperatures on the Moon base will range from −173°C (280°F) to 112°C (234°F), depending on whether it is plunged into complete darkness or direct Sunlight. For the base to operate throughout the long lunar night, its photovoltaic and solar dynamic generators will have to be augmented by a nuclear dynamic power system. NASA currently favours radioisotope thermonuclear generators like those used aboard the Voyager and Galileo craft. The habitation areas will have to be suitably shielded from these potentially dangerous man-made radiation sources, as well as from natural hazards such as cosmic rays and bursts of intense solar radiation. It is envisaged that Moon bases may eventually be buried under the lunar soil as a protective measure. Another suggestion is that lava tubes – snake-like ridges formed from dried out lava flows – could readily be converted into habitable compartments. They would have the additional advantage of shielding their occupants from the extremes of heat and cold on the lunar surface.

Ironically, the constant bombardment of the lunar surface by cosmic radiation may one day work in the colonists' favour, for a component of this radiation is the valuable isotope, helium-3. On Earth, helium-3 is a by-product of thermonuclear fuel processing which could be used as a cleaner and more efficient fuel for nuclear reactors were it not so rare. On the Moon, however, it is ubiquitous and waiting to be mined. It also has another great benefit: every tonne of helium-3 extracted from the Moon yields 3,300 tonnes of water – a rare commodity on the lunar surface.

The Moon provides scientists with an exciting range of possibilities: hard vacuum accelerators could be constructed far more easily than on Earth, as could networks of laser reflectometers to measure gravity waves in space: an observatory on the far side of the Moon would weigh 100 times less than an instrument of equivalent resolving power on Earth. Isolated from the increasingly radio-noisy planet Earth, a network of radio dishes linked as interferometers (see page 26) could be built up on the lunar surface putting unprecedented resolving power at the disposal of radio astronomers.

▼ **Astronomy from the Moon** would give us a new perspective on the universe. University of Arizona astronomers have proposed this transit telescope which uses lightweight reflectors. A "transit" refers to the passage of a celestial body across an observer's local meridian. From the Moon, a transit telescope would be used for highly accurate measurements of the Solar System.

► **2020 vision**: NASA's current concept of a lunar outpost consists of an inflatable habitat dome attached to a "construction shack" used during its building. Coiled bags of lunar soil at the base of the dome give additional protection against radiation. Behind the dome, leading toward the horizon, is a "road" cleared to a landing pad. Power for the base is provided by the solar power system (top right).

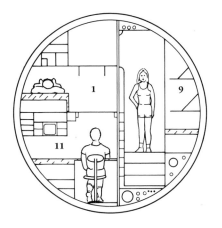

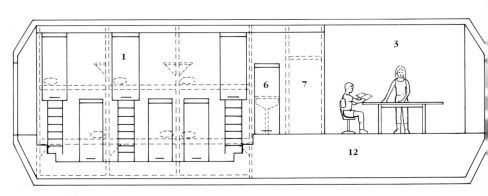

Habitat module

1. Private Quarters
2. Corridor
3. Galley
4. Kitchen
5. Toilet
6. Bathroom
7. Shower
8. Storage Compartments
9. Temporary Bunks
10. Sink
11. VDU Screen
12. Life Support System

▼ **In 1988**, students at the International Space University considered constructing a lunar base using modules from Freedom which will be available by the year 2000. Such modules could easily form the basis of a tentative outpost on the Moon within the first decade of the 21st century. Four modules – dedicated to habitation, power generation, life science and geophysics research – could be assembled on the lunar surface. Orbital Transfer Vehicles would jockey the modules into orbit around the Moon where they would be linked together. A lander stage would then be used to lower the whole structure onto the surface. Cross-sections through the habitat module are shown here in elevation and plan.

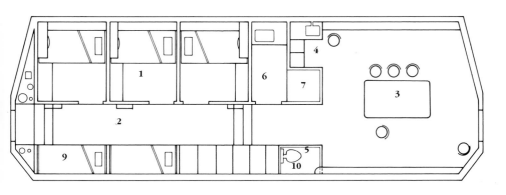

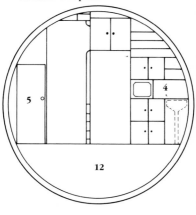

Some time in the next century the first human will set foot on Mars. A journey to the Red Planet will place a new set of psychological demands on future space travellers: all sentimental and physical attachments to the Earth will have to be put on ice. The isolation factor – which the National Commission on Space described as "severing the umbilical with the home planet" – will have to be given serious consideration if future missions to Mars are to stand any chance of success.

Prolonged spaceflight is already known to have debilitating physiological effects, indeed the risk of dying on a flight to Mars is thought to be so great as to warrant carrying an onboard mortuary. The biggest dangers come from repeated exposure to radiation and progressive bone demineralization. Solar flares – which remain unpredictable (see page 34) – throw vast plumes of lethal radiation into the Solar System. In August 1972, in the course of an hour, such a flare generated a skin dosage equivalent to over four times the recommended lifetime maximum for Freedom astronauts: unshielded, this could have been lethal. Storm shelters – either lead-lined, or surrounded by water-filled bags – may provide one solution, but to assess their effectiveness, we will need to gather more data on how human physiology is affected by radiation in space.

Astronauts on long space journeys are likely to suffer from progressive bone demineralization: weight-bearing bones are not compressed under zero-gravity conditions and the resulting calcium loss can lead to kidney stones and even cranial difficulties. These problems could be eradicated by building spacecraft with artificial gravity – and whilst the idea of their spindle-like arms rotating gracefully around a central hub does have a certain attraction, it carries its own set of drawbacks. Rotating structures can also cause disorientation, nausea and fatigue, as well as sleep and mood disturbances.

Previous experience with long-duration missions has emphasized the importance of balancing the daily workload with physical exercise, rest and relaxation in order to prevent boredom and fatigue. But the prospect of exercise regimens lasting up to four hours per day – which has been proposed for Mars missions – is unlikely to gladden the heart of any astronaut.

The psychological difficulties peculiar to life in space have been well documented. In 1985, Soviet cosmonaut Vladimir Vasyutin became fatigued and listless while attempting to stretch the then endurance record toward the 300-day mark aboard Salyut 7. At the end of his stay aboard Mir, Yuri Romanenko repeatedly lost his temper with ground controllers over changes to work schedules. Similarly, when NASA tried to load the final Skylab crew with additional work, they literally went on strike. Skylab astronaut Bill Pogue was later to say "I'm a fallible human being, I cannot operate at 100 percent efficiency, I am going to make mistakes." Apart from Antarctic Bases, there are very few situations similar to space in which the effects of long-term isolation of groups of people can be tested. Without sufficient data, psychologists are left to argue over the structure of hierarchal roles within the crew, the need for privacy and even how to suppress the normal sex urge in adults. But these unexplored parts of the human psyche must be understood if humankind is to extend its domain into space.

Unlike the three days or so it took to reach the Moon, a return journey to Mars will take around three years. The technology base and expertise needed for such a journey would require a long-term financial commitment. In 1986, the National Commission on Space suggested that it would cost 0.5% of the US Gross National Product over a thirty-year period. Such a commitment would fund more than just another space spectacular: it would be the next evolutionary step for the human race.

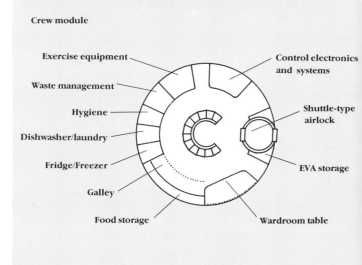

Crew module

Exercise equipment

Waste management

Hygiene

Dishwasher/laundry

Fridge/Freezer

Galley

Food storage

Control electronics and systems

Shuttle-type airlock

EVA storage

Wardroom table

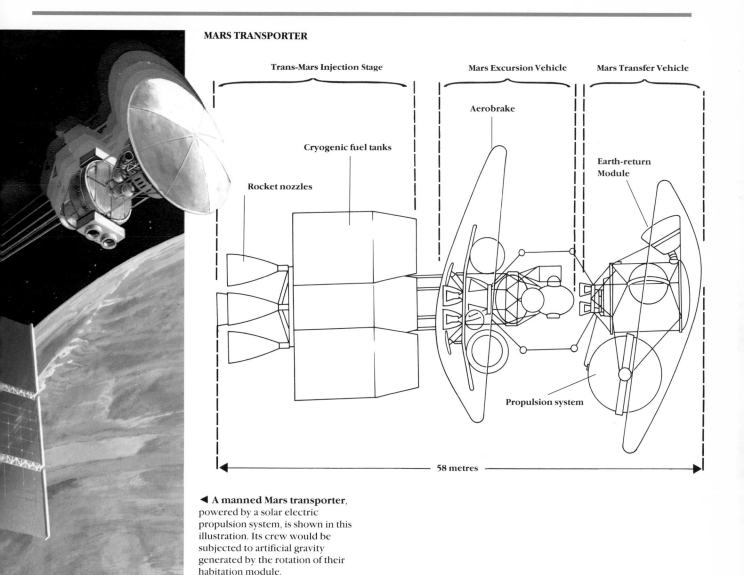

MARS TRANSPORTER

Trans-Mars Injection Stage

Mars Excursion Vehicle

Mars Transfer Vehicle

Aerobrake

Cryogenic fuel tanks

Earth-return Module

Rocket nozzles

Propulsion system

58 metres

◀ **A manned Mars transporter,** powered by a solar electric propulsion system, is shown in this illustration. Its crew would be subjected to artificial gravity generated by the rotation of their habitation module.

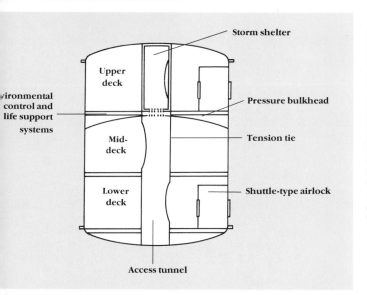

Storm shelter

Upper deck

Environmental control and life support systems

Pressure bulkhead

Mid-deck

Tension tie

Lower deck

Shuttle-type airlock

Access tunnel

◀ **Home from home**: Initially crews of four astronauts will travel to and from Mars in the single, pressurized crew module. It can be seen at the front end of the whole Mars craft above. The module is 7.6 m (24 feet) in diameter and 9 m (29 feet) long. An internal pressure bulkhead means that in the event of an emergency, the crew could retire to the relative safety of the upper third of the module. The module has a life support system which recycles water and oxygen. Each crew member has a private compartment similar to those on board the space station Freedom.

▲ **Chariots of fire**: The first settlers on the Red Planet will travel to and from Mars in vehicles such as those shown above. Each vehicle has three distinct parts: high-efficiency cryogenic engines (left); a Mars lander into which the crew transfers on arrival at Mars (centre); and the Mars Transfer Vehicle (right) in which they live in transit. Each transporter craft is assembled at the Freedom station in low Earth orbit. The vehicle as a whole is placed on a Mars transfer orbit by the propulsion system (fully known as the Trans-Mars Injection Stage) which has five main engines and up to three additional strap-ons. The landers and transfer vehicles have large aerobrakes, which can reduce the amount of mass that has to be lifted from Earth by up to 50%.

MARS 2: EXPRESS RETURN

The laws of interplanetary mechanics are immutable. They set their own limits to journeying to and from the Red Planet: complex gravitational interactions between Earth, the Sun and Mars mean that opportunities to launch missions there occur only every 26 months or so. Furthermore, orbital irregularities make some of these opportunities better than others. The flight profiles of missions to Mars must be planned around these restrictions if bases are to be established on the planet.

Planetary dynamics permit two "types" of Mars mission – short and long stay. The former, launched when the Earth and Mars are on roughly opposite sides of the Sun, involve a stay of 100 days on the Martian surface and a round trip of 500 days duration. Short-stay missions would be used to set up the Mars base: the first flight would carry a crew of four who would live in a temporary habitat facility. The second, unmanned, flight would deliver a permanent residence, as well as airlock, power and support systems, and thus pave the way for the first long-stay manned mission to the planet. These missions – launched when Mars and the Earth are the same side of the Sun – are more efficient in terms of energy, but involve a longer wait (typically 600 days) before a return is possible.

In the past, interplanetary spacecraft have carried large quantities of fuel to decelerate them into orbit around their target planets: Viking 1, for example, used over two-thirds of its onboard propellant to achieve its orbit of the Red Planet. The capacity of any supply craft is therefore limited by the need to carry this "deadweight" fuel – a serious problem for the occupants of a future Mars base. However, engineers have now devised a powerful technique – known as aerobraking – which increases cargo capacity by eliminating this dependence on retrofire fuel. A suitably designed spacecraft can "dip into" a planet's atmosphere and burn off speed through frictional heating. This technique could allow up to 45 percent more cargo to be carried to and from Mars. The beauty of aerobraking is that it could also be used when returning to Earth.

The disadvantage of aerobraking is that flight control systems have to be more sophisticated to compute, and continually recompute, the spacecraft's complex trajectory – a tightrope between too steep a dive (resulting in burn-out) or too shallow (resulting in the craft "bouncing" out of the atmosphere). After

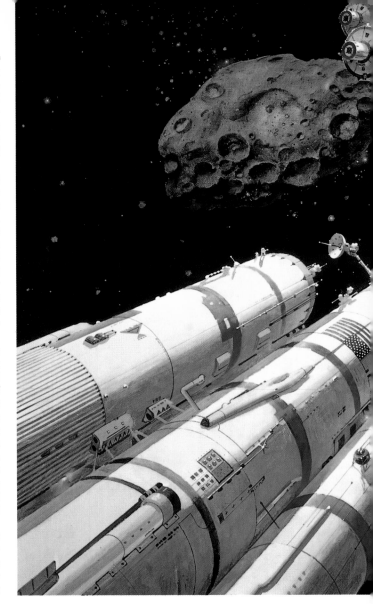

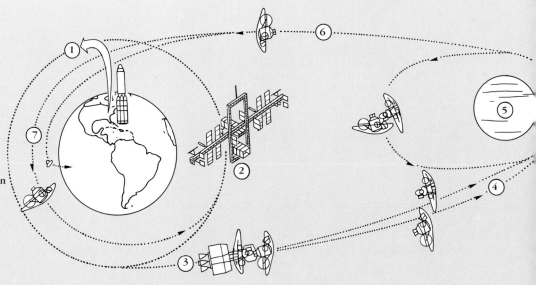

A mission profile for early base emplacement on Mars.

1. Cargo and crew of the Mars-bound vehicle are prepared at Freedom "transport node".

2. Mars Transfer Vehicle, housing a crew of four, is mated with rest of vehicle.

3. Trans-Mars Injection Stage fires to send whole craft toward the Red Planet.

4. Mars Lander separates and arrives on Mars 7 days before Transfer Vehicle, which remains in Mars Orbit.

5. Crew transfer to/from surface in the Lander.

6. Crew return to Earth in Transfer Vehicle.

7. Transfer Vehicle aerobrakes and crew either return to Freedom or to Earth.

◀ **Martian chronicles**: Once an efficient transport system between the Earth and Mars has been set up, a transportation depot similar to that pictured here could be in

place in Mars orbit. In the foreground, space-suited astronauts perform important servicing work before the transporters return to Earth.

How to get there. The gravitational interactions between Earth, Mars and the Sun will be exploited by the Mars colonists. Large transportation vehicles will regularly ply the "interplanetary highways" mapped out below.

▶ The traditional route between the two worlds takes 2.7 years in total. Stopover time on Mars varies between 330 and 520 days.

1. Conjunction Class

2. VISIT-1

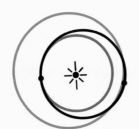

▲ The first cyclical orbit has a period of roughly 1.25 years, and encountering Mars near to its perihelion, when it is closest to the Sun.

3. VISIT-2

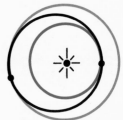

▲ With a period of 1.5 years, these VISIT orbits encounter Mars at aphelion, thereby increasing the time available for rendezvous.

4. "Up" escalator

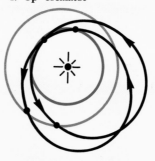

▲ Up/Down Escalator orbits have more frequent and regular encounters with both planets. The 'Up' Escalator minimizes the Earth-Mars transit time to six months.

5. "Down" escalator

The "return" leg (Mars-Earth) is minimized: gravity assists from the more massive Earth are used on both escalator orbits to match the orbital rotation of both planets.

---

extended periods of weightlessness, crew members could be debilitated by the sharp deceleration on re-entry. NASA has therefore set the limits to entry speed at 8.5 kilometres per second (5.3 miles per second) for Mars and 12.5 kilometres per second (7.8 miles per second) for Earth. During the 1990s, the potential for aerobraking techniques will be tested in earnest.

A quirk of interplanetary mechanics may allow the first colonists to benefit from an "interplanetary bus service" between the Earth and Mars. A spacecraft orbiting the Sun between the orbits of the two planets can ply a trajectory that regularly intersects the orbits of both. Powerful number-crunching computers have shown that, with only occasional navigational tweaks, four supply craft could give Mars colonists a reasonably regular supply service. By altering these cycling (VISIT) orbits, a subtle variation known as an escalator orbit can be achieved which would minimize the transit time to and from Mars.

Crews returning from Mars, or replacements heading out from Earth, would use transfer vehicles to reach the supply ship: similarly, cargo vehicles could hook up to the "cosmic ski-lift" as it passed by. The main drawback is that the timing involved in catching up with and undocking from the supply ships is critical. Error margins are minute – and for Mars colonists, missing the bus home would have serious repercussions.

MARS 3: TO MARS – TOGETHER ?

In July 1985, five middle-aged men took centre stage in a Washington DC auditorium. All five were old friends: ten years earlier they participated in the Apollo-Soyuz Test Project, the only large-scale collaborative space venture between the superpowers. In the intervening years, astronauts Stafford, Brand and Slayton along with cosmonauts Kubasov and Leonov had retired from flight status, though were still involved in space enterprises. They used the tenth anniversary of their flight to make a clarion call for further cooperation, culminating in a joint mission to Mars. Subsequently, they have been amongst the most vociferous proponents of the "Together to Mars" lobby.

Four years later, George Bush stood in the same auditorium and committed the US to an eventual Mars outpost, emphasizing the need for America to achieve pre-eminence in space. Yet with the opening up of the Eastern Bloc, conditions for a joint venture are at their most favourable for years. Mikhail Gorbachev has discussed a joint mission to Mars on several occasions. But is such an enterprise really likely?

The pros and cons of space collaboration must be carefully assessed, for the savings in cost made possible by sharing technology and expertise march hand in hand with the dilution of control and increasing management complexity. But without doubt, the challenges of Mars colonization could be best tackled by combining Soviet and American know-how: the Soviets have extensive experience of long-term spaceflight (see page 54) while American space technology is more sophisticated.

Soviet-American collaboration could provide a solution to the dilemma at the heart of NASA's plans for a base on Mars – cargo capacity. It has been estimated that anywhere between 550 and 850 tonnes of vehicle elements and fuel will be needed each year to maintain extended stays on the Martian surface: the trans-Mars injection stage propellant tank (the fuel stage to boost a spacecraft to Mars) alone requires around 135 tonnes of launch capacity. The various other elements, including aerobrakes and individual engines, will have to be lifted up to Freedom before their onward journey to Mars.

Given that the Space Shuttle can carry a maximum of around 30 tonnes, one can understand why NASA is exploring the possibility of using "big dumb boosters" to increase payload capacity. A variant shown here, the Shuttle C, could hoist perhaps 70 tonnes, and its big brother, the Heavy Lift Launch Vehicle could handle around 120 tonnes. Yet a continent away, such a vehicle already exists: the Soviet Energia booster is capable of lifting 140 tonnes into low Earth orbit. NASA could easily adapt its vehicle elements to be flown atop the Soviet craft.

On a Mars outpost, a closed-environment life support system – one which generates oxygen from exhaled carbon dioxide, drinking water from body wastes and allows basic foodstuffs to be grown – is a necessity. The development of such a system would also benefit from close cooperation between the superpowers. Experiments run aboard Mir have acquainted Soviet scientists with the demands of growing plants hydroponically in orbit, while genetic manipulation techniques developed in the United States can be used to engineer durable strains of crop plants.

The universe of political reality is far more perplexing than that which spacefaring pioneers wish to traverse. Forecasting the political climate between the superpowers is infinitely more difficult than predicting the future in space. Apollo-Soyuz stands as a curiosity in the history of space, the crowning glory of détente. But the precedent for collaboration between the superpowers has been set: it is to be hoped that unbridled nationalism will not confound what could become a great political triumph. Mars, for so long associated with war, would be transformed into a potent symbol of peace and harmony.

▼ **Base camp**: Paul Hudson's painting "Winter Morning on Mars" depicts perhaps the greatest hope for space exploration in the next century – a joint superpower mission to Mars. The Stars and Stripes and Hammer and Sickle flown together are an evocative symbol of peaceful cooperation.

▶ **The first humans** to walk on the surface of Mars explore Noctis Labyrinthus ("Labyrinth of the Night") at the eastern end of Valles Marineris canyon complex.

▶ **Shuttle C**, an unmanned variant of the Shuttle system, could lift nearly 70 tonnes into low Earth orbit. Though it will be ready as early as the mid-1990s, greater cargo-carrying capacity will be needed to supply Mars bases.

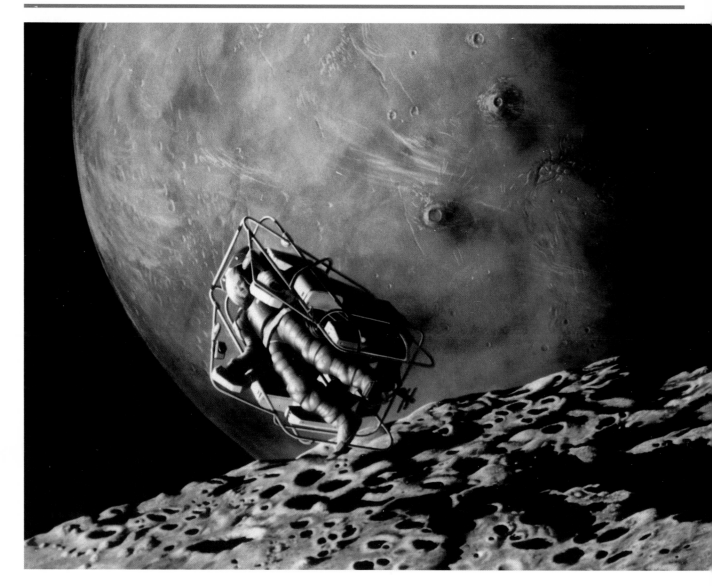

On March 22nd 1989, an asteroid about half a kilometre across passed within 690,000 kilometres (430,000 miles) of the Earth. This celestial "near miss" was nothing new, as asteroids have passed precariously close before, and doubtlessly will again. Astronomers estimate that one of around a thousand near-Earth asteroids have a statistical chance of colliding with our planet during the next half million years or so.

If it had hit the Earth, this asteroid – provisionally named Asteroid 1989CF – could have caused an explosion equivalent to 100,000 megatonnes of TNT, gouging out a crater 20 kilometres (12.4 miles) wide in the Earth's surface. But over the next 100 years, the attention of the spacefaring nations will be focussed not so much on these potentially cataclysmic statistics, as on the wealth of mineral resources that the asteroids offer.

The near-Earth asteroids are remnants of primordial interplanetary detritus which has been swept up by the gravitational influence of the inner planets. To date, around a hundred such objects, less than a kilometre (0.62 miles) in diameter, have been discovered. By astronomical convention, they are assigned a catalogue number until a name is decided upon: so in due time, asteroid 1989CF will join a cast of cosmic characters with names like Ra-Shalom, Belulia, Quetzalqoatl, Tetzcatlipoca, Geographos and even Midas. The last of these names appropriately alludes to the riches that these objects may hold. There might not necessarily be gold in the asteroids, but we might find the next best thing – precious minerals and high-grade metals.

Our current picture of asteroidal composition is based on spectroscopic studies from the ground and the analysis of meteorites. Missions in the late 1990s and early next century will reveal their true chemical nature. Most asteroids fall into one of two classes: dark, carbonaceous or dense, silicate. The carbonaceous ones – similar in nature and composition to the small Martian moons, Phobos and Deimos – make up around 75 percent of the total asteroid population. Another 15 percent are silicate, and the rest stony or more exotic. Exactly what "exotic" means in this context is open to debate, but our knowledge of the chemical conditions in the asteroid belt between Mars and Jupiter allows us to make some informed guesses. The rationale behind sending probes to the asteroids becomes abundantly clear when one considers that a typical stony body around half a kilometre (0.3 miles) across may contain 7 billion tonnes of iron, a billion tonnes of nickel and enough cobalt to supply the Earth

◀ **Tentative foothold**: Two astronauts explore the rugged surface of Phobos, the larger Martian moon. Possibly a captured asteroid, Phobos may be of the carbonaceous chondrite class, so that up to 20% of the moon's weight may contain water. It has been suggested that oxygen, water and propellants could be manufactured on Phobos. An oxygen producing plant would have a mass of 50 tonnes.

▼ **Strip-mining**: A near-Earth asteroid is the target for mineral extraction. This illustration from Gerard O'Neill's Space Studies Institute shows a manufacturing vehicle furnishing the elements for a solar power satellite (in the foreground). This sort of large scale manufacturing could be a reality by the middle of the 21st century.

for 3,000 years, even at today's prodigious rates of consumption. Other metals, such as titanium and aluminium, may also be present as high-grade ores.

The near-Earth asteroids present us with a unique opportunity. Due to a quirk of interplanetary mechanics, less energy is needed to reach them than is required to land on the surface of the Moon. It would be an easy matter to adapt the cargo-carrying vehicles that will service the Mars and Moon bases to reach Quetzalqoatl and its cosmic cohorts. As with Phobos and Deimos, the energy needed to land on asteroids is minimal: instead of vast propulsion units, something as simple as airjets could be used to rendezvous with such objects.

Experience on Earth has shown humans to be destructive animals, influencing their environment far more pervasively than perhaps they ought. Astronomers are acutely aware of the irrevocable damage that could result from the exploitation of the asteroids. So before any strip-mining is permitted, the International Astronomical Union wants assurances from the spacefaring nations that the isotopic record of the primordial Solar System will be preserved, and not destroyed by the polluting influence of the first mining expeditions.

As every diligent schoolchild knows, Christopher Columbus set sail in three small ships in search of Asia and accidentally discovered the Americas. As an allegory for space exploration, this story has a number of flaws, not least the fact that Amerigo Vespucci had visited the continent some years earlier. Nevertheless, Columbus' ships – *Nina*, *Pinta* and *Santa Maria* – have provided the names and the inspiration for an ambitious project to celebrate the 500th anniversary of the Spanish explorer's famous voyage. The three spacecraft will set sail into space, using the power of the Sun rather than wind to propel them. The craft – known as solar sails – will take part in an international competition, known as the Columbus 500 Space Sail Cup, which promises to prove a concept which may enable asteroid mining to become a reality (see page 98). For the three latter-day sailing ships will race each other to Mars as part of an interplanetary Americas Cup.

The idea of a solar sail is not new: the Russian scientist Konstantin Tsiolkovskii discussed the principle back in the 1920s. Stated simply, when sunlight shines on an object, solar photons exert pressure on it which tends to drive it away from the Sun. The catch is that the forces generated are tiny: on Earth they are "drowned out" by the twin vexations of gravity and air resistance. But in space, both these impediments disappear and solar sailing becomes possible.

In the 1970s, NASA considered using solar sails to explore Halley's Comet. Their designs – vast square-sail affairs – were conservative, limited as they were by the technology and materials of the day. Since then, lighter materials, better construction methods and folding techniques have given rise to a new generation of solar sails. The Columbus 500 project, instituted by an arm of Congress, will endorse three designs – one each from the Americas, Europe and Australasia – but others will be allowed to enter.

The commission has already approved the design shown opposite, which was put forward by a British company – Cambridge Consultants Limited. The Cambridge design was praised for its elegance and relative simplicity of unfurling, apparently inspired by its chief designer's interest in origami. The whole structure takes about an hour to extend to its full size of 60,000 square metres (72,000 square yards) and thereafter accelerates from 0 to 60 kilometres per hour (0 to 37 miles per hour) in around three hours.

The solar sail is not without its drawbacks, the most obvious being that the pressure of photons on the sail decreases in proportion to the square of its distance from the Sun. At the distance of the Earth, the Cambridge Solar Sail would accelerate at 2 millimetres (0.08 inches) per second per second, assuming totally efficient reflection: twice as far from the Sun, acceleration would drop to a quarter this value. As yet we have no experience of designing attitude and stability controls as well as precise navigation and manoeuvrability systems for football pitch-sized objects. The first part of the Columbus 500 project must demonstrate that the solar sail can be controlled before it embarks on its epic voyage to Mars.

At first glance the solar sail's acceleration appears to be pitifully low, but it must be remembered that it is continual and incremental: the journey to Mars would take around 300 days – about the same as for a chemically-fuelled rocket. The obvious attraction of solar sailing through the inner Solar System is that it provides a cheap, renewable and non-polluting method of visiting the asteroids. Returning to Earth is no problem, for like the mariners of yore, the sail could be tacked into the sunlight, and its course through space altered by changing the sail's angle of reflection accordingly.

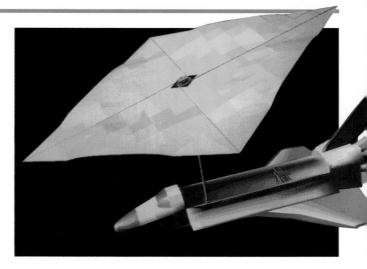

▲ **A solar sail design** proposed by the World Space Foundation is shown above being deployed from the payload bay of a shuttle. This computer-aided design was proposed in 1986 to test deployment mechanisms for sails.

► **Orbital origami:** The Cambridge design for a sail to participate in the Columbus 500 Solar Sail Cup is shown in the main illustration. The sail unfolds to its full size in less than an hour.

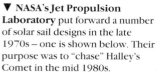

▼ **NASA's Jet Propulsion Laboratory** put forward a number of solar sail designs in the late 1970s – one is shown below. Their purpose was to "chase" Halley's Comet in the mid 1980s.

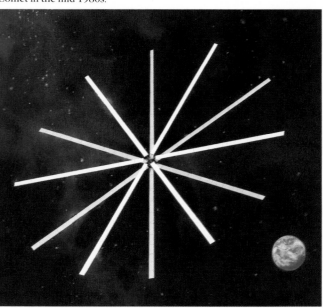

THE FAR FUTURE

"The Earth is the cradle of humanity, but mankind will not stay in the cradle forever."

Konstantin Tsiolkovskii

"To everything there is a season, and a time to every purpose under the heavens A time to be born, and a time to die."

Ecclesiastes, 3.1

"Space is almost infinite. As a matter of fact we think it is infinite."

Vice-President Dan Quayle

"One of these days we can ride to the stars on a jet of annihilated matter and mirror matter. And then James Kirk and Montgomery Scott, Pavel Chekov and Janice Rand, Leonard McCoy and Hikaru Sulu will no longer be science fiction."

Robert L. Forward and Joel Davis, *Mirror Matter*

◄ **Quest without end**: Future generations will extend human presence beyond the Solar System. Seen here is a dark cloud surrounding the star Rho Ophiuchi, made up of interstellar grains of dust and hydrogen out of which young stars are forming.

ISLAND EARTHS

When Gerard K. O'Neill wrote a short note to the scientific journal *Nature* in August 1974, pointing out that mankind's prodigious rate of land usage could be sustained if land could be manufactured in space, he was unconsciously echoing the thoughts of earlier pioneers. Konstantin Tsiolkovskii, Robert H. Goddard, J.D. Bernal, and Dandridge Cole had all written about colonies in space, but not with O'Neill's eloquence or singularity of vision. Many applauded what Isaac Asimov was later to call the end of "planetary chauvinism", and very quickly the notion of vast islands in space became ingrained in the public conscience. These hollowed-out, spinning colonies where the inhabitants would look upwards to see the other side of the colony; and where terrestrial day and night would be simulated by ingenious arrangements of mirrors, featured in O'Neill's seminal work *The High Frontier*, published in 1977.

In the late 1970s, these "Island Earths" were all the rage. The general idea was to build and deploy them in stable Lagrangian orbits between the Earth and the Moon. Mass drivers – vast electromagnetic guns – on the Moon would be used to "shoot" raw materials and supplies to the island inhabitants. Understandably enough, O'Neill called his first habitat – a sphere less than 500 metres (550 yards) in diameter – "Island One". The island would be rotated about twice a minute, thus providing an artificial gravity environment for the few thousand people living on its inside surface.

The next element of O'Neill's scheme was "Island Two", an industrial-size structure some 1,800 metres (2,000 yards) in diameter, housing 140,000 people in several separate villages. Finally, "Island Three" was also considered: 6.4 kilometres (4 miles) in diameter and 32 kilometres (20 miles) in length, this design afforded several million island occupants a land area of 1,300 square kilometres (500 square miles). Later in the seventies, a group at Stanford University came up with a similarly gargantuan colony – two kilometres (1.25 miles) across and weighing over ten million tonnes.

Curiously, these visionary structures were proposed when the US space programme was passing through the nadir which followed Apollo's demise. Not surprisingly, the political paymasters were bleakly unimpressed by the concept of island colonies. "Not a penny for this nutty fantasy!" Senator William Proxmire was heard to retort. O'Neill started the "Islands" project partly as a reaction to what he saw as a growing lack of faith in technology in grass-roots America. O'Neill's islands, one felt, were the very apotheosis of hip philosophy, a sort of bohemian utopia in the sky. Yet these supposedly carefree island colonists were supposed to act as brokers for solar power satellites. This obvious dichotomy

▼ **Island One**, home to 10,000 people, is shown in comparison to lesser leviathans of the modern age, the Empire State Building (left) the *Hindenburg* and the *Queen Mary* (mid-picture). The occupants live in the rotating sphere at the centre of this sectional drawing. The entire colony rotates around the long axis to provide Earthly gravity conditions at the equator. Non-rotating docking ports at either end allow spacecraft to dock with the structure. The whole structure would have to be built in orbit from lunar materials.

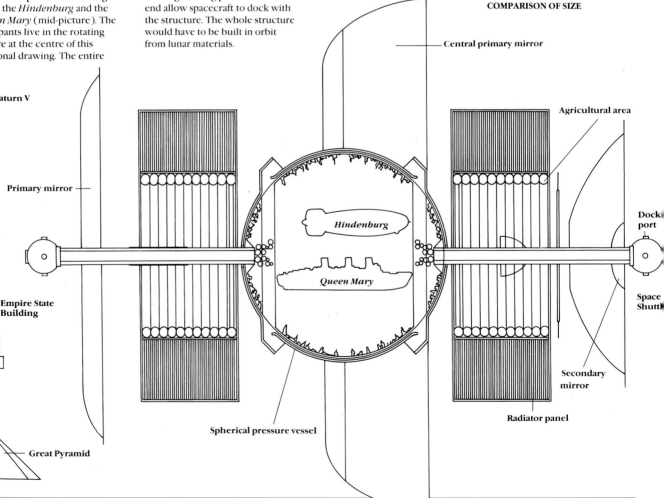

COMPARISON OF SIZE

Saturn V

Central primary mirror

Agricultural area

Primary mirror

Hindenburg

Queen Mary

Docking port

Empire State Building

Space Shuttle

Secondary mirror

Spherical pressure vessel

Radiator panel

Great Pyramid

between purpose and function was one of the more puzzling aspects of O'Neill's grandiose plan.

Subsequently, O'Neill set up the Space Studies Institute which has continued to refine the principles behind island colonies. In 1985, O'Neill was asked to serve on the National Commission on Space – its purpose being to chart America's future in space. In a new chapter to *The High Frontier* written in 1988, O'Neill pointed out that the Commission had discussed solar power satellites, space colonies, self-replicating machines, mass-drivers and the vitally important closed-environment life support systems, which would be essential for self-contained biospheres.

My own feeling is that O'Neill's work was stuck between a pillar and a post. Island colonies are no longer new, and have been supplanted by less ambitious schemes such as planetary bases. And by the time we develop the technology and infrastructure to make island colonies possible, the lure of interstellar travel may divert our interest – and our funds. Perhaps the island colony will go down in the history books as a visionary idea that ultimately ran out of time.

▲ **Celestial plants**: The study and development of Biospheres and Closed Environmental Life Support Systems will be a matter of survival in any sort of space colony. Here engineers at Biosphere 2, a research facility in the Arizona Desert, work towards a self-sufficient "closed-loop" system. Waste products of fish in the tanks shown here fertilize the plants; unused portions of the plants feed the fish; human waste products are also fed back into the system. The goal is to create semi-independent life systems which require only solar radiation as an external input.

◀ **A utopia in the sky**: Island Three Habitats, also known as O'Neill Cylinders, would be more than 6.4 km (4 miles) in diameter and 32 km (20 miles) long. In the foreground is the central hub in which up to a million inhabitants could be housed in a "landscape" of forests, lakes and rivers. Publicity material from the Space Studies Institute paints an even more utopian picture: "As people grow older and less able or willing to fight the pull of gravity, they can move to a part of the settlement nearer the axis [of the Habitat]". Those who would be considered "disabled" by full Earth gravity standards would be given a new lease of life. Such activities as human powered flight are also possible along the zero gravity axis of rotation.

Big isn't always beautiful. That statement is particularly relevant to the future of space exploration, for during the 21st century, microminiaturized spacecraft will be put to use as pathfinders in the more difficult and dangerous corners of the Solar System. The long-term aim is for self-replicating machines, which utilize the resources of the Solar System, to extend human influence to Pluto and beyond – perhaps even to other star systems.

Recent advances in nanotechnology – the technology of very small systems – have been fuelled by the desire to reduce launch costs and by research into the Strategic Defence Initiative (Star Wars) in the United States. In Britain, Smith Associates have put forward plans for a vast fleet of orange-sized spacecraft: in low Earth orbit such a network could act as a telecommunications relay, effectively replacing the multi-million pound communications satellites now in geostationary orbit. Electromagnetic railguns – powerful magnetic fields originally developed to launch Star Wars projectiles into the upper atmosphere – could also be used to launch miniature vehicles at accelerations of up to 200,000 g to anywhere within the Solar System.

The miniature craft could provide the answer to cost-effective planetary exploration. Jim Burke of the Jet Propulsion Laboratory has patented the design for a mechanical "maple-seed" which could spiral down through the atmospheres of Mars, Venus and Titan, taking television pictures all the while. The payload, itself a miracle of miniaturization, would weigh only around one kilogram (two pounds). Exploration of the outer Solar System could be achieved far more quickly, far more efficiently and certainly less expensively than currently possible.

In the longer term, even more remarkable concepts are in the offing: "smart" robots, sometimes called Santa Claus or von Neumann machines, may one day be found throughout the Solar System. First postulated by John von Neumann, a mathematician at the Institute of Advanced Study in Princeton, these machines will be able to replicate themselves by utilizing raw materials to hand. When they were described in von Neumann's *Theory of Self-Replicating Automata*, the robots existed as no more than mathematical abstractions in a perfect system. Yet four decades later, self-replicating robots – albeit rather primitive ones – are used industrially. Japan's Fanuc Corporation has robot-building factories that employ the same robots in the manufacturing process. It has been envisaged that von Neumann machines could

land on the asteroids and build replicas of themselves. Some machines would act as transporters, others as raw material processors and "job shops" where all the elements could be assembled. It would never be possible to have 100 percent efficiency in reproduction, as the machines would be subject to wear and tear, and the resources to manufacture sophisticated electronic components may be absent.

In any event, total self-replication is not necessary to exploit the resources of the Solar System. In 1986, the US National Commission on Space suggested that the "Model T Ford" approach be adopted to maximize the industrial "seeding" of space. The same design of machine, deliberately kept simple, could be mass produced: such small, labour-intensive devices could easily and cheaply be transported into space. To further reduce design complexity, these machines would be controlled remotely from the Earth – though in practice this would be unfeasible beyond the Moon as the signal would take too long to reach its destination. If these principles are adhered to, it is possible that "Model T" machines will one day be found on nearly all the bodies of the Solar System. The inventor of the original Model T, Henry Ford, once remarked that history was bunk: what would he have made of this vision of the future?

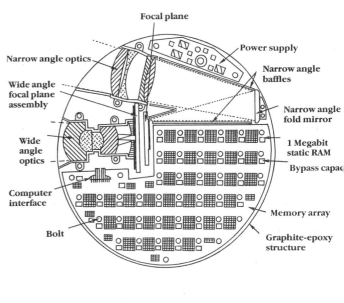

MICROSPACECRAFT CAMERA

15 centimetres

▲ **A conceptual design** for a camera which could be carried aboard microminiaturized explorer spacecraft, is shown above. Weighing less than 1 kg (2.2 pounds), it would give a resolution of 7 m (25 ft) from a distance of 100 km (62 miles).

◄ **Robotic self-replication** is no idle fantasy, though we are still far from von Neumann's vision. At the Fanuc Corporation factory near Mount Fuji in Japan, the robotic workforce is capable of manufacturing 500 "steel collar" workers per month.

◄ **Star Wars** technology could be adapted for peace-time use. The photograph shows a technician working on a section of the Advanced Test Accelerator, a device capable of accelerating a high intensity beam of electrons to an energy of 50 million electron volts. Stationed in Earth orbit, the accelerator could be used to fire a high energy particle beam at distant objects – most notably ballistic missiles. But such a beam could also be used from the Earth to push a microminiaturized spacecraft into orbit.

► **This insect-like robot**, developed at the Massachusetts Institute of Technology, weighs less than 1 kg (2.2 pounds). It has six infrared sensors and a "brain" made up of four microprocessors. These robots could be delivered to Mars or the asteroids on sample-return missions.

Ross 248 in the constellation of Taurus and AC +79 3888 in the constellation of Camelopardus are particularly unremarkable stars. On the face of it, both ought to be condemned to the obscurity of a listing in one of the more esoteric star catalogues. Yet they will one day enter the record books as the first stars to be visited by spacecraft sent from Earth.

Four man-made artefacts are slowly, yet inexorably, heading for these stars. After successfully completing their missions to the outer planets, Pioneers 10 and 11 plus Voyagers 1 and 2 are heading out of the Solar System. Pioneer 10 will reach Ross 248 in just under 33,000 years' time, while Voyager 1 will pass AC +79 3888 40,000 years from now. Even this lengthy time period has been "condensed" because these stars are heading towards our Solar System anyway. Mohammed will reach these mountains because they are coming towards Mohammed.

The scale of even our neck of the galactic woods indicates how colossal a task it will be to reach the stars. Voyager 1, for example, is travelling at the quite respectable hypervelocity of 3.5 Astronomical Units (AU) per year. The AU is a convenient astronomical yardstick: one AU is equivalent to the average distance between the Sun and Earth, some 150 million kilometres, or 93 million miles. At the speed of Voyager 1, it would take just under 80,000 years to reach Alpha Centauri – the nearest star system to the Earth.

Clearly, speedier interstellar envoys are needed. With this in mind, scientists at the Jet Propulsion Laboratory are planning the launch of an unmanned precursor mission toward the stars. The technology for this mission – known as Thousand Astronomical Units, or TAU for short – is expected to come on line within the next thirty years. TAU will be propelled out of the Solar System at roughly 20 AU per year by a nuclear electric power source. This propulsion system employs a small (around 150 kilowatt) nuclear

reactor to generate electricity which is in turn used to expel charged ions of an inert reaction mass such as xenon. Although TAU's speed will be limited by the capacity of its propellant tanks, its nuclear electric propulsion system is far more powerful than the best chemical rockets currently available, and is capable of producing exhaust velocities of up to 70 kilometres per second (43 miles per second).

TAU's main purpose is to carry out astrophysical studies – to investigate the particles and fields of interstellar space. Its instruments will include astrometric telescopes which will give astronomers a different perspective on stellar motion, and maybe even a highly sensitive radio antenna. Stanford radio astronomer Von Eshleman has suggested that an interstellar precursor mission could use the Sun as a gravitational lens to amplify possibly intelligent radio emissions from space.

There is, of course, no signpost telling a star-bound craft it has left the Solar System. Most astronomers consider the heliopause – the region at which the solar wind reaches the particles from other stars – to be the best astronomical equivalent. By the time TAU is launched, the four probes now en route for the stars may have encountered this region, which is believed to be between 75 and 150 AU from the Sun. However, both Pioneers 10 and 11 will have passed out of communication range with the Earth by the end of the 1990s. A similar fate will befall the Voyagers around the year 2015. Thereafter all four will become little more than cosmic "messages in bottles". Both Pioneers bear a plaque showing from whence they came, whereas the more sophisticated Voyagers carry gold-plated videodiscs (cartridges and instructions thoughtfully provided) on which the sights and sounds of planet Earth are faithfully preserved. But quite what alien civilizations might make of the sounds of wolves baying and Melanasian pan pipes, we cannot say.

▼ **TAU, the Thousand** Astronomical Unit interstellar precursor mission is shown in this schematic diagram from the Jet Propulsion Laboratory. The nuclear reactor and ion-thrusters of the nuclear electric propulsion system are located at the left. At the front end (right) is a possible Pluto orbiter to be dispatched as TAU leaves the Solar System. The propulsion system would be fired

for nearly a decade, after which the craft would separate into two. The "astronomy" spacecraft (shown opposite) would communicate with the Earth via the larger "Spin Science Communications" craft. A 10 watt optical laser system would relay information back to Earth. Even at 1,000 Astronomical Units, it would be capable of transmitting data to the ground at a rate of 20 kilobits/s.

▶ **A unique vantage point** will be afforded TAU when it is the full 1,000 Astronomical Units away from Earth. Its astronomy satellite will have a unique perspective on the Milky Way and our Solar System. The main "tube" of the craft will house a 1.5 m (5 ft) diameter telescope.

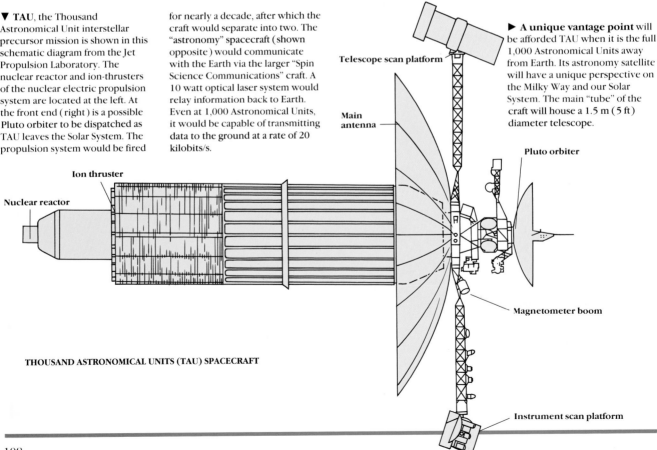

Telescope scan platform

Main antenna

Pluto orbiter

Magnetometer boom

Instrument scan platform

Ion thruster

Nuclear reactor

THOUSAND ASTRONOMICAL UNITS (TAU) SPACECRAFT

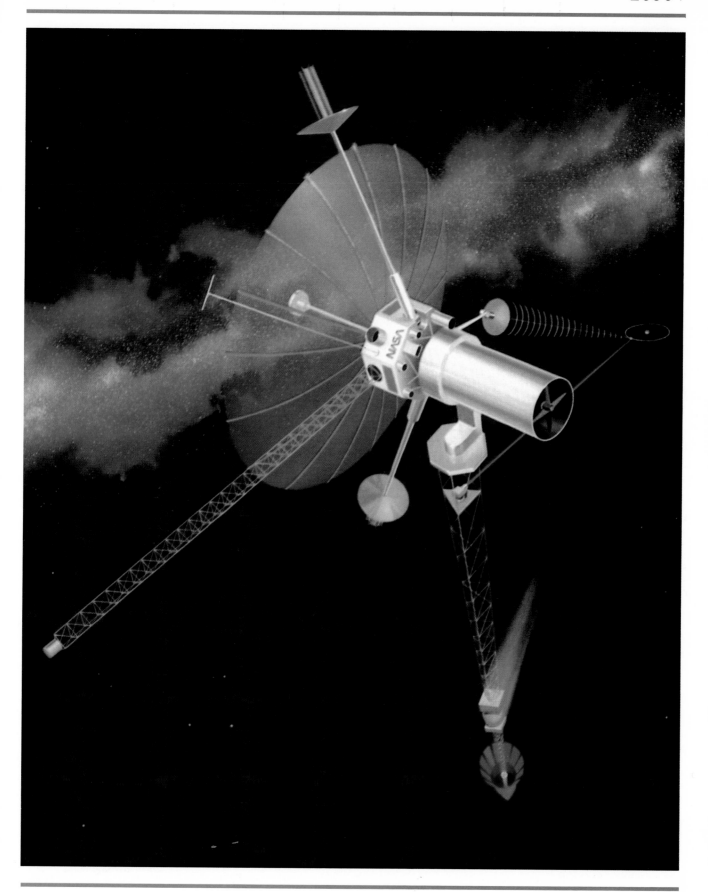

▲ Fusion power: The Antares laser system has been developed for Star Wars research. Two converging beams from a carbon dioxide laser are fired at a gold target the size of a full stop. These nuclear fusion experiments can yield up to 25 terawatts of power in a 250 nanosecond pulse.

▶ Aim and fire: At the Joint European Torus in Culham, Oxfordshire, scientists attempt to produce controlled fusion reactions. An intensely hot plasma confined within the torus, briefly simulates conditions at the Sun's core. Further advances in technology will be required before fusion power can be harnessed to travel to the stars.

In the late 1950s, a casual bystander at the Point Loma cliffs near San Diego would have witnessed some remarkable sights. The testing of a vehicle, which looked for all the world like a pogo stick with a dish beneath it and used the force of small explosions to push it upwards, would have been a glorious spectacle to behold. The vehicle – part of the US army's Project Orion – was a prototype designed to test the principle of a nuclear fission-powered rocket. Sadly, the technical problems of this early attempt to harness the untold energies of nuclear power proved insurmountable. One cynical observer compared the Orion concept to putting a "firecracker under a tin can and watching it blow sky-high".

In the annals of space travel, Project Orion is just one of many false starts in the quest for astronautics' holy grail: efficient and effective propulsion systems capable of opening up the Solar System to colonization and allowing travel to the stars. Some of the more ingenious designs are outlined on the following pages. Reading through them, the words of a Project Orion scientist may spring to mind: "This is not nuts, this is supernuts!" Yet if we are to colonize the Solar System and venture to the stars, then such seemingly far-fetched technologies will have to be developed.

The signing of the partial nuclear test ban in the early 1960s effectively rendered Orion obsolete. Thereafter approaches became more modest, concentrating on ion drives and nuclear electric propulsion (see page 108): both of these have the merit of being within reach of current technical capabilities. Both use charged particles accelerated by electric fields, rather like the electron gun inside a television set, to build up an incremental thrust far greater than that from a conventional chemical rocket. To improve efficiency, metals like mercury which can readily be ionized are used, and a nuclear reactor or a thermionic electrical generator provides additional energy.

In the late 1970s, the British Interplanetary Society considered the large-scale engineering challenge of reaching the stars, and came up with the Daedalus concept. A vast 60,000 tonne vehicle would make a one-way trip to Barnard's Star powered by fusion microexplosions. High energy electron beams would "ignite" pellets of helium-3 at a rate of 250 explosions a second, thereby creating enough force to build up to 12.2 percent the speed of light within four years of launch. On reaching Barnard's Star some forty years later, robotic probes would explore the star and its possible planetary companion(s).

The main drawback of Daedalus was the wear and tear that it would inevitably suffer during its journey. Highly autonomous robots or "wardens" – well beyond today's technology – would be needed to maintain the vehicle. The other problem with the concept was how to feed its huge appetite for helium-3. The Daedalus team believed that the atmosphere of Jupiter could be "mined" for this fuel – an idea also far beyond current capabilities.

Energy generated by fusion could also be harnessed by ramjets far larger and more powerful than those which will take aerospaceplanes into Earth orbit (see page 82). A vast "scoop" would literally "gulp" hydrogen atoms from interstellar space. The hydrogen atoms would then be used as fuel for an onboard fusion reactor, the power from which would expel the resultant helium atoms and thus drive the vehicle forward. The advantages of such a propulsion system are obvious: theoretically it has an inexhaustible supply of fuel and so can accelerate up to near-light velocities, allowing return trips to other galaxies within a single human lifetime. The development of an instellar ramjet would, however, require enormous technological advances: controllable fusion is a long way off; and the hydrogen "scoop" itself would need to be around 100 kilometres (62 miles) in diameter – representing a formidable engineering problem.

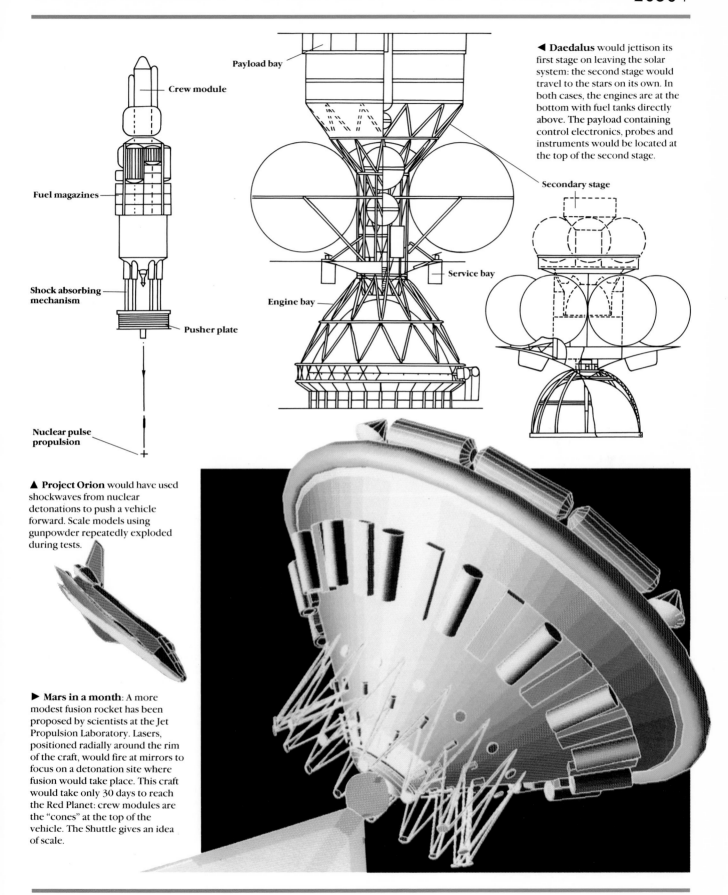

Crew module

Fuel magazines

Shock absorbing
mechanism

Pusher plate

Nuclear pulse
propulsion

Payload bay

Service bay

Engine bay

◀ **Daedalus** would jettison its
first stage on leaving the solar
system: the second stage would
travel to the stars on its own. In
both cases, the engines are at the
bottom with fuel tanks directly
above. The payload containing
control electronics, probes and
instruments would be located at
the top of the second stage.

Secondary stage

▲ **Project Orion** would have used
shockwaves from nuclear
detonations to push a vehicle
forward. Scale models using
gunpowder repeatedly exploded
during tests.

▶ **Mars in a month**: A more
modest fusion rocket has been
proposed by scientists at the Jet
Propulsion Laboratory. Lasers,
positioned radially around the rim
of the craft, would fire at mirrors to
focus on a detonation site where
fusion would take place. This craft
would take only 30 days to reach
the Red Planet: crew modules are
the "cones" at the top of the
vehicle. The Shuttle gives an idea
of scale.

Antimatter propulsion has been staple fare for connoisseurs of science fiction for many years. Viewers of the television series *Star Trek* would regularly see chief engineer Scottie forever exasperated by the state of his beloved "dilithium crystals" as the *Enterprise* continued its infinitive-splitting voyage through the intergalactic realms. The surprising thing is that antimatter does exist, and if properly harnessed, may one day allow us to journey to the stars in a matter of months.

Antimatter is composed of antiparticles: each type of sub-atomic particle has an equivalent antiparticle which "mirrors" its charge, spin and parity (or "symmetry"), but is identical to it in all other respects. So for example, the positron – the first antiparticle to have been discovered – has the same mass as an electron, but carries a positive charge. When antimatter and matter come into contact, they annihilate each other totally and their combined mass is converted into energy. Compared to nuclear fission, where only 0.1 percent of the mass of the fissionable material is converted into energy, or even fusion, where this figure rises to 0.5 percent, matter-antimatter annihilation is a remarkably efficient way of generating energy from a small mass, making it ideal for space propulsion systems.

To create antimatter, the high-energy tools of the particle physicist are needed. For example, if pairs of protons are smashed together at tremendous velocity in a particle accelerator they will yield three more protons and an antiproton. These rare particles are then stored in superconducting coils which magnetically "bottle" them in the laboratory. It has been estimated that one milligram of antimatter would be sufficient to make a propulsion system possible. To date only micro-milligrams of antiprotons have been created in particle accelerators. At present day prices this "magic milligram" would cost around US$100 billion to produce. But there is hope: in 1986, the Los Alamos National Laboratory reported that antiproton production rates were increasing by a factor of ten every two years – by early next century, as much as a gram of the precious material may have been produced.

To harness this prodigious source of energy in a viable propulsion system, the physicist Robert L. Forward has proposed a "magnetic nozzle" which forces pions produced by proton-antiproton reactions into a stream, thus converting their momentum into acceleration for the vehicle. Forward also suggested that the pions could be used to heat up a supply of inert propellant – possibly hydrogen or water – which could then be directed into an exhaust, translating 50 percent of the annihilation energy into thrust. Even this level of efficiency would far outstrip that of a chemically-fuelled propulsion system. Forward estimated that to send a one-tonne spacecraft to Alpha Centauri at one tenth the speed of light would require only 18 kilograms (40 pounds) of antimatter and four tonnes of inert propellant.

Though the theories underlying antimatter propulsion have

been explored, the practicalities may be more difficult to deal with. The antimatter "fuel" must be stored in a magnetic container light enough to be taken into space – such technology has yet to be developed. Furthermore, there are many dangers involved: when protons and antiprotons annihilate, a veritable pot pourri of subatomic particles and gamma rays results as the pions interact "downstream". In a particle accelerator, these products can be effectively contained, but in space they would stream out of the craft and react further in the vacuum of space, forming a vast ionized plume thousands of kilometres long. If this plume were inadvertently directed towards any living creatures – on the Earth, on a planetary base, in a colony, or even in another antimatter-propelled vehicle – the effect would be lethal. Perhaps antimatter vehicles would have to be restricted to outside the Solar System, with "proceed with extreme caution" navigational beacons charting their course!

▶ **The antimatter rocket** is the fastest and most efficient form of interstellar propulsion known. Technologically, it may be beyond our reach – but only just. In the design shown here, matter/antimatter annihilation would take place in the "rim" of the cone-shaped spacecraft. Superconducting coils would then channel the pions produced toward the nozzle at the rear of the craft. A Shuttle is shown for scale.

The advantage of the pion rocket is that large quantities of fuel would not need to be carried, even on lengthy journeys to the stars.

◀ **Matter/antimatter annihilation** is an extremely efficient way of generating energy. In this false colour bubble chamber photograph, an antiproton (pale blue) meets a proton. Eight highly energetic particles are produced in this encounter: 4 positive pions (red) and 4 negative pions (green).

▲ **The first Shuttle's futuristic namesake**, the *Enterprise,* here shown head to head with a hostile vessel, used a putative antimatter propulsion system to take it to light speeds. Chief engineer Montgomery Scott (pictured above) was the man charged with the awesome task of tending to the craft's engines.

In the first half of the 21st century, solar sail technology will make journeying within the Solar System quite routine (see page 100). In the second half of the century, suitable modification of these techniques, together with the development of even lighter and more efficient materials may well allow solar sails to embark on journeys across the interstellar oceans.

Because the intensity of solar radiation decreases in proportion to the square of the distance from the Sun, the only way that an interstellar sail could gain sufficient speed to escape the Solar System would be to pass precariously close to our parent star. It has been estimated that a sail with a radius of one kilometre (0.62 miles) carrying a mass of around 60 kilograms (130 pounds) would have to pass within one Sun radius in order to reach Alpha Centauri. Total journey time would be around 350 years.

A big-brother of this design could tow a heavier – perhaps even human – payload to the stars. An "ark" with a mass of 10,000 tonnes could accommodate 1,000 people, but the sail needed to carry it would have to be nearly 400 kilometres (250 miles) in diameter. Nearing the Sun, the passengers would be protected by a thick layer of asteroidal material – a shield covering the sail's occupants – of similar dimensions. The construction of a suitable, yet sufficiently light, shield would itself constitute a monumental engineering feat. In theory, an ark of these proportions could be accelerated up to 0.14 percent of the speed of light, at which speed it would reach Alpha Centauri in around 1,350 years.

The physicist Robert L. Forward has proposed an intriguing variant of the solar sail concept, which he calls "Starwisp". The theory is that a perforated sail could be driven through interstellar space by a focussed microwave beam, provided that the perforations were smaller than the wavelength of the incident radiation. This proposal has the advantage that any spare capacity from existing solar power satellites could be used to generate the microwaves, which could then be focussed by an orbiting Fresnel lens. A microwave beam with a total power of 10,000 megawatts could take the vehicle to 20 percent of the speed of light within a few days, and to Alpha Centauri within 20 years. On reaching its destination, Starwisp could be "zapped" with microwaves to power its instruments: using the perforated sail as an antenna, information could then be transmitted back to Earth.

Starwisp would have a sail one kilometre (0.62 miles) in diameter but its instruments would weigh only 16 grams (0.56 ounces) – a quarter of that devoted to intelligent microminiature electronics. However it is unlikely that Starwisp could ever be adapted to take humans to the stars since the perforated sail needed for such a craft would have to be the size of Jupiter!

At present, these revolutionary ideas rank alongside that "old faithful" of interstellar transport – the black hole – in terms of their viability. Black holes are the natural end product of larger (twice Sun-size) stars which collapse inward on themselves at the end of their lives, causing disruptions in the space-time continuum. Many theorists – most notably the Soviet scientist Nikolai Kardashev – have proposed using these disruptions as "underground stations" to connect the farthest corners of our galaxy.

One obvious drawback is something which is becoming increasingly familiar to commuters on London's tube system – you have no idea where you will end up or when you will arrive. Calculations also show that the gravitational tides induced over a human body entering a black hole would stretch the traveller to spaghetti-like proportions. Some authorities believe that atom-size black holes, having a mass comparable to that of an asteroid, were formed during unusual conditions in the primordial universe. These objects, or even specially manufactured "designer black holes", may one day be put to use as "stargates" by future civilizations.

SAILING TO THE STARS

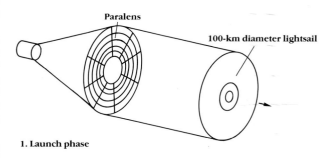

Paralens

100-km diameter lightsail

1. **Launch phase**

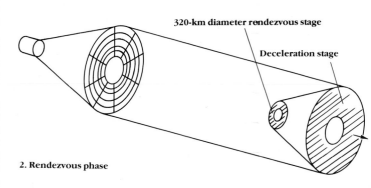

320-km diameter rendezvous stage

Deceleration stage

2. **Rendezvous phase**

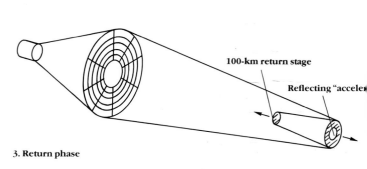

100-km return stage

Reflecting "accele▸

3. **Return phase**

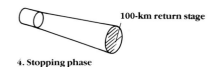

100-km return stage

4. **Stopping phase**

▲ **Forward vision:** American physicist Robert L. Forward has proposed many ingenious ways of travelling to the stars. The scheme shown here is a "Big Brother" of Starwisp which uses laser light, focussed by a "paralens" to push a sail to the stars. The sail shown here has an initial diameter of 1,000 km (620 miles). As it approaches its target star, a smaller sail, 100 km (62 miles) across, separates out and is slowed down by laser light reflected by the large annular "decelerator". The light reflected by the annular ring could then propel the sail on its return journey to our Solar System. The sail would be stopped in our Solar System by direct reflection of laser light by the returning portion of the spacecraft.

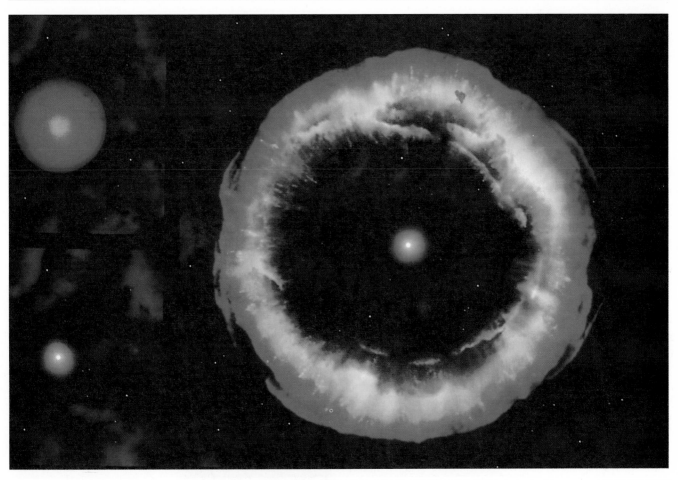

▶ **Every home should have one**: For a civilization that could utilize antimatter propulsion and sail to the stars pushed by lasers, creating a black hole would probably cause few difficulties. Well, probably: there is no conclusive proof that black holes do exist, but some sort of "singularity" could be formed in the space-time continuum. Astronomers believe that black holes are created when larger stars collapse in on themselves after they run out of "fusionable fuel" – the hydrogen which is converted into helium. To use black holes as the ultimate underground stations – "wormholes" in the space-time continuum – they will have to be carefully constructed. Many theoretical physicists wax eloquently on the possibilities of this rather bizarre method of transportation.

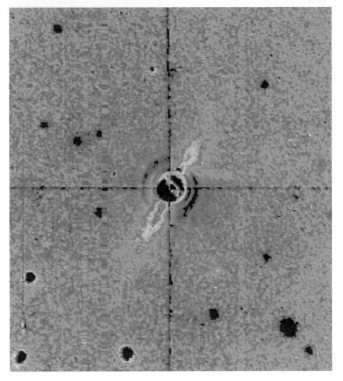

▲ **Target for tonight**: Beta Pictoris, some 80 light years distant, is believed to be surrounded by a planetary system. By suppressing light from the star itself (by use of a masking device seen at the centre of the image). American astronomers detected a faint disk of dust surrounding the star. Image analysis reveals the extent of the dust to be 100,000 million km (61,000 million miles). This dust is most likely to be associated with the formation of new planets. Observations from Hubble Space Telescope and its successors may reveal clearer evidence of other planetary systems. Whilst we may not be "spoilt for choice", astronomers should be able to identify likely targets for the first interstellar missions to investigate.

One of the most evocative pictures of the space age is that of the Earth and Moon appearing as twin crescents in the field of view of Voyager 2 as it headed out toward Jupiter. It was twelve years before the hardy probe returned a similar view of Neptune and its largest moon Triton. Future space travellers will be able to appreciate both views within a matter of weeks rather than years.

However unlikely it may now seem, sometime during the second half of the twentieth century, the technology to allow mankind to travel to the stars will become available. The history of Atlantic crossing provides a suitable analogy for the hurdles we now face. In August 1492, Christopher Columbus set out from Spain in search of India: his flagship *Santa Maria* and two other vessels reached the Americas over two months later. By the middle of the 19th century, the SS *Great Britain* had cut that journey time down to a matter of days. The first commercial airliners completed the trip in a day, and today, one can hop on Concorde and arrive within three hours.

But the distances involved are so great that if an interstellar *Santa Maria* sets off, it could well be overtaken by an interstellar Concorde a few centuries later. This phenomenon means that future societies may prefer to bide their time, rather than embark on journeys to the stars as soon as they become technically possible. Princeton theorist Freeman Dyson has suggested that stellar travel will not be attempted until countries' Gross National Products have increased to a thousand times their current values.

The American authors Eugene Mallove and Gregory Matloff outlined the four basic approaches to interstellar travel. In the summary below, the term "world ship" refers to vast, rotating, cylindrical spacecraft, an order of magnitude larger than O'Neill's Island Three concept (see page 104).

- **Low speed world ship.** The journey would take millennia. Generations would be born and die on the world ship before the destination was reached.
- **Biomedical extension of lifespan.** The extension of human longevity through the use of genetic engineering techniques would allow all the crew members to reach their destination star system regardless of the velocity of the world ship.
- **Suspended animation.** New biological techniques would allow travel to the stars of virtually infinite duration.
- **The twins paradox.** A world ship would travel at near-light speed, so the relativistic effect of "fast clocks run slow" would dilate time to shorten perceived journey length.

After the technology to travel to the stars becomes available, the next question is obvious: where should humanity head for?

Within 21 light years there are around a hundred stars – the first calling ports in our neck of the galactic woods – which we could investigate. The Alpha Centauri system consists of three stars and is roughly 4.3 light years away. The nearest of the triumvirate is the red dwarf known as Proxima. The main star of the system, Alpha Centauri A, is a yellow-coloured star like our Sun, though much more massive and luminous. A fainter, orange-coloured star known as Alpha Centauri B orbits Alpha Centauri A with a period of around 80 years.

Next closest after Alpha Centauri is Barnard's Star, another red dwarf, whose proper motions through space suggest there may be a planet – or planets – orbiting it. But the likelihood of life having evolved there is remote because Barnard's Star was never hot enough for nuclear reactions to begin. For any vague hopes of life-like conditions, we must travel to either Epsilon Eridani (10.8 light years distant) or Tau Ceti (11.8 light years). Both were "targeted" in the first radio search for artificial signals in 1960 – Project Ozma – and there appeared to be no obvious signs of advanced civilization. It may be that we will have to journey there ourselves to get a definite answer.

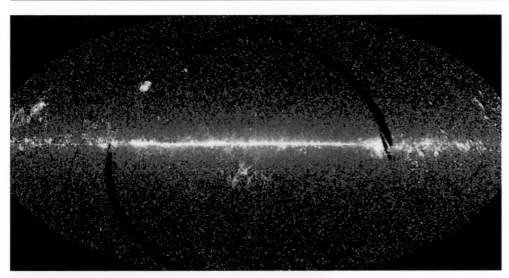

◀ **Our galactic home**: An all-sky survey of the Milky Way by the IRAS satellite, launched in 1983, revealed no signs of artificial "heat sources". In the early 1990s, ESA's Infra-Red Space Observatory will return measurements with a thousand times greater resolution than this mosaic. Over the next century, even more advanced telescopes will increase that resolution still further. If, for example, an advanced civilization were able to dismantle its planetary system and constructs a Dyson sphere – a "shell" around its parent star – then terrestrial astronomers would be able to identify it from its very peculiar infrared signature.

Groombridge 34 A/B (11.6 light years)

Ross 248 (10.3 light years)

Procyon (11.4 light years)

LAL 21185 (8.1 light years)

61 Cygni A/B (11.2 light years)

Wolf 359 (7.6 light years)

Epsilon Eridani (10.7 light years)

Ross 128 (10.9 light years)

Tau Ceti (11.9 light years)

4 6 8 10 12 light years

Barnard's Star (5.9 light years)

Proxima Centauri (4.3 light years)

Luytens 726-8 A/B (8.9 light years)

Lac 9352 (11.7 light years)

Ross 154 (9.5 light years)

Alpha Centauri A/B (4.3 light years)

Epsilon Indus (11.2 light years)

◀ **Unimagined vistas**: Stars outside our Milky Way may prove difficult to reach in the immediate future. But if "wormholes" can be exploited, future generations may yet see sights like this one. Our Sun is a particularly unremarkable member of the Milky Way: yet, the presence of life on our planet makes us, at the moment, unique.

◀ **Neptune and Triton** (far left) were captured by the cameras of Voyager 2 in late August 1989, as it successfully completed its final planetary encounter.

▲ **Neighbours**: Nearby Stars out to 12 light years are shown in this schematic diagram. They are probably the only ones which mankind could conceivably reach during the next hundred years if the technology becomes available to travel beyond the Solar System. Barnard's Star, Epsilon Eridani and Tau Ceti are the most likely to possess planetary systems. Astronomer Bruce Campbell has found evidence to suggest that a planet, one to ten times the size of Jupiter, is in orbit around Epsilon Eridani.

MAN AND SUPERMAN

Advances in genetic engineering are expected to result in fundamental social change in the next century. For the first time, human beings will have the ability to alter the course of their own evolution. This issue poses many ethical and moral dilemmas which will be faced by the next generation. However these problems are resolved, it is clear that the control of evolutionary processes will be a highly significant factor in the human colonization of the Solar System.

When we consider the possible outcome of human evolution in space, we are hampered by the lack of available data. In the past, space biology experiments have yielded some strange results, but it would be premature to take their implications literally. For example, studies of young rats on the Spacelab 3 mission in 1985 revealed that their bones did not grow as long as control samples back on Earth. But this does not mean that babies born in space would necessarily have shortened and widened bones and hence appear short and fat.

In very general terms, we can describe how the human body could change over many generations to cope with the rigours of zero gravity. The following outline is at best rudimentary because the technology to affect the change will not be available until the end of the next century. The "designer astronaut" outlined here would be a true *Homo sapiens astronautica*.

Since the supporting role of the skeleton would be minimal, the spine could become more flexible and act as the main counterpoint for "levers" like the arms and legs. The pelvic girdle, would no longer be load-bearing and so could become less dense. The feet, freed of their locomotive duties, could take on a manipulative function like the hands.

A distant product of evolution in space could well be a human being possessing all the life supporting functions of a spacesuit. If people are to venture out into a vacuum or live in other atmospheres, some sort of oxygen store will be necessary: two additional internal lungs would probably solve the problem. When free oxygen was available from the blood, an oxygen bearing lung would inflate, later filling the normal lungs when oxygen was not available. The second additional lung, working in tandem with the oxygen storing lung, would store waste carbon dioxide. The oxygen would be used to release energy through the normal aerobic metabolism of food. Without changing the very tenets of biochemistry, there seems to be very little chance of altering this process to make space travellers less reliant on regular feeding, so a system of storing food reserves, probably in the form of fatty deposits, may develop.

In vacuum or very thin atmospheres, the human body would have to contend with the absence of pressure. The human frame in vacuum does not make for an appealing sight — the body effectively expands and ruptures. To ensure this does not happen, internal tissues would have to be "sealed off" from the environment by a thickened, more resilient skin. Since the future human space dweller would be living off "internal" oxygen for long periods at a time, the necessity for a mouth and nose in constant contact with the atmosphere would be removed. However, eyes would still be needed, so the cornea could develop a thick transparent protective layer.

Clearly, all this change could not be accommodated in the space of a few hundred years. But, as the phrase has it, nature isn't in a hurry. In an interview with *Omni* magazine in 1978, Princeton theorist Freeman Dyson pointed out that it takes up to a million years for a new species to evolve, ten million for a new genus, one hundred million for a class and a billion for a phylum. "In five billion years or less, we've evolved from some sort of primordial slime into human beings ... what could happen in another ten billion years?"

In the long-term colonization of the planets, human beings must either adapt themselves to the new physical conditions (see page 118) or adapt the conditions to suit themselves. The latter is generally known as terraforming, modifying the conditions on the planets to enable humans to make a home in previously inhospitable environments. Ironically, the worsening environmental crisis on our own planet means that the concept of terraforming could well be tested on the Earth first.

The problems of global warming could be tackled by building a thin reflecting shield from lunar materials and placing it in a Lagrangian orbit between the Earth and Moon. If it were able to reduce incident solar radiation by a mere two percent, it could offset a global temperature rise of four degrees Celsius or so. James Early of the Lawrence Livermore Laboratory in California has calculated that a ten micron thick reflecting shield, fashioned from glass manufactured from lunar soil, with a diameter of 2,000 kilometres (1,240 miles) would do the trick. However, the cost of such an enterprise would be in the region of one to ten trillion US dollars. Would it be worth it?

The inner planets are almost crying out to be terraformed. The "Goldilocks" situation where Venus is far too hot, Mars too cold and Earth just right, could easily be changed – though it would take millennia. The concept of terraforming Venus was first proposed by Olaf Stapledon in his novel *The Last and First Men,* published in 1930. He suggested electrolysing the Venusian "oceans" to produce hydrogen that would be propelled into space, thereby reducing the atmosphere's stranglehold on the planet. In the 1960s, Carl Sagan proposed that genetically-engineered blue-green algae be deposited on to the surface of Venus to convert carbon dioxide into oxygen. But at present, around a thousand launches would be needed to carry out an operation of this scale. A more recent suggestion is that sunshades

– either shields in orbit or vast films of mylar in the atmosphere itself – be placed over the planet.

To make Mars habitable, the greenhouse effect would have to be positively encouraged. The introduction of "greenhouse gases" such as fluorine and chlorine would produce a rise in surface temperature which would in turn cause the release of carbon dioxide gas and water vapour – themselves greenhouse gases – from the polar caps and permafrost. Another way of vapourizing carbon dioxide on the planet's surface would be to use thermonuclear devices. This man-made phase would take around a century, and the result would be a warmer, wetter climate. However, the main component of the atmosphere would still be carbon dioxide: genetically-engineered plants like mosses and lichens deployed on the Martian surface could convert this into oxygen. To build up the fertility of Martian soils, the planet would have to be seeded with organisms capable of fixing free atmospheric nitrogen. The development of a biosphere on Mars would not happen overnight – we may have to wait up to 100,000 years before the planet becomes truly habitable.

The principles of terraforming could also be applied in the outer Solar System. In theory, Jupiter's moons Ganymede and Callisto could be made habitable, particularly as they have sub-surface reserves of water. The first step would be to stellify Jupiter – to cause it to implode in a controlled manner so that it would undergo thermonuclear fusion and warm its local surroundings. The raw materials for fusion are readily available on Jupiter, and a "designer" black hole could be used to trigger the sequence of events. Something similar was shown in the film *2010,* when Dave Bowman reappeared from the stargate and declared that "something wonderful will happen". In reality, to create a biosphere for Ganymede and Callisto, something tedious would happen as the whole process would run into millennia.

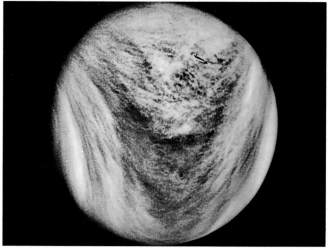

◄ **From red to green**: Mars is particularly suitable for terraforming as it may have reserves of water locked up as ice, as well as water vapour in the form of clouds. The clouds are shown in this Viking view of a cyclonic system over the north pole.

▲ **From hot to cold**: The dense clouds of Venus may prove difficult to disperse without using genetically engineered algae.

► **By use of orbiting reflectors** it may be possible to counter the effects of greenhouse gases.

"It is difficult to say what is impossible, for the dream of yesterday is the hope of today and the reality of tomorrow." These words came from Robert Goddard in the 1920s, but are as valid today as they were then. Concepts like solar power satellites, antimatter propelled vehicles and interstellar world ships may seem as fanciful now as journeys to the Moon appeared in Goddard's day. Yet it is instructive to recall that in the 1920s Goddard's prescience was met with unequivocal scorn from the scientific community. President Roosevelt called a handful of leading scientific authorities into the White House. Their task was to consider America's technological future – yet they singularly failed to anticipate jet aircraft, radar, atomic power and, of course, space travel.

So perhaps the predictions contained in this last section of this book are not as fanciful as they seem. Quite what can be achieved beyond the next hundred years will doubtlessly be even more mind-boggling. One of the most intriguing possibilities is that some form of extraterrestrial life will be discovered in the 21st Century. The philosopher Philip Morrison has written that any evidence of extraterrestrial intelligence takes us from being a unique miracle into a universal statistic – initially of two. At various times since the 1960s, searches have been instigated which have hoped to take us from the miraculous into the statistical. Radio observatories have listened out for alien signals from space – but to no avail.

Since 1983, Paul Horowitz of Harvard University has used a signal analyser called META to listen in to 8 million channels centred on a frequency of 1 GHz (21 centimetres). At this "magic frequency", atomic resonances for naturally-occurring hydrogen and the hydroxyl radical (OH-) occur. This second guesses our inter stellar brethren, assuming that they would concentrate their efforts to communicate with other life forms on the constituents of water, upon which life ultimately depends. The META project is administered by The Planetary Society, and was officially opened by Steven Spielberg, who contributed some of his earthly riches to the project. In October 1991, a replica of META will be opened in Argentina to extend the search for extraterrestrial life into the southern hemisphere sky.

A year after that – perhaps on the 500th anniversary of Columbus's discovery of the New World – NASA's own Search for Extra Terrestrial Intelligence (SETI) project will begin. Covering the 1 to 10 GHz bands, SETI will adopt two different approaches. Sun-like stars will be monitored using the fixed Arecibo dish in Puerto Rico; and radio telescopes similar to those which have tracked the Voyagers will perform systematic sky searches, from both the northern and southern hemispheres. The project is likely to last ten years: by the end of this time, we will have narrowed down the possibility that extraterrestrial beings – or at least those who can communicate by radio – exist.

The search for extraterrestrials will continue with greater sensitivity using radio telescopes in Earth orbit and on the Moon.

The Soviet radio astronomer, Nikolai Kardashev, has suggested there are three stages by which we can gauge a civilization's development. The first is that it uses the resources of its home planet; the second, the resources of a whole system; and thirdly, the resources of a galaxy. Thus far there seems to be no evidence that there are any advanced civilizations routinely dismantling galaxies. Freeman Dyson has put forward the idea that the resources of a planetary system could be used to build a sphere around the parent star, upon which the civilization could then live. Such "Dyson Spheres" would make themselves known by particularly peculiar "heat signatures" in whole sky surveys using the new generation of infrared telescopes.

If contact is ever made, perhaps it would be possible to arrange with any friendly, neighbourhood aliens to communicate human perceptions and feelings across the vast distance of intergalactic space. This has been proposed by Soviet space scientist Konstantin Feoktistov, who was one of the first civilians to fly in space. He has suggested that at some point in the future, it may be possible to "download" the contents of the human mind and electronically send them across the vast realms of space. All that would be required is a "carrier" at the other end to reconstitute the human mind.

No matter how intensive the search for extraterrestrials, the results may prove inconclusive. In the same way that we cannot devise a single experiment to prove the origins of the universe, so too the existence of life in space is difficult to ascertain. Any number of bizarre theories have been proposed to explain why extraterrestrials are noticeable by their absence. Perhaps we are part of an intergalactic quarantine experiment: if we do not destroy ourselves, perhaps we will be initiated into the superior fraternity. Another theory suggests that we cannot detect advanced civilizations because they communicate by other means, perhaps using neutrinos or tachyons.

Alexander Pope once declared that "among the stars lies the proper study of mankind": perhaps the great writer got it the wrong way round. "Among mankind lies the proper study of the stars" seems more apt. If human beings succeed in voyaging to the stars, then that expansion will diversify the human species as never before.

Even if we are alone in the universe, it is surely inevitable that through our own progeny we will ensure the longevity of our species. No matter how diverse a species humanity eventually becomes, we may – in all our wanderings between the stars – face a variety of human beings in the future. Perhaps it will be an even greater miracle that the aliens will be us.

▲ **Quest without end**: Radio telescopes, like this one operated by NASA, will be used to search for extraterrestrial intelligence. More advanced systems will become available as the century progresses.

▶ **The infinite realm**: This cluster of galaxies in the southern constellation of Fornax forms part of an even greater supercluster of galaxies. It may be a target for future missions.

design changes 76, 77
docking with Columbus 70
flight profile 83
future role 76
French Guiana 68
Friendship 7 spacecraft 8
fuel requirements
  hypersonic planes 15
  missions to Mars 96
  orbit entry 94
fusion power 110, 111
fusion rocket 111

G
Gagarin, Yuri Alexeyich 8, 9
Galileo (astronomer) 44, 46
Galileo orbiter/probe 13, 15, 44-5
Gamma Ray Observatory 25
Ganymede 44, 120
Gemini series 9
Giotto 48, 50
Glaser, Peter 86
Glavkosmos 12, 54
Glenn, John 8
global monitoring 13-14, 28-31, 74-5
global warming 13-14, 120
Goddard, Robert 16
Gorbachev, Mikhail 96
gravitational waves 36
gravity
  artificial 92, 93
  on Columbus 70
  and industrial processes 72
  on Island Earths 105
  lunar 90
  on Mars 40
  and tissue culture 70
Great Britain 69
  HOTOL 80, 82
  microminiaturized spacecraft 106
  Project Juno 56, 84
Great Red Spot 44
greenhouse effect 13
Grigg-Skjellerup 50
Group for Psychological Support 56
guest astronauts 54, 56

H
habitation modules
  Freedom space station 64, 65, 76, 77
  lunar base 91
  Mars transporter 93
  Mir space station 54
Haldej 51
Halley's Comet 13, 48, 50, 100
Hamburga 50
Harmonia 51
heatshields, aerospaceplane 82
Heavy Lift Launch Vehicle 96

heliopause 108
heliosphere 34
helium-3 on the Moon 90
Hermes spaceplane 13, 15, 68-9, 70, 73
Hipparcos astrometry satellite 25
HOrizontal Take-Off and Landing vehicle (HOTOL) 80, 82
Horowitz, Paul 122
HOTOL see HOrizontal Take-Off and Landing vehicle
Hubble Space Telescope 14, 15, 21-3, 25
Huygens, Christiaan 46
Huygens probe 46, 47
Huygens/Cassini project 46, 47
hydroponic growth in space 96
hypersonic spaceplanes 15, 80-1, 82-3

I
industrialization of space 15, 60
Infra-Red Astronomical Satellite (IRAS) 12
Infra-Red Space Observatory 14, 24, 117
Infra-Red Telescope Facility 25
interferometry, astronomy by 26, 90
International Space Year 14
International Ultraviolet Explorer 25
International VLBI Satellite (IVS) 26, 27
interstellar propulsion 112
interstellar ramjet 110
interstellar travel 108, 114, 116
Io 44
ion drives 110
IRAS see Infra-Red Astronomical Satellite
Irwin, Jim 10
Ishtar Terra 32
Island Earths 104-5
isolation factor 56, 92
Italy 69
IVS see International VLBI Satellite

J
Japan
  Freedom space station 62
  lunar bases 88-9
  orbital hotel 84
  radio astronomy projects 26, 27
  self-replication robots 106
  space platform 74, 75
Jet Propulsion Laboratory 108
Juewa 51

Jupiter 11, 46
  magnetic field 36
  space probes 15, 44, 45
  terraforming 120

K
Kardashev, Nikolai 122
Kennedy, John F. 9
Khrushchev, Nikita 10
Kizim, L.D. 12
Komarov, Vladimir 9
Korolev, Sergei 9, 10
Korund IM furnace 54, 72
Krikalev, Sergei 56
Krystal 54, 72
Kubasov, Valery 96
Kvant (Quantum) 54

L
Laika 8
laser reflectometers 90
Laser Retro Reflector (LRR) 30
Leonov, Alexei 9, 11, 96
life support systems on space stations 63, 93, 96
lifespan, biomedical extension of 116
Lomonosov 25
low speed world ship 116
LRR see Laser Retro Reflector
Luna 9 space probe 9
Luna 24 space probe 11
lunar bases 88-9, 90
lunar day and night 77, 90
lunar probes 9, 11, 88
lunar soil 89
Lunik 3 space probe 8
Lyman/FUSE (Far Ultraviolet Spectroscopic Explorer) 25

M
McCandless, Bruce 12
McDonnell Douglas 73
Magellan orbiter 13, 32, 33
magnetic fields
  Jupiter 36
  Mars 38
  solar 36
Manned Manoeuvering Unit 12
manned vs unmanned spaceflight 62
Mariner 2 space probe 8
Mariner 4 space probe 9
Mariner 9 space probe 10
Mariner 10 space probe 10
Mars 14, 38-43, 92-7
  data-gathering by balloons 40
  data-gathering by robots 42-3
  gravity 40
  joint mission to 96
  long stay missions 94
  mission profile 94

possibility of life on 38
short stay missions 94
supply service to 95
surface features 38, 40
surface sampling 38
terraforming 120
Mars '94 orbiter 14, 38, 40, 41
Mars lander vehicle 93
Mars Observer space probe 14, 38, 39, 40
Mars rover 15, 42-3
Mars Transfer Vehicle 93
Mars transporter 93
materials science experiments 70, 72-3
matter-antimatter annihilation 112, 113
Maxwell Montes 32
medical problems on space stations 65
META project 122
meteorites 48
microgravity 72-3
microgravity experiments 54, 70, 73
microminiaturized spacecraft 106
mineral extraction
  asteroids 98-9
  Moon 89
Mir space station 15, 54-61
  advertising on board 13
  design 54
  food supplies 56
  guest astronauts 56
  technical deficiencies 58-9
  work/rest routine 56
Mission to Planet Earth 28, 75
Montgolfier hot-air balloon 40
Moon
  Apollo project 9-10, 11, 19
  lunar bases 88-9, 90
  lunar probes 9, 11, 88
  mineral extraction 89
  Soviet/US race to 10
Munarov, Musa 56, 113
MUSES-A lunar probe 88

N
nanotechnology 106
NASA see National and Aeronautics Space Administration
NASA/ESA joint missions
  Huygens/Cassini project 46
  Ulysses solar probe 14, 15, 34, 36-7
NASP aerospaceplane 82
National Aeronautics and Space Administration (NASA)
  Apollo programme 9-10, 11, 19
  CRAF 15, 47, 48, 50

126

ACKNOWLEDGEMENTS

I would like to thank the many scientists, engineers and managers who so freely gave of their time during the writing of this book. Those who formally read through the manuscripts are listed at the start of the book. In particular, I would like to thank the two consultants who read through material as the book took shape, my old friend Peter Muller and my new friend, Gordon Oswald. Naturally any errors are my sole responsibility.

The public relations officers of NASA and ESA were, as ever, most helpful. Bill Sheehan, Associate Administrator for Communications at NASA Headquarters, was instrumental in arranging for Admiral Truly to write the foreword. His colleagues Debbie Rahn, Paula Cleggett-Haleim and Charles Redmond were also on hand to provide information. Other NASA personnel were always ready with information, especially Jurrie van der Woude and Mary Beth Murrill at JPL.

Beatrice Lacoste, Head of Press Relations at ESA, and Mike Blackwell and David Williams of the British National Space Centre were valued sources of information. I must thank Neil Pattie of British Aerospace who arranged for me to visit the United States for the launch and deployment of Hubble Space Telescope. Conversations with Rob Staehle, Tom McDonough, Mike Klein and Kerry Nock improved the quality of my writing immeasurably.

Further information

Keeping up with activities in space is made easier by two widely-available magazines: *Spaceflight News* appears monthly in Britain, and *Final Frontier* bimonthly in the US. One could do no worse than regularly obtain these periodicals for their breadth of coverage and constant quality.

The world's largest space interest group is The Planetary Society. It is directly sponsoring research into Mars balloons and SETI. Its Planetary Report is available through membership at: The Planetary Society, 65 North Catalina Avenue, Pasadena CA 91106, USA.

The World Space Foundation, also based in Pasadena, is involved with many aspects of solar sailing and can be contacted at: World Space Foundation, Box Y, South Pasadena, CA 91030, USA.

The Space Studies Institute, set up by Gerard O'Neill, is active in developing new initiatives: Space Studies Institute, Box 82, Princeton, NJ 08542, USA.

Photographic credits

Theo Pirard of the Space Information Center in Pepinster, Belgium was instrumental in locating Soviet material. Mike Gentry and Lisa Vasquez of Media Services at Johnson Space Center and Marie Jones at NASA Headquarters provided many of the NASA pictures. Simon Vermeer at ESA Headquarters in Paris provided all the ESA material used. Anne Pennaneach of the Centre Spatial de Toulouse, also endured badly written faxes in franglais to provide CNES material for this book. And finally, Humphrey Price, manager of the Advanced Propulsion Systems group at JPL, provided the illustrations of fusion and antimatter vehicles at remarkably short notice. The flap photograph of the author was taken by Andi Spicer.

European Space Agency: 14 (right). 15 (left, right). 35. 37. 47 (main picture). 67 (centre, bottom). 68. 73 (all).
NASA/Goddard Space Flight Center: 29 (top, bottom left). 75 (bottom right).
NASA/Headquarters: 6, 30. 77 (top). 91 (top right). 94 (top right).
NASA/Johnson Space Center: 8 (Centre right, top right). 9 (all). 10 (all). 11 (top left, bottom left, top right). 12 (bottom left, centre bottom, right). 13 (top left, bottom left, centre left). 28 (bottom right). 29 (bottom right). 33 (top, bottom left). 34 (bottom right). 52. 64. 65. 74 (bottom). 77 (bottom). 91 (top). 97 (top right). 98. 118. 121.
NASA/Jet Propulsion Laboratory: 11 (bottom right, bottom centre). 12 (top left). 13 (top right). 31 (bottom left). 32 (top right). 38 (bottom right). 47 (bottom left). 51 (bottom). 100 (bottom right). 106 (right). 109. 115 (bottom). 116 (left). 117 (top). 120 (both). 122.
NASA/Kennedy Space Center: 14 (left and insert). 20. 66.
Space Telescope Science Institute: 22. 24 (top left). 51 (top). 115 (top). 116 (right).

p. 8 (top left, bottom left, centre left, bottom right) Novosti
p. 13 (centre right, bottom left) CNES
p. 16 (left) British Library, (right) Kobal Collection
p. 17 (left) Kobal Collection, (right) © Hergé/Casterman, reproduced by kind permission of Methuen Children's books
p. 18 (top left) Chesley Bonestell/Space Art International, (centre right) Fred Freeman/Space Art International
p. 19 (both) Kobal Collection
p. 32 (bottom) United States Geological Survey, Branch of Astrogeologic Studies, Flagstaff, Arizona
p. 38 (bottom right) United States Geological Survey, Branch of Astrogeologic Studies, Flagstaff, Arizona
p. 45 (bottom right) NASA/Smithsonian
p. 48 (insert) CNES
p. 54 CNES

p. 55 Space Commerce Corporation
p. 56 (both) Novosti
p. 57 Novosti
p. 58 CNES/Novosti
p. 59 CNES/Novosti
p. 60 Novosti
p. 61 Novosti
p. 67 (graph, top) Office of Technology Assessment, US Congress
p. 69 (top left) CNES, (illustrations) Aérospatiale
p. 72 McDonnel Douglas
p. 74 (top) National Center for Atmospheric Research, Boulder, Colorado
p. 78 Carter Emmart
p. 83 (top) NASA/Wright Patterson Air Force Base
p. 85 (insert) Kuku Kurita/Gamma/Frank Spooner Pictures
p. 86 Peter Menzel/Science Photo Library
p. 87 (bottom) Peter Menzel/Science Photo Library
p. 90 (centre) University of Arizona
p. 96 Paul Hudson/Orbital Sciences Corporation
p. 97 (insert, bottom) Martin Marietta
p. 99 (bottom right) Space Studies Institute
p. 100 (top) Rob Staehle/World Space Foundation
p. 102 Royal Observatory, Edinburgh and Anglo-Australian Telescope Board
p. 105 (both) Space Studies Institute
p. 106 (bottom left) Kuku Kurita/Gamma/Frank Spooner Pictures
p. 107 (top) Lawrence Livermore National Laboratory/Science Photo Library, (bottom) Massachusetts Institute of Technology
p. 110 (both) Alexander Tsiaras/Science Photo Library
p. 111 (bottom) Humphrey Price/Jet Propulsion Laboratory
p. 112 Humphrey Price, Jet Propulsion Laboratory
p. 113 (top right, bottom right) Kobal Collection, (left) Lawrence Berkeley Laboratory/Science Photo Library
p. 123 Royal Observatory, Edinburgh and Anglo-Australian Telescope Board

COMPUTER BOOK SERIES FROM IDG

Photoshop® 4 For Windows® For Dummies®

Cheat Sheet

Selection Tricks

Note: All selection tricks are performed with selection tools. (There's a shocker.)

Draw straight lines	Alt+click with lasso tool
Add to selection outline	Shift+drag
Deselect specific area	Alt+drag
Deselect all but intersected area	Shift+Alt+drag
Deselect entire image	Ctrl+D
Select everything	Ctrl+A
Hide selection outlines	Ctrl+H
Delete floating selection	Delete
Move selection outline only	Drag or press an arrow key

Moving Selections

Note: Use the move tool to perform the following tricks. Or press Ctrl and use any other tool except the hand or pen tool.

Nudge selection one pixel	arrow key
Nudge selection ten pixels	Shift+arrow key
Clone selection	Alt+drag

More Fun with Selections

Fill selection with foreground color	Alt+Backspace
Fill selection with background color	Ctrl+Backspace
Display Fill dialog box	Shift+Backspace
Cut selection	Ctrl+X
Copy selection	Ctrl+C
Paste image last cut or copied	Ctrl+V
Reapply last filter	Ctrl+F
Reapply filter and change settings	Ctrl+Alt+F
Adjust brightness and contrast	Ctrl+L

Layer Tricks

Convert floating selection to layer	Ctrl+Shift+J
Clone selection to a new layer	Ctrl+J
Cut selection to a new layer	Ctrl+Shift+J
Change opacity of floater or layer in 10% increments	1, ... , 9, 0
Activate layer that contains specific image	Alt+right-click with move tool
Activate next layer up	Alt+]
Activate next layer down	Alt+[
Hide all layers but one	Alt+click on eyeball
Select the contents of active layer	Ctrl+click on layer name in Layers palette

...For Dummies: #1 Computer Book Series for Beginners

COMPUTER BOOK SERIES FROM IDG

Photoshop® 4 For Windows® For Dummies®

Cheat Sheet

Painting and Editing Tricks

Increase brush size	]
Select largest brush size	Shift+]
Decrease brush size	[
Select smallest brush size	Shift+[
Change opacity of tool in 10% increments	1, ... , 9, 0
Paint or edit in straight lines	click, Shift+click
Change eraser style	E
Reveal saved image with eraser	Alt+drag
Finger paint with smudge tool	Alt+drag

Navigation Tricks

Scroll image	spacebar+drag
Zoom in	Ctrl+spacebar+click
Zoom in and change window size	Ctrl+plus
Zoom out	Alt+spacebar+click
Zoom out and change window size	Ctrl+minus
Scroll up or down one screen	PageUp/PageDown
Move to upper-left corner of image	Home
Move to lower-right corner of image	End

Daily Activities

Cancel operation	Esc
Close image	Ctrl+W
General preferences	Ctrl+K
Display last preferences panel used	Ctrl+Alt+K
Open image	Ctrl+O
Print image	Ctrl+P
Quit Photoshop	Ctrl+Q
Save image to disk	Ctrl+S
Undo last operation	Ctrl+Z

Toolbox Shortcuts

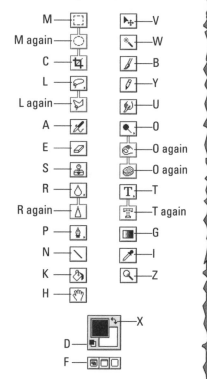

Palette Shortcuts

Brushes palette	F5
Color palette	F6
Layers palette	F7
Info palette	F8
Options palette	Enter
All palettes, status bar, and toolbox	Tab
Just palettes	Shift+Tab

...For Dummies: #1 Computer Book Series for Beginners

Readers Rave about Previous Editions of Photoshop For Dummies:

"Easy to use, simple language, starts from scratch. Not just tips and tricks. I bought it to have on hand for those I train."

— Carolyn Boyle, Orlando, Florida

"Simple, straightforward, good beginner overview (with which to start) and eventual development of more advanced details."

— Allen J. Monczyk, Brooklyn, New York

"Great book to start learning a complex program . . . I laughed, I cried."

— Robert G. Kopp, Plano, Illinois

"It broke down all of the complicated jargon into simple English. It allowed me to use my program to the fullest extent."

— Jesse Stenbak, Keene, New Hampshire

"The manual that came with Photoshop was so boring and long winded that reading this book was a pleasure."

— Marlene Colon, Highlands, New Jersey

"I loved it being so down to earth, and no 'nerd speak'."

— Caron Green, Campbell, California

"This is fun and easy enough to read that I can read it on it's own rather than using it only as a reference to solve problems while at the computer."

— Roberta Brenner, Van Nuys, California

"It's actually interesting and enjoyable to read from cover to cover as well as informative. I learned Photoshop 3.0 in no time at all!"

— Daniel Timiraus, Miami, Florida

"Of all the IDG books I have, this one has to be the champion. I thoroughly enjoyed it. It is far easier to understand than Photoshop 3 manuals."

— Seif Jaiwaji, Edmonton, Alberta

"Sense of humor is right up my alley . . . funnier than Don Rickles at his best moments on the old *Tonight Show*."

— Ken Funk, New York, New York

PHOTOSHOP® 4
FOR
WINDOWS®
FOR
DUMMIES®

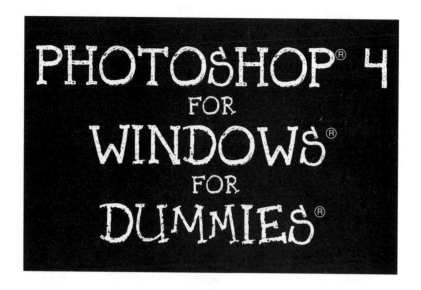

by Deke McClelland

Revised by

Julie King

IDG Books Worldwide, Inc.
An International Data Group Company

Foster City, CA ♦ Chicago, IL ♦ Indianapolis, IN ♦ Southlake, TX

Photoshop® 4 For Windows® For Dummies®

Published by
IDG Books Worldwide, Inc.
An International Data Group Company
919 E. Hillsdale Blvd.
Suite 400
Foster City, CA 94404
www.idgbooks.com (IDG Books Worldwide Web site)
www.dummies.com (Dummies Press Web site)

Library of Congress Catalog Card No.: 96-80227

ISBN: 0-7645-0102-X

Printed in the United States of America

10 9 8 7 6 5 4 3

1B/QT/QZ/ZX/IN

Distributed in the United States by IDG Books Worldwide, Inc.

Distributed by Macmillan Canada for Canada; by Transworld Publishers Limited in the United Kingdom; by IDG Norge Books for Norway; by IDG Sweden Books for Sweden; by Woodslane Pty. Ltd. for Australia; by Woodslane Enterprises Ltd. for New Zealand; by Longman Singapore Publishers Ltd. for Singapore, Malaysia, Thailand, and Indonesia; by Simron Pty. Ltd. for South Africa; by Toppan Company Ltd. for Japan; by Distribuidora Cuspide for Argentina; by Livraria Cultura for Brazil; by Ediciencia S.A. for Ecuador; by Addison-Wesley Publishing Company for Korea; by Ediciones ZETA S.C.R. Ltda. for Peru; by WS Computer Publishing Corporation, Inc., for the Philippines; by Unalis Corporation for Taiwan; by Contemporanea de Ediciones for Venezuela; by Computer Book & Magazine Store for Puerto Rico; by Express Computer Distributors for the Caribbean and West Indies. Authorized Sales Agent: Anthony Rudkin Associates for the Middle East and North Africa.

For general information on IDG Books Worldwide's books in the U.S., please call our Consumer Customer Service department at 800-762-2974. For reseller information, including discounts and premium sales, please call our Reseller Customer Service department at 800-434-3422.

For information on where to purchase IDG Books Worldwide's books outside the U.S., please contact our International Sales department at 415-655-3200 or fax 415-655-3295.

For information on foreign language translations, please contact our Foreign & Subsidiary Rights department at 415-655-3021 or fax 415-655-3281.

For sales inquiries and special prices for bulk quantities, please contact our Sales department at 415-655-3200 or write to the address above.

For information on using IDG Books Worldwide's books in the classroom or for ordering examination copies, please contact our Educational Sales department at 800-434-2086 or fax 817-251-8174.

For press review copies, author interviews, or other publicity information, please contact our Public Relations department at 415-655-3000 or fax 415-655-3299.

For authorization to photocopy items for corporate, personal, or educational use, please contact Copyright Clearance Center, 222 Rosewood Drive, Danvers, MA 01923, or fax 508-750-4470.

 is a trademark under exclusive license to IDG Books Worldwide, Inc., from International Data Group, Inc.

About the Author

Deke McClelland is the author of more than 30 books about desktop publishing and graphics programs for the Mac and for Windows including IDG Books' bestselling *Macworld Photoshop 3 Bible, CorelDRAW! 6 For Dummies, Photoshop 4 For Macs For Dummies,* 2nd Edition, *Macworld FreeHand 4 Bible,* and he is the coauthor of *PageMaker 6 For Windows For Dummies,* 2nd Edition, and *Photoshop 3 For Windows 95 Bible.*

He is also contributing editor to *Macworld* magazine and frequently pops up in *Publish* and *PC World.* He received the Ben Franklin award for the Best Computer Book in 1989 and won prestigious Computer Press Awards in 1990, 1992, and 1994. When he isn't writing, he hosts the television series Digital Gurus for the Jones Computer Network. In his few minutes of spare time, Deke lives with his wife and aging cat in Boulder, Colorado.

ABOUT IDG BOOKS WORLDWIDE

Welcome to the world of IDG Books Worldwide.

IDG Books Worldwide, Inc., is a subsidiary of International Data Group, the world's largest publisher of computer-related information and the leading global provider of information services on information technology. IDG was founded more than 25 years ago and now employs more than 8,500 people worldwide. IDG publishes more than 275 computer publications in over 75 countries (see listing below). More than 60 million people read one or more IDG publications each month.

Launched in 1990, IDG Books Worldwide is today the #1 publisher of best-selling computer books in the United States. We are proud to have received eight awards from the Computer Press Association in recognition of editorial excellence and three from *Computer Currents'* First Annual Readers' Choice Awards. Our best-selling *...For Dummies*® series has more than 30 million copies in print with translations in 30 languages. IDG Books Worldwide, through a joint venture with IDG's Hi-Tech Beijing, became the first U.S. publisher to publish a computer book in the People's Republic of China. In record time, IDG Books Worldwide has become the first choice for millions of readers around the world who want to learn how to better manage their businesses.

Our mission is simple: Every one of our books is designed to bring extra value and skill-building instructions to the reader. Our books are written by experts who understand and care about our readers. The knowledge base of our editorial staff comes from years of experience in publishing, education, and journalism — experience we use to produce books for the '90s. In short, we care about books, so we attract the best people. We devote special attention to details such as audience, interior design, use of icons, and illustrations. And because we use an efficient process of authoring, editing, and desktop publishing our books electronically, we can spend more time ensuring superior content and spend less time on the technicalities of making books.

You can count on our commitment to deliver high-quality books at competitive prices on topics you want to read about. At IDG Books Worldwide, we continue in the IDG tradition of delivering quality for more than 25 years. You'll find no better book on a subject than one from IDG Books Worldwide.

IDG BOOKS WORLDWIDE

John Kilcullen
CEO
IDG Books Worldwide, Inc.

Steven Berkowitz
President and Publisher
IDG Books Worldwide, Inc.

*Eighth Annual
Computer Press
Awards ≥1992*

*Ninth Annual
Computer Press
Awards ≥1993*

*Tenth Annual
Computer Press
Awards ≥1994*

*Eleventh Annual
Computer Press
Awards ≥1995*

IDG Books Worldwide, Inc., is a subsidiary of International Data Group, the world's largest publisher of computer-related information and the leading global provider of information services on information technology. International Data Group publishes over 275 computer publications in over 75 countries. Sixty million people read one or more International Data Group publications each month. International Data Group's publications include: **ARGENTINA:** Buyer's Guide, Computerworld Argentina, PC World Argentina; **AUSTRALIA:** Australian Macworld, Australian PC World, Australian Reseller News, Computerworld, IT Casebook, Network World, Publish, Webmaster; **AUSTRIA:** Computerwelt Osterreich, Networks Austria, PC Tip Austria; **BANGLADESH:** PC World Bangladesh; **BELARUS:** PC World Belarus; **BELGIUM:** Data News; **BRAZIL:** Annuário de Informática, Computerworld, Connections, Macworld, PC Player, PC World, Publish, Reseller News, Supergamepower; **BULGARIA:** Computerworld Bulgaria, Network World Bulgaria, PC & MacWorld Bulgaria; **CANADA:** CIO Canada, Client/Server World, ComputerWorld Canada, InfoWorld Canada, NetworkWorld Canada, WebWorld; **CHILE:** Computerworld Chile, PC World Chile; **COLOMBIA:** Computerworld Colombia, PC World Colombia; **COSTA RICA:** PC World Centro America; **THE CZECH AND SLOVAK REPUBLICS:** Computerworld Czechoslovakia, Macworld Czech Republic, PC World Czechoslovakia; **DENMARK:** Communications World Danmark, Computerworld Danmark, Macworld Danmark, PC World Danmark, Techworld Denmark; **DOMINICAN REPUBLIC:** PC World Republica Dominicana; **ECUADOR:** PC World Ecuador; **EGYPT:** Computerworld Middle East, PC World Middle East; **EL SALVADOR:** PC World Centro America; **FINLAND:** MikroPC, Tietoverkko, Tietoviikko; **FRANCE:** Distributique, Hebdo, Info PC, Le Monde Informatique, Macworld, Reseaux & Telecoms, WebMaster France; **GERMANY:** Computer Partner, Computerwoche, Computerwoche Extra, Computerwoche FOCUS, Global Online, Macwelt, PC Welt; **GREECE:** Amiga Computing, GamePro Greece, Multimedia World; **GUATEMALA:** PC World Centro America; **HONDURAS:** PC World Centro America; **HONG KONG:** Computerworld Hong Kong, PC World Hong Kong, Publish in Asia; **HUNGARY:** ABCD CD-ROM, Computerworld Szamitastechnika, Internetto online Magazine, PC World Hungary, PC-X Magazin Hungary; **ICELAND:** Tolvuheimur PC World Island; **INDIA:** Information Communications World, Information Systems Computerworld, PC World India, Publish in Asia; **INDONESIA:** InfoKomputer PC World, Komputek Computerworld, Publish in Asia; **IRELAND:** ComputerScope, PC Live!; **ISRAEL:** Macworld Israel, People & Computers/Computerworld; **ITALY:** Computerworld Italia, Macworld Italia, Networking Italia, PC World Italia; **JAPAN:** DTP World, Publish in Asia; **IRELAND:** ComputerScope, PC Live!; **ISRAEL:** Macworld Israel, People & Computers/Computerworld; **ITALY:** Computerworld Italia, Macworld Italia, Networking Italia, PC World Italia; **JAPAN:** DTP World, Macworld Japan, Nikkei Personal Computing, OS/2 World Japan, SunWorld Japan, Windows NT World, Windows World Japan; **KENYA:** Hi-Tech Information, Macworld Korea, PC World Korea; **KOREA:** Hi-Tech Information, Macworld Korea, PC World Korea; **MACEDONIA:** PC World Macedonia; **MALAYSIA:** Computerworld Malaysia, PC World Malaysia, Publish in Asia; **MALTA:** PC World Malta; **MEXICO:** Computerworld Mexico, PC World Mexico; **MYANMAR:** PC World Myanmar; **NETHERLANDS:** Computer! Totaal, LAN Internetworking Magazine, LAN World Buyers Guide, Macworld Netherlands, Net, WebWereld; **NEW ZEALAND:** Absolute Beginners Guide and Plain & Simple Series, Computer Buyer, Computer Industry Directory, Computerworld New Zealand, MTB, Network World, PC World New Zealand; **NICARAGUA:** PC World Centro America; **NORWAY:** Computerworld Norge, CW Rapport, Datamagasinet, Financial Rapport, Kursguide Norge, Macworld Norge, Multimediaworld Norge, PC World Ekspress Norge, PC World Nettverk, PC World Norge, PC World ProduktGuide Norge; **PAKISTAN:** Computerworld Pakistan; **PANAMA:** PC World Panama; **PEOPLE'S REPUBLIC OF CHINA:** China Computer Users, China Computerworld, China InfoWorld, China Telecom World Weekly, Computer & Communication, Electronic Design China, Electronics Today, Electronics Weekly, Game Software, PC World China, Popular Computer Week, Software Weekly, Software World, Telecom World; **PERU:** Computerworld Peru, PC World Profesional Peru, PC World SoHo Peru; **PHILIPPINES:** Click!, Computerworld Philippines, PC World Philippines, Publish in Asia; **POLAND:** Computerworld Poland, Computerworld Special Report Poland, Cyber, Macworld Poland, Networld Poland, PC World Komputer; **PORTUGAL:** Cerebro/PC World, Computerworld/Correio Informático, Dealer World Portugal, Mac*In/PC*In Portugal, Multimedia World; **PUERTO RICO:** PC World Puerto Rico; **ROMANIA:** Computerworld Romania, PC World Romania, Telecom Romania; **RUSSIA:** Computerworld Russia, Mir PK, Publish, Seti; **SINGAPORE:** Computerworld Singapore, PC World Singapore, Publish in Asia; **SLOVENIA:** Monitor; **SOUTH AFRICA:** Computing SA, Network World SA, Software World SA; **SPAIN:** Communicaciones World España, Computerworld España, Dealer World España, Macworld España, PC World España; **SRI LANKA:** Infolink PC World; **SWEDEN:** CAP&Design, Computer Sweden, Corporate Computing Sweden, Internetworld Sweden, it.branschen, Macworld Sweden, MaxiData Sweden, MikroDatorn, Natverk & Kommunikation, PC World Sweden, PCaktiv, Windows World Sweden; **SWITZERLAND:** Computerworld Schweiz, Macworld Schweiz, PCtip; **TAIWAN:** Computerworld Taiwan, Macworld Taiwan, NEW ViSiON/Publish, PC World Taiwan, Windows World Taiwan; **THAILAND:** Publish in Asia, Thai Computerworld; **TURKEY:** Computerworld Turkiye, Macworld Turkiye, Network World Turkiye, PC World Turkiye; **UKRAINE:** Computerworld Kiev, Multimedia World Ukraine, PC World Ukraine; **UNITED KINGDOM:** Acorn User UK, Amiga Action UK, Amiga Computing UK, Apple Talk UK, Computing, Macworld, Parents and Computers UK, PC Advisor, PC Home, PSX Pro, The WEB; **UNITED STATES:** Cable in the Classroom, CIO Magazine, Computerworld, DOS World, Federal Computer Week, GamePro Magazine, InfoWorld, I-Way, Macworld, Network World, PC Games, PC World, Publish, Video Event, THE WEB Magazine, and WebMaster; online webzines: JavaWorld, NetscapeWorld, and SunWorld Online; **URUGUAY:** InfoWorld Uruguay; **VENEZUELA:** Computerworld Venezuela, PC World Venezuela; and **VIETNAM:** PC World Vietnam.   3/24/97

Dedication

To Elizabeth, who came home from a low-brow evening of bingo to cart her klutz of a husband off to the hosipital. That's just the kind of loving person she is.

Author's Acknowledgments

Thanks to the many folks who loaned me products and support, including John Leddy and Mark Hamburg at Adobe; Charles Smith at Digital Stock; Tom Hughes at PhotoDisc; and the helpful folks at Palmer's.

Thanks also to Diane Steele for providing advice and support, to Beth Jenkins and the art department for their expertise and cooperation, to Ted Padova for keeping an eye out for the technical foibles, and to Jennifer Ehrlich for keeping the whole shebang on track and in good shape. Finally, special thanks to Julie King for the excellent job of adapting this book for the Windows platform.

Publisher's Acknowledgments

We're proud of this book; please send us your comments about it by using the Reader Response Card at the back of the book or by e-mailing us at feedback/dummies@idgbooks.com. Some of the people who helped bring this book to market include the following:

Acquisitions, Development, and Editorial

Project Editor: Jennifer Ehrlich

Acquisitions Editor: Gareth Hancock

Media Development Manager: Joyce Pepple

Copy Editor: Michael Bolinger

Technical Editor: Ted Padova

Editorial Manager: Kristin A. Cocks

Editorial Assistant: Chris H. Collins

Production

Project Coordinator: Sherry Gomoll

Layout and Graphics: Theresa Sánchez-Baker, Theresa Ball, Brett Black, Cameron Booker, Linda Boyer, Elizabeth Cárdenas-Nelson, Angela F. Hunckler, Todd Klemme, Jane Martin, Drew Moore, Brent Savage, Michael Sullivan

Proofreaders: Melissa D. Buddendeck, Rachel Garvey, Nancy Price, Robert Springer, Carrie Voorhis

Indexer: Sherry Massey

General and Administrative

IDG Books Worldwide, Inc.: John Kilcullen, CEO; Steven Berkowitz, President and Publisher

IDG Books Technology Publishing: Brenda McLaughlin, Senior Vice President and Group Publisher

Dummies Technology Press and Dummies Editorial: Diane Graves Steele, Vice President and Associate Publisher; Judith A. Taylor, Product Marketing Manager; Kristin A. Cocks, Editorial Director; Mary Bednarek, Acquisitions and Product Development Director

Dummies Trade Press: Kathleen A. Welton, Vice President and Publisher

IDG Books Production for Dummies Press: Beth Jenkins, Production Director; Cindy L. Phipps, Manager of Project Coordination, Production Proofreading, and Indexing; Kathie S. Schutte, Supervisor of Page Layout; Shelley Lea, Supervisor of Graphics and Design; Debbie J. Gates, Production Systems Specialist; Robert Springer, Supervisor of Proofreading; Debbie Stailey, Special Projects Coordinator; Tony Augsburger, Supervisor of Reprints and Bluelines; Leslie Popplewell, Media Archive Coordinator

Dummies Packaging and Book Design: Patti Sandez, Packaging Specialist; Lance Kayser, Packaging Assistant; Kavish + Kavish, Cover Design

◆

The publisher would like to give special thanks to Patrick J. McGovern, without whom this book would not have been possible.

◆

Contents at a Glance

Cartoons at a Glance

By Rich Tennant • Fax: 508-546-7747 • E-mail: the5wave@tiac.net

page 167

page 7

page 217

page 51

page 291

page 107

Table of Contents

Introduction

· ·

*W*hy in the world is Photoshop such a popular program? Normally, graphics software is about as much of a hit with the general public as a grunge rock band is with the senior-citizen set. And yet Photoshop — a program that lets you correct and modify photographs on your computer screen — has managed to work its way into the hearts and minds of computer users from all walks of life. What gives?

Wouldn't you know it, I just happen to have a couple of theories. First, when you work in Photoshop, you're not drawing from scratch, you're editing photos. Sure, tampering with a photograph can be a little intimidating, but it's nothing like the chilling, abject fear that seizes your soul when you stare at a blank screen and try to figure out how to draw things on it. Simply put, a photograph inspires you to edit it in precisely the same way that an empty piece of paper does not.

Second, after Photoshop hooks you, it keeps you interested with a depth of capabilities that few pieces of software can match. Unlike so many programs that have caught on like wildfire over the years but are actually a pain in the rear to use — I won't name any, but I bet you can think of a few — Photoshop is both powerful and absorbing. After several years with the program, I am continually discovering new things about it, and I've enjoyed nearly every minute of it. (Okay, so a couple of stinky minutes sneak themselves in every once in a while, but that's to be expected. Photoshop is a computer program, after all, and we all know that computers are cosmic jokes whose only reason for being is to mock us, ignore our requests, and crash at the least opportune moments. In fact, considering that it's a computer program, Photoshop fares remarkably well.)

Why a Book ...For Dummies?

Just because Photoshop is a pleasure to use doesn't mean that the program is easy to learn. In fact, it's kind of a bear. A big, ornery, grizzly bear with about 17 rows of teeth and claws to match. This program contains so much that it honestly takes months of earnest endeavor to sift through it all. By yourself, that is.

When you go into battle armed with this book, however, Photoshop sucks in its teeth, retracts its claws, and lies down like a lamb. In fact, studies show that if you just hold the book up to the computer screen, Photoshop behaves 50 percent better, even if you never read a single page.

If you do read a page or two, Photoshop not only behaves, it makes sense. The truth is, I wrote this book with the following specific goals in mind:

- ✔ To show you what you need to know at the precise pace you need to know it.

- ✔ To show you how to do the right things in the right way, right off the bat.

- ✔ To distract you and shove little facts into your head when you're not looking.

- ✔ To make the process not only less painful, but a real adventure that you'll look back on during your Golden Years with a wistful tear in your eye. "Oh, how I'd like to learn Photoshop all over again," you'll sigh. "Nothing I've done since — whether it was winning the lottery that one time or flying on the inaugural commuter shuttle to the moon with the original cast of *Star Trek* — seemed quite so thrilling as sifting through Photoshop with that crazy old *...For Dummies* book."

Okay, maybe that's an exaggeration, but prepare yourself for a fun time. In a matter of days, you'll be doing things that'll make your jaw hang down and dangle from its hinges. And don't worry, it's all perfectly legal throughout the 50 states as well as Puerto Rico, the Virgin Islands, and Guam.

Don't You Have Another Photoshop Book?

While you were browsing the bookstore shelves deciding which book on Photoshop to buy, you may have noticed another book by yours truly: *Photoshop 3 Bible for Windows 95.* That 800-page tome covers just about everything there is to know about Photoshop.

Some folks get a little worried when they see an 800-page book, though. They look forward to reading the 800 pages with the same dread they normally reserve for eating 800 pieces of dry toast. As people who have read the *Bible* know, the pages are anything but dry and laborious; in fact, they're more like 800 tasty cookies. "Make it fatter, and throw in a free forklift so I can tote it around my house," is the typical response I get. But even so, the *Bible* is something that this book is not. It's exhaustive. It assumes that you just can't get enough Photoshop knowledge.

Photoshop 4 For Windows For Dummies looks at things from a different angle. It points out the features you need to know and shows you exactly how to use them. You don't want to make Photoshop your life — not yet, anyway — but you don't want the thing to just sit there and beep at you in between completely destroying your photograph, either. You'd like to reach a certain satisfying level of comfort, like the one you've recently achieved with your cat now that he's no longer clawing the furniture apart. Becoming comfortable and productive with Photoshop is what this book is all about.

What's in This Book?

This book comprises a bunch of independent sections designed to answer your questions as they occur. Oh, sure, you can read the book cover-to-cover and it will make perfect sense. But you can also read any section completely out of context and know exactly what's going on.

To help you slog through the information, I've broken up the book into six major parts. Each of these parts contains three or four chapters, and these chapters are divided into sections and subsections. Graphics abound to illustrate things that would take 1,000 words to explain, and you'll even find two sets of glorious color plates — 16 pages in all — to show off special issues related to color.

To give you an overview of the kind of information you're likely to find in these pages, here's a quick rundown of the six major parts.

Part I: What the . . . ? Aagh, Help Me!

The first stage of using any computer program is the worst. You don't know what you can do, you don't know how good the program is, you don't even know how to ask a reasonably intelligent question. These first three chapters get you up and running in record time.

Chapter 1 introduces you to image editing, explains where to find images to edit, and provides a quick glimpse of what's new in Version 4 of Photoshop. Chapters 2 and 3 take you on a grand tour of the Photoshop interface and image window and give you all the information you need to navigate both.

Part II: The Care and Feeding of Pixels

Before you can edit a digital photograph, you have to know a few things about the nature of the beast. What's a pixel, for example, and why is getting rid of one so dangerous? What's the difference between a color image and a grayscale image — other than the obvious? And how do you save or print your image after you get done editing it? All these questions and many more are answered in Chapters 4 through 7.

Part III: Tiptoe through the Toolbox

Photoshop offers fewer tools — pencils, paintbrushes, and the like — than most graphics programs. But these tools are remarkably capable, allowing you to perform pages and pages of tricks while expending minimum effort. Learn how to smear colors, get rid of dust specks, erase mistakes, and do a whole lot more in Chapters 8 through 11.

Part IV: Select before You Correct

The selection tools let you cordon off the portion of the photograph you want to edit. Select the face, for example, and Photoshop protects the body, no matter how randomly you drag or how spastic your brushstrokes. Chapters 12 through 14 help you understand how selections work and how to use them to your advantage.

Part V: So, You Say You're Serious about Image Editing

Now we step into the really incredible part of the Photoshop playground. In Chapter 15, I introduce you to layers, a Photoshop feature that adds flexibility, creative opportunity, and security to your image-editing life. In Chapter 16, you find out how to create text effects and add them to your image. And in Chapters 17 and 18, I show you the commands that professionals use to sharpen focus, change brightness and contrast, correct colors, and generally make an image look three times better than it did when you started. Very exciting stuff.

Part VI: The Part of Tens

Chapters 19 through 21 contain the ultimate Photoshop Top Ten lists. Find out the most essential Photoshop shortcuts, the most amazing special-effects tricks, and the answer to that age-old question, "Now that I've finished mucking up my image in Photoshop, what do I do with it?"

What's with All the Margin Icons?

When you're driving, road signs are always warning you about bad things. Slow, Detour, Stop, Dip — these are all signs that I, for one, hate to see. I mean, you never see good signs like Go Ahead and Speed, No Traffic This Way, or Free Money Up Ahead.

This book isn't like that. Using friendly little margin icons, I highlight good things and bad things, and the good things outnumber the bad. For example, you'll find several times more Tip icons than Warning icons. So don't shy away from the road signs in this book; welcome them into your reading ritual with open arms. Here's your field guide to icons:

I hate computer jargon as much as the next red-blooded American. But sometimes, I have to use it because there's no word for this stuff in normal, everyday, conversational English. It's a crying shame, I know, but at least I warn you that something nerdy is coming your way with this icon.

Photoshop has very few obvious shortcuts and a ton of hidden ones. That's where the Tip icon comes in. It says, "Hey, whoa there, here's a juicy one!"

This icon calls your attention to special little reminders of things I've mentioned in the past or things I want you to bear in mind for the future.

Photoshop is a kind and gentle program. But every once in a while, it pays to be careful. The Warning icon tells you when to keep an eye out for trouble.

This icon points out features or commands that have changed or are new in Version 4. If you're upgrading to Version 4 from an earlier version of Photoshop, pay attention to this road sign, because lots of things are different now.

Now and then, I feel compelled to share something with you that has nothing whatsoever to do with your learning Photoshop or any other computer program. It's just my way of showing that I care.

Where Do I Go Now?

When I was in grade school, I don't think that a year went by that our teacher didn't show us how to handle our new books. Open the book once in the center and then open the first quarter and the last quarter, each time gently creasing the spine. Never fold the pages or roll them so that they won't lie flat. And be sure to read the words from the beginning to end, just as the author meant them to be read. A book, after all, is a Special Thing to Be Treasured.

Well, I'll tell you what, this isn't your teacher's book and it isn't my book either. This is your book, so you treat it and read it any way you please.

- ✔ Break the spine first thing out. The pages lie flatter that way.
- ✔ When you have a question, look it up in the index. Feel free to shut the book and get on with your life when you're done (though I do my best to snag you and make you read longer).
- ✔ If you're just curious about what the book has to offer, look up whatever topic interests you in the table of contents and read a few pages.
- ✔ If you want to learn everything the book has to offer in what I consider the optimum order, turn the next page and start reading at your own pace.
- ✔ If you come across something important, don't hesitate to fold the page, slap a sticky note on it, circle the text with a highlighter pen, or rip out the page and tack it to the wall.
- ✔ And when you've gleaned everything there is to glean, house-train your new puppy with the pages or use them for kindling.

I just want you to know that you have my permission to learn in any way that suits you. Respecting a book is a waste of energy; respecting yourself and your needs is what counts.

How to Bug Me

Want to send me a line of congratulations or complaint? Fill out the registration card in the back of this book, and the folks at IDG Books Worldwide, Inc. will pass it along to me. Or send me an e-mail at either of these addresses:

America Online: DekeMc

Internet: DekeMc@InternetMCI.com

I'm not very regular about checking my mail, mind you — I do it once a week if I'm feeling particularly diligent, less frequently otherwise. But I never fail to answer, eventually.

Part I
What the . . . ? Aagh, Help Me!

The 5th Wave   By Rich Tennant

IF BOB DYLAN HAD PURSUED A CAREER IN COMPUTERS.

@RICHTENNANT

"PUT HIM IN FRONT OF A TERMINAL AND HE'S A GENIUS, BUT OTHER-
WISE THE GUY IS SUCH A BROODING, GLOOMY GUS HE'LL NEVER
BREAK INTO MANAGEMENT."

In this part . . .

A lot has been written, spoken, and tapped out in Morse code about the value of information. To hear some folks tell it, information is now the top commodity in the industrialized world. Well, I don't know if that's true or not — personally, you can give me money over information any day of the week. "There's always more room in my billfold than my head," is my saying. But being dumb on any subject is no fun. I mean really dumb — as in, you don't even know what questions to ask in order to get answers.

Well, I've been this dumb myself, and frankly, I remain this dumb about all kinds of subjects. If you're not sure how to ask an intelligent question about Photoshop, take heart. These first three chapters answer that most impossible of all questions to express, "What the . . . ? I mean . . . ? You know, if the . . . ? Aagh, help me!" For example, you find out what Photoshop is, take a quick, all-expenses-paid jaunt through its tools and commands, and learn how to open and view images.

By the end of Chapter 3, you won't know everything there is to know about Photoshop — otherwise, I could have dispensed with the 18 chapters that follow it — but you will know enough to phrase a few intelligent questions. And please remember that as you read these chapters, there's no shame in being a dummy. I mean, it must be more than coincidental that the initials for *Photoshop For Dummies* are Ph.D.

Chapter 1

Meet Dr. Photo and Mr. Shop

· ·

· ·

*P*hotoshop is arguably the most comprehensive and most popular photo editor around. In fact, I don't know a single computer artist who doesn't use Photoshop on an almost daily basis, regardless of what other programs he or she may also use.

I assume that you've at least seen if not used, Photoshop before, and that you have a vague idea of what it's all about. But just so that we're all clear on the subject, the primary purpose of Photoshop is to make changes to photographic images that you somehow managed to get on disk. (For some clever ideas on acquiring such images, see the section "Where Do I Find Images to Abuse?" later in this chapter.)

If you've only used Photoshop for a week or so, you may have mistaken it for a fairly straightforward package. Certainly, on the surface of the program, Photoshop comes off as rather friendly. But lurking a few fathoms deep is another, darker program, one that is distinctly unfriendly for the uninitiated but wildly capable for the stout of heart. My analyst would no doubt declare Photoshop a classic case of a split personality. It's half man, half monster; half mild-mannered shoeshine boy, half blonde-grabbing, airplane-swatting King Kong; half kindly old gent with white whiskers chewing on a pipe, half green-gilled invader from another planet chewing on your . . . well, perhaps you don't want to know. In short, Photoshop has a Dr. Jekyll-and-Mr. Hyde thing going, only it's way scarier.

As you may recall from the last time you saw *Abbott and Costello Meet Dr. Jekyll and Mr. Hyde* — indisputably the foremost resource of information on this famous tale — this Jekyll character (not to be confused with the similarly named cartoon crow) is normally your everyday, average, nice-guy scientist. Then one day, he drinks some potion or gets cut off in traffic or something and changes into his ornery alter ego, known at every dive bar in town by the surname Hyde. Photoshop behaves just the same way, except that no magical transformation is required to shift between the program's Jekyll half and its Hyde half. Both personalities coexist simultaneously in what you might call harmony.

This chapter explores both sides of the Photoshop brain. It also introduces you to the personality changes found in the latest incarnation of the program, Version 4. Finally, I get you started on the road to image-editing bliss by explaining where to find images to edit in the first place.

The Bland but Kindly Dr. Photo

To discover the benevolent Dr. Jekyll half of Photoshop, you need look no farther than the standard painting and editing tools. Shown in Figure 1-1, these tools are so simple, they're practically pastoral, the kind of household appliances your great-grandmother would have been comfortable with. The eraser erases, the pencil draws hard-edged lines, the airbrush sprays a fine mist of color, and so on. These incredibly straightforward tools attract new users just as surely as a light attracts miller moths (except new users don't give off quite so much dust when you squish them).

Figure 1-1: Many of the Photoshop tools have an old-world rustic charm that's sure to warm the cockles of the most timid technophobe.

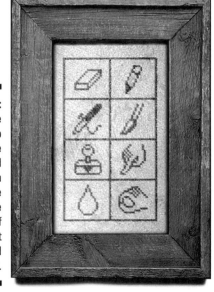

But you quickly discover that on their own, these tools aren't super-duper exciting, just like the boring Dr. Jekyll. They don't work much like their traditional counterparts — a line drawn with the pencil tool, for example, doesn't look anything like a line drawn with a real pencil — and they don't seem to be particularly applicable to the job of editing images. Generally speaking, you have to be blessed with pretty major hand-eye coordination to achieve good results using these tools.

The Ghastly but Dynamic Mr. Shop

When the standard paint and editing tools don't fit the bill, you try to adjust the performance of the tools and experiment with the other image controls of Photoshop. Unfortunately, that's when you discover the Mr. Hyde half of the program. You encounter options that have meaningless names such as Dissolve, Multiply, and Difference. Commands such as Image Size and Canvas Size — both of which sound harmless enough — seem to damage your image. And clicking on icons frequently produces no result. It's enough to drive a reticent computer artist stark raving insane, as illustrated in Figure 1-2.

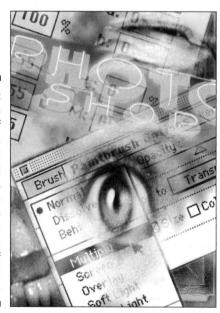

Figure 1-2: When you tire of playing with the standard paint and edit tools, you run smack dab into a terrifying collection of options and commands.

The net result is that many folks return broken and frustrated to the under-equipped and boring but nonthreatening painting and editing tools that they've come to know. It's sad, really. Especially when you consider all the wonderful things that the more complex Photoshop controls can do. Oh sure, the controls have weird names and they may not respond as you think they should at first, but after you come to terms with these slick puppies, they perform like you wouldn't believe.

In fact, the dreaded Mr. Hyde side of Photoshop represents the core of this powerful program. Without its sinister half, Photoshop is just another rinky-dink piece of painting software whose most remarkable capability is keeping the kids out of mischief on a rainy day.

The Two Phunctions of Photoshop

Generally speaking, the two halves of Photoshop serve different purposes. The straightforward Jekyll tools mostly concentrate on *painting,* and the more complex Hyde capabilities are devoted to *image editing.* Therefore, to tackle this great program, you may find it helpful to understand the difference between the two terms.

Painting without the mess

Painting is just what it sounds like: You take a brush loaded with color and smear it all over your on-screen image. You can paint from scratch on a blank canvas or you can paint directly on top of a photograph. The first option requires lots of talent, planning, and a few dashes of artistic genius; the second option requires an opposable thumb. Okay, that's a slight exaggeration — some lemurs have been known to have problems with the second option — but most people find painting on an existing image much easier than creating an image from scratch.

Take Figure 1-3, for example. Here's a rather drab fellow drinking a rather drab beverage. (Though you may guess this man to be Dr. Jekyll armed with the secret potion, most scholars consider it highly doubtful that even Jekyll was this goofy.) I introduce this silly person solely to demonstrate the amazing functions of Photoshop.

Were you to paint on our unsuspecting saphead, you might arrive at something on the order of the image shown in Figure 1-4. I invoked all these changes using a single tool — the paintbrush — and just two colors — black and white. Suddenly, a singularly cool dude emerges. No planning or real talent was involved; I simply traced over some existing details in the image. Better yet, I haven't permanently damaged the image, as I would if I tried the same thing using a real-life paintbrush. Because I saved the original image to disk (as explained in Chapter 6), I can restore details from the original image at whim (the subject of Chapter 11).

Figure 1-3:
The unadorned "I Love My Libation" poster boy of 1948.

Figure 1-4:
A few hundred strokes of the paintbrush result in a party animal to rival Carmen Miranda.

Editing existing image detail

The remade man in Figure 1-4 is the life of the party, but he's nothing compared to what he could be with the aid of some image editing. When you edit an image, you distort and enhance its existing details. So rather than painting with color, you paint with the image itself.

Figure 1-5 demonstrates what I mean. To achieve this grotesque turn of the visual phrase, I was obliged to indulge in a liberal amount of distortion. First, I flipped the guy's head and stretched it a little bit. Well, actually, I stretched it a lot. Then I further exaggerated the eyes and mouth. I rotated the arm and distorted the glass to make the glass meet the ear. Finally, I cloned a background from a different image to cover up where the head and arm used to be. The only thing I painted was the straw (the one coming out of the guy's ear). Otherwise, I lifted every detail from one of two photographs. And yet, this man's very own mother wouldn't recognize him, were she still alive today.

Mind you, you don't have to go quite so hog-wild with the image editing. If you're a photographer, for example, you may not care to mess with your work to the point that it becomes completely unrecognizable. Call you weird, but you like reality the way you see it. Figure 1-6 shows a few subtle adjustments that affect neither the form nor composition of the original image. These changes merely accentuate details or downplay defects in the image.

Figure 1-5:
Image
editing
has no
respect for
composition,
form, or
underlying
skeletal
structure.

Figure 1-6:
If Figure 1-5
is a little too
disgusting
for your
tastes, you
can apply
more
moderate
edits to your
image.

Just for the record, here are a few common ways to edit photographs in
Photoshop:

- ✔ You can *sharpen* an image to make it appear in better focus, as in the first
  image in Figure 1-6. Generally, sharpening is used to account for focus
  problems in the scanning process, but you can sometimes sharpen a
  photograph that was shot out of focus.

- ✔ If you want to accentuate a foreground image, you can blur the focus of the
  background. The image on the right side of Figure 1-6 is an example.

- ✔ If a photograph is too light or too dark, you can fix it in a flash through the
  miracle of color correction. You can change the contrast, brighten or dim
  colors, and actually replace one color with another. Both of the images in
  Figure 1-6 have been color-corrected.

- ✔ Using the Photoshop selection and move tools, you can grab a chunk of
  your image and physically move it around. You can also clone the selection, stretch it, rotate it, or copy it to a different image.

And that's only the tip of the iceberg. The remaining chapters of this book
explore Photoshop as both a painting program and an image editor. Most
chapters contain a little bit of information on both topics, but as a general rule,
the first half of the book stresses painting, and the second half spends more
time on image editing. Rip the book in half and you may very well have the
makings of a late-night horror flick.

It's New! It's Improved!

Someday, the folks at Adobe may come out with an upgrade to Photoshop that completely tames the Mr. Hyde half of the program. But Version 4 isn't the upgrade to do it, which is good for me because it allows me to continue with my colorful dual-personality analogy. Version 4, it turns out, is one part helpful, unbelievably great upgrade and one part exercise in frustration.

On one hand, Version 4 includes some incredibly useful new features. On the other, Version 4 trashes some time-honored shortcuts and techniques used in earlier versions of the program, a development that is sure to confuse and annoy veteran Photoshop users.

The good news is that Version 4's good side more than compensates for its bad side. So in the interest of focusing on the positive, here are just some of the improvements Version 4 brings you:

✔ The new Navigator palette, discussed in Chapter 3, gives you a faster and more convenient way to zoom in and out on an image and view different areas of the image.

✔ Speaking of zooming, you can now zoom in and out with greater flexibility. Whereas previous versions of Photoshop let you zoom only in preset increments determined by the program, Version 4 lets you specify any zoom ratio you want. Chapter 3 zooms in on the topic further.

✔ Grids and guides, long offered in page-layout programs, are now offered in Photoshop, too. Covered in Chapter 3, grids and guides serve as handy tools for lining things up within an image.

✔ A new type mask tool makes it easy to use type as a selection outline. If that sounds like Greek to you, don't panic; Chapter 16 explains all.

✔ The Float command, a popular editing device in earlier versions, is gone. Photoshop now automatically creates a new layer for you when you perform certain actions, such as adding text to an image or cutting and pasting one part of an image into another. Version 4 also brings you adjustment layers, which enable you to color correct all the layers in an image in one fell swoop — and in a way that takes the risk out of color correction. Chapters 15 and 18 have the details.

✔ Following the latest software trend, Photoshop now offers context-sensitive menus. To translate that into English, you can click the right mouse button — an action more commonly known as right-clicking — to quickly display a list of commands related to whatever it is you're trying to accomplish at the moment. See Chapter 2 for the lowdown.

✔ On top of all these goodies, Photoshop 4 also offers improved gradient (blend) capabilities, as discussed in Chapter 14, and provides you with a ton of new filters, as discussed in Chapter 17.

If you're used to working in Photoshop 3, some of these changes may confuse you at first, but they make the editing process much easier after you get the hang of things. Of course, if you've never used Photoshop before, you won't even be aware of Version 4's bad side — ignorance is bliss, as they say.

Where Do I Find Images to Abuse?

Recapping this book's top news so far: Photoshop is first and foremost an image editor. Although you can paint images from scratch, you're more likely to use the program to edit photographs that have been captured to disk.

Herein resides the problem. We all know how to turn photographs from our cameras into colorful pieces of paper that we can then slap into albums or frames for public display. (In other words, we all know how to get our film processed.)

But few of us have scanned a photograph to disk. You can't go to the local Piggly Wiggly, for example, and say, "Pardon me, I'd like to process this roll of film to disk so that I can open it up on my Mac." The cashier would look at you as if you had popped out of the pages of the *Sun*. "Blood Sucking Vampire from Outer Space Requests Film-to-Disk Transfer!" reads the headline in her mind. "Top Scientists Baffled by Implications!"

Now that I've mentioned the *Sun*, I would be delinquent if I failed to acknowledge this proud publication's contributions to the field of image editing. In the last few years of grocery shopping, I have yet to see a front page item in the *Sun* that was not edited to the fullest extent possible. Whether it's featuring an image of a 400-pound baby, a housewife with fingers growing out of her ears, or a real-life alien that looks enough like E.T. to be a hand puppet, the *Sun* can't be beat for ghoulish manipulation of everyday photos. Its motto — "We will let no image go unmolested" — tugs at the heartstrings of old hacks and burgeoning image editors alike. We salute you, *Sun*!

Anyway, when it comes to finding images to edit in Photoshop, grocery stores are out. But you can still find plenty of affordable options if you look in the right places:

> ✔ You can purchase collections of photos on CD-ROM. These collections range in price from less than 25 cents to several dollars per image. Some of my favorite image vendors are PhotoDisc (206-441-9355); Digital Stock (619-794-4040); and ColorBytes (303-989-9205). Most of the images in this book come from these vendors, in fact (see Appendix B for specific image credits). Figure 1-7 shows two vintage images taken from Volume 13, "Italian Fine Art, Prints, and Photographs," from PhotoDisc.

Figure 1-7:
Two PhotoDisc images from an era when little kids were encouraged to climb on the furniture and barbers forgot to remove their hats.

- If you're hooked into the Internet or an online service such as CompuServe or America Online, you can find zillions of photos to download. The problem is, most of these images are of dubious quality and/or pornographic. If you want high-quality, general-purpose images, you have to subscribe to a specialized service such as PressLink Online/MediaStream (800-717-7706); Comstock (212-353-8600); and The Picture Exchange (800-579-8737). Unfortunately, these services are extremely expensive. They charge hourly online and download fees in addition to the cost of the photos themselves.

- You can take your own photo into your local Kinko's or some other copy shop or service bureau and scan the image to disk — assuming, of course, that you aren't lucky or rich enough to have a scanner available in your own office. Kinko's charges $9.95 per image.

- A better (and cheaper) method for scanning images is to scan them to a Photo CD, which costs between $1 to $3 a shot plus the price of the CD itself, which is usually in the neighborhood of $10. One CD can hold about 100 images, and you don't have to worry about scanning all 100 images at the same time. You can scan just a few and then keep adding to the CD as needed. To find a place where you can scan images to Photo CD, look in the Yellow Pages under "Photo Finishing — Retail." Be sure to shop around; prices vary widely from vendor to vendor. Also, be aware that having your images scanned to CD may take a few days, so plan ahead.

Chapter 2

Canvassing the On-Screen Canvas

. . . .

In This Chapter

▶ Launching Photoshop

▶ Taking some first, tentative looks at the Photoshop interface

▶ Learning mouse terminology

▶ Working with the program window

▶ Switching between Photoshop and other programs

▶ Choosing commands

▶ Using dialog boxes and palettes

▶ Picking up tools from the toolbox

. . . .

*I*f you're brand new to Photoshop — and/or to computers in general — this is the chapter for you. It explains the basic stuff you need to know before you can begin using the program to distort the faces of all your family members.

Even if you're already familiar with the basic interface of Photoshop, give this chapter the once-over to get acquainted with new features in Version 4 and to make sure that we're speaking the same language. Here is where we calibrate brains, so to speak.

Giving Photoshop the Electronic Breath of Life

Before you can use Photoshop, you have to start up — or *launch* — the program. Here's how to do it if you're using Windows 95:

1. **Start your computer.**

2. **Click on the Windows 95 Start button.**

3. **Click on the Programs item in the Start menu.**

   Windows displays a submenu showing all your program groups.

4. **Click on the Adobe item in the submenu.**

   You get another submenu listing all your Adobe programs.

5. **Click on the Adobe Photoshop 4.0 item.**

   It's the one that uses that famous Adobe eyeball as its icon.

6. **Hope it works.**

   If you see the Photoshop splash screen — a kind of billboard that provides garish graphics and some copyright information — you're in business. If your computer complains that it doesn't have enough memory to open Photoshop or you see some equally discouraging message, scream loudly and hope that the resident computer expert is in close proximity. You need help.

To launch Photoshop in Windows 3.1, open the Adobe program group in Program Manager and then double-click on the Adobe Photoshop 4.0 icon, just as you launch any other program.

After your computer stops making little shicka-shicka noises and your screen settles down, you see the Photoshop program window shown in Figure 2-1. (The figure shows the window in Windows 95, as do all the figures in this book. Your screen will look slightly different if you're using Windows 3.1, but not much.) I cover the various elements of the window later in this chapter.

Don't freak out and start running around the room in a frenzy if you're a little fuzzy on what I mean by *click, menu,* and a few other terms. I cover all this stuff in fairly hefty detail, in short order, and in this very same chapter.

Making Sense of the Mouse and the Cursor

Ever hung around one of those lopsided couples — the kind made up of one person who says "Jump" and another who says "How high?" Well, your mouse and the *cursor* — that little arrow that moves around on-screen (caught in the act in Figure 2-1) — have this same dynamic going on. In fact, the cursor's only goal in life is to emulate everything the mouse does. If the mouse moves, the cursor moves. If the mouse stops, the cursor stops. The little guy has no mind of its own. It's kind of sad, actually. You want to grab the cursor and say, "Take hold of your life, man, and quit being such a victim!"

But the cursor is the cursor. There's no sense in trying to change it, so you may as well exploit it. By taking advantage of this skewed relationship, you can control the way Photoshop and other Windows programs behave. Throughout

Toolbox   Title bar   Cursor   Menu bar

Minimize
Restore
Close

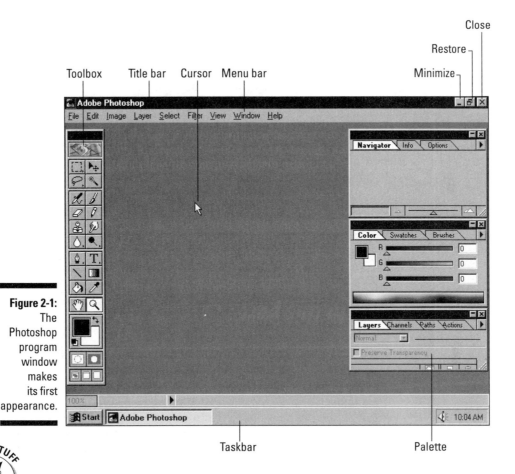

Figure 2-1:
The
Photoshop
program
window
makes
its first
appearance.

Taskbar   Palette

TECHNICAL STUFF

Why does Photoshop give your computer Alzheimer's?

If your computer says that it's out of memory, it just means that a part of the machine is filled to capacity. Memory — known in computer dweeb circles as *RAM* (random access memory, pronounced *ram,* like the goat) — allows your computer to run programs. Photoshop needs lots of RAM — it requires a minimum of 16MB and prefers to have even more. If you can't launch Photoshop because of a memory error, you have three options:

✔ Free up RAM by quitting all other programs that are currently running.

✔ Restart your computer by choosing the Shut Down command from the Windows 95 Start menu and then choosing the Restart the Computer option. After your computer restarts itself, try to launch Photoshop again.

✔ Buy and install more RAM.

If you've never tried to upgrade the RAM in your machine before, seek out expert advice from your local computer guru.

this book, I ask you to do certain things with the cursor, but you perform these actions by using your mouse. For example, if I instruct you to move the cursor, you move the mouse, which makes the cursor move in kind.

Here's a quick look at some other things I ask you to do with the mouse that the cursor has no choice but to go along with:

- ✔ To *click* is to press the left mouse button and immediately release it without moving the mouse. For example, you click on an icon in the top portion of the toolbox to select a tool.

- ✔ To *double-click* is to press and release the left mouse button twice in rapid succession without moving the mouse.

- ✔ To *right-click* is to click the right mouse button instead of the left one. (There's one you didn't need me to tell you.)

- ✔ To *press and hold* is to press the left mouse button and hold it down for a moment without moving the mouse. This action is sometimes called *mousing down,* although I think this sounds too much like an aerobic exercise. I refer to this operation very rarely — for example, when some item takes a moment or two to display.

- ✔ To *drag* is to press the left button and hold it as you move the mouse. You then release the button to complete the operation. In Photoshop, for example, you drag with the pencil tool to draw a free-form line.

- ✔ Traditionally, the left mouse button is the primary button — the one you use to do most jobs in a computer program. But some left-handed folks like to switch their mouse buttons so that the right button is the primary button. If you fall in that camp, remember that, when I tell you to click or double-click, you should click your right mouse button. And if I tell you to right-click, you should left-click instead.

- ✔ To *crush* the mouse is to set it on the floor and stack heavy rocks on it. You are rarely called on to perform this technique. In fact, I recommend crushing only to very desperate performance artists, and then only if swinging the mouse around by the cord and shouting, "Somebody's going to lose an eye!" fails to get a rise.

You can also use the keyboard and mouse in tandem. For example, in Photoshop, you can draw a perfectly horizontal line by pressing the Shift key while dragging with the line tool. Or you can press Alt and click on the rectangular marquee tool in the upper-left corner of the toolbox to switch to the elliptical marquee tool. Such actions are so common that you often see key and mouse combinations joined into compound verbs, such as Shift+dragging, Alt+clicking, or Shift+Alt+crushing.

Working with Windows

In Photoshop, as in most other Windows programs, you have two kinds of windows: the program window, which contains the main Photoshop work area, and image windows, which contain any images that you create or edit. Figure 2-1 shows you the program window; for a look at image windows, see Chapter 3.

Photoshop windows — both program and image — contain the same basic elements as those in other Windows programs. But just in case you need a refresher or you're new to this whole computing business, here's how the Photoshop program window works if you're using Windows 95:

- ✔ Click on the Close button in the upper-right corner of the window to shut down Photoshop. If you have any open images that haven't been saved, the program prompts you to save them. (For details on saving images, see Chapter 6.)

- ✔ Click on the Minimize button to reduce the program window to a button on the Windows 95 taskbar (labeled in Figure 2-1). To redisplay the program window, just click on the taskbar button.

- ✔ You can also use the taskbar buttons to switch between Photoshop and other running programs. Click on the button of the program you want to use.

- ✔ The appearance of the Restore/Maximize button changes depending on the current status of the window. If you see two boxes on the button, as in Figure 2-1, the button is the Restore button. Click on this button to shrink the window so that you can see other open program windows. You can then resize the window by placing your mouse cursor over a corner of the window until you see a double-headed arrow. When you see the arrow, drag the window to resize it. To move the window around, drag its title bar.

- ✔ After you click on the Restore button, it changes to the Maximize button, which looks like a single box. Click on the button to zoom the program window so that it consumes your entire screen. After the window zooms, the button changes back to the Restore button. Click on the button to restore your screen to its former size.

If you're using Windows 3.1, the Minimize button looks like a downward-pointing arrow and reduces your window to a small icon. Double-click on the icon to redisplay the window. The Maximize button looks like an upward-pointing arrow and zooms your window so that it fills up your whole screen. The Restore button shows a stacked pair of arrows, one pointing up and one pointing down. You don't have a Close button, unfortunately; the quickest way to close your program window (and Photoshop) is to press the keyboard shortcut for the Exit command, Ctrl+Q (as in Quit). This shortcut also works in Windows 95, by the way.

Maneuvering through Menus

As do all Windows programs, Photoshop sports a menu bar at the top of its window (labeled in Figure 2-1). Each word in the menu bar — File, Edit, Image, and so on — represents a menu, which is simply a list of commands that you can use to open and close images, manipulate selected portions of a photograph, hide and display palettes, and initiate all kinds of mind-boggling, sophisticated procedures.

I explain the most essential Photoshop commands throughout the course of this book. But before I send you off to cope with a single one of them, I feel compelled to provide some background information on how to work with menus.

- To choose a command from a menu, click on the menu name and then click on the command name. Or you can press and hold on the menu name, drag down to the command name, and release the mouse button at the desired command.

- Some commands bring up additional menus called *submenus*. For example, if you choose File➪Preferences, you display a submenu offering still more commands. If I ask you to choose File➪Preferences➪General, you choose the Preferences command under the File menu to display the submenu and then choose the General command from the submenu, all in one, beautiful, continuous movement. When you do it just right, it's like something out of *Swan Lake*.

- Did you notice that I underlined some letters in the commands I discussed in the last paragraph? Those letters are called *hot keys*. If you prefer using the keyboard to using the mouse, you can press hot keys in combination with the Alt key to choose a command. For example, to display the File menu, press Alt+F. To then choose the Preferences command from the File menu, press F again — no Alt key needed this time. You can also use hot keys to access options inside dialog boxes (explained later in this chapter), by the way.

In addition to using hot keys, you can access some commands by pressing *keyboard shortcuts*. For example, to initiate the File➪Open command, you can press the keyboard shortcut Ctrl+O — that is, press and hold the Ctrl key, press the O key, and then release both keys.

Most keyboard shortcuts are listed along the right side of a menu. Some keyboard equivalents select tools and some perform other functions. Either way, I keep you apprised of them throughout this book. If you take the time to memorize a few keyboard shortcuts here and there, you can save yourself a heck of a lot of time and effort. (For the most essential shortcuts, read Chapter 19. Also, tear out the Cheat Sheet at the front of this book and tape it up somewhere within easy ogling distance.)

✔ Version 4 offers you yet another way to access some commands. If you right-click inside an image window, you display a *context-sensitive menu.* In nongeek-speak, a context-sensitive menu is a mini-menu that contains commands that are related to the current tool, palette, or image, as shown in Figure 2-2.

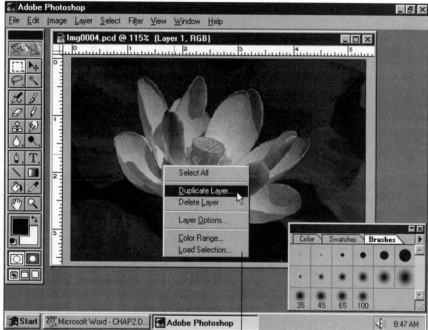

Figure 2-2: Right-click inside the image window to access context-sensitive menus.

Context-sensitive menu

Talking Back to Dialog Boxes

Photoshop reacts immediately to some menu commands. But for other commands, the program requires you to fill out a few forms before it processes your request. If you see an ellipsis (three dots, like so . . .) next to a command name, that's your clue that you're about to see such a form, known in computer clubs everywhere as a *dialog box.*

Figure 2-3 shows a sample dialog box. As the figure demonstrates, a dialog box can contain any or all of six basic kinds of options. The options work as follows:

✔ A box in which you can enter numbers or text is called an *option box.* Double-click in an option box to highlight its contents and then replace the contents by entering new stuff from the keyboard.

✔ Some option boxes come with *slider bars*. Drag the triangular slider to the left or right to lower or raise the associated numerical value. (All without hydraulics, mind you.)

✔ You can select only one circular *radio button* from any gang of radio buttons. To select a radio button, click on the button or on the option name that follows it. The selected radio button is filled with a black dot; all deselected radio buttons are hollow.

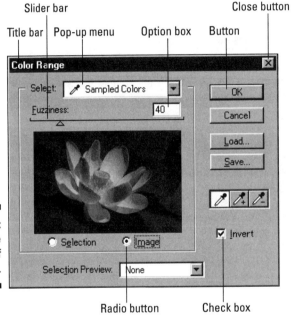

Slider bar   Close button

Title bar | Pop-up menu   Option box   Button

Figure 2-3:
The
anatomy of
a dialog box.

Radio button   Check box

✔ Although you can select only one radio button at a time, you can usually select as many *check boxes* as you want. Really, go nuts. To select a check box, click on the box or on the option name that follows it. A check mark fills the box to show that it's selected. Clicking on a selected check box turns off the option.

✔ To conserve space, some multiple-choice options appear as *pop-up menus*. Click on the down-pointing arrow to display a menu of option choices. Then click on the desired option in the menu to choose it, just as if you were choosing a command from a standard menu. As with radio buttons, you can select only one option from a pop-up menu at a time.

✔ Not to be confused with the radio button, the normal, everyday variety of *button* allows you to close the current dialog box or display others. For example, click on the Cancel button or the Close button to close the dialog box and cancel the command. Click on OK to close the dialog box and execute the command according to the current settings. Clicking on a button with an ellipsis (such as <u>L</u>oad . . . and <u>S</u>ave . . .) displays yet another dialog box.

As you can with menus, you can select options and perform other feats of magic inside dialog boxes from the keyboard. The following shortcuts work in most dialog boxes:

✔ To advance from one option box to the next, press the Tab key. To back up, press Shift+Tab.

✔ You can also move from option to option by using the hot keys (those underlined letters in the option names). Press Alt plus an option's hot key to move to that option.

✔ Press Enter to select the button surrounded by a heavy outline (such as OK in Figure 2-3).

✔ Press the up-arrow key to raise an option box value by one; press the down-arrow key to decrease the value by one. Pressing Shift+↑ and Shift+↓ raise and lower the value by ten, respectively.

✔ If you change your mind about choices you make in a dialog box, you can quickly return things to the settings that were in force when you opened the dialog box. In most dialog boxes, pressing the Alt key magically changes the Cancel button to a Reset button. Click on the Reset button to bring back the original values.

If a dialog box gets in the way of your view of an image, you can reposition the box by dragging its title bar.

Playing Around with Palettes

Photoshop 4 offers free-floating *palettes* that you can hide or leave on-screen at whim. The *palettes,* which are basically dialog boxes that can remain on-screen while you work, provide access to options that affect the performance of tools, change the appearance of images, and otherwise assist you in your editing adventures. I cover the specifics of using the options in the most popular palettes in chapters to come, but here's a brief introductory tour of how palettes work:

✔ As illustrated by the palette shown in Figure 2-4, palettes may contain the same kinds of options as dialog boxes — pop-up menus, option boxes, and so on. For information on using these options, see the preceding section.

✔ Each of the palettes is actually a collection of palettes sharing the same palette window. For example, the Layers, Channels, Paths, and Actions palettes are all housed in the same palette window (see Figure 2-4). To switch to a different palette in a palette window, click on its tab.

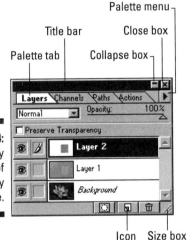

Figure 2-4:
The many elements of a healthy palette.

Palette menu

Title bar   Close box

Palette tab   Collapse box

Icon   Size box

✔ Click on the Close box on the right side of the title bar to — guess what — close the palette. (To make the palette come back, choose the desired palette from the window menu.)

✔ Press Tab to hide or display the currently open palettes, the toolbox, and the status bar (covered in Chapter 3). Press Shift+Tab if you want to hide or display all the palettes but leave the toolbox and status bar as is. Note that this trick doesn't work if an option box inside a palette is active — that is, if the option box is highlighted or if the cursor is blinking inside it. In this case, pressing Tab and Shift+Tab moves you from option to option throughout all open palettes. To deactivate the option box, just click outside it or press Enter to make the option box value take effect. You can then use the Tab/Shift+Tab shortcuts to hide and display palettes.

✔ To hide and display individual palettes; press their keyboard shortcuts: F5 for the Brushes palette, F6 for the Color palette, F7 for the Layers palette, and F8 for the Info palette.

✔ Some palettes contain icons, just like the toolbox does. Click on an icon to perform a function, such as changing the brush size or deleting a selected image.

✔ Drag the title bar at the top of the palette to move the palette around on-screen.

✔ Shift+click on a title bar to snap the palette to the nearest edge of the screen. For example, if the palette is near the right side of the screen, Shift+clicking on its title bar moves it all the way over to the right, giving you more space to view your image on-screen.

✔ Some palettes have a size box, as labeled in Figure 2-4. Drag the size box to resize the palette. To return the palette to its default size, click on the collapse box.

✔ If the palette is already at its default size, clicking on the collapse box shrinks the palette so that only the most essential options at the top of the palette are visible. Click on the collapse box again to bring all the options into full view.

✔ Alt+click on the collapse box to hide all but the title bar and the palette tabs. Or double-click on a palette tab. The advantage is that you free up screen space without closing the palettes altogether.

✔ You can break any palette off into its own window by dragging the palette tab out of the current window, as shown in Figure 2-5. You can also combine palettes into a single palette window by dragging a tab from one palette into another.

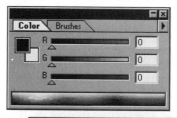

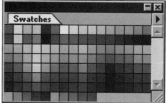

Figure 2-5:
Drag the palette tab (left) to break the palette off into its own little palette apartment.

✔ Want to know my favorite application of this technique? Drag the Swatches palette out of the Color/Swatches/Brushes palette window to create a separate Swatches palette. Then close the Swatches palette altogether. See, the Swatches palette isn't very useful, so you may as well get it off the screen. Now you can drag the Options palette into the same palette window as the Color and Brushes palette, enabling you to access all three of these very vital palettes quickly while using up a minimum of on-screen space.

✔ Press and hold on the right-pointing arrowhead on the right side of the palette, just below the title bar — phew, I need a breather — to display the palette menu. Here's yet another place to find commands, just in case you manage to master all of the others. Yeah, right.

Opening Up Your Toolbox

I think that you're ready to move on to the tempestuous world of the toolbox. As shown in Figure 2-6, the items in the toolbox fall into three basic categories — tools, color controls, and icons. Future chapters explain in detail how to use the various gizmos in the toolbox, but here's a basic overview of what's in store:

✔ The top two-thirds or so of the toolbox is devoted to an assortment of tools that you can use to edit images, just as you might use an assortment of pencils and paintbrushes to paint a picture. To select one of these tools, click on its icon. Then use the tool by clicking on or dragging it inside your image.

✔ A tiny, right-pointing triangle in the bottom-right corner of a tool icon indicates that more tools are hidden away on a *flyout* menu behind that icon. To display the flyout menu and reveal the hidden tools, press and hold the mouse button on the icon. Drag across the row of tools until your cursor is hovering over the tool you want to use and then release the mouse button.

✔ You can also Alt+click on a tool icon to cycle through all the tools hidden beneath it.

✔ The bottom third of the toolbox contains color selection options and other icons. These icons respond immediately when you click on them.

✔ If you've been clicking away on the toolbox icons and haven't seen any results, don't panic. Your copy of Photoshop isn't broken; the icons just don't do anything unless you have an image open. To find out how to open images, see Chapter 3.

✔ Actually, one of the icons in the toolbox does do something with no image on-screen. If you click on the very top icon in the toolbox — the one with the ghostly looking eyeball in it — you display a splash screen that contains a scrolling list of the names of the people who developed the program.

If you have Netscape Navigator or another Web browser installed on your computer, clicking on the Adobe icon in the top-left corner of the splash screen launches your browser and displays an Adobe Web page that resides on your hard drive. The page includes links that you can use to access the Adobe Web site after you log on to the Internet.

✔ When you get bored with playing with the splash screen, click inside it to put it away.

✔ You can also access all the tools and icons and two of the color controls from the keyboard. For example, to select the blur tool, you just press the R key. To select the sharpen tool, which shares the flyout menu with the blur tool, you press R again. Other keyboard equivalents are shown in Figure 2-6.

✔ One exception to the preceding tip: Choosing tools from the flyout menu in the top-left corner of the toolbox, which contains marquee tools and the crop tool, actually involves two shortcut keys. Press M to switch between the rectangular and elliptical marquee tools, but press C to select the crop tool. You can't select the single-row and single-column marquee tools from the keyboard.

✔ If you can't remember the name of a particular tool, pause your cursor over its icon for a second or two. A little label appears to tell you the name of the tool and its keyboard equivalent.

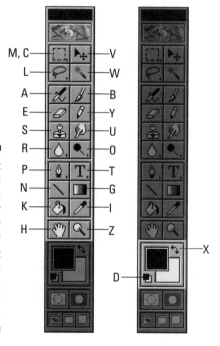

Figure 2-6: Select a tool or activate a color control or icon by clicking on it or by pressing the keys listed here.

Chapter 3

Now the Fun Really Begins

• •

In This Chapter

▶ Opening and closing images

▶ Creating a new, blank image

▶ Mastering your image windows

▶ Moving around your image

▶ Zooming in and out

▶ Changing views

▶ Turning on grids and guides

• •

*W*hen you first start Photoshop, you're presented with a plethora of tools, menus, and palettes, as illustrated in Chapter 2. Until you open up an image, those contraptions are intriguing, yet ultimately worthless — it's like having an easel, a full set of brushes, and a whole paintbox full of paints, but no canvas. And with Photoshop, you can't even amuse yourself by creating a political mural on your neighbor's garage door, as you can with traditional paint. No, if you want to become a digital Picasso (or Rembrandt, or Monet, or whatever artistic legend you choose), you need to open an image.

This chapter explains how to open existing images and also how to create a new, blank canvas for an image you want to paint from scratch. Then the chapter explains the myriad ways you can display your image on-screen in order to view your masterpiece from just the right perspective.

Don't Just Sit There, Open Something

If you're a longtime computer buff, you might expect opening an image to be a relatively straightforward process. You just choose File⇨Open or press Ctrl+O and select the image file you want to display, right?

Well, opening files in Photoshop involves a little complication: The steps for opening a Photo CD image are different than the steps for opening images saved in other file formats. The following sections give you the lowdown on opening both types of images.

The term *Photo CD image* can be a little confusing; it refers to images saved in the Kodak Photo CD file format, not simply to images that come from a CD. A Photo CD image has the letters PCD tagged onto the end of its filename.

Opening a non-Photo CD image

To open an image that's stored in any format except the Kodak Photo CD format, walk this way:

1. Choose File⇨Open.

If choosing the commands from the menu is too much work — and it is — just press Ctrl+O. The Open dialog box rears its useful head, as shown in Figure 3-1. (The dialog box looks slightly different if you're using Windows 3.1. Also, your dialog box may not offer all the options in the figure or the options may have different names. But the basic components work the same.)

2. Select the disk or folder that contains your image from the Look In pop-up menu.

After you select a disk or folder, the contents of that disk or folder appear in the box beneath the pop-up menu. Double-click on a folder in the box to display its contents, if necessary, until you find the file you want to open.

3. Click on the image you want to open.

After you locate your image, click on its name in the list to select it.

The new version of Photoshop now offers image previews, something that was lacking in earlier Windows versions of the program. The preview appears at the bottom of the Open dialog box, enabling you to take a gander at the image before you go to the trouble of opening it. But previews are available only in certain circumstances. If no preview appears, see the "Where's my preview?" sidebar, in this chapter.

Click on the Details button to display pertinent information about each image, including its size and type and the date it was last edited.

4. Click on the Open button.

Or press the Enter key or press Alt+O. Alternatively, you can simply double-click on the image to open it.

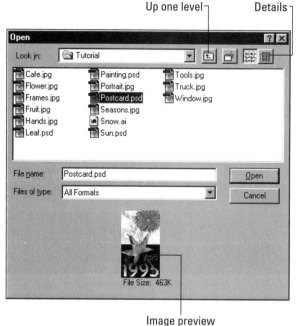

Figure 3-1:
This dialog
box lets you
locate and
open images
on your hard
drive or
some other
disk.

That's all there is to it. Your image is now open and ready to abuse. But before you have at it in earnest, here are a few additional notes on opening images:

✔ To close a folder and view the contents of the folder that contains it, click on the Up One Level button at the top of the Open dialog box.

✔ Click on the Look In pop-up menu to display the list of folders that contains the current folder. For example, if the items in the pop-up menu read Elephant, Digestive Systems, Food-Processing Enzymes, then the Food-Processing Enzymes folder resides inside the Digestive Systems folder, which is on the Elephant disk.

✔ If you can't find a file in a certain folder, it may be because Photoshop doesn't think it can open the file. To see all files in a folder, whether Photoshop can open them or not, select the All Formats option from the Files of Type pop-up menu. If the file appears, go ahead and try to open it. It may not work, but it's worth a try.

✔ Here's a trick to try if you're using Windows 95: You can preview an image even when Photoshop isn't running by right-clicking on the image file in My Computer or Explorer. When you right-click, choose Properties from the menu that appears. Then click on the Photoshop Image tab of the resulting dialog box. Unfortunately, this trick only works for images saved in Version 4 and in the native Photoshop format. (Formats are explained in Chapter 6.)

Where's my preview?

You wouldn't think that a little thing like an image preview would deserve its own sidebar, but in order for previews to appear in the Open dialog box, the planets must be in perfect alignment:

✔ You must be currently using Windows 95 or Windows NT.

✔ The image must have been saved in Photoshop 4. Earlier Windows versions of Photoshop didn't support image previews.

✔ The image must have been saved to disk with the Save Thumbnail check box selected in the Save dialog box, as explained in Chapter 6. This check box is turned on by default, but it's possible that someone (maybe you?) fooled with the default settings in the Preferences dialog box. For information on how to get your previews saved automatically again, see Chapter 6.

Opening a Kodak Photo CD image

As mentioned earlier, opening a Kodak Photo CD image involves a different process than opening other types of images. Here's the scoop:

1. **Choose File⇨Open or press Ctrl+O.**

2. **Select the Photo CD disk from the Look In pop-up menu.**

   The disk will have some meaningless machine-assigned name like PCD0196.

3. **Open the Photo_CD folder.**

   Inside, you find several weirdly named files.

4. **Open the Images folder.**

   Here's where the real images live. They all have dumb names like IMG0001.PCD;1 and so on. Luckily, every Photo CD disk comes with two or three sheets of tiny thumbnail printouts so that you know which image is associated with each file number.

5. **Double-click on the image you want to open.**

   After what may seem like an interminable amount of time — don't give up and think that your computer has crashed — the dialog box shown in Figure 3-2 appears.

6. **Click on the Source button.**

   Here's the tricky part. The Photo CD interpreter built into Photoshop wants more than anything to make sure that the colors in the image are correctly converted from the disk to your screen. Therefore, you have to tell Photoshop a source and destination for the image. It's kind of weird, but just do as I tell you and you can't go wrong.

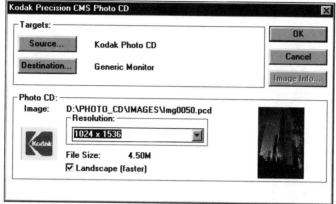

Figure 3-2:
This dialog
box rears its
pesky head
when you
try to open a
Photo CD
file from the
Images
folder.

7. **Select the proper film type.**

   If the image you want to open was scanned from a 35mm slide, select the
   Universal Ektachrome or Universal Kodachrome option, depending on the
   film used to shoot the photo. If the image came from a film negative, select
   the Color Negative option. (If you're opening an image from a commercial
   CD, such as one from Digital Stock, you can assume that the Source option
   should be set to Universal Ektachrome.)

   Press Enter to go back to the dialog box shown in Figure 3-2.

8. **Click on the Destination button.**

   It's right there below Source.

9. **Select Generic Monitor from the pop-up menu.**

   This choice converts the scan to a standard color Photoshop image. Press
   Enter when you finish.

10. **Select an option from the Resolution pop-up menu.**

    The option you select depends on the amount of memory available to your
    computer. I suggest starting with 1024 x 1536. If that gives your computer
    fits after the next step, try selecting the 512 x 768 option, which creates an
    image that's roughly big enough to fill a 17-inch monitor. The smallest
    option, 128 x 192, results in an image that's too tiny for even an ant to edit.

11. **Press Enter or click on OK.**

    Photoshop opens the Photo CD image. If you get an out-of-memory error,
    try opening the image again and selecting a smaller resolution option, as
    described in the preceding step.

If an image opens up lying on its side, you can shift it to an upright position by rotating it. Choose Image⇨Rotate Canvas⇨90° CW (clockwise) if the image is resting on its left side; choose Image⇨Rotate Canvas⇨90° CCW (counter-clockwise) if the image is taking a nap on its right side. (The latter is more common.) If the image turns upside down, choose Edit⇨Undo and then choose the command that you didn't choose the first time.

After you open an image for the first time, the Source and Destination options remain set. This means that you can skip Steps 6 through 9 when opening future Photo CD images.

I Want to Start from Scratch!

To create a new image instead of opening an existing one, choose File⇨New or press Ctrl+N. Photoshop displays the New dialog box. There, you can name your file; specify the width, height, and resolution (as discussed in Chapter 4); and set the color mode (as discussed in Chapter 5). However, you'll probably have little reason to create a new image unless you just want to play around with the painting tools. Photoshop is, after all, made primarily for editing existing images.

Behold the Image Window

After you open up an image, Photoshop displays the image on-screen inside a new image window. Several new elements appear when you open an image, as labeled in Figure 3-3. The following list explains all:

- ✔ The title bar lists the title of your image, hence the name. The added bonus of the title bar is that you can drag it to move the window to a different location on-screen. Easy stuff.

- ✔ Just like the main Photoshop program window, each image window has a Close button, Minimize button, and Maximize/Restore button. The buttons work just as they do for the program window (explained in Chapter 2), with one exception. The Minimize button reduces the image window so that only a small title bar is left on-screen. Click on the Restore button to bring the image back into view.

- ✔ Alternatively, you can choose File⇨Close or press Ctrl+W to close an image. You know, W as in *hasta la vista, window.* (If you've made some changes to the image, Photoshop asks you whether you want to save the new and improved image, a process explained in great detail in Chapter 6.)

Scroll box ┐

Title bar   Image area   Man scaring sea life   Scroll arrow ┐

Figure 3-3:
An image
from Digital
Stock's
"Active
Lifestyles 2"
collection.

Page preview box   Status bar   Scroll bar ┘

└ Magnification box

✔ To change the size of the image window, place your cursor over a corner of the window. When a double-headed arrow appears, drag the corner. The image remains the same; you're just changing the size of the window that holds the image. Give it a try and see what I mean.

✔ The status bar gives you information about your image and hints about the tool or command you're using.

✔ Don't see the status bar on your screen? Choose Window➪Show Status Bar to display it. Remember that the status bar disappears when you press Tab to hide the palettes and the toolbox, as explained in Chapter 2.

✔ At the left end of the status bar is the magnification box, which lets you zoom in and out on your image, as explained later in this chapter.

✔ Next to the magnification box is the page preview box, which shows how much memory your image is consuming, measured in digital chunks called *bytes.* The first number is the size of the image as the image will be sent to the printer; the second number reflects the size of the image with layer information included. I discuss file size and resolution and all those other thorny issues in Chapter 4 and explain layers in Chapter 15. For the time being, don't worry about the preview box too much. I just didn't want to leave you wondering, "What in the Sam Hill is this thingie here?"

✔ If you click and hold the mouse button down on the page preview box, Photoshop displays a window that shows you where the image will appear on the page when you print the image. The big X indicates the image in the preview.

✔ Hold down Alt as you click on the page preview box, and Photoshop displays a box showing the height, width, resolution, and number of channels in the image. (Channels are discussed in Chapter 5.)

✔ The scroll bars let you navigate around and display hidden portions of the image inside the window. Photoshop offers two scroll bars, one vertical bar along the right side of the image and one horizontal bar along the bottom.

✔ If you click on a scroll arrow, you nudge your view of the image slightly in that direction. For example, if you click on the right-pointing scroll arrow, an item that was hidden on the right side of the photograph slides into view. Click in the gray area of a scroll bar to scroll the window more dramatically. Drag a scroll box to manually specify the distance scrolled.

✔ Using the scroll arrows isn't the only way to move around your image; in fact, it's probably the least efficient method. For some better options, check out the techniques presented in the section "The Screen Is Your Digital Oyster," coming up next.

✔ The area inside the title bar and scroll bars is the *image area.* The image area is where you paint and edit and select details and, otherwise, have at your image. Obviously, we look at the image area a lot throughout the many pages of this book.

You can open as many images on-screen as your computer's memory and screen size allow. But only one image is active at a time. To make a different window active, just click on it or choose its name from the bottom of the Window menu.

The Screen Is Your Digital Oyster

The Photoshop toolbox includes two navigation tools: the hand tool, which lets you scroll the image inside the window with much more ease than the silly scroll bars afford, and the zoom tool, which lets you move closer to or farther away from your image. The hand tool and the zoom tool are called navigation tools because they don't change the image; they merely move your view of the image so that you can get a better look-see.

Version 4 offers a new, additional navigation aid, appropriately called the Navigator palette. The palette gives you a super-convenient way to zoom and scroll your image; in fact, after you are familiar with the palette, you may not use the hand and zoom tools at all. But in the interest of fair play, I present all of your various options for moving around in your image in the upcoming sections.

Using the hand tool

If you're familiar with other Windows programs, you need to know something about Photoshop: The scroll bars are useless. Keep away from them. I want you to promise me you'll always use the hand tool or the new Navigator palette (explained shortly) instead. Promise? Good. As for you new users, I don't worry about you because I'm going to teach you right.

Consider the following example: Figure 3-4 shows another Digital Stock image — this time from the "Children and Teens" collection. The top view in the figure shows a young lad in obvious distress. The problem is that the picture is wider than my screen, so I can't see what's causing him such grief.

To view the rest of the scene, I select the hand tool by clicking on its icon in the toolbox. Then I position my Photoshop hand over the hand in the picture, as shown in the top example in Figure 3-4, and drag to the left. The image moves with the hand cursor, as shown in the bottom example, and reveals the source of the boy's torment.

Dragging with the hand tool is like turning your head to view a new part of your surroundings. You can drag at any angle you please — up, down, sideways, or diagonally.

You can also select the hand tool by pressing the H key. To temporarily access the hand tool when another tool is selected, press the spacebar. As long as the spacebar is down, the hand tool is available. Releasing the spacebar returns you to the selected tool.

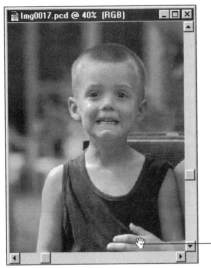

—Hand cursor

Figure 3-4:
Dragging
with the
hand tool
reveals that
a bad
haircut isn't
the only
thing a kid
has to worry
about.

Using keyboard shortcuts

As in most other programs, you can also use keyboard shortcuts to move about your image. Press Page Up or Page Down to scroll up or down an entire screen. Press Shift+Page Up or Shift+Page Down to scroll in smaller increments. Press Home to go to the upper-left corner of the image and press End to move to the lower-right corner.

Zooming in and out on your work

When you first open an image, Photoshop displays the entire image so that it fits on-screen. But you may not be seeing the details in the image as clearly as you want. The first view is sort of like being far away from the image. If you want to inspect it in more detail, you have to step closer.

Photoshop gives you several ways to zoom in and out on your work, as described in these next few sections.

Zooming doesn't change the size at which your image prints. It just affects the size at which you see the image on-screen. Zooming is like looking at some eentsey-teentsey life-form under a microscope. The creature doesn't actually grow and shrink as you vary the degree of magnification, and neither does your image.

The zoom tool

Using the zoom tool is one avenue for changing your view of an image. Every time you click on your image with the tool, you magnify the image to a larger size. Here's an example of how it works:

1. **Select the zoom tool.**

   Click on the zoom tool in the toolbox. It's the one that looks like a magnifying glass. You can also press the Z key to grab the zoom tool.

2. **Click in the image area.**

   Photoshop magnifies the image to the next preset zoom size (the increments are set by Photoshop), as demonstrated in the second example of Figure 3-5. The program centers the magnified view about the point at which you click. In Figure 3-5, for example, I clicked between the girl's eyes.

3. **Repeat.**

   To zoom in farther still, click again with the zoom tool, as demonstrated in the bottom example of Figure 3-5.

A setting in the Zoom Tool Options palette determines whether Photoshop resizes your image window to match the image when you zoom with the zoom tool. To display the palette, select the zoom tool and press Enter. If you want your image windows to be resized when you zoom, select the Resize Windows to Fit option. The only hitch comes when the window bumps into a palette — when the window hits a palette that's anchored to the side of the screen (as opposed to floating in the middle of the screen), Photoshop thinks that it's hit some sort of wall and stops zooming. To get around the problem, press Tab to hide all the palettes and the toolbox and then zoom. Press Tab again to bring back the palettes and the toolbox.

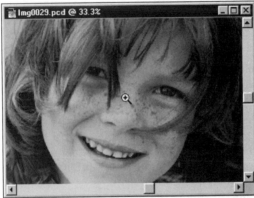

Figure 3-5:
Clicking
with the
zoom tool
magnifies
your image
in preset
increments.

Here's some other zoom-tool stuff to tuck away for future reference:

- Alt+click with the zoom tool to zoom out on your image.

- You can also zoom in and out from the keyboard: Press Ctrl++ (the Ctrl key followed by the plus key) to zoom in; press Ctrl+- (Ctrl+minus) to zoom out. Note that Photoshop zooms your window in and out to match the image size when you use this shortcut, regardless of the setting in the Zoom Tool Options palette. If you don't want the window itself to resize, press Ctrl+Alt++ or Ctrl+Alt+- to do your zooming from the keyboard.

- As you zoom, Photoshop displays the *zoom factor* in the title bar. A zoom factor of 100 percent shows you one screen pixel for every pixel in your image. (Pixels are explained thoroughly in the next chapter.)

Keep in mind that a 100-percent zoom ratio doesn't necessarily correspond to the printed size of your image, contrary to what you might expect. If you want to view your image at its printed size, use the Print Size command, explained in the next section.

- To magnify just one section of an image, drag with the zoom tool to surround the area with a dotted outline. Photoshop fills the image window with the area that you surrounded.

- To temporarily access the zoom tool while another tool is selected, press Ctrl+spacebar. Press Ctrl+Alt+spacebar to get the zoom out cursor. In either case, releasing the keys returns you to the previously selected tool.

The View commands

Version 4's new View menu offers some more ways to change the magnification of your image. The first two zoom commands on the menu, Zoom In and Zoom Out, aren't of much interest; they do the same thing as clicking and Alt+clicking with the zoom tool, except that you can't specify the center of the new view as you can with the zoom tool. But you may find the other three View commands helpful at times:

- Choose View⇨Actual Pixels or press Ctrl+Alt+0 (zero) to return to the 100 percent zoom ratio. This view size shows you one pixel on your monitor for every pixel in the image, which is the most accurate way to view your image. (For background information on all this pixel stuff, read Chapter 4.)

- Choose View⇨Fit on Screen or press Ctrl+0 (zero) to display your image at the largest size that allows the entire image to fit on-screen.

- You can also choose the Actual Pixels view by double-clicking on the zoom tool icon in the toolbox. Double-click on the hand tool icon to change to Fit on Screen view.

- Choose View⇨Print Size to display your image on-screen at the same size that it will print. Note that Photoshop just provides an approximation of the print size; your actual printed piece may be slightly smaller or larger.

The magnification box

The zoom tool and View commands are great when you want to zoom in or out to one of the preset Photoshop zoom ratios. But what if you want more control over your zooming? The answer awaits in the magnification box in the lower-left corner of the Photoshop window (labeled back in Figure 3-3).

To enter a zoom ratio, just double-click on the magnification box and type in the zoom ratio you want to use. If you know exactly what zoom ratio you want, press Enter to make Photoshop do your bidding. But if you want to play around with different zoom ratios, press Shift+Enter instead. That way, Photoshop zooms your image but keeps the magnification box active so that you can quickly enter a new ratio if the first one doesn't work out. When you're satisfied, press Enter.

When you use the magnification box, the image window size doesn't change as you zoom, regardless of whether the Resize Windows to Fit option is selected in the Zoom Tool Options palette.

Navigating by palette

The Navigator palette, shown in Figure 3-6, is one of the handiest additions to Version 4. To display the palette, choose Window⇨Show Navigator. Or press F8 to display the Info palette and then click on the Navigator palette tab. To make the palette smaller or larger, drag on the size box in the palette's lower-right corner.

The palette provides a handy, all-in-one tool for scrolling and zooming. It's especially useful when you're working on a large image that doesn't fit entirely on-screen when you're zoomed in for detail work. Here are the how-tos for using the palette:

✔ In the center of the palette, you see a thumbnail view of your image, as in Figure 3-6. The palette shows your entire image, even if it's not all visible in the main image window.

✔ See the box that surrounds a portion of the thumbnail? That's called the view box. The area within the box corresponds to the portion of your image that's visible in the main image window. As you drag the box, Photoshop scrolls your image in the main image window to display the area that's surrounded by the box. You can also click on an area in the thumbnail to move the view box over that portion of the image.

✔ Press and hold Ctrl, and the cursor in the palette changes to a zoom cursor. If you drag the view box with the cursor (keep pressing Ctrl), you resize the view box, which in turn zooms the image in the image window.

View box   Size box ⌐

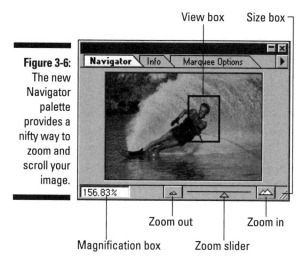

Figure 3-6:
The new
Navigator
palette
provides a
nifty way to
zoom and
scroll your
image.

Zoom out   Zoom in

Magnification box   Zoom slider

✔ The palette also contains a magnification box, as labeled in the figure. The box works just like the one in the image window; just enter a zoom factor and press Enter.

✔ To zoom in or out in the preset Photoshop increments (as with the zoom tool), click on the Zoom In or Zoom Out buttons, labeled in Figure 3-6.

✔ You can also zoom by dragging the Zoom slider — drag left to zoom out and drag right to zoom in.

If you don't like the color of the view box, you can change it. Click on the right-pointing arrow in the upper-right corner of the palette and choose the Palette Options command. Then choose a new color from the Color pop-up menu.

Filling up the screen with your image

The three icons at the bottom of the toolbox let you change the way the window fills the screen. These icons appear labeled in Figure 3-7.

✔ Click on the leftmost icon to view the window normally, with scroll bars and title bar and all that stuff. This is the default setting.

✔ Click on the center icon to eliminate the scroll bars and title bar and fill the screen with your image. Any portions of the screen that aren't consumed by the image appear gray. The toolbox, palettes, status bar, and menu bar remain visible.

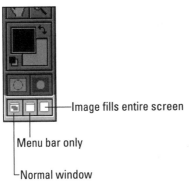

Figure 3-7:
Those weird little icons at the bottom of the toolbox change your on-screen landscape.

—Image fills entire screen

Menu bar only

Normal window

✔ If you want to take over still more screen real estate, click on the rightmost icon to hide the menu bar. Now any portions of the screen that don't contain the image are black. The only desktop elements that remain available are the palettes, toolbox, and status bar.

✔ As covered in Chapter 2, you can press Tab to hide the toolbox, the palettes, and the status bar; press Tab again to redisplay them. To hide and redisplay the palettes only, press Shift+Tab.

You can cycle through the different screen modes by pressing the F key instead of clicking on the toolbox icons if you prefer. Press F once to select the second icon, press F again to select the third icon, and press F a third time to return to the first icon.

Tools for the Terribly Precise

If you've ever used a page layout program such as PageMaker or QuarkXPress, you're no doubt familiar with the concept of *grids* and *guides,* which are new to Photoshop 4. Shown in Figure 3-8, grids and guides are on-screen devices that help you align elements in your image. For example, in the figure I used a horizontal guide to position my text exactly 2 inches from the left edge of the image and 11 inches from the top of the image.

In addition to grids and guides, Photoshop also offers rulers that run across the top and left sides of the image window. Grids, guides, and rulers come in handy when you're feeling the urge to be especially precise with your work.

Guide   Move guide cursor   Ruler   Grid line

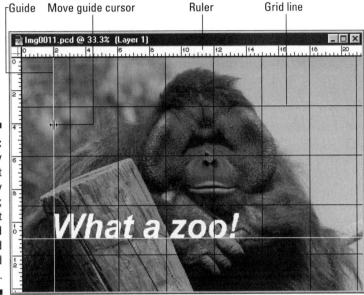

Figure 3-8:
Our furry
friend isn't
really
fenced in;
he's just
covered
with grid
lines and
guides.

Switching on the rulers

To display rulers, choose View⇨Show Rulers or press Ctrl+R. To hide the rulers, choose View⇨Hide Rulers or press Ctrl+R again.

You can specify the unit of measurement used by the rulers. For example, if you want to use picas instead of inches, choose File⇨Preferences⇨Units & Rulers. Or just double-click on a ruler. In the Rulers section of the dialog box that appears, select a new unit of measure from the Units pop-up menu.

Using guides

Guides are horizontal and vertical lines that you create to help you align elements in your image. Guides don't print; they're creatures of the on-screen world only. You can create as many guides as you need.

Before you can create a guide, you have to display the rulers by choosing View⇨Show Rulers or pressing Ctrl+R. Then drag from one of the rulers to "pull out" a guide. Drag from any point on the horizontal ruler to create a horizontal guide; drag from the vertical ruler to create a vertical guide. Release the mouse button at the spot where you want to place the guide.

Here are some more guides to using guides:

✔ After you create a guide, you can reposition it. First, select the move tool (it's the top right tool in the toolbox) by clicking on its icon in the toolbox. Then place the cursor over the guide until you see the double-headed arrow, as in Figure 3-8, and drag the guide to its new home. Alternatively, you can Ctrl+drag the guide with any other tool except the hand or pen tool. (The Ctrl key temporarily accesses the move tool when any tool but the hand or pen tool is selected.)

✔ To remove a guide, drag it out of the image window using the move tool or Ctrl+drag with any other tool but the pen or hand tool. To get rid of all guides, choose View➪Clear Guides.

✔ To lock a guide in place, choose View➪Lock Guides or press Ctrl+Alt+;. To unlock the guides so that you can move them again, choose View➪Lock Guides or press Ctrl+Alt+; again.

✔ When you drag an image element near a guide, the element "snaps" into alignment with the guide — as if the guide had some sort of magnetic pull. If you don't want stuff to snap to guides, choose View➪Snap to Guides or press Ctrl+Shift+;. Choose the command again to turn snapping back on. (A check mark next to the command name means that the feature is turned on.)

✔ To change the color of the guides, choose File➪Preferences➪Guides & Grid, double-click on a guide with the move tool or Ctrl+double-click on the guide with any other tool but the hand or pen tool. In the Guides section of the dialog box that appears, you can choose a color and line style for your guides. Press Enter to exit the dialog box and make your changes official.

Turning on the grid

Unlike guides, which you can position willy-nilly in the image window, the grid positions lines across your image in preset intervals. You can't move grid lines, but you can change the spacing and color of the lines.

To turn on the grid, choose View➪Show Grid or press Ctrl+" (quote). To change the spacing and appearance of the grid lines, choose File➪Preferences➪Guides & Grid. Photoshop presents you with a dialog box in which you can choose a color and line style for the grid lines, specify how far apart you want to space the lines, and choose whether you want to subdivide the grid with secondary grid lines or not. You can also choose a unit of measurement for the grid.

Like guides, the lines of a grid have "snapping" capabilities — anything you drag near a grid line automatically snaps into alignment with that line. You turn snapping on and off by choosing View➪Snap to Grid or by pressing Ctrl+Shift+". A check mark next to the command name in the menu means that snapping is turned on.

Part II
The Care and Feeding of Pixels

The 5th Wave   By Rich Tennant

"I THINK YOU'VE MADE A MISTAKE. WE DO PHOTO RETOUCHING, NOT FAMILY PORTRAI... OOOH, WAIT A MINUTE-I THINK I GET IT!"

In this part . . .

1 can't tell you how disappointed I was the first time I dissected a frog. Here we had been looking at all the cool pictures of the animal's colorful innards, and the moment we got the critter open, everything was various shades of pale beige. Where are the blue veins? And the red arteries? And the purple muscles and organs, and the bright yellow fat cells? Is my frog defective?

That's the problem with real life — it's never as interesting as the pictures. But an electronic image is different. It's not some natural miracle that tests the minds of our best scientists and absolutely baffles the brains of junior high school students; it's something designed by humans expressly to be understood by other humans. So you can be sure that the dissection that takes place in Chapters 4 through 7 will look the same on your computer screen as it does in my figures, except more colorful.

The chapters in this part tell you how to manage the colored specks — called *pixels* — that make up the image, how color and black-and-white images work, and how to save and print the image when you're done editing. These chapters aren't obscure experiments, they're straightforward journeys through features that you use every time you open Photoshop. Even better, you won't have to put up with the nauseating smell of formaldehyde.

Oh, and one more thing: The publisher wants me to tell you that no frogs were killed or inconvenienced in the making of this book. One parrot was made to take notation, but that's it.

Chapter 4

Sizing Up Your Image

· ·

In This Chapter

▶ Taking a close look at the pixels in an image

▶ Using the Image Size dialog box

▶ Understanding resolution

▶ Matching the width of an image to page columns

▶ Changing the number of pixels in an image

▶ Resizing the canvas independently of the image

· ·

*I*mages that you create and edit in Photoshop — or in any other image editor, for that matter — are made up of tiny squares called *pixels.* Understanding how pixels work in an image can be enormously confusing to beginning image editors. Unfortunately, managing your pixel population correctly is essential to turning out professional-looking images, so you really do need to come to grips with how pixels work before you can be successful with Photoshop.

This chapter explains everything you need to know to put pixels in perspective, including how the number of pixels in an image affects its quality, printed size, and size on disk. I also show you how to reduce or enlarge the size of the on-screen canvas on which all your pretty pixels perch. In other words, this chapter offers pages of particularly provocative pixel paragraphs, partner.

The Version 4 Image Size dialog box, which is Grand Central Station for controlling pixels, has some important differences from the one in earlier versions of Photoshop. Be sure to pay special attention to information marked with the Version 4 icon if you've upgraded from an earlier version.

Welcome to Pixeltown

Imagine, if you will, that you are the victim of a terrifying scientific experiment that has left you 1 millimeter tall. After recovering from the initial shock that such terrifying scientific experiments tend to produce on one's equilibrium, you discover that you are sitting on a square tile that's colored with a uniform shade of blue. Beyond your tile are eight other blue tiles, one to your right and one to your left, one in front and one behind, and four others in diagonal directions. In other words, the tiles are aligned in a perfect grid, just like standard floor tiles. You notice upon further inspection that each of the blue tiles differs slightly in shade and tone. As you slowly turn, it becomes evident that you're surrounded by these colored tiles for as far as your infinitesimally tiny, pin-prick eyes can see.

You cry out in anguish and fling your dust-speck body about in the way that folks always do when plagued by these terrifying scientific experiments. As if in answer to your pitiful squeals, you start to grow. In a matter of moments, you increase in size to almost 5 centimeters tall. A bug that was considering devouring you has a change of mind and runs away. You can now see that you sit in the midst of a huge auditorium and that all the tiles on its vast and unending floor are colored differently, gradually changing from shades of blue to shades of green, red, and yellow. You continue to grow: Ten centimeters, 20, 50, a full meter tall. The tiles start to blend together to form some kind of pattern. Two meters, 5, 10. You've now grown several times beyond your normal height, reaching 20 meters tall. Your massive head bursts through the flimsy ceiling of the room.

When you reach the height of a 50-story building, your growth spurt comes to an end. You look down at the ruined auditorium, whose walls have been shredded to rubble by the great edges of your tremendous feet, and you notice a peculiar thing. You stand not on a floor, but on a picture, as rich in color and detail as any you've seen. The tiles, which now appear dot-sized to you, have merged together to create a seamless blend. You had expected the result to have the rough appearance of a mosaic — requiring a heavy dose of imagination to compensate for occasionally choppy transitions — but in fact it looks exactly like a continuous photograph.

The vision inspires you to claw at your temples, fling your arms about in circles, and shriek, "What's happening to me?!" The answer, of course, is nothing. Well, okay, your body may be stretched out of shape, but your eyes are working fine. You see, when you get far enough away from a perfect grid of colored tiles — whether via a terrifying scientific experiment or more conventional means — the tiles disappear, and an overall image takes shape.

What does this little trip down sci-fi lane have to do with Photoshop? Well, a lot, actually. Like the image on the auditorium floor, your Photoshop image is made up of a grid of colored squares. In this case, the squares are called *pixels*.

By now, you're probably thinking, "Fine, images are made up of a bunch of itsy-bitsy square pixels. So what? Who cares? Quit wasting my time, darn you." The truth is, these tiniest of image particles are at the heart of what makes Photoshop and your electronic images tick.

Every single painting and image-editing function in Photoshop is devoted to changing either the quantity or the color of pixels. That's all Photoshop does. I know, it sounds so simple that you figure I must be joking, exaggerating, or just plain lying. But as Salvador Dali is my witness, it's the absolute truth. Photoshop is merely an extremely sophisticated pixel counter and colorer, nothing more.

Screen Pixels versus Image Pixels

Like the tiles in the preceding story, each pixel in a computer image is perfectly square, arranged on a perfect grid, and colored uniformly — that is, each pixel is one color and one color only. Put these pixels together, and your brain perceives them to be an everyday, average photograph.

The display on your computer's monitor is also made up of pixels. Like image pixels, screen pixels are square and arranged on a grid. A typical 13-inch monitor measures 640 screen pixels wide by 480 screen pixels tall. These screen pixels are kind of tiny, so you may not be able to make them out. Each one generally measures $1/72$ inch across.

To understand the relationship between screen and image pixels, open an image. After the image comes up on-screen, double-click on the zoom tool in the toolbox or choose <u>V</u>iew⇨<u>A</u>ctual Pixels. The title bar on the image window lists the zoom ratio as 100 percent, which means that you can see one pixel in your image for every pixel displayed by your monitor.

To view the image pixels more closely, enter a value of 200 percent in the magnification box in the lower-left corner of the Photoshop window (double-click on the box to activate it). A 200 percent zoom factor magnifies the image pixels to twice their previous size, so that one image pixel measures two screen pixels tall and two screen pixels wide. If you change the zoom factor to 400 percent, Photoshop displays four screen pixels for every image pixel, giving you a total of 16 screen pixels for every image pixel (4 screen pixels tall by 4 screen pixels wide). Figure 4-1 illustrates how different zoom factors affect the appearance of your image pixels on-screen.

Remember that the zoom factor has nothing to do with the size at which your image will print — it only affects how your image looks on-screen. If you want to see your image on-screen at its approximate print size, choose <u>V</u>iew⇨<u>P</u>rint Size.

100%   200%

400%   800%

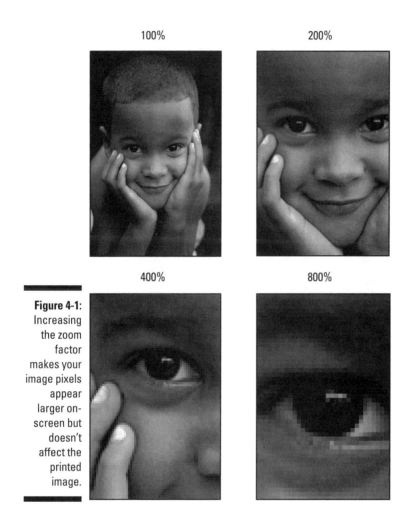

Figure 4-1: Increasing the zoom factor makes your image pixels appear larger on-screen but doesn't affect the printed image.

Image Size, Resolution, and Other Tricky Pixel Stuff

A Photoshop image has three primary attributes related to pixels: file size, physical dimensions, and resolution, as explained in the following list. You control these attributes through the Image Size dialog box, shown in Figure 4-2. To display the dialog box, choose Image➪Image Size.

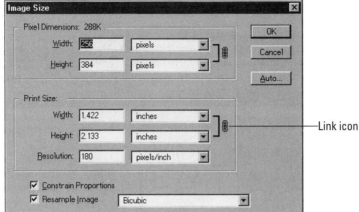

—Link icon

Figure 4-2:
You control
file size,
image
dimensions,
and
resolution
through the
Image Size
dialog box.

If you just want to get a quick look at the dimensions and resolution of an image, press Alt as you press and hold the mouse button on the page preview box in the lower-left corner of the Photoshop window (next to the magnification box). Photoshop displays a little box listing the dimensions, resolution, and other scary stuff.

✔ The *file size* of the image is a measure of how many pixels the image contains. The image in Figure 4-1 is 256 pixels wide and 384 pixels tall, for a total of 98,304 pixels. Most of the images you create will contain hundreds of thousands or even millions of pixels.

Photoshop refers to file size as *pixel dimensions.*

✔ The *resolution* of an image refers to the number of pixels that print per inch. For example, the resolution of the first image in Figure 4-1 is 180 pixels per inch (ppi). That may sound like an awful lot of pixels squished into a small space, but it's about average.

✔ Not to be confused with file size, the *dimensions* of an image are its physical width and height when printed, as measured in inches, centimeters, or your unit of choice. You can calculate the dimensions by dividing the number of pixels by the resolution. For example, the little boy in Figure 4-1 measures 256 pixels ÷ 180 pixels per inch = $1^3/_8$ inches wide, and 384 pixels ÷ 180 ppi = $2^1/_8$ inches tall. Measure him with a ruler and you see that this is indeed the case.

No problem, right? I mean, okay, this stuff is a little technical, but it's not like it requires an advanced degree in cold fusion to figure out what's going on. And yet, the Image Size dialog box may well be the most confusing Photoshop dialog box. You can even damage your image if you're not careful. So be extremely careful before you make changes in the Image Size dialog box (the upcoming sections tell you everything you need to know to stay out of trouble).

Depending on your printer, you may be able to simply reduce or enlarge your image for printing via a scaling option in the printer's Properties dialog box, which you access by choosing File⇨Page Setup to display the Page Setup dialog box and then clicking on the Properties button. Photoshop then scales your image to the new size during the print cycle only. Your image isn't permanently altered as it is when you use the Image Size dialog box. For more information, see Chapter 7.

Resolving resolution

Although the Resolution option box is positioned unceremoniously toward the bottom of the Image Size dialog box, it's one of the most critical values to consider if you want your images to look good.

The Resolution value determines how tightly the pixels are packed when printed. It's kind of like the population density of one of those ridiculously large urban areas cropping up all over the modern world. Take Lagos, Nigeria, for example, which is a city of nearly 10 million souls — more than London, Paris, or Shanghai. Lagos, in case you're curious, is the fastest-growing major metropolitan area in the world, with an annual population explosion of 5 percent. (If that doesn't sound so bad, consider that it would put Lagos at 33 million people in the year 2020, which would be more than Tokyo, the current topper.) The population density of Lagos is second only to Hong Kong, at roughly 150,000 people packed into each square mile (on average, that's 15 times as crowded as New York City).

In order to increase the population density, you have to either increase the number of people in a city or decrease the physical boundaries of the city and scrunch everyone closer together. The same goes for resolution. If you want a higher resolution (more pixels per inch), you can either decrease the physical dimensions of the image or increase the file size (pixel dimensions) by adding pixels to the image. For example, the two images in Figure 4-3 have the same file size, but the smaller image has twice the resolution of the larger image — 180 pixels per inch versus 90 ppi.

Conversely, population density goes down as people die off or as the boundaries of the city grow. For example, if we were to mandate that Lagos spread out evenly over the entire 360,000 square miles of Nigeria, the population density would temporarily drop to 28 people per square mile (assuming, of course, that the other 110 million Nigerian residents happened to be on vacation at the time). Likewise, when you increase the dimensions of an image or delete some of its pixels, the resolution goes down.

Figure 4-3:
Two images
with the
exact same
number of
pixels but
subject
to two
different
resolutions.

Before you get the mistaken idea that this analogy is completely airtight, I should in all fairness mention a few key differences between a typical image and Lagos:

- ✔ Although I've never been there, I imagine that Lagos has its crowded spots and its relatively sparse areas. An image, by contrast, is equally dense at all points. Unlike population density, therefore, resolution is constant across the board.

- ✔ An image is always rectangular. Having misplaced my aerial map of Lagos, I can't swear to its shape, but I imagine that it's rather free-form.

- ✔ Population density is measured in terms of area — you know, so many folks per square mile. Resolution, on the other hand, is measured in a line — pixels per linear inch. So an image with a resolution of 180 pixels per inch contains 32,400 pixels per square inch. (That's 180 squared, in case you're wondering where I got the number.)

✔ The pixels in an image are absolutely square. The people in Lagos are shaped rather arbitrarily, with undulating arms and legs jutting out at irregular and unpredictable angles.

✔ You have total control over the size and resolution of an image. Like it or not, Lagos is entirely out of your hands.

Changing pixel dimensions

The top two option boxes in the Image Size dialog box enable you to change your image's *pixel dimensions* — the number of pixels wide by the number of pixels tall. (The number of pixels in your image is also known as the *file size*.) Unless you want to risk ruining your image — or you really, really know what you're doing when it comes to pixels — avoid these option boxes like the plague.

Lowering the Pixel Dimensions values can be dangerous because what you're really doing is throwing away pixels, and when you delete pixels, you delete detail. Figure 4-4 shows what I mean. The physical size of all three images is the same, but the detail drops off from one image to the next. The first image contains 64,000 pixels and is printed at a resolution of 140 ppi; the second contains $^1/_4$ as many pixels and is printed at 70 ppi. The third contains only 4,000 pixels and has a resolution of 35 ppi. Notice how details such as the shadows from the girl's eyelashes and the distinction between individual hairs in her eyebrows become less pronounced and more generalized as the pixel population decreases.

Increasing the file size (by raising the Pixel Dimensions values) isn't such a hot idea, either, because Photoshop can't generate image elements out of thin air. When you raise the Pixel Dimensions values, Photoshop adds pixels by averaging the preexisting pixels in a way that may result in image softening and never results in the miraculous reconstruction of detail.

If changing the pixel dimensions is so dangerous, you may wonder why Photoshop gives you the option to do so at all. Well, although I don't recommend ever adding pixels to an image, you may need to lower the pixel dimensions on occasion. If your file size is really large — that is, your image contains a ton of pixels — you may want to toss some of the pixels overboard.

In an ideal world, you'd want as many pixels as possible because more pixels means greater image detail. But the more pixels you have, the more disk space the image consumes, which can be a problem if you're working with limited computing resources. Large file sizes can also slow Photoshop down substantially. Also, if you're publishing your image on the Internet, you may want to reduce your file size so that users can download the image more quickly. Finally, you may need to lower the pixel dimensions in order to make an image print at the size you want.

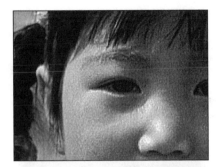

Figure 4-4:
Three
images,
each of
which
contains
fewer pixels
and is
printed at a
lower
resolution
than the
image
above it.

Even when you dump pixels from an image, however, you shouldn't attack the job from the Pixel Dimensions options boxes; I show you a better way in the steps within the section "Using the Image Size dialog box safely."

In some particularly nerdy circles, changing the number of pixels in an image is called *resampling.* The idea is that you sample the photograph when you scan it — as if that makes a lick of sense — so any adjustment to the quantity of pixels after scanning is resampling. Photoshop uses the term *resampling,* but I prefer to call it *resizing,* because this gives folks a fighting chance of understanding what I'm talking about. But just be aware that there are computer aficionados out there who will gladly stick their noses high in the air, trade shocked stares with one another, and mutter pronouncements such as "Don't tell me she has mouse privileges," or "Gad, did you hear what it said?" These things must be endured.

Yeah, okay, but what resolution should I use?

The Auto button in the Image Size dialog box is supposed to generate a perfect Resolution value based on the line screen that your printer will use. The only problem is, no one knows what a line screen setting is. Rather than bother with trying to explain this arcane bit of printing technology to you at this point — what with your head already spinning with Lagos population data — I decided to come up with both ideal and acceptable values for certain kinds of print jobs. See whether these work for you.

Type of Job	Ideal Resolution	Acceptable Setting
Full-color image for magazine or professional publication	300 ppi	225 ppi
Full-color slides	300 ppi	200 ppi
Color image for laser printing or overhead projections	180 ppi	120 ppi
Color images for multimedia productions and World Wide Web pages	72 ppi	72 ppi
Black-and-white images for imageset newsletters, flyers, and so on	180 ppi	120 ppi
Black-and-white images for laser printing	120 ppi	90 ppi

Keep in mind that there are no hard-and-fast rules about resolution settings. You can specify virtually any resolution setting between the ideal and acceptable settings and achieve good results. (If your commercial printer or service bureau tells you that you're getting bad results because your resolution doesn't match some exact ideal, consult a different company; this excuse is an example of a bad carpenter blaming his tools.) Even if you go with a Resolution value that's lower than the suggested acceptable setting, the worst that can happen is you'll get fuzzy or slightly jagged results. But there is no wrong setting.

Changing the physical dimensions of the image

The Width and Height boxes in the Print Size portion of the Image Size dialog box reflect the actual printed size of your image and the approximate size of your image when distributed over the World Wide Web. (Because monitors can vary from user to user, the actual size of the image may change a little when viewed on different monitors.)

The pop-up menus next to the Width and Height options let you change the unit of measure displayed in the option boxes. For example, if you select Picas from the Print Size Width pop-up menu, Photoshop converts the Width value from inches to picas. (A pica is an obscure typesetting measurement equal to ¹/₆ inch.) The Percent option in the pop-up menu enables you to enter new Width and Height values as a percentage of the original values. Enter a value larger than 100 percent to increase the print size; enter a value lower than 100 percent to reduce the print size.

When you change the print size of the image, either the Resolution value or the number of pixels in the image automatically changes, too, which can affect the quality of your image. For more information, read the section "Resolving resolution," earlier in this chapter. And for details on how to change the print size without ruining your image, see the section "Using the Image Size dialog box safely," later in this chapter.

Matching images to columns

What is the meaning of the Columns option in the Print Size Width pop-up menu? Oh, man, you would ask that. All right (sigh), I suppose I'd better tell you.

You see, Photoshop is capable of precisely matching the width of an image to the columns in a printed document. So for the sake of argument, say that you're working on an image that you eventually want to place into PageMaker. This specific PageMaker document happens to be a three-column newsletter. Each column is 2 inches wide, and the gutter (space) between each column is ¹/₄ inch wide.

To match Photoshop column settings to those in PageMaker, you would choose File⇨

Preferences⇨Units & Rulers and enter the column specs — in this case, 2 and 0.25 — into the Column Size option boxes, highlighted in the following figure. (Select inches from the pop-up menus if you want to use inches.) From that point on, a Column in the Image Size dialog box conforms to your settings. One column, for example, would be 2 inches wide; two columns would be 4¹/₄ inches wide — 4 inches for the two columns and the extra ¹/₄ inch for the gutter.

Columns is not an option in the Height pop-up menu (inside the Image Size dialog box), because columns run up and down, not left to right. In other words, columns make no sense as a system of measurement for height.

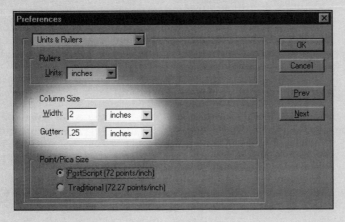

Keeping things proportionate

Both pairs of Width and Height option boxes in the Image Size dialog box list the dimensions of your image in the current unit of measure. If you enter a different value into either option box and click on the OK button (or press Return), Photoshop resizes your image to the dimensions. Pretty obvious, eh?

But strangely, when you change either the Width or Height value, the other value changes, too. Are these twins separated at birth? Is there some new cosmic relationship between Width and Height that is known only to outer-space aliens and the checkout clerk at your local grocery store? No, it's nothing more than a function of the Constrain Proportions check box, which is turned on by default. Photoshop is simply maintaining the original proportions of the image.

If you click on the Constrain Proportions button and turn it off, Photoshop permits you — in a very generous spirit, I might add — to adjust the Width and Height values independently. Notice that the little link icon (labeled back in Figure 4-2) disappears, showing that the two options are now maverick independents with reckless disregard for one another. You can now create stretchy effects like the ones shown in Figure 4-5. In the first example, I reduced the Width value by a factor of two and left the Height value unchanged. In the second example, I did the opposite, reducing the Height value and leaving the Width value unaltered.

However, in order to deselect the Constrain Proportions check box, you have to select the Resample Image check box. As explained later, in the section "Using the Image Size dialog box safely," when the Resample Image check box is selected, Photoshop either adds or deletes pixels from your image to compensate for the changes to the width and height of the image. Because adding pixels can make your image look like mud, never increase the width or height value with Constrain Proportions deselected. It's okay to decrease the width and height values, as long as the Resolution value stays in the acceptable range (see the "Yeah, okay, but what resolution should I use?" sidebar in this chapter for recommended resolution values).

Using the Image Size dialog box safely

As mentioned in the section "Resolving resolution," you have three image attributes — size, resolution, and dimension — all vying for your attention and all affecting each other. These attributes, in fact, are like three points on a triangle. Change any one of the points, and at least one of the others has to change proportionately. If you decrease the file size (number of pixels), for example, either the physical dimensions (printed size) or resolution (number of pixels per inch) must also decrease. If you want to increase the physical dimensions, you have to increase the file size — add pixels, in other words — or decrease the resolution.

Figure 4-5:
Known to
friends and
family as Kid
Squishums,
this
versatile
little tyke is
the result of
deselecting
the
Constrain
Proportions
check box.

Thinking about all the possible permutations can drive you crazy, and besides, they aren't the least bit important. What is important is that you understand what you can accomplish with the Image Size dialog box and that you know how to avoid mistakes. So now that I've provided all the background you need, it's finally time for me to offer a modicum of fatherly advice:

- Changing the Pixel Dimensions (file size) values can be deadly, as explained in the section "Changing pixel dimensions." To avoid changes to file size, deselect the Resample Image check box at the bottom of the Image Size dialog box. When you deselect the option, the Image Size dialog box changes, and the Width and Height options in the Pixel Dimensions portion of the dialog box become unavailable to you. A link icon also connects the Print Size Width, Height, and Resolution option boxes, showing that changes to one value affects the other two values as well.

- In order to turn off the Constrain Proportions option box, you have to turn on the Resample Image option box. If you make changes to the image width and height values, Photoshop will resample the image. If you're lowering the width and height values, you'll probably be okay, but if you try to raise the width and height values, you're likely to muck things up.

- Want a surefire method to tell whether you've changed the file size? Your image looks different on-screen after you change the Resolution or Print Size values and exit the Image Size dialog box. As long as the file size remains unchanged, you won't see any difference — none, zilch, zippo — on-screen. On-screen, Photoshop just shows your image pixels with respect to screen pixels; resolution and dimension enter into the equation only when you print the image. Therefore, you want the image to look the same on-screen after you get done fiddling around with the Image Size command.

- If you manage to mess everything up and change one or more settings in the Image Size dialog box to settings that you don't want to apply, you can return to the original settings by Alt+clicking on the Cancel button. Pressing Alt changes the word Cancel to Reset; clicking resets the options. Now you have your original settings back in place so that you can muck them up again. If you already pressed Enter to exit the Image Size dialog box, choose Edit⇨Undo or press Ctrl+Z right away to undo your changes.

- Whatever you do, be sure to use the Bicubic setting in the Resample Image pop-up menu. I'd tell you what *bicubic* means, but you don't want to know. Suffice it to say, it keeps Photoshop running smoothly.

- If you want to change the unit of measure that displays by default in the Image Size dialog box pop-up menus, choose File⇨Preferences⇨ Units & Rulers and select a different option from the Units pop-up menu.

After all the warnings I've given you so far, you may think that changing the image size is something that you never want to do. But as mentioned earlier, you may in fact want to reduce the image size on some occasions — to get the image to print at a certain size, to enable your computer to handle the image, or to make the image faster to download from the Internet. The following steps show you how to reduce your image size without turning your image into a worthless pile of goo.

Before you follow these steps, choose <u>F</u>ile⇨Sav<u>e</u> As to save a backup copy of your image. The steps result in Photoshop tossing away pixels, and after you delete pixels, you can't get them back. So always make a copy of the original in case things don't work out or you decide you want to use the original again at a later date.

1. **Open the image at the highest resolution possible.**

   For example, if you're opening a Photo CD image, select the 2048 by 3072 option from the Resolution pop-up menu. If that doesn't work — Photoshop may complain that you don't have enough memory to pull it off — try again and select the 1024 by 1536 option. Whatever works, go for it.

2. **Choose <u>I</u>mage⇨<u>I</u>mage Size to open the Image Size dialog box.**

3. **Note the values in the Pixel Dimensions <u>W</u>idth and <u>H</u>eight option boxes.**

   You may want to write 'em down — they're important.

4. **Enter your desired print width and height in the Print Size option boxes.**

   If you want Photoshop to retain the original proportions of your image, make sure that the Constrain Proportions option box is checked.

5. **Enter your desired resolution in the <u>R</u>esolution option box.**

   Check the "Yeah, okay, but what resolution should I use?" sidebar in this chapter for some suggestions on acceptable resolution values if you need help.

6. **Check the Pixel Dimensions values.**

   Did either of the values get bigger? If so, you need to either reduce your Print Size width and height values or lower the resolution. Otherwise, Photoshop adds pixels to your image, and you won't be happy with the results.

   If the Pixel Dimensions values got smaller, on the other hand, proceed to Step 7.

7. **Make sure that the Resample <u>I</u>mage check box is selected.**

8. **Make sure that the Bicubic option is selected in the Resample <u>I</u>mage pop-up menu.**

9. **Click on the OK button.**

   Photoshop resizes — or, if you prefer, resamples — your image in accordance with your perfect settings. If you don't like the results, press Ctrl+Z or choose <u>E</u>dit⇨Undo *immediately* to put things back to the way they were.

What Does This Canvas Size Command Do?

There's one more command related to the topic of image sizing that you should know about: Image⇨Canvas Size. Unlike the Image Size command, which stretches or shrinks the photograph, the Canvas Size command changes the size of the page — or canvas — on which the image sits. If you increase the size of the canvas, Photoshop fills the new area outside the image with white (or the background color). If you make the canvas smaller, Photoshop crops the image.

When you choose Image⇨Canvas Size, the dialog box shown in Figure 4-6 pops up out of its virtual hole. You can play with the options found inside the dialog box as follows:

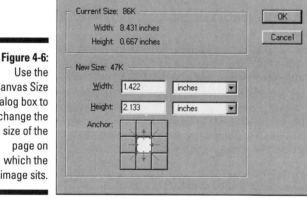

Figure 4-6:
Use the
Canvas Size
dialog box to
change the
size of the
page on
which the
image sits.

✔ Enter new values into the Width and Height option boxes as desired. You can also change the unit of measurement by using the pop-up menus, just as in the Image Size dialog box.

✔ You can't constrain the proportions of the canvas the way you can inside the Image Size dialog box. Therefore, the Width and Height values always operate independently.

✔ The Anchor section shows a graphic representation of how the current image sits inside the new canvas. By default, the image is centered in the canvas. But you can click inside any of the other eight squares to move the image to the upper-right corner, center it along the bottom edge, or place it where you like.

✔ If you reduce either the Width or Height value and press Enter, Photoshop asks you whether you really want to crop the image. If you click on the Proceed button (or press Enter) and decide you don't like the results, you can always choose Edit⇨Undo or press Ctrl+Z to restore the original canvas size.

Chapter 5
Auntie Em versus the Munchkins (Death Match)

• •

In This Chapter

▶ Understanding RGB color theory

▶ Viewing independent color channels

▶ Defining colors using the Color palette

▶ Selecting colors that will print

▶ Lifting colors from an image with the eyedropper

▶ Converting color images to grayscale

• •

*I*n case you're wondering what the title of this chapter means, it's all about color — the same kind of color that Dorothy encountered when she passed over the weather-beaten threshold of her old Kansas porch onto a path of lemon-yellow bricks in that beloved classic, *The Wizard of Oz*. As you might imagine, Auntie Em represents the world of black and white, and the Munchkins represent the wonderful world of color.

With that in mind, you might think that Auntie Em is pretty well doomed. I mean, how can one woman cope with an entire Oz full of rowdy Munchkins? And how can drab black and white compete with rich, beautiful color?

Well, I'm rather fond of black and white myself. To me, the absence of color offers its own special attractions. It's the mysterious essence of a torch-lit castle on a stormy night. It's the refreshingly personal vision of a 16mm short-subject film you stumble across one evening on Bravo. It's the powerful chiaroscuro of an Ansel Adams photograph or a Rembrandt oil. In an age when every screen, page, and billboard screams with color that's more vivid than real life, black and white can beckon the eye like an old friend.

But on the off chance you think all that's a pretentious load of hooey, I can tell you one area in which Auntie Em kicks major Munchkin keister, and that's cost. Despite the increasing influence of computers in print houses, color printing remains extremely expensive. Major four-color magazines — including the ones I write for — spend more on ink than they do on their writers. The color medium costs more than the message, and that's a sad fact.

Though by no means free, black-and-white images are substantially less expensive to reproduce. Only one ink is involved — black. Other supplies, such as film and plates for the printing press, are kept to a minimum. Black-and-white printing is also incredibly versatile. You can print black-and-white images with any laser printer, you can photocopy black-and-white images using cheap equipment, and you can fax black-and-white images with relatively little loss in quality. And finally, black-and-white images require one-third of the overhead when you're working in Photoshop, meaning that you can edit black-and-white images that contain three times as many pixels as color images without Photoshop complaining that it's out of memory. I'd say that this is one match in which Auntie Em can be counted on to hold her own. No surprise, really. Farm women are well-known troupers, while the Munchkins — to hear Judy Garland tell it — were a bunch of randy booze hounds.

Whether you choose black and white, color, or — like most folks — vacillate between the two, this chapter tells you how it all works. You find out how to use color, create colors that you can apply with the painting tools, and switch between color modes. Not bad for a chapter based on an old MGM musical, eh?

Looking at Color in a Whole New Light

To understand color in Photoshop, you have to understand a little color theory. To this end, I want you to do me a favor and open some random color image that you have sitting around. Chances are that you'll see the telltale initials RGB inside parentheses in the image title bar. (If you don't, try opening a different image.) These initials mean that all colors inside the image are created by blending red, green, and blue light.

Red, green, and blue? That doesn't sound particularly colorful, does it? But in fact, these colors are the primary colors of light. The red is a vivid scarlet, the green is so bright and tinged with yellow that you might be tempted to call it chartreuse, and the blue is a brilliant Egyptian lapis. It just so happens that these colors correspond to the three kinds of cones inside your eyeball. So in theory, your monitor projects color in the same way your eyes see color.

Surfing the color channels

To get a hands-on feel for the inner workings of a color image, follow these steps:

1. **Open an RGB image.**

   Oh, you already did that. My mistake.

2. **Choose File⇨Preferences⇨Display & Cursors.**

   The Preferences dialog box shown in Figure 5-1 appears.

   The Preferences dialog box actually contains several panels of options. You switch between the panels via the pop-up menu at the top of the dialog box. Another way to display the dialog box is to press Ctrl+K, which brings up the Preferences dialog box with the General preferences panel showing. Then press Ctrl+3 or choose Display & Cursors from the pop-up menu to display the options shown in Figure 5-1. After you close the dialog box, you can redisplay the last panel you visited by pressing Ctrl+Alt+K.

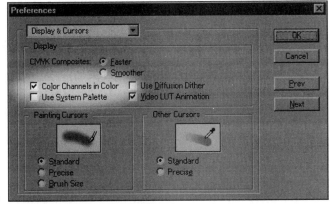

Figure 5-1: Select the Color Channels in Color option to better see how the primary colors work.

3. **Select the Color Channels in Color check box and then press Enter.**

   Highlighted in the figure, this option makes the individual layers of red, green, and blue color appear in red, green, and blue. These layers of color are called *channels*.

4. **Press Ctrl+1 to view the red channel.**

   You see a black-and-red image. Notice that the RGB in the title bar changes to Red to show that you're viewing the red channel. This image is the one being sent to the red cones in your eyes.

5. Press Ctrl+2 to view the green channel and then press Ctrl+3 to view the blue channel.

These images are the ones being sent to your green and blue cones.

6. Press Ctrl+~ (tilde) to return to the full-color RGB view.

The tilde key, by the way, is found in the upper-left corner of the keyboard, next to the 1 key. To type an actual tilde, you have to press the Shift key, but you don't need to press Shift to invoke the full-color view shortcut. The shortcut really should be Ctrl+` (grave) because pressing the key without Shift accesses the grave mark. But Photoshop prefers to label this shortcut Ctrl+~, so I follow suit.

At any rate, when you press Ctrl+~, you can see the red, green, and blue channels all mixed together.

The keyboard shortcut for viewing the channels together has changed in Version 4. The old shortcut, Ctrl+0, now switches you to the Fit on Screen view.

Pretty nifty, huh? Here's another way to think about it: If you were to take the images you saw in the red, green, and blue channels, print them to slides, put each of the slides in a different projector, and shine all three projectors at the same spot on a screen so that the images precisely overlapped, you would see the full-color image in all its splendor. Check out Color Plate 5-1 for the pictorial representation.

Now try something different. Choose File⇨Preferences⇨Display & Cursors (or press Ctrl+Alt+K to redisplay the Display & Cursors panel of the Preferences dialog box) but this time, turn off the Color Channels in Color check box. Now look at the color channels once more by pressing Ctrl+1, Ctrl+2, and Ctrl+3. Each channel looks like a standard black-and-white image. Figure 5-2, for example, shows the contents of the red, green, and blue channels as they appear in black and white.

Mixing red, green, and blue to create color

Every channel contains light areas and dark areas, just like a black-and-white image. With the Color Channels in Color check box turned off, you can better see these light and dark areas without a bunch of distracting colors getting in your way (which is why the option is off by default). The light and dark pixels from each channel mix together to form other colors.

The following list explains how corresponding pixels from the different channels mix together to form a single full-color pixel.

Color Plate 5-1:
The red, green, and blue color channels in Photoshop act like slides in separate projectors pointed at the same spot on a screen. You may find it hard to believe that three primary hues could mix together to produce so many colors, but it's true.

Color Plate 5-2:
This shows the way light, dark, and medium pixels in the red, green, and blue channels mix to form various sample colors. Altogether, you can create more than 16 million color variations.

Color Plate 5-3:
Pure white light from the sun (or a man-made light source) is made up of red, green, and blue light. When light passes through the cyan, magenta, or yellow printing ink, the ink filters out the red, green, or blue light and lets the other two pass through.

Color Plate 7-1:
The cyan, magenta, and yellow channels as they appear when inked in their proper colors (top row). Each color channel takes on new depth and detail when combined with black (middle row). During the commercial printing process, the cyan image is first combined with magenta (bottom left), and then yellow (bottom center), and then black (bottom right).

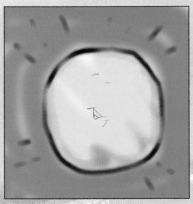

Color Plate 8-1:
When I used the paintbrush tool to paint in the sun with yellow and the sky with blue, the paint obscured the sun's face and rays. When I started over again and lowered the Opacity setting to 40 percent, I just got weaker color (right).

Multiply

Screen

Overlay

Difference

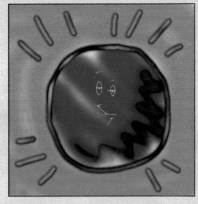

Color Plate 8-2:
The results of applying yellow and blue with the paintbrush using each of four brush modes.

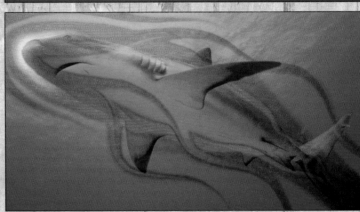

Color Plate 9-1:
Using the smudge tool, I turned a common, household-variety shark into a red-hot shark torpedo. In the Smudge Tool Options palette, I turned on the Finger Painting check box, set the brush mode to Color, and set the Pressure slider bar to 90 percent.

Color Plate 10-1:
By cloning from the top left image onto the bottom left image with the rubber stamp tool, I was able to merge the two images to create the strange but nonetheless believable specimen on the right.

Tolerance: 32

Tolerance: 90

Tolerance: 180

Color Plate 12-1:
By raising the Tolerance value in the Magic Wand Options palette, I instructed
Photoshop to select a wider range of colors around the point at which I clicked (just to
the right of the forward giraffe). In this case, 90 seems to be the best setting.

One base color, Fuzziness: 200

Color Plate 12-2:
The result of clicking just to the right of the monster's nose and applying the Color Range command with a Fuzziness setting of 200. In the right image, I filled the selection with white and then deselected it.

Three base colors, Fuzziness: 60

Color Plate 12-3:
By Shift-clicking in the image while inside the Color Range dialog box and lowering the Fuzziness value, I selected more of the blue sky and made the selection outline less blurry.

Color Plate 14-1:
I filled the area behind the jar with custom gradients created using the Gradient Editor.

Color Plate 15-1:
To create this composition, I combined eight images and blended them together using various modes and Opacity settings from the Layers palette. I selected all the images using the Color Range command, tinted the astronaut using the Variations command, and erased, scaled, and rotated a few others.

Red

Green

Blue

Figure 5-2:
The black-
and-white
channels
that
combine to
make a full-
color image.

✔ A light pixel from the one channel mixed with dark pixels from the other two channels produces the color from the first channel. For example, if the red is light, and green and blue are dark, you get a red pixel.

✔ Light pixels from the red and green channels plus a dark pixel from the blue channel form yellow. This may sound weird — two colors, red and green, mixing to form a lighter color — but that's exactly how things work in the upside-down world of RGB. Because you're mixing colors projected from a monitor, two colors projected together produce a still lighter color.

✔ With me? No? Well, say that you had a flashlight with a red bulb and your friend had one with a green bulb. I don't know, maybe it's Christmas or something. At any rate, if you were to point your flashlight at a spot on the ground, the spot would turn red. No surprise there. But if you then said, "Look, Nancy, it's the missing key from the old Smithers' place," and your friend pointed her green flashlight at the same spot, the spot wouldn't get darker, it would get lighter. In fact, it would turn bright yellow. "Gee wizikers, Ned, do you suppose this means Mrs. Johnson is innocent after all?" I'm afraid we'll never know.

✔ Light pixels from the green and blue channels plus a dark pixel from the red channel make a bright turquoise color called cyan. Light red and blue pixels plus a dark green pixel make magenta.

✔ By a strange coincidence, cyan, magenta, and yellow just happen to be the main ink colors used in the color printing process. Well, actually, it's not coincidence at all. Color printing is the opposite of color screen display, so the two use complementary collections of primary hues to produce full-color images. The difference is, because cyan, magenta, and yellow are pigments, they become darker as you mix them. Yellow plus cyan, for example, make green. This won't affect how you edit RGB images, but I thought you might find it interesting.

   ✔ Light pixels from all three channels mix to form white. Dark pixels all
     around form black. Medium pixels make gray.

Although all this is highly stimulating, I have a feeling that it would make more
sense if you could see it. If you're the visual type, take a look at Color Plate 5-2.
The left side of the figure shows the RGB combinations I just discussed. The
right half shows RGB mixes that result in other colors, including orange, purple,
and so on. Give it the once-over and see whether you can't feel your brain grow
by leaps and bounds.

Using the Channels palette

Keyboard equivalents such as Ctrl+1 and Ctrl+2 aren't the only way to access
different channels. You can also use the Channels palette. Choose Window⇨
Show Channels to display the Channels palette, shown in Figure 5-3. Here's how
to use the palette:

   ✔ To switch to a different channel in the palette, simply click on its name.
     Figure 5-3 finds me clicking on the Red channel.

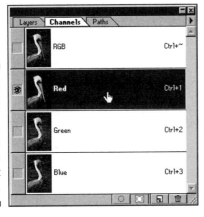

Figure 5-3:
Click on a
channel
name in the
Channels
palette to
view that
channel.

   ✔ To return to the full-color RGB view, click on the top item in the Channels
     palette or press Ctrl+~ (tilde).

     The Channels palette includes little thumbnails of the contents of each
     channel. To change the size of these thumbnails, choose Palette Options
     from the palette menu — click on that little right-pointing arrowhead just
     beneath the title bar — and select a different Thumbnail Size icon.

Being Your Own L.J. Grand Master Funky Glow

In case you're hip-hop impaired, L.J. stands for Light Jockey, and that's exactly what you have to be to create colors in Photoshop. In other words, to define a color, you have to specify the quantities of red, green, and blue that go into it.

Uh, just so you don't go and make a fool of yourself the next time your kid's friends come over by saying something painfully embarrassing like, "Hey, check me out, I'm L.J. Grand Master Funky Glow!" I thought I should admit that L.J. isn't a real hip-hop term. I just made it up. I mean, for all I know, L.J. means lemon juice or lantern jaw in today's imaginative middle-school lingo. "You're what, Dad? A lentil jar?"

Juggling foreground and background colors

In Photoshop, you can work with two colors at a time: a foreground color and a background color. Some tools and commands paint your image with the foreground color; others splash it with the background color.

The two colors are displayed in the lower portion of the toolbox. As shown in Figure 5-4, the foreground color is on top and the background color is on the bottom. To get some idea of how these colors work, read the following list. (Skip the following list if you'd like to remain ignorant.)

- ✔ The foreground color is applied by the painting tools, such as the airbrush, paintbrush, and pencil.

- ✔ When you use the eraser tool, you're actually painting with the background color.

- ✔ When you increase the size of the canvas using Image⇨Canvas Size (as explained in Chapter 4), Photoshop fills the empty portion of the canvas with the background color.

- ✔ The gradient tool creates a rainbow of colors between the foreground and background colors (assuming that you use the default gradient option, Foreground to Background, as explained in Chapter 14).

The toolbox includes a few icons that enable you to change the foreground and background colors, swap them around, and so on.

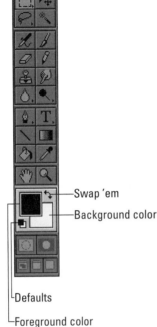

Figure 5-4:
The small
collection
of color
icons in the
toolbox.

—Swap 'em

—Background color

└Defaults

└Foreground color

✔ Click on the foreground icon to display the intensely complex Color Picker dialog box, which is filled with about 17 thousand options you don't need to know anything about.

✔ Press Esc to leave that dialog box. Then pick up a Bible or some other holy relic and swear that you'll never go back there again. The next section tells you a better option for defining the foreground and background colors.

✔ Click on the background color to go to that same terrible dialog box. Hey, didn't I specifically instruct you to stay out of there?

✔ Click on the defaults icon (labeled in Figure 5-4) to restore the foreground color to black and the background color to white.

✔ Click on that little two-way arrow icon — childishly labeled *swap 'em* in the figure — to swap the foreground and background colors with each other.

✔ You can also access the default and swap 'em icons from the keyboard. Press D to restore the default colors, black and white. Press X to swap the foreground and background colors.

Defining colors

You can define the foreground and background colors in Photoshop in three ways:

- ✔ You can click on the foreground or background color icon in the toolbox and battle your way through the Color Picker. If you read the preceding section, you know that I think that this option is a real stinkeroo and should be avoided at all costs.

- ✔ You can use the handy-dandy Color palette. The Color palette is pretty much the same thing as the Picker palette found in Version 3 and just one "s" away from the Colors palette found in Version 2.5. You wouldn't think there would be so much controversy about naming this particular palette, would you?

- ✔ You can lift colors from your image using the eyedropper tool.

Using the Color palette

To define colors using the Color palette, shown in Figure 5-5, choose Window⇨ Show Color or press the F6 key. You should see three slider bars labeled R, G, and B (for Reginald, Gertie, and Bert). If you don't, choose RGB Sliders from the palette menu. (Click on the right-pointing arrow in the upper-right corner of the palette to display the menu.)

┌Foreground color

┌Background color

Figure 5-5:
The Color
palette fully
adorned
with its
cheerful
RGB slider
bars.

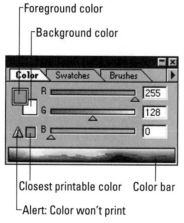

Closest printable color   Color bar

└Alert: Color won't print

Here's how you go about changing a color using the Color palette:

1. **Decide which color you want to change.**

   The palette offers its own foreground and background color icons, as labeled in Figure 5-5. Click on the icon for the color you want to change. A double outline surrounds the icon to show that it's selected.

2. **Drag the little RGB slider bar triangles to change the color.**

   Think of red, green, and blue as ingredients in baking the perfect color. You can add 256 levels of each of the primary hues, 0 being the darkest amount of the hue, 255 being the lightest, and 128 being smack dab in the middle. For example, if you set the R slider to 255, the G slider to 128, and the B slider to 0, you get a vibrant orange, just like the one shown in the upper-right corner of Color Plate 5-2.

   If you've never mixed colors using red, green, and blue, it can be a little perplexing at first. For example, folks often have a hard time initially accepting that all yellows and oranges are produced by mixing red and green. I encourage you to experiment. Better yet, I order you to experiment.

3. **Click on the triangular alert icon if desired.**

   If a little triangle with an exclamation point appears in the lower-right corner of the palette, Photoshop is pointing out that the color you have mixed will not print exactly as you see it on-screen. The closest printable color appears inside a little square to the right of the alert icon. Click on either the icon or the square if you want to use the printable color instead.

Just a few other things I want to pass along about the Color palette:

- If you can't get the knack of using the RGB slider bars, you can also select a color by clicking inside the color bar at the bottom of the palette. By default, all the colors in the bar are printable. (To make sure that this is true, Ctrl+click on the color bar, select CMYK Spectrum from the Style pop-up menu, and press Enter.)

- Alt+click in the color bar to change the opposite color. For example, if the foreground color is active, Alt+click to select the background color. If the background color is active, Alt+click to select the foreground color.

- If you want to set the foreground or background color to a shade of gray, you can set all sliders to the same value. Or better yet, choose Grayscale Slider from the palette menu and adjust the single K slider. (*K* stands for black, remember?)

Why won't my color print?

You may be wondering why you can define a color that won't print. Isn't a color on the screen the same as a color on the page? No, and the reason has to do with the differences between the principles of colored light and colored pigments. (Hold on, this is a long but mighty interesting topic — if I do say so myself.)

As I mentioned earlier, your monitor creates white by mixing the lightest amounts of red, green, and blue. In the Color palette, for example, you set all sliders to 255 to get white. This is just the opposite of how things work on a printed page.

Color printing exploits the fact that sunlight, household light bulbs, fluorescent and halogen lamps, and other so-called "white light" sources contain the entire spectrum of visible light, including all shades of red, green, and blue. The primary printing inks that I alluded to earlier in this chapter — cyan, magenta, and yellow (CMY) — are actually color filters. When white light hits cyan ink printed on a white page, for example, the cyan ink filters out all traces of red and reflects only green and blue, which (as I mentioned earlier) mix to form cyan. Similarly, magenta is a green light filter, and yellow is a blue light filter, as illustrated in supreme detail in Color Plate 5-3.

In a perfect world, RGB and CMY would be exact opposites. Photoshop would simply print the red channel in cyan ink, the green channel in magenta ink, and the blue channel in yellow ink, and everything would come up roses. But on the off chance that you haven't learned this important lesson yet, the world is not perfect. In the case of color, it's half near perfect and half totally whacked.

The culprit is color purity. The basic rule of thumb is that red, green, and blue light represent pure colors, and cyan, magenta, and yellow inks are impure. What does this mean? Well, scientific types have been able to split white light into its precise red, green, and blue components since Isaac Newton discovered the spectral powers of a common prism in 1666. The red you see on-screen may not exactly match the red you see on a neighbor's screen, but it comes awfully darn close.

Unfortunately, the world's technicians have had a harder time coming up with pure inks. Not only do the specific tints of commercial-grade cyan, magenta, and yellow vary widely, the most accurate of them isn't right on. You can't split a chemical dye into its primary color components. So like economics and child rearing, CMY inks represent an imprecise science.

To balance things out, color printing throws in one additional ink, black. (Black is the *key* color — the ink that materializes out of thin air to help out the other inks — which is why color printing is sometimes called CMYK.) Black ensures deep shadows, neutral grays, and — of course — nice, even blacks.

But even with black, CMYK can't measure up to RGB. There are just too many random elements involved. Is the paper absolutely white? Are the inks as pure as they can be? Are you viewing the page under ideal lighting conditions? Because the answer to all three questions is generally no, CMYK can produce fewer colors than RGB. Tech-heads say that CMYK has a smaller *gamut,* which is just a fancy word for range. (Can you imagine a bunch of nerdy computer guys out on the lone prairie singing, "Home, home on the gamut"?) Bright reds, oranges, greens, blues, and purples all fall outside the CMYK range. In fact, by comparison to RGB, CMYK is dull.

But all things are relative. It's highly doubtful that the word "dull" comes to mind when viewing a typical glossy magazine ad because it looks very colorful compared to the surrounding magazine color. But if you were to hold it up to the same image on an RGB screen, you'd be surprised at how lackluster it looks.

The upshot of all this? Just one thing. Don't worry that the closest printable color (the little box in the Color palette) looks duller than the RGB color you want to use. It very likely won't look dull when the image is printed. All the colors in Color Plate 5-3 were printed, after all, and they don't look dull. Just accept the duller color and go on with life.

Lifting colors with the eyedropper tool

You can also change the foreground or background colors by lifting them from the image. Just select the eyedropper tool — on the right side of the toolbox just above the zoom tool — and click inside the image on the color you want to use. If you have more than one image open, you can even click inside a different image than the one you're working on.

Here's some stuff to know about this incredibly easy-to-use tool:

- ✔ You can press I (for I-dropper) to select the eyedropper tool instead of clicking on its toolbox icon.

- ✔ The eyedropper affects whatever color is selected in the Color palette. So if the foreground color icon is selected, the eyedropper tool changes the foreground color, and if the background icon is selected — well, you get the idea.

- ✔ To select the opposite color — in other words, to select the background color when the foreground color icon is active or the foreground color when the background color icon is active — Alt+click with the eyedropper.

- ✔ You can temporarily access the eyedropper when another tool is selected by pressing the Alt key. As long as the key is down, the eyedropper is available. This trick doesn't always work; in fact, it only works when you're using the type, paint bucket, gradient, line, pencil, airbrush, or paintbrush tool. But it can come in handy.

- ✔ If you use the preceding tip, you can only change the active color in the Color palette. You need the Alt key to change the opposite color, so you can't use the key to temporarily access the eyedropper. You have to select the eyedropper for real (click on its icon or press I) and then Alt+click. (If your keyboard offers two Alt keys, it doesn't help to press both of them.)

Going Grayscale

Now that I've wasted most of the chapter on the colorful Munchkins, you may be wondering when I'm ever going to get around to discussing the much-lauded Auntie Em. Friends of Kansas, take heart, the heralded hour of black-and-white images has arrived.

The first thing to understand about black-and-white images is that the black-and-white world offers more colors than just black and white. It includes a total of 256 unique shades of gray and is therefore more properly termed *grayscale*. Each one of these shades is a color in its own right, which is why the term "black and white" can inspire fisticuffs among some grayscale devotees.

Secondly, all the stuff I told you about creating colors holds true for grayscale image editing as well. You have a foreground and background color. You can define colors in the Color palette. (Be sure to choose Grayscale Slider from the palette menu so that you have to use just one slider bar.) And you can lift colors from a grayscale image using the eyedropper tool.

But some aspects of grayscale editing are different than full-color editing, which is what led me to write the next two sections.

The road to grayscale

Most images that you'll come across will be in color. Most commercial images and all Photo CD images are in color. Scans from a commercial quick-printer or service bureau may be either in color or in grayscale, but you never know. My point is that working in grayscale generally requires a conversion inside Photoshop.

Unlike a three-channel RGB image, a grayscale image includes only one channel of imagery. That's why the red, green, and blue channels all appear in black and white — each is its own grayscale image. If you plan on printing in black and white, you should jettison all the extraneous color information, for two reasons. First, it's easier for Photoshop to keep track of one channel than three. In fact, given the same image size and resolution, Photoshop performs faster and with fewer problems when editing a grayscale image than when editing in color. Second, you can better see what your printed image will look like. When you're designing an image to be printed in black and white, color just gets in the way.

To convert a color image to grayscale, just choose Image⇨Mode⇨Grayscale. Photoshop asks you whether you want it to discard color information. You can answer OK or chicken out and cancel. That's all there is to it. You now have a single-channel grayscale image. No matter what color you choose in the Color palette, the color appears gray in the foreground and background color icons. (If you don't like the results of your conversion to grayscale, you can go back to the full-color original by choosing Edit⇨Undo or pressing Ctrl+Z.) But you have to choose the command *immediately* after you apply the Grayscale command — if you choose some other command or apply a painting or editing tool, you won't be able to undo the color conversion. And after that color is gone, it's gone for good; you can't bring it back by choosing one of the other commands on the Mode menu.

Before you change a color image to grayscale, you may want to make a backup copy of the original image, just in case you ever want to have the image available in color some day. For details on saving images, see Chapter 6.

When you choose Image⇨Mode⇨Grayscale, Photoshop merges all three RGB channels together to create the new colorless image. But what if the contents of any one of the RGB channels strikes you as just right and you want to simply dump the other two? The answer is to just go to that channel (press Ctrl+1, Ctrl+2, or Ctrl+3) and choose Image⇨Mode⇨Grayscale. This time Photoshop asks you whether you want it to discard all the other channels. If the channel you see on-screen is the one you want to keep, press Enter to give Photoshop the go-ahead. Otherwise, click on Cancel and go back to channel surfing.

Figure 5-6 shows an example of the difference between converting all channels in an image and retaining just one. In the first image, I chose Image⇨Mode⇨Grayscale in the RGB view to merge all channels. The result is washed out, with little distinction between lights and darks. I didn't like it, so I chose Edit⇨Undo to restore my RGB image. Then I tiptoed through the channels to find something better, and wouldn't you know, the red channel looked just right. So after pressing Ctrl+1, I again chose Image⇨Mode⇨Grayscale to toss out the green and blue channels, thus arriving at the second image in Figure 5-6.

Figure 5-6: The difference between converting a color image to grayscale (left) and throwing away all but the red channel (right).

More grayscale tips from Auntie Em

That's basically all there is to tell about grayscale images. Future chapters explain how to edit color and grayscale images, and Chapter 18 explains how to make automated adjustments, such as changing brightness and contrast. So I'll wrap things up with four last-minute grayscale tidbits:

✔ If you decide to convert a single channel from an RGB image to grayscale, you'll almost always want to use either the red or green channel. The red channel is generally lighter than the other two because skin tones gravitate toward red. The green channel is the detail channel, full of nice edges. Blue is the dark and dank channel. Except for skies and oceans, not much in this world is blue. Also, your eye contains fewer blue cones than red or green ones. So many scanners generate some pretty cruddy detail in the blue channel, knowing that you won't be able to see it.

✔ To add color to a grayscale image, convert back to RGB by choosing Image⇨Mode⇨RGB Color. Photoshop won't add a bunch of colors to the image, but it will allow you to add colors of your own.

✔ If your color image contains more than one layer (as explained in Chapter 15), the layers are flattened (merged together) when you convert to grayscale. So before you go ahead with the conversion, do all editing that involves layers and also make a backup copy of the layered image.

✔ If you're using an 8-bit monitor — that is, a monitor that can display only 256 colors — you're better off editing grayscale images. When you edit full-color RGB images, Photoshop shows only 256 of the 16 million possible colors at a time, resulting in *dithering,* an effect in which a random pattern of pixels is used to emulate lots more colors. When you edit a grayscale image, however, you can see every shade just right. Don't worry that Photoshop converts your entire screen to grays, including Finder icons and all other background items. This is a normal effect of editing in grayscale on an inexpensive computer system.

Chapter 6

Save Before You Say Good Night

*I*f you've used a computer before, you may be wondering why I devote an entire chapter to saving files. After all, you just press Ctrl+S and you're done, right? Well, if we were talking about any other program, I'd have to agree with you. If this book were about Microsoft Word, for example, I'd say, "Not to worry, Dear Reader, saving a file is so simple, a newborn lemur could pull it off with the most cursory supervision from a parent or older sibling." If this book were about PageMaker, I'd add, "Saving makes tying your shoes look like a supreme feat of civic engineering," all the while gently smiling and donning a cardigan sweater in a manner not unlike Mr. Rogers.

But this book is about Photoshop. And Photoshop, as you may or may not be aware, enables you to save images in more flavors than Willy Wonka manages to squeeze into an Everlasting Gobstopper. In the software world, these flavors are called *file formats,* and each one has a different purpose.

This chapter offers a thorough explanation of the saving process, including an exhaustive — well, okay, pretty decent review of the various file formats you can use. With this chapter by your side, Ctrl+S can be a pretty easy command, after all.

Save an Image, Save a Life

I don't know you from Adam — or Eve for that matter — but I'm guessing that you're the kind of person who doesn't like to spend hours editing an image only to see your work vanish in a poof of on-screen smoke as the result of some inexplicable and unforeseen computer malfunction. If you are indeed that kind of person, learning to save your image is essential. By saving your image early and often, you improve your chances of weathering any digital storm that may come your way.

Saving for the very first time

After applying the first few edits to your image, save it under a new name and — if necessary — specify where you want to store it on disk. If you do this, the original image remains untouched, allowing you to return to it at a later date for inclusion in a different project. Here's how to save your customized image without harming the original:

1. **Choose File⇨Save As.**

   The dialog box shown in Figure 6-1 appears. (The dialog box may look slightly different if you're using Windows 3.1.)

   You can also open the dialog box by pressing Ctrl+Shift+S.

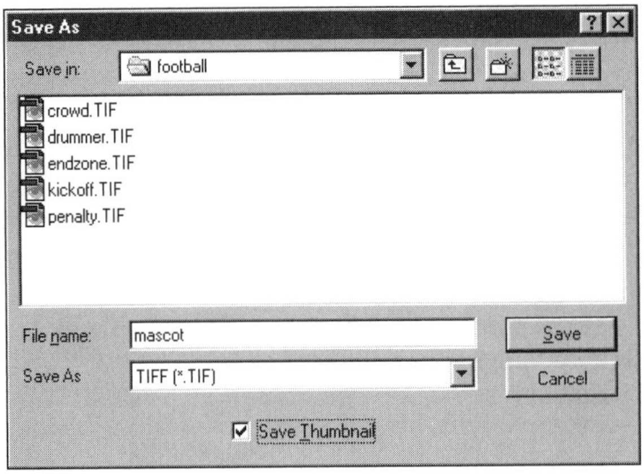

Figure 6-1:
Use this dialog box to name your image and decide where you want the image to hang out on disk.

Save As
Save in: football
crowd.TIF
drummer.TIF
endzone.TIF
kickoff.TIF
penalty.TIF
File name: mascot   Save
Save As: TIFF (*.TIF)   Cancel
☑ Save Thumbnail

2. Enter a name into the File <u>N</u>ame option box.

In Windows 95, filenames can include as many as 255 characters (although a 255-character filename is beyond excessive, if you ask me). Windows 3.1 filenames can consist of only eight characters. In both cases, the filename is followed by a three-character file extension (such as TIF) that indicates the file format (explained shortly). Don't use any spaces or special characters, such as ampersands or brackets, in your filenames. Stick with regular letters and numbers to be safe. You don't have to enter the extension because Photoshop does that for you.

If you use Windows 95 and plan on sharing your images with friends or co-workers who still use Windows 3.1 or earlier, stick with the Windows 3.1 naming conventions. Long filenames get truncated (cut off) in Windows 3.1, leading to some ambiguous filenames. Also, be aware that not all programs support long filenames yet, so it's a good idea to also use Windows 3.1 naming rules if you plan to open your image in another program.

3. Select a format from the Save As pop-up menu.

This is the point at which you have to deal with the image flavors I touch on in the introduction to this chapter. The pop-up menu provides all kinds of options, such as TIFF, JPEG, PICT, and others. I discuss the ramifications of the important formats later in this chapter.

Some formats are restricted to certain kinds of images. For example, you can only save images that contain layers (as explained in Chapter 15) in the Photoshop format. If a format is grayed out in the Save As pop-up menu, that format isn't available for the kind of image you're trying to save.

4. Use the Save <u>I</u>n pop-up menu to select the folder in which you want to save the image.

The controls in this menu are explained in the "Don't Just Sit There, Open Something" section of Chapter 3.

5. Click on the <u>S</u>ave button or press Enter.

6. If another dialog box appears, fill out the options and press Return.

Most formats present additional dialog boxes that enable you to modify the way the image is saved. I explain this in more detail later.

Your image is now saved! Come heck or high water, you're protected.

The Save Thumbnail check box at the bottom of the dialog box is important if you want to be able to see image previews in the Open dialog box, as explained in Chapter 3. If you don't turn on the Save Thumbnail option when you save an image, you don't get a preview when you later try to open that image.

To make sure that Photoshop always saves previews, choose File⇨ Preferences⇨Saving Files. When the Preferences dialog box appears, select the Always Save option from the Image Previews pop-up menu. Press Enter to exit the dialog box. Now the Save Thumbnail option is selected by default in the Save As dialog box, and you don't have to worry about it anymore. The only time *not* to save a preview is when you're extremely limited on disk space; saving images with previews requires a bit more disk space than saving them without previews. The file-saving process also takes longer when you save with previews.

Join the frequent-saver program

After you name your image and save it to disk for the first time, press Ctrl+S or choose File⇨Save every time you think of it. In either case, Photoshop updates your image on disk, without any dialog boxes or options popping up and demanding your attention. Then, when something goes wrong — notice that I said when, not if — you don't lose hours of work. A few minutes, maybe, but that comes with the territory.

Creating a backup copy

If it takes longer than a day to create an image, you should make backup copies. The reasoning is, if you invest lots of time in an image, you're that much worse off if you lose it. By creating backup copies — Dog1, Dog2, Dog3, and so on, one for each day that you work on the project — you're that much less likely to lose mass quantities of edits. If some disk error occurs or you accidentally delete one or two of the files, one of the backups will probably survive the disaster, further protecting you from developing an ulcer or having to seek therapy.

At the end of the day, choose File⇨Save As. The Save dialog box appears, as when you first saved the image. Change the filename slightly and then click on the Save button. Way to be doubly protected!

You can also use Save a Copy command to make a backup copy of an image, but that command offers a few extra options specifically designed for saving images that have multiple layers. Ignore it for now. For more information on working with layers, see Chapter 15.

Photoshopper's Guide to File Formats

Even though the Save As pop-up menu appears at the bottom of the Save As dialog box — as if it were an afterthought or something — selecting a format is a critical decision. So you need to pay attention to the sections to come, even if the subject is a rather dry one — which it is. Get a Jolt cola if you need one, but don't skip this information.

What is a file format, anyway?

Glad you asked. A *file format* is a way of saving the electronic bits and pieces that make up a computer file. Different formats structure those bits and pieces differently. In Photoshop, you can choose from about a zillion file formats when you save your image to disk, which makes things a tad bit confusing.

Luckily, you can ignore most of the file format options. The Amiga IFF and Raw formats, for example, sacrifice colors and other image information, so avoid them. The Pixar, Targa, and Scitex CT formats are very sophisticated formats used by very sophisticated (and well-funded) creative types, so you can forget about those formats, too. In fact, you probably will have use for only a handful of formats: TIFF, JPEG, EPS, and the native Photoshop format. (For the technically curious, native formats are explained in the sidebar, "Why are there so many different formats?") If you plan on publishing your image on the World Wide Web, you may also want to use the CompuServe GIF format at times, too.

The following sections explain the most important file formats and when to use them.

Why are there so many different formats?

Why don't we have just one format instead of dozens? Because back in the early days of home and office computing, every program saved its stuff in its own unique way. Computer geeks came up with the name *native format* to refer to a program's unique file format.

At first, programs couldn't decipher data that was stored in any format but their own. But over time, that changed. For example, PC Paintbrush was an early painting program in the DOS world. The native format for PC Paintbrush was called PCX. (Who knows what the *X* stands for? Xavier, maybe.) PC Paintbrush became so popular that a groundswell of images emerged in the PCX format. In an effort to attract users, other programs started supporting PCX, making it a de facto standard.

Photoshop supports PCX as well as BMP — the native format for Microsoft Windows Paint. However, it's very unlikely that you'll want to save an image in either of these native formats today. Unless you need to open your image in the rare program that supports only BMP or PCX, you're better off using TIFF, JPEG, or one of the other more mainstream formats. BMP is the format of choice, however, for creating graphics for use as Windows system resources, such as your desktop wallpaper.

Photoshop also offers its own native format, which can be a good option in some scenarios. For the lowdown on this format, see the section, "BMP: The wallpaper format" later in this chapter.

TIFF: The great communicator

One of the best and most useful formats for saving Photoshop images is TIFF (pronounced *tiph*), which stands for Tagged Image File Format. TIFF was developed to serve as a platform-independent standard so that both Macintosh and Windows programs could take advantage of it.

When you select the TIFF option from the Save As pop-up menu and click on the Save button, Photoshop displays another dialog box, shown in Figure 6-2. In the area labeled Byte Order, you can tell Photoshop whether to save the TIFF image for use on the Macintosh or with a Windows program. Unless you're going to open your image in a Mac program, select IBM PC. (Why are these options labeled Byte Order? Just to confuse you.)

Figure 6-2:
The options
that appear
when you
save a
TIFF file.

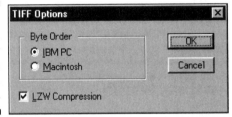

The TIFF Options dialog box also offers a check box labeled LZW Compression. If you check the box, Photoshop compresses your image file so that it takes up less room on disk. Unlike some types of compression, LZW Compression doesn't sacrifice any data to make your file smaller. It's known as a *lossless compression scheme.*

Most programs that support TIFF also support LZW. For example, you can import a compressed TIFF image into either PageMaker or QuarkXPress. Only obscure programs don't support LZW, so there's really no reason not to select this option.

JPEG: The space saver

Photoshop also supports the JPEG (pronounced *jay peg*) format. JPEG stands for some Joint Photographers convention, but that doesn't really matter. What matters is that the JPEG format uses *lossy compression.* Lossy is the computer nerd's way of saying that stuff is lost during the compression process — namely, some of the data that makes up your image.

The good news, however, is that you probably won't miss what's not around anymore — sort of like when you were a kid and you "lost" your little brother at the park. You may notice a slight difference in your on-screen image after you save the file using JPEG, but when the image is printed, the compression is virtually undetectable.

Like LZW compression, JPEG compression saves you lots of disk space. In fact, a JPEG image takes up less space on disk than a compressed TIFF file — half as much space, maybe a tenth as much, depending on your settings. JPEG isn't supported by as many programs as TIFF, but it's becoming more and more common.

So should you use JPEG or TIFF? My philosophy is this: Save in TIFF when you're editing an image. Then, when you think you're finished editing, save in JPEG at the Maximum setting. You generally won't see the results of JPEG right away. But editing an image can bring out its weaknesses, and JPEG definitely weakens an image. So it's best to go to JPEG after you finish editing. This is not a hard-and-fast rule — I've edited plenty of JPEG images without incident — but it's a good rule of thumb.

Also, if you want to distribute your image on the World Wide Web, you have to save it in either the JPEG or GIF format. TIFF isn't an option for Web publishing.

When you choose the JPEG option in the Save As dialog box and press Enter, the dialog box shown in Figure 6-3 appears. Here's a rundown of the options you need to worry about:

Figure 6-3:
When
saving a
JPEG file,
select the
Maximum
option or, if
space is
limited,
select the
High option.

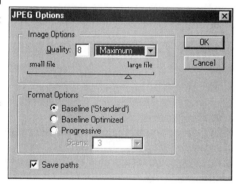

✔ The Quality pop-up menu lets you choose the amount of compression that is applied to your image and therefore the quality of your saved image. The higher the image quality, the less the file is compressed and the more space it takes on disk.

✔ The Quality option box and the slider bar beneath the box give you other ways to choose your compression setting. The slider bar and option box give you access to 11 settings (0 through 10), whereas the pop-up menu gives you access to only four. But unless you're a real control freak like me, you can just select one of the pop-up menu options.

✔ For print images, choose the Maximum or High option from the Quality pop-up menu. The Maximum option is best because it preserves the most image data, but High is okay if you're really short on disk space.

✔ If you plan to publish your image on the World Wide Web, choose the Medium option from the pop-up menu. The Medium option is the standard because it can retain a fair amount of image data while still substantially reducing file size. But before you save your image using this option, make a backup copy using the Maximum or High setting first. Because of how much image data is dumped with the Medium setting, you won't be able to successfully edit the image after you save it using that setting.

✔ Another option for images published on the Web is to save them as *progressive* JPEG files. A progressive image initially appears on the Web-surfer's monitor at a very low quality and then improves as more and more image data is downloaded. If you want to save your image in this way, select the Progressive radio button at the bottom of the dialog box. The Scans pop-up menu lets you choose the number of intermediate images the browser displays before the image appears in full. Be aware that not all browsers support progressive images.

✔ If you want to save an image for the Web but you don't want to create a progressive image, choose the Baseline Optimized radio button. For regular print graphics — that is, graphics that aren't going to be distributed over the Web — use the default setting of Baseline — ('Standard').

GIF: For Webbies only

GIF, which was developed for CompuServe specifically for transferring images via modem, is one of two options you can consider when you want to distribute your image online, whether on CompuServe, America Online, or the World Wide Web. (The other format is JPEG, discussed in the preceding section.)

Computer hacks are divided on how you pronounce GIF. Some folks swear that the proper pronunciation is with a hard "G" — as in one *t* short of a *gift*. Other experts insist that you say it with a soft *g,* so that the word sounds just like that famous brand of peanut butter. Regardless of which camp you decide to join, GIF is best used for high-contrast images, screen shots, and text. The biggest drawback to GIF is that it can only save images with 256 colors or less; the advantage is that GIF results in crisper image details than JPEG.

If your image contains more than 256 colors, choose Image➪Mode➪Indexed Color to reduce the number of colors before you save in the GIF format. In the Indexed Color dialog box, choose Adaptive from the Palette pop-up menu. For Color Depth, start with the lowest possible setting (the smallest number of bits per pixel) and see what happens to your image. If it turns to muck, press Ctrl+Z to undo things and choose the next highest Color Depth setting. Use the lowest setting that keeps your image reasonably intact.

You need to do similar experimentation with the Dither option. The best choice is None, but if that setting wrecks your image, choose Diffusion. You can ignore the Colors setting entirely; Photoshop handles that one for you automatically.

When you save an image to the GIF format, you're presented with a dialog box containing just two radio buttons, Normal and Interlaced. The Interlaced setting results in an image that appears gradually when it is downloaded, like a progressive JPEG image. If you don't want your image to be downloaded in this way, choose Normal.

The GIF format also enables you to create images that include transparent areas that allow other parts of your Web page to show through. If you want to give this trick a try, see the sidebar "Meet GIF89a."

EPS: The 1 percent solution

EPS (pronounced *E-P-S*) stands for Encapsulated PostScript. PostScript is a page-description language used by LaserWriters, Linotronic imagesetters, and hundreds of other printers. While TIFF and JPEG can save only images, the EPS format accommodates anything that the printer can print. Unfortunately, an EPS image takes up about three times as much disk space as the same image saved in the TIFF format — even more if the TIFF image is compressed.

For the most part, EPS is used by high-end professionals producing high-end projects. EPS is also the format to use if you want to create expert color separations from QuarkXPress. In other words, you can ignore the EPS format 99 percent of the time and use TIFF instead.

Meet GIF89a

Photoshop 4 includes a command on the File⇨Export menu that enables you to create a transparent GIF image for use on the World Wide Web. Using this command — which has the user-friendly name of GIF89a Export — you can make portions of an image transparent so that a background pattern on your Web page can be seen through the image.

After choosing the Indexed Color command to reduce your image to 256 colors, as described in the section "GIF: For Webbies only," choose File⇨Export⇨GIF89a Export. In the dialog box that appears, click in the image preview on each color that you want to make transparent. Or click on the color swatches at the bottom of the dialog box. Ctrl+click on a color if you change your mind and want to make the color opaque again.

If you choose the Interlace check box, your image is drawn incrementally when a Web surfer downloads it, just like a progressive JPEG image.

After you press Enter to exit the dialog box, Photoshop prompts you to save the image by displaying a dialog box that looks and works just like the regular Save As dialog box (but has the name Export GIF89). Give your image a name, specify where you want to store the image on disk, click on Save, and you're done.

BMP: The wallpaper format

As mentioned earlier in this chapter, BMP is a popular format for saving graphics that that you want to make part of your computer's systems resources, such as the wallpaper that you see behind your desktop. (Chapter 21 gives you the step-by-step procedure for turning one of your Photoshop images into wallpaper.) Programmers also use BMP to create images that appear in Help files.

When you save a file in the BMP format, the dialog box shown in Figure 6-4 appears. Don't worry about changing the radio button settings; use the defaults that Photoshop picks for you. If you're creating wallpaper, don't select the Compress (RLE) check box; Windows doesn't recognize files saved using this compression scheme. Otherwise, the compression scheme is a lossless (good) one, so select Compress (RLE) if you can.

Figure 6-4:
The BMP
format is
used mostly
to create
wallpaper
for the
Windows
desktop.

What about the native Photoshop format? The Save As pop-up menu in the Save As dialog box offers one other important format choice: the native Photoshop format.

The Photoshop format is the only format that saves the layers in your image; all the others "flatten" (merge) the layers together. The Photoshop format is also the only format that can save grids and guides (explained in Chapter 3).

If you need to open a Photoshop 4 image in earlier versions of the program, you can use the Photoshop format without worry. Version 3 can open files saved in the Version 4 native format. By default, Photoshop 4 also saves a version of your image that can be opened by programs that recognize Version 2.5 files. But unless and until you need to take advantage of this feature — which is likely to be never — choose File⇨Preferences⇨Saving Files and deselect the 2.5 Compatibility check box in the Preferences dialog box. When the option is deselected, your images consume less space on disk.

Like TIFF, the Photoshop formats offer a lossless compression scheme. And Photoshop can open and save images faster in its native format than in any other format. But very few programs other than Photoshop support the native format. So use the native format when you don't plan on importing the image into another program and you don't need JPEG compression.

What format to use when

Ooh, you cheated, didn't you. You skipped right over the sections on how formats work and why they were invented. Instead of reading all that juicy background information I offered up — information that would help you make your own decision about which format to use — you want me to make the decision for you.

Okay, fine. You plunked down good money so that I would make things easy for you, so I suppose that I can give you a break just this once. Think of the following list as your Cliff's Notes to File Formats. Just don't blame me when you're standing around at a cocktail party and the discussion turns to JPEG compression versus TIFF, and you don't have an intelligent word to offer.

✔ If you are just going to use the image in Photoshop, save it in the Photoshop format. You can open images saved in this format in Version 3 as well as in Version 4. You can open images in Version 2.5 as well (if you turn on the 2.5 Compatibility check box in the Preferences dialog box as discussed in the preceding section), but layers, grids, and guides won't be available to you in Version 2.5.

✔ If your image contains layers (as explained in Chapter 15) and you want to preserve those layers, choose the Photoshop format.

✔ If you want to import your image into another program, use TIFF, as long as you have the available disk space.

✔ If you want to import your image into another program and you don't have the available disk space, use JPEG.

✔ If you want to import your image into a program that doesn't support either TIFF or JPEG, resort to EPS.

✔ If you're creating a photograph for online distribution, use JPEG. For high-contrast graphics or partially transparent images, use GIF.

✔ If you're creating wallpaper to amuse your coworkers or just yourself, use BMP and turn off RLE compression.

Good Night, Image, Don't Let the Programming Bugs Bite

To put Photoshop to bed for the night, choose File⇨Exit or press Ctrl+Q (as in *quit*). Photoshop may display a message asking you whether you want it to save the changes you made to your image. Unless you have some reason for doing otherwise, press Enter to select the Yes button. The program then shuts itself down.

If you don't want to save your changes, press the N key, which is the same as clicking on the No button. If you decide that you aren't ready to say good-bye to Photoshop after all, click on the Cancel button.

Chapter 7

Going to Hard Copy

· ·

· ·

*I*n case you don't already know, *hard copy* is a term for the printed page. The on-screen image is just a figment of your computer's imagination. The final printed piece is something tangible that you can really sink your teeth into (assuming that you're extremely hungry).

In this chapter, I explain how to go from on-screen, imaginary image to hard copy. But I have to confess that there's a lot that I don't know. For example, I don't know what kind of printer you're using, I don't know what kind of cabling is installed, and I don't even know where the printer is located in your home or office. In other words, I'm suffering from a terrific deficit of knowledge. With this in mind, I ask for your sympathy and understanding as I explain — very briefly — how to print from Photoshop using an everyday, generic printer.

For starters, I am going to be totally rash and assume the following:

✔ You have a printer. If I've said it once, I've said it, I don't know, two or three times: You have to have a printer to print.

✔ Your printer is plugged in, it's turned on, and it doesn't have a 16-ton weight sitting on top of it. In other words, your printer works.

✔ The printer is properly connected to your computer. A cable running out of your computer and into your printer is a good sign.

✔ The proper printer software is installed on your computer.

> ✔ Your printer is stocked with ribbon, ink, toner, paper, film, chew toys, little bits of felt, springlike gizmos that go "bazoing," or whatever else is required in the way of raw materials.

If you've used your printer before, everything is probably ready to go. But if something goes wrong, I advise that you call your local printer wizard and ask for assistance. Or you can try walking into the boardroom and wringing your hands and weeping in a cloying but professional way. This strategy has been known to produce the desired effects.

This May Be All You Need to Know

When things are in working order, printing is not a difficult process. Though it involves slightly more than picking up your mouse and saying "print" into it, printing does not require a whole lot of preparation. In fact, a quick perusal of the following steps may be all you need to get up to speed:

1. **Turn on your printer.**

   And don't forget to remove that printer cozy your uncle knitted for you.

2. **Choose File⇨Save or press Ctrl+S.**

   Although this step is only a precaution, it's always a good idea to save your image immediately before you print it because the print process is one of those ideal opportunities for your computer to crash. Your computer derives a unique kind of satisfaction by delivering works of art from the printer and then locking up at the last minute, all the while knowing that the image saved on disk is several hours behind the times. If you weren't the brunt of the joke, you'd probably think that it was amusing, too.

3. **Select a printer, paper size, and page orientation.**

   You accomplish all this inside the Page Setup dialog box, which you can display by choosing File⇨Page Setup, pressing Ctrl+Shift+P, or clicking on the Setup button in the Print dialog box (which you display by choosing File⇨Print or pressing Ctrl+P).

4. **Check that the image fits on the page.**

   After you select a printer and set the paper size and orientation, press Enter to close the Page Setup dialog box. Then press and hold on the page preview box in the lower-left corner of the Photoshop window to see a little preview of the printed page. The page preview box is just to the right of the magnification box. (If you can't remember where the preview box is located, flip to Figure 3-3 for a refresher.)

If the image doesn't fit on the page, you can reduce the image by using the Image Size command, discussed in Chapter 4. Or, depending on your printer, you may also be able to scale (reduce) your image for printing in the Page Setup dialog box. Scaling the image through the Page Setup dialog box changes the image size for printing only; the Image Size command permanently resizes your image.

5. Choose File⇨Print or press Ctrl+P.

Photoshop displays the Print dialog box, covered in detail later in this chapter. In this dialog box, you can specify how many copies of the image you want to print.

6. Press Enter.

Experts say that this is the easiest step. Well, one guy got a blister on the end of his finger, but otherwise the vote was unanimous.

Congratulations: You now have what is commonly known as a brand-new, 1-gram-baby piece of output. But on the off chance that you're unclear on how a couple of the preceding steps work or you're simply interested in excavating every possible nugget of information from this book, I encourage you to probe the depths of the rest of this chapter.

Choosing a Printer and Paper Size

If you have only one printer hooked up to your computer, you can skip this section entirely. But if you're part of a network or you have more than one printer available to you, you need to tell Photoshop which printer you want to use.

To select a printer, open the Page Setup dialog box. You can do this in several ways: Choose File⇨Page Setup; press Ctrl+Shift+P; or click on the Setup button inside the Print dialog box (choose File⇨Print or press Ctrl+P to open the dialog box). However you go about it, a dialog box similar to the one shown in Figure 7-1 appears. (Your dialog box may look slightly different depending on your printer and which version of Windows you're using.)

To select a printer, just choose the printer name from the Name pop-up menu. Choose the paper size and printer tray from the two pop-up menus in the middle of the dialog box. (Other options in this dialog box are discussed in other sections in this chapter.) Click on OK or press Enter to exit the dialog box.

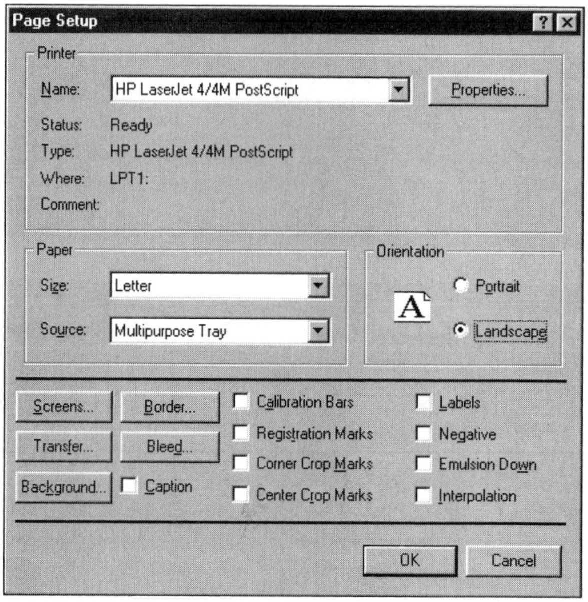

Figure 7-1:
You select a printer, paper size, and page orientation in this dialog box.

Getting Image and Paper in Sync

Before you send your image to the printer, you need to make sure that the image you want to print actually fits on a piece of paper. To see whether all is well in this regard, click and hold on the page preview box in the lower-left corner of the image window. As shown in Figure 7-2, Photoshop displays a preview of how your image fits on your chosen paper size.

The white area in the page preview represents the size of the page; the rectangle with an X through it represents the image. (All right, so the image preview isn't particularly accurate when it comes to showing actual images, but it's good enough for showing the dimensions.) If the rectangle with an X fits entirely inside the white area, as in Figure 7-2, your image fits on the page. If the X exceeds the boundaries of the white area, the image is too big for the page and needs to be reduced. After you know whether the image fits or not, you can release your mouse button.

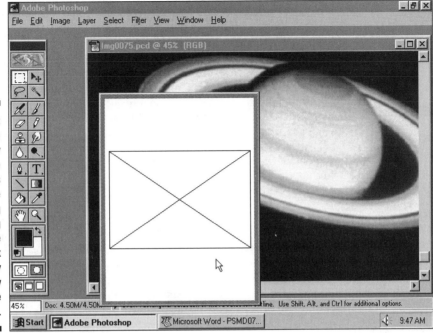

Figure 7-2:
You can
preview
how the
image fits
on the page
by clicking
and holding
on the page
preview box
(hidden by
the preview
in the
figure).

If the image doesn't fit, you have some work to do. One way to get the image to fit the paper is to reduce the image size. Another possibility is to rotate the image on the page. For example, if the image is wider than it is tall, you might want to print it out horizontally by rotating the page 90 degrees. Here's a closer look at these two options:

✔ To rotate the image on the page, choose File⇨Page Setup or press Ctrl+Shift+P to display the Page Setup dialog box, shown back in Figure 7-1. (Or open the Print dialog box by pressing Ctrl+P and then click on the Setup button.) Though your dialog box may not look exactly like the one shown in Figure 7-1, you should find two Orientation radio buttons: Portrait and Landscape. If you choose Portrait, your image prints upright on the page; if you choose Landscape, Photoshop rotates the image so that it prints out sideways on the paper.

✔ The specific options found inside the Page Setup dialog box vary depending on the kind of printer you're using. Some printers offer Scaling options that let you reduce or enlarge the image for printing only. To hunt down this option, click on the Properties button in the Page Setup dialog box. When the Properties dialog box appears, click on the Graphics tab. If you see a Scaling option, you're in business. Enter any percentage below 100 percent to reduce the dimensions of the printed image. The printer still prints all pixels in the image; the pixels are just smaller.

✔ The Scaling value remains in effect until you open up the Properties dialog box and change it. So if you don't want to scale future print jobs, be sure to change the setting back to 100 percent after you print the current image.

✔ If you can't find a Scaling option, you have to abandon the Page Setup dialog box and reduce your image by using Image➪Image Size instead. Be sure to deselect the Resample Image check box so that you don't affect the number of pixels in the image. Then increase the Resolution value or decrease the values in the Print Size Width and Height option boxes. (You can find a complete explanation of the Image Size dialog box in Chapter 4.)

After trying one of these options, click and hold on the page preview box again to see whether you're making any progress. If the image still doesn't fit, move on to the second option and give it a try.

Keep in mind that any changes made inside the Page Setup dialog box have absolutely no effect on anything about your image except how it prints. You can't do any permanent damage via this particular dialog box, so feel free to change settings recklessly and without regard to personal safety.

Changes made inside the Image Size dialog box are another story. As I explain in Chapter 4, you can easily do permanent damage if you forget to deselect the Resample Image check box.

Sending the Image to the Printer

After you confirm that the image fits inside the page, choose File➪Print or press Ctrl+P to display the Print dialog box, shown in Figure 7-3. If the image is still too large for the page, Photoshop displays an error message to warn you that a portion of your image will be cut off the page and to ask whether you want to proceed. If you say no, the error message disappears, and you can then resize the image to fit the page, as discussed earlier in this chapter. If you say that you want to go ahead and print anyway, the Print dialog box appears.

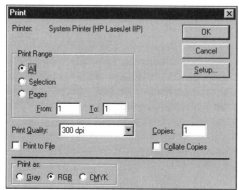

Figure 7-3:
The Print
dialog box.

What I love about the Print dialog box is that you can ignore almost all of it. Only a couple of options are the least bit useful:

✔ If you want to print more than one copy of the image, enter how many copies you want into the Copies option box.

✔ If you selected a portion of your image by using one of the tools I don't get around to discussing until Chapter 12, you can print the selected area only by selecting the Selection radio button. If you just want to take a quick look at an isolated area, this option can save time.

✔ When you're printing a full-color image, the Print As radio buttons — Gray, RGB, and CMYK — appear. If you have a color printer, leave this option set to RGB. If you're printing to a black-and-white device, you can speed things up by selecting Gray. Don't ever select CMYK.

✔ The CMYK option doesn't create color separations, incidentally. To accomplish that feat, read the next section.

✔ If you need to visit the Page Setup dialog box to choose a printer, set image orientation, or adjust other print settings, you can do it by clicking on the Setup button. Clicking on the button is the same as choosing File➪Page Setup.

That's it. Don't worry about the other options in the dialog box. Just click on the OK button or press Enter, and you're off. Depending on the size of the image, it should print in a matter of a few minutes.

Printing CMYK Color Separations

So far, I've explained how to print *composite* images, in which all colors are combined together on a single page. Unfortunately, composite images are a poor solution if you intend to make more than, say, 50 copies of an image. Oh, sure, you can print multiple pages directly from your color printer or reproduce them with one of those mondo-expensive photocopiers, but the colors don't always fare very well, and the cost per page is exceedingly high. Using either solution, a print run of 1,000 copies could cost you $500 or more, and you wouldn't get professional quality for your money.

The more accepted solution is to print *color separations.* You print four pages, one each for the primary printing colors cyan, magenta, yellow, and black. Then you let your commercial printer — the person, not the machine — combine the color separations to create mass quantities of colorful pages. This process is the same one used to create magazines, newspapers, and other professional color publications.

To print color separations of a full-color image from Photoshop, you have to go through these steps:

1. **Save your image to disk.**

   Before diving into CMYK, you want to make sure that your RGB image is backed up and safe from harm. Chapter 6 provides assistance with the saving process if you need help.

2. **Choose Image⇨Mode⇨CMYK Color.**

   Photoshop converts the image from the world of RGB to the world of CMYK. After the conversion, you have a four-channel image with one channel each for cyan, magenta, yellow, and black. You can even view the channels if you want by pressing Ctrl+1, Ctrl+2, Ctrl+3, and Ctrl+4. (This channel thing is explained in Chapter 5.)

3. **Inside the Page Setup dialog box, select the check boxes shown selected in Figure 7-4 and press Enter.**

   You can display the Page Setup dialog box directly by choosing File⇨Page Setup. Or you can open it from inside the Print dialog box (File⇨Print) by clicking on the Setup button.

   For the record, select Calibration Bars, Registration Marks, Corner Crop Marks, Center Crop Marks, and Labels. These five options print a series of alignment markings that will prove very useful to your commercial printer. (If you're printing to a non-Postscript printer, some of these options may not be available; select the ones that are.)

   Be sure to select *all* these check boxes. If you miss any of them, your commercial printer may have problems lining up the images on the press, and your pages may come out like a page from the Sunday comics.

4. **Inside the Print dialog box, select the Print Separations check box and press Enter.**

   (If the Print dialog box isn't already open, press Ctrl+P or choose File⇨Print to display it.)

   The Print Separations check box takes the place of the Print As radio buttons when you print a CMYK image. Selecting this check box (as shown in the background dialog box in Figure 7-4) tells Photoshop to print each channel from the image to a separate page.

When printed, each page looks like a standard black-and-white printout, but don't let that worry you. When you take the pages to your commercial printer, a technician photographically transfers your printouts to sheets of metal called *plates.* Each plate is inked with cyan, magenta, yellow, or black ink. The technician prints all the pages with the cyan plate first; then runs the pages by the magenta plate; then the yellow plate; and finally, the black plate. The inks mix together to form a rainbow of greens, violets, oranges, and other colors.

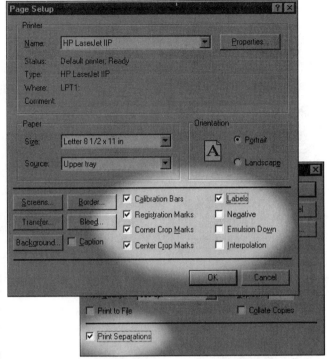

Figure 7-4:
Check these
check boxes
to print
color
separations
from
Photoshop.

For example, Figure 7-5 shows four color separations for the full-color photograph that appears in Color Plate 5-1. (Compare these separations to the red, green, and blue channels I included back in Figure 5-2 to get a feel for the dramatic changes that occur when you convert from RGB to CMYK.) Color Plate 7-1 shows the separations as they appear when inked with cyan, magenta, yellow, and black. I also show a few examples of how the inks look when combined.

Cyan   Magenta

Figure 7-5:
The black-
and-white
contents of
the cyan,
magenta,
yellow, and
black
channels as
they appear
when
printed to
separate
sheets of
paper.

Yellow   Black

Part III
Tiptoe through the Toolbox

NATIONAL ENQUIRER
PHOTO IMAGING
WORKSHOP

"Remember, Charles and Di can be pasted next to anyone but each other, and your Elvis should appear bald and slightly hunched- nice Big Foot, Brad.- keep your two-headed animals in the shadows and your alien spacecrafts crisp and defined."

In this part . . .

*I*n real life, a paintbrush is a fairly static tool. You dip it in paint and drag it across the canvas; in return, it paints a line. The line varies depending on how much paint you dabbed onto the brush and how hard you press, but your options are limited. In Photoshop, on the other hand, a single tool is capable of literally hundreds of variations. You can change the size of the brush tip, the angle of the brush, the translucency of the paint, and the way colors mix, all at the drop of a hat. You can even paint straight lines and change the brush strokes from hard-edged to soft.

If painting isn't your primary interest, Photoshop provides an assortment of editing tools for smearing colors, changing their focus, lightening or darkening pixels, and adjusting the intensity of colors. You'll also find a rubber stamp tool for cleaning up dust and hairs on an image and an eraser for eliminating mistakes. All these tools go beyond anything that's available in real life, providing a degree of flexibility and forgiveness that natural media simply do not offer.

But my favorite thing about Photoshop is the convenience. No wiping up spills, no soaking brushes, and no opening windows to clear the fumes. You just paint what you want and erase what you don't want. Everything you do on-screen is imaginary — until you print the image, you haven't changed one scrap of real-life material — so spills, strains, and fumes are a thing of the past. And when it comes time to clean up for the day, you just press Ctrl+Q and you're finished. Who says things aren't better now than they used to be?

Chapter 8

Paint Me Young, Beautiful, and Twisted

∙ ∙

In This Chapter

▶ Using the pencil, paintbrush, and airbrush

▶ Drawing straight lines with the painting tools

▶ Changing the brush size

▶ Creating your own custom brush

▶ Selecting brushes from the keyboard

▶ Creating translucent brush strokes

▶ Painting with strangely named brush modes

∙ ∙

*O*kay, here's a big assumption: As a novice or casual Photoshop user, you fall into one of two camps: artist or nonartist. Some people are so comfortable with a pencil or paintbrush that they feel like they were born with the device. But a much larger group of Photoshop users falls into a camp that modern sociologists call "artistically challenged."

Take this quick test to determine where you fall:

✔ After doodling in the phone book, are you so horrified by the results that you rip out the page, pour ketchup on it, and feed it to your dog?

✔ When you're asked to draw a map to your house, do you try to lie your way out of the situation by asserting that you have no idea where your house is located and you doubt very seriously that you live anywhere?

✔ Do you have recurring dreams in which you suddenly remember that today is the day your final project is due in the art class you've forgotten to attend all year? And as you attempt to quickly paint a lounging model, you notice that the model is fully clothed and you're the one who's naked?

If you answered "Yes" to any of the preceding questions, you can safely assume that you belong to the nonartist camp. If you answered "Yes" to any two of the questions, you are so firmly entrenched in the nonartistic tradition that completing a dot-to-dot picture seems like an immense and terrifying project. And if you answered "Yes" to two of the questions and "Oh, wow, I had that exact dream just last night!" to the third, I am obliged by the code of computer ethics to ask you one more question: Are you sure that your analyst isn't overcharging you?

Whatever your level of artistic skill, though, there will probably come a time when you'll want to rub a couple of the Photoshop painting tools against an image. Sure, it'll be scary. But you'll be prepared, thanks to this chapter.

Doodling with the Pencil, Paintbrush, and Airbrush

Photoshop offers just three painting tools, the bare minimum for artists and nonartists alike. Shown in Figure 8-1, they work like so:

- The pencil tool draws hard-edged lines of any thickness.
- The paintbrush draws soft lines with slightly blurry edges to create more natural transitions.
- The airbrush paints soft lines like the paintbrush. The only difference is that this tool pumps out color continuously even when you hold it in place — as long as the mouse button is down. By contrast, the pencil and paintbrush tools only paint as you drag.

You can select each of the painting tools from the keyboard. Press A to select the airbrush, B to select the paintbrush, and Y to select the pencil. In Photoshop 3, the P key selected the pencil tool. But that keyboard shortcut is now assigned to the pen tool, which earned a spot in the toolbox in Version 4.

The pen tool, by the way, doesn't draw beautiful, flowing lines that look as if they're emanating from a kazillion-dollar status pen. In Photoshop, you use the pen tool to create *paths*. Paths enable you to select a portion of your image by creating a sort of connect-the-dots outline. Because paths are an advanced and frankly frustrating topic — geared only for hard-core users — I don't cover them in this book.

By default, Photoshop displays a little paintbrush, airbrush, or pencil cursor when you select the painting tools. If you press the Caps Lock key, however, the cursor changes to a crosshair cursor that makes it easier to see what you're doing. Use the crosshair when the standard cursor gets in your way. Press Caps Lock again to return to the standard cursor.

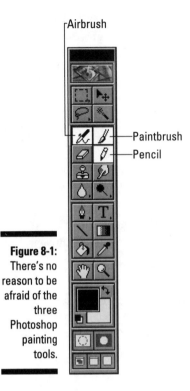

Airbrush

Paintbrush

Pencil

Figure 8-1: There's no reason to be afraid of the three Photoshop painting tools.

If you prefer, you can make your cursor match the brush size exactly. (The upcoming section "Switching the brush size" explains how to change brush sizes.) To make the cursor reflect the brush size, press Ctrl+K to display the Preferences dialog box. Then choose Display & Cursors from the top pop-up menu or press Ctrl+3 to get to the cursor options. Select Brush Size from the Painting Cursors radio buttons and press Enter.

The painting tools are small, nonpoisonous, and good with children. So why not take them for a walk and see how you like them? The following steps show you how to use the paintbrush, pencil, and airbrush to create the friendly Mr. Sun image shown in Figure 8-4 (go ahead, flip forward to take a look).

1. **Choose File⇨New (Ctrl+N) to create a new canvas.**

   Photoshop displays a dialog box that asks what size to make the new canvas. The dialog box offers Width, Height, and Resolution options, just like the Image Size dialog box discussed in Chapter 4.

2. **Make the canvas about 400 pixels wide by 400 pixels tall.**

That's about 5¹/₂ x 5¹/₂ inches with a Resolution value of 72 ppi or 4 x 4 inches with a Resolution of 100 ppi. Alternatively, you can select Pixels from the Width and Height pop-up menus, enter 400 into each, and forget about the Resolution value. Also, choose the RGB Color option from the Mode pop-up menu.

3. Press Enter.

The new empty canvas appears in a new window.

4. Select the paintbrush tool.

Click on its icon in the toolbox or press the B key. That's B for buff, as in, "Boy howdy, Biff, this brush is beaucoup buff!" That's what the programmers told me, anyway.

5. Draw a circle in the middle of your new canvas.

A rude approximation of a circle is fine. Experts agree that a lumpy circle has more personality.

6. Now paint some rays coming off the circle.

Figure 8-2 shows more or less how your image should look so far.

Figure 8-2: The beginnings of a sun, drawn exclusively with the paintbrush tool.

7. Now select the pencil tool.

To access the pencil from the keyboard, press Y, as in "Yellow number 2."

8. Draw a little face inside the sun.

Using the pencil, you get hard-edged lines, as in Figure 8-3.

Figure 8-3:
A face
drawn with
the pencil
tool.

9. **Select the airbrush tool.**

   Press A for . . . hey! Here's a shortcut that actually makes sense.

10. **Change the foreground color to orange.**

    Use the RGB slider bars in the Color palette (press F6 to display the palette). Max out the R slider to 255, set the G slider to 150, and leave the B slider at 0.

11. **Click and hold — without moving your mouse — inside the sun.**

    Notice that the airbrush continuously pumps out paint. Neither the paintbrush nor the pencil do this.

12. **Paint some shading in the lower-right region of the sun.**

    Figure 8-4 shows what I mean. The airbrush is useful for shading images. Of course, the real sun can't possibly have a shadow, but it doesn't have a face either, so I think that we can allow room for some personal expression.

That's good enough for now. You may want to save this image because I come back to it later in this chapter. Then again, if something goes wrong and you don't save the sun, no biggie. You can always re-create it or experiment with a different image.

Remember that at any stage in the previous exercise — or during any other painting mission you may embark on — you can eliminate the last brush stroke by choosing Edit⇨Undo or pressing Ctrl+Z. Everyone makes mistakes, and the Undo command is there to correct those errors.

Figure 8-4:
Use the
airbrush to
paint a
highly
unrealistic
shadow on
the sun.

Performing Special Painting-Tool Tricks

Dragging with a tool inside the image window is obviously the most common way to paint in Photoshop. But it's not the only way, as the following list makes clear:

- ✔ To create a perfectly straight line, click at one point in the image with any of the three painting tools and Shift+click at another. Photoshop automatically creates a straight line between the two points.

- ✔ Continue Shift+clicking at various points in the image to create a straight-sided polygon. This method is great for creating triangles, five-pointed stars, and all sorts of other geometric shapes.

- ✔ To create a straight line that is exactly vertical or horizontal, click and hold with one of the painting tools, press and hold the Shift key, and then drag with the tool while the Shift key remains down. In other words, press Shift immediately after you begin to drag and hold Shift throughout the length of the drag. If you release the Shift key while dragging, the line returns to its naturally free-form and wiggly ways.

- ✔ You can also use the line tool to draw straight lines. But using the Shift key in combination with the painting tools is usually a better option, because the painting tools give you more flexibility. You can vary the softness of your lines if you use the painting tools, but you can't if you use the line tool. The only time I use the line tool is to create lines with arrowheads at the end. To create this kind of line, double-click on the line tool in the toolbox to display the Line Tool Options palette, which contains options that enable you to specify the placement of the arrowhead, the shape of the arrowhead, and the width of your line. Then drag with the tool to create the line.

✔ Alt+click to lift a color from the image. Then drag to start painting with that color. (As I discuss in Chapter 6, pressing Alt when you're using a painting tool accesses the eyedropper.)

Choosing Your Brush

If the preceding two sections covered everything there is to know about the painting tools, Photoshop would be a royal dud. But as we all know, Photoshop is not a dud — far from it — so there must be more to the painting tools than I've shown you so far. (This is classic Sherlock Holmes-style deductive reasoning at work here.)

You can modify all three tools to a degree that no mechanical pencil or conventional paintbrush can match. For starters, you can change the size and shape of the tip of the tool, as explained in the next few sections. You can draw thick strokes one moment and then turn around and draw thin strokes the next, all with the same tool.

Switching the brush size

To change out one tool tip — called a brush size, or just plain brush — for a different one, choose Window⇨Show Brushes or press the F5 key. Photoshop displays the Brushes palette, shown in Figure 8-5. Here you can find a total of 16 brush sizes (assuming default settings), all free for the taking.

Most brush size icons are shown at actual size, but the last four are too large to fit inside their little boxes. The numbers below the icons represent the diameters of the brushes. (In case that year of high-school geometry has altogether removed itself from your brain, diameter is merely the width of a circle measured from side to opposite side.)

To change the brush size associated with the pencil, paintbrush, or airbrush tool, select the desired tool and then click on an option in the Brushes palette. The left column of Figure 8-6 shows how each of the predefined brushes affects the performance of the paintbrush tool. (In each case, an icon from the Brushes palette is shown directly to the left of a stroke created with that brush.) Notice that the first six brushes have soft edges, while the remaining ten have downright blurry edges.

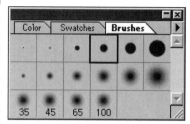

 In Photoshop, soft edges are said to be *antialiased* (pronounced *an-tie-ay-lee-ast*), while blurry edges are *feathered.* Both terms are proof positive that computer professionals actually don't want to be understood by the greater public. They prefer to speak in their own private code.

Figure 8-6 also shows the effect of some of the brushes on the pencil and airbrush tools. As you can see, the pencil tool draws a harsh, jagged line no matter which brush you select. Even the feathered brushes produce jagged lines when used with the pencil. The airbrush generally produces softer lines than the paintbrush.

Making your own brush

You might think that 16 brushes would be enough to keep you happy well into your declining years. But I assure you, one day you'll want a brush size that's a little thicker than Option A and a little thinner than Option B. You'll have to modify one or the other to come up with a custom brush of your own.

To edit a brush, you can select one of the options in the Brushes palette and then choose the Brush Options command from the palette menu. But I recommend that you just double-click on a brush icon and be done with it. In response to your double-click, Photoshop displays the Brush Options dialog box, shown in Figure 8-7. Here's how you modify the brush:

✔ Drag the Diameter slider to make the brush bigger or smaller. If you know the exact width value, enter it into the option box on the right side of the slider. This value is measured in pixels.

✔ The Hardness value represents the blurriness of the brush size. A value of 100 percent is soft, like the first six options in the Brushes palette. Anything else is progressively fuzzier. The ten feathered options in the Brushes palette have Hardness values of 0 percent.

 ✔ Don't change the Spacing value. And don't even think about turning off the Spacing check box. The Spacing option determines how many dollops of paint are applied to your canvas and is better left unmolested.

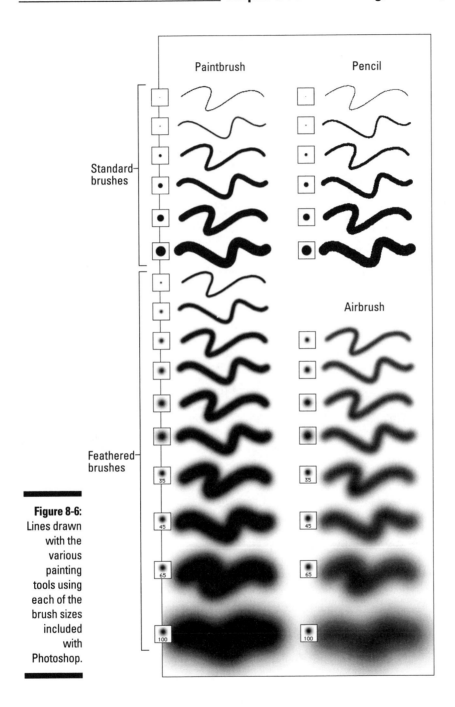

Figure 8-6:
Lines drawn
with the
various
painting
tools using
each of the
brush sizes
included
with
Photoshop.

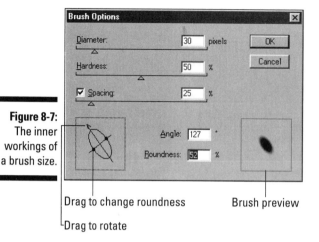

Figure 8-7:
The inner
workings of
a brush size.

Drag to change roundness   Brush preview

Drag to rotate

✔ Before I tell you about the Angle option, which comes next, I need to explain how Roundness works. (You see, the Angle value doesn't have any effect unless you first change the Roundness value.) The Roundness option lets you make the brush oval instead of round. A value of 100 percent is absolutely circular, as are all the predefined brushes; anything less results in a shape that is shorter than it is wide.

✔ If you want an oval brush to be taller than it is wide or some other variation on its present state, you can rotate it by changing the Angle value. Keep in mind that 360 degrees represents one complete counterclockwise turn, so 90 degrees is a quarter-turn, 180 degrees is a half-turn, -90 degrees is a clockwise quarter-turn, and so on.

✔ I never use the Angle and Roundness option boxes to change the values. Instead, I use that diagram in the lower-left corner of the dialog box. Drag one of the two circular handles on either side of the circle to make the brush oval. To rotate the brush, either drag the gray arrowhead or just click at the position where you want the arrow to point. The labels in Figure 8-7 tell the story.

As you change the settings, the preview box in the lower-right corner of the dialog box shows what the brush will look like. If the diameter of the brush is too large for the preview to fit in its box — 74 pixels or larger — Photoshop automatically reduces the preview and displays a zoom ratio above the box. A zoom ratio of 1:2, for example, means that you're seeing the preview at half-size.

When you finish editing the brush, press Enter to accept your changes.

Going nuts with the Brushes palette

Whenever I explain some feature or other associated with Photoshop, I'm tempted to say, "But wait, there's more!" like some daft Ginsu Knife salesman. But that's because there always is more. Photoshop is never satisfied to supply you with anything short of everything. You have to admire that in a program.

Here's what I mean:

✔ You don't need to manually click on a brush icon in the Brushes palette to select it. You can change the brush size from the keyboard, even when the Brushes palette is hidden. Press the right bracket key ( ]) to select the next brush in the Brushes palette. Press the left bracket key ([ ) to select the previous brush.

✔ To select the very first brush size option — something that comes in especially handy when using the pencil tool — press Shift+[. To select the last option, press Shift+].

✔ To delete a brush size option from the palette, Ctrl+click on it. (When you press the Ctrl key, you get a miniature pair of scissors. That's how Photoshop tells you that you're ready to clip a brush into oblivion.)

✔ To add a new brush icon, click in the empty area in the lower-right corner of the Brushes palette. The dialog box from Figure 8-7 appears, though it's titled New Brush instead of Brush Options. Change the settings as desired and press Enter.

✔ You can load additional custom brushes from disk by choosing the Load Brushes command from the palette menu. (Click on the right-pointing arrow in the palette to display the menu.) When you choose the command, you see a dialog box similar to the standard Open dialog box. Go inside the Photoshop folder and then inside the Brushes folder, and you find a file called ASSORTED.ABR. That's a fun one. Click on Open to add the custom brushes to the Brushes palette.

✔ To get rid of any changes made to the brush size options in the Brushes palette, choose Reset Brushes from the palette menu. After the message appears, click on the OK button or press Enter.

Exploring More Painting Options

The Options palette represents the heart and soul of the Photoshop tool modification options. Although the Brushes palette controls only one aspect of a painting tool, the Options palette lets you modify tools in a whole bunch of ways. You can modify nearly every tool in the toolbox to some extent using the Options palette.

Ogling the Options palette

To get to the Options palette, you can choose Window⇨Show Options. Or you can press F8 and then click on the Options tab in the Info palette. Both of those methods are the sucker's routes for displaying the Options palette. Here are two better ways:

✔ Double-click on the toolbox icon for the tool you want to modify.

✔ If the tool you want to modify is already selected, just press the Enter key. Photoshop not only displays the Options palette, it highlights the first option box in the palette so that you can immediately enter the option value without selecting the option box first.

Figure 8-8 shows the Paintbrush Options palette that appears when the paintbrush is active. With a few exceptions, these options are the same ones that appear when the pencil and airbrush tools are selected. Here's how they work:

✔ The pop-up menu in the upper-left corner of the palette provides access to a bunch of different brush modes, which control how the foreground color applied by the tool mixes with the existing colors in the image. The modes have confusing and seemingly meaningless names such as Multiply, Hard Light, and Difference, so beginners tend to avoid them like the plague. I show you some fun tricks you can perform with some of the modes in the next section.

Figure 8-8:
The
Paintbrush
Options
panel is
headquarters
for
modifying
the painting
tools.

Brush modes

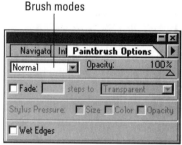

✔ Available when you use the pencil or paintbrush, the Opacity slider bar controls the translucency of the foreground color. A setting of 100 percent ensures that the paint is opaque, so that you can't see the colors underneath. (When you use a feathered brush, the edges are translucent even at 100 percent, but the center is opaque.) Any Opacity setting lower than 100 percent makes the brush translucent.

✔ If you're still a little fuzzy on how the Opacity slider works, it may be because you're a visual learner. Figure 8-9 shows four lines drawn with the paintbrush, two using a standard soft brush and two using a feathered brush. In each case, one line is set to 100 percent Opacity and the other is set to 40 percent.

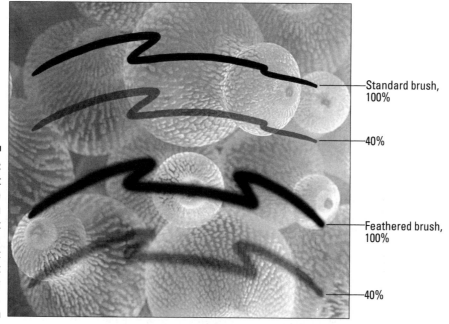

Standard brush, 100%

40%

Figure 8-9:
Here's what it looks like when you paint over sea anemone at different Opacity settings.

Feathered brush, 100%

40%

✔ When the airbrush is selected, the Opacity slider bar changes to the Pressure slider bar. Rather than producing translucent lines at lower settings, the airbrush applies less paint. It's as if you tightened the nozzle on a real airbrush.

✔ You can change the Opacity or Pressure value in 10-percent increments by pressing a number key. As long as one of the painting tools is selected, pressing 9 changes the Opacity to 90 percent, 8 changes it to 80 percent, and so on. Press the 0 key to change the Opacity back to 100 percent. If you want a more precise setting — say, 75 percent — just type the value quickly.

✔ Fade does not rank among the most useful Photoshop options. It fades out the line over the course of several "steps," which are those dollops of paint I discuss a few pages back, in the context of the Spacing option in the Brush Options dialog box. Skip it.

✔ The Stylus Pressure check boxes affect how pressure-sensitive tablets work in Photoshop. But if you've never even seen a pressure-sensitive tablet, let alone have one hooked up to your computer, don't give these options another thought.

✔ The Wet Edges check box appears only when the paintbrush tool is selected. When selected, this option makes your lines translucent with dark edges, as if the lines were drawn with a magic marker. Give it a try. For a variation on the effect, choose the Multiply mode from the brush modes pop-up menu.

✔ When the pencil is selected, the check box changes to Auto Erase. This option draws in the background color whenever you click or drag on a pixel painted in the foreground color (the accepted practice in other painting programs). It's very useful for making touch-ups with the single-pixel brush — click to add the foreground color, click again to change it to the background color. I almost always leave this option on because it lets you add and erase color with a single tool.

Experimenting with brush modes

Of all the controls in the Options panel, the brush modes in the pop-up menu make the least sense. Don't worry, I'm not going to list every one of them and explain how it works. That would just fry your brain, and you need your brain for other chapters. Instead, I demonstrate a few specific effects you can achieve using brush modes and let you experiment with the others at your own pace.

For example, consider the sun image shown back in Figure 8-4. Suppose that you want to color in the sun with yellow and the sky with blue.

The problem is, if you try to color in the sun and sky with one of the painting tools — even the airbrush — you end up covering the face inside the sun and the rays outside the sun. You can't fix the problem by lowering the Opacity value because it just results in washed out colors, and you still obscure some of the sun's detail.

The two images in Color Plate 8-1 show what I'm talking about. In the left image, I've painted in the sun and sky with the paintbrush tool at 100 percent Opacity. Obviously a bad move. In the right image, I changed the Opacity to 40 percent and tried again. It looks like I smeared chalk all over the image. Yuk.

The solution is to select a brush mode. Change the Opacity back to 100 percent by pressing the 0 key. Then select Multiply from the brush modes pop-up menu in the Options palette. Miraculously, you can now paint both sky and sun without covering up the rays and the face. This is because the Multiply option darkens colors as if you had painted with watercolors. It mixes the colors together to create darker colors. The top left example in Color Plate 8-2 shows the result.

Here are some other brush modes that you may find interesting:

✔ The Screen mode is the exact opposite of Multiply. Rather than mixing colors together to create darker colors, you mix them together to create lighter colors. In the upper-right example of Color Plate 8-2, I was able to apply color exclusively inside the black outlines and orange shadow. When I painted over white areas, nothing happened, because any color mixed with white just makes more white.

✔ Does that make sense? Let me take another stab at it. Multiply mixes colors as if they were pigments, which is why the colors get darker. (Remember my discussion of CMYK colors from Chapter 5? Well, it's just like that.) By contrast, Screen mixes colors as if they were lights — just like RGB colors — which is why they get lighter.

✔ The Overlay mode darkens dark colors and lightens light colors, resulting in a heightening of contrast. In the case of our sun, Overlay creates halos around the black lines because it darkens the inside of the lines and lightens the feathered edges. The bottom-left example in Color Plate 8-2 shows what I'm talking about.

✔ The Difference brush mode is the loopiest mode of them all and the most likely to surprise you. It creates a photo-negative effect by mixing colors and finding their opposites. Check out the final example in Color Plate 8-2 to see the resulting plum sun against a tomato sky. Way cool.

✔ You can also have some fun experimenting with Difference's cousin, Exclusion. It sends all blacks to white, all whites to black, and all medium colors to gray.

✔ Use the Color brush mode to colorize grayscale images or change the color of portions of RGB images. Suppose that you want to change the color of the sky in the upper-left example of Color Plate 8-2 from blue to green. You can't use the Normal mode because that would wipe out the rays and the other lines. And you can't use Multiply again because that would further darken the sky. The answer is the Color mode, which replaces a color with the foreground color without harming underlying detail.

✔ The Color Dodge and Color Burn brush modes offer an interesting new twist on the dodge and burn tools discussed in Chapter 9. In case you haven't discovered the dodge and burn tools yet, you drag with the dodge tool to lighten a portion of your image and drag with the burn tool to darken a portion of your image. If you use one of the painting tools and the Color Dodge mode, you can both lighten your image and infuse it with color. Using Color Burn, you can darken and infuse with color. For example, to darken your image and give it a greenish tint, you would paint with green using the Color Burn brush mode.

✔ To paint normally again, just select the Normal brush mode.

I'd rate six of the brush modes discussed above — Multiply, Screen, Overlay, Difference, Color, and Normal — as super-useful, the kinds of modes you want to get to know on a first-name basis. Exclusion, Color Dodge, and Color Burn are also worth some attention. The others aren't nearly so useful. In fact, they're mostly boring and obscure. With that in mind, I encourage you to freely experiment with the ones discussed here to the exclusion of all the others.

If brush modes seem a little daunting at first, don't give up. Just keep on plugging away. Remember, everything's daunting at some time. Heck, walking upright on two legs once seemed impossible, and yet look how well you do that today. Sure, not as well as some folks, but you're still learning. Keep your chin up.

Chapter 9
Making a Mockery of Reality

In This Chapter

▶ Using the edit and crop tools

▶ Clipping away unwanted portions of your image

▶ Selecting different focus and toning tools

▶ Smudging an image to remove imperfections

▶ Creating an oil-painting effect

▶ Using the blur tool instead of the smudge tool

▶ Making sense of the dodge and burn tools

▶ Adjusting color saturation with the sponge

*B*ack in the old days, retouching a photograph was a formidable task. If you wanted to remove the reflection from someone's glasses, sharpen the focus of a detail, or tidy up a wrinkle or two, you had to actually take paint or airbrush to the photo and hope for the best. Anyone short of a trained professional would more often than not make a complete mess of the project and wish to heck it had never been started. Even the pros found it difficult to match flat colors on a palette to the ever-changing landscape of a photograph.

The beauty of Photoshop is that you can paint not only with specific colors — as explained in the previous chapter — but also with colors and details already found in the image. Using the editing tools — smudge, blur, sharpen, dodge, burn, and sponge — you can subtly adjust the appearance of pixels by shifting them around, boosting contrast between them, or lightening and darkening them. The results are edits that blend in with their surroundings.

With the Photoshop crop tool and Image⇨Crop command, you can also snip away unwanted portions of your image. Never before has it been so easy to cut relatives you hate out of your family photos.

"Photo-retouching menace spreads wave of panic"

A certain line of popular logic argues that because of computer programs such as Photoshop, we as viewers have no idea which portions of a photograph to believe and which not to believe. But the truth is, photo manipulation is anything but new. Folks have been retouching photographs throughout the latter half of the previous century and all of this one. Old magazines, for example, are rampant with flagrantly augmented advertisements and subtly adjusted editorial photographs. These sorts of changes have generally been accepted as an ethical synthesis of photography and art.

That's fine, goes the argument, but now the edits are incredibly believable and sometimes even impossible to detect. Well, I hate to burst a bubble, but today's startling fiction is tomorrow's obvious fakery. In other words, viewer sophistication improves over time. Can you imagine being frightened half to death by a radio broadcast of "War of the Worlds" or shocked and amazed by the realism of *The Creature from the Black Lagoon*? And yet, these were exactly the reactions of previous generations. Even relatively recent films such as *Star Wars* and *Jaws* are beginning to show their age. Darth Vader wears a cheesy plastic mask with fingerprints all over it, and the mechanical great white shark appears limited to two movements — bite and blink.

Just as special-effects engineers are constantly raising the bar and making their predecessors look bad, future image-editing techniques will put current solutions to shame. So despite what you may hear about the terrifying miracles of computer technology, don't be surprised if the masterpiece of seamless image editing that you create today gets mixed reactions several years from now. "Gips, Gramps," your granddaughter may react (employing a bit of kiddy vocabulary that should hit full stride around 2025), "That's so fakey!"

Photoshop not only enables you to retouch images in ways that traditional photographic techniques simply don't allow, but also offers a built-in safety net. You can undo any change you make or simply revert back to your original image if you don't like how your retouched image turns out. In other words, Photoshop is a real pleasure for modern retouching enthusiasts. After you finish this chapter, you'll be so inspired to enhance and modify photographic details that you'll welcome problem images with open arms.

Trimming Excess Gunk Off the Edges

In Chapter 4, I explain how to change the size of your image without changing the elements therein — in other words, how to turn that 8 x 10 wedding photograph into a nifty wallet-size snapshot without trimming off anyone's vital body parts. But suppose that your spouse up and runs off to Lagos with your next-door neighbor? What do you do then? Why, you use the crop tool to cut the cretin out of the picture, that's what.

The sharp edges of the crop tool

Novice photographers have a habit of worrying about getting too much imagery into their pictures. This can be a dangerous concern. In your effort to cut out background flack, you may overcompensate and cut off Grandma's head or the right half of little Joey's body. The fact is, it's better to have too much stuff in your photos than too little, for the simple reason that excess stuff can be cut away, but missing stuff has to be reshot. Since photography was invented, production artists have been taking knives and scissors to just about every image that passes over their light tables in an effort to clip away the extraneous gook around the edges and home in on the real goods. Called *cropping,* this technique is so pervasive that professional photographers purposely shoot subjects from too far away knowing that someone, somewhere, will slice the image and make it right.

Inside Photoshop, you can cut away the unpalatable parts of an image using the crop tool. The crop tool used to have its own single-family home in the toolbox but now is forced to share a cramped apartment with the marquee tools in the top-left corner of the toolbox. To select the crop tool without messing with the toolbox, press C.

The crop tool has changed a lot since the last version of Photoshop. Here's how to use the new, improved crop tool:

1. **Drag with the tool around the portion of the image you want to retain.**

   In Figure 9-1, I dragged around the floating spaceman. A dotted rectangle called a *marquee* follows your drag to clearly show the crop boundaries. Don't worry if you don't surround your image elements just right; you get the chance to edit the boundary in the next step.

   If you press the spacebar during your drag, Photoshop stops resizing the crop boundary and starts moving the entire boundary. This technique can be helpful when you're trying to position the boundary precisely. (You can also move the boundary after you create it, though.)

2. **Drag the crop boundaries as desired.**

   After you release your mouse button, Photoshop displays square handles around the edges of the marquee, as shown in Figure 9-1. If the marquee is not the right size, drag a handle to change the crop boundary. Your cursor changes to a double-headed arrow when you place it over a handle, indicating that you have the go-ahead to drag the handle. You can drag as many handles as you please — one at a time, of course — before cropping the image.

Handle   Resize cursor   Crop boundary

Figure 9-1:
Drag the
square
handles to
change the
crop
boundary.

If you move the cursor outside the crop boundary, the cursor changes to a curved, double-headed arrow. Dragging then rotates the crop boundary.

3. **After you get the crop boundary the way you want it, double-click inside the boundary to crop the image.**

   Or just press Enter. Photoshop throws away all pixels outside the crop boundary, as shown in Figure 9-2. If you rotated the crop boundary in Step 2, Photoshop rights the rectangular area and thus rotates the image, as illustrated in Figure 9-3.

Figure 9-2:
Up close
and
personal
with a
spaceman.

Figure 9-3: If the photograph isn't straight, you can rotate the crop boundary to match (top) while telling Photoshop to crop and straighten the image at the same time (bottom).

Rotate cursor ┘

When you rotate an image in this way, Photoshop *resamples* your image — that is, it rearranges the pixels to come up with the rotated image. As I discuss in Chapter 4, resampling can damage your image. For best results, don't rotate your image more than once. Also, make sure that the Interpolation option in the General panel of the Preferences dialog box is set to Bicubic. (Press Ctrl+K to display the dialog box.)

More good news about cropping

Cropping is easy and fun for the whole family. You can do it at home or at work, with friends or by yourself, in the car or while performing household chores. Learn how you can make cropping an everyday part of your new life. Here's how to order:

 ✔ Sorry, I misplaced the real intro to this section and nobody seems to be able to find it. But before I hunt around, I just want to mention briefly that the next few items explain more cropping techniques that you might find useful.

✓ If you change your mind about wanting to crop your image, press Esc to get rid of the cropping boundary.

✓ If you try to drag with the crop tool when a portion of the image is selected (as discussed in Chapter 12), Photoshop deselects the image but doesn't respond to your drag. You have to drag a second time to make Photoshop sit up and take notice.

✓ To move the cropping boundary in its entirety, just drag inside the boundary.

✓ In addition to using the crop tool, you can crop an area selected with the rectangular marquee tool (discussed in Chapter 12) by choosing Image⇨Crop. I take advantage of this alternative quite often because Photoshop can slow down and react lethargically when you edit the crop marquee.

The only trick is that the selected area has to be exactly rectangular. If one side is even slightly crooked — which might happen if you modify the selection outline slightly — the Crop command doesn't work. Also, the Feather option in the Marquee Options palette must be set to 0. (To display the palette, double-click on the marquee tool icon in the toolbox.)

✓ The Fixed Target Size option in the Crop Tool Options palette is useful for cropping one image so that it's the exact same size as another image. Suppose that you want to make Image A the same size as Image B. First, open Image B, turn on the Fixed Target Size option, and click on the Front Image button. Next, open Image A and use the crop tool as you normally would. When you press Enter to execute the crop, Photoshop automatically resizes the image to match Image B.

✓ You can also crop an image by using the Canvas Size command, as discussed at the end of Chapter 4. You may want to consider this method if you need to trim your image on one or more sides by a precise number of pixels to get the image to a certain size. The Canvas Size command can also come in handy if you want to crop a very small area — say 3 pixels worth — along one or more edges of the image and you have trouble selecting the area with the crop marquee. You can reduce the size of the canvas using Image⇨Canvas Size to eliminate the offensive pixels.

Touching Base with Retouching Tools

When push comes to shove, the editing tools are more like the painting tools than unlike them. You use an editing tool by dragging with it, just as you do with a painting tool. You change the size of the tool tip by selecting an option from the Brushes palette. You modify the performance of an editing tool from the Options palette. You can even apply brush modes and Opacity settings. (Brush modes, the Brushes palette, and the Options palette are all introduced in Chapter 8, in case your response to these last few sentences was "Huh?")

But the editing tools are sufficiently different than their painting cousins to confuse and perplex the unsuspecting neophyte. Moreover, unlike the pencil, paintbrush, and airbrush, the editing tools don't have any common real-world counterparts. I can't say, "the Photoshop smudge tool works just like the conventional smudge tool that's hanging out in your garage right next to the leaf rake," because almost no one has a smudge tool hanging in the garage or anywhere else.

What do the editing tools do, exactly?

Editing tools would be extremely useful in real life, if only someone would get around to inventing them. Take the task of touching up the walls in your rec room. (Come on, everyone has a rec room!) Using paintbrushes and rollers alone, this job can be a nightmare. The paint on the walls and the paint in the can may no longer exactly match. If you have to scrape away any dry paint, you'll have a heck of a time matching the texture. And knowing you, you may very well trip over something and spill paint all over the carpet.

But scan the walls of the rec room into Photoshop, and your problems are solved. Even if you have to retouch both paint and wallpaper, the editing tools, labeled in Figure 9-4, can handle the job without incident:

- Use the smudge tool to smear colors from a pristine area of the wall over the bare spots and the stains. You can smear the paint as far as you want, just as if it were still wet and in infinite supply. This is the editing tool you'll use most. It's discussed further in the section "Smudging Away Imperfections."

- If the transitions between elements in the wallpaper are a little ragged — for example, if the pixels in the little polka-dot mushrooms don't seem to blend naturally with those in the cute little frogs sitting beneath them — you can smooth the pixels out with the blur tool, which looks like a water drop. This tool blurs the edges between colors so that the colors blend together.

- To rebuild textures, drag with the sharpen tool — which looks like a pointy cone of some sort. The sharpen tool increases the amount of contrast between colors and builds up edges.

- Together, the blur and sharpen tools are known as *focus tools.* The former downplays focus; the latter enhances it. Both tools are eloquently explained later in this chapter in the section "Focusing from the hip."

- To lighten a dark area in the wallpaper, drag with the dodge tool, which looks like a circle on the end of a stick. This tool lightens up the area evenly.

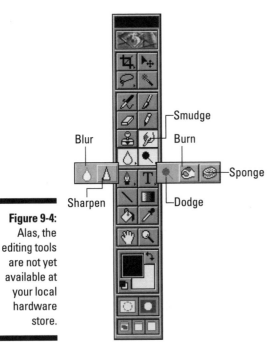

Blur

Smudge

Burn

Sponge

Sharpen

Dodge

Figure 9-4:
Alas, the
editing tools
are not yet
available at
your local
hardware
store.

✔ If an area on the wall has become faded over the years, you can darken it using the burn tool, which looks like a hand in the shape of an O.

✔ Are the colors just too darn garish? Or has the color been drained right out? I admit, these aren't common rec room problems, but if they do occur, you can take up the sponge tool to remedy them.

✔ The dodge, burn, and sponge tools are called *toning tools,* meaning that they change the colors in an image. The last two sections in this chapter are devoted to the toning tools.

See, don't you wish you had a crack at using these tools in real life? Seems to me that Bob Vila or that *Home Improvement* guy should get to work on them.

Uncovering hidden editing tools

When you first saw Figure 9-4, you may have noticed that the toolbox in my figure doesn't look anything like the one on your screen. In order to show you all the tool icons, I enhanced the screen shot (using Photoshop, of course).

By default, the smudge, blur, and dodge tools appear in the toolbox. As discussed in Chapter 2, the little arrow in the bottom-right corner of the blur and dodge tools means that additional tools lurk behind the icons, on a flyout menu. To get to the hidden tools on the flyout menu, press and hold on the icon and then drag across to the tool you want to use. Or just Alt+click on the icon to cycle through the tools on the menu.

You can also cycle through the tools by using their shortcuts: Press R to select the tool that's currently showing in the blur/sharpen compartment of the toolbox; press R again to switch to the tool that's hidden. Likewise, you can press O (that's the letter O, not zero) to cycle through the dodge, burn, and sponge tools. To select the smudge tool from the keyboard, press U (as in smUdge).

Keep tapping the R key to make the blur and sharpen icons do a little hula dance. This trick keeps me amused for hours.

Because the effects of the edit tools can be a little difficult to predict — especially for beginners — be sure to press Ctrl+S to save your image before you pick up an edit tool. And after you achieve the effect you want with the tool, save your image again before moving on to the next editing step. That way, if you mess up, you can use File⇨Revert to restore your image to the last-saved version.

Smudging Away Imperfections

The shark image shown in Figure 9-5 provides an ideal subject for demonstrating the powers of the proudest Photoshop editing tool, the smudge tool. Like so many rough-and-tumble sharks that occupy the inner cities of our oceans, this guy is no stranger to the occasional toothy brawl. Frankly, his face is a mess. If he were old enough to shave, I'd say that he had problems operating a razor. But because he's at that violent age where his friends think it's fun to rip an innocent tuna to shreds, I'm guessing that these marks are war wounds.

But whatever caused his scars, I can fix them with the help of the smudge tool. As you may recall from my earlier rec room analogy, the smudge tool pushes color from one portion of your image into another. When you drag with this tool, Photoshop "grabs" the color that's underneath your cursor at the start of your drag and smears it in the direction of your drag.

Figure 9-5:
This shark is
on the road
to ruin.

The smudge tool is a great contraption for smearing away scars, wrinkles, overly large noses, droopy ears, and all the other things that plastic surgeons keep their eyes out for. Figure 9-6 shows a magnified view of me using the smudge tool on the shark. The various sharkish defects are smoothed away to the point that the guy looks like he's made out of porcelain.

Smearing with style

Notice that in Figure 9-6 I rubbed with the grain of the detail. I traced along the shark's gills, rubbed along the length of its fins, and dragged up its snout, all in short, discreet strokes. I was planning on saying say something about how you don't want to rub a shark the wrong way, but my editor told me to lay off the puns. So I'll just point out that you get more naturalistic results if you carefully trace along the details of your subject and don't simply drag haphazardly all over the place.

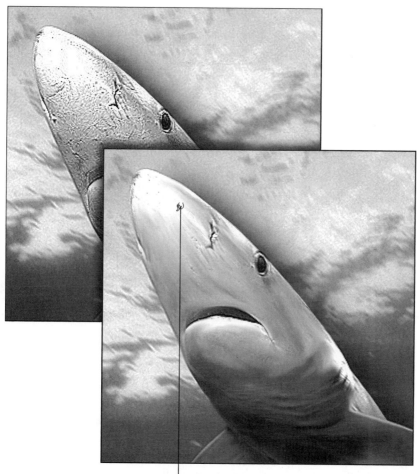

Figure 9-6:
As these before (top) and after (bottom) photos prove, the smudge tool can take years off a shark's face.

Smudge cursor

Retouching with the smudge tool requires a certain amount of discretion. If you really go nuts and drag over every single surface, you get an oil-painting effect, like the one shown in Figure 9-7. Don't get me wrong — you can create some cool stuff this way, but excessive smudging is not the same as retouching.

Figure 9-7:
You can
convert a
photo into
an oil
painting by
dragging all
over the
place with
the smudge
tool.

Smudge-specific controls

You can modify the performance of the smudge tool as follows:

✔ Click and Shift+click to smudge in a straight line. Or Shift+drag to smudge horizontally or vertically. These Shift+click and Shift+drag techniques work for all the edit tools, by the way.

✔ Select another brush size in the Brushes palette to enlarge or reduce the size of the smudge brush. You can likewise change the brush size for all the edit tools. To display the Brushes palette, press F5. (For more on changing brushes, see Chapter 8.)

✔ Double-click on the smudge tool icon in the toolbox to display the Smudge Tool Options palette, shown in Figure 9-8. Or, if the smudge tool is selected, just press Enter to display the palette.

✔ Adjust the Pressure slider below the default setting of 50 percent to create more subtle retouching effects. Increase the Pressure setting to make the effect more pronounced.

✔ Remember that you can change the brush size from the keyboard by pressing the bracket keys and change the Pressure setting by pressing the number keys, as I explain in the preceding chapter.

Figure 9-8:
The options
that affect
the smudge
tool.

✔ The brush modes pop-up menu (in the upper-left corner of the Smudge Tool Options palette) doesn't offer the Multiply, Screen, Overlay, or Difference options I discuss at the end of Chapter 8. Instead, you get two options, Darken and Lighten, which let you smear only those colors that are darker or lighter than the original colors in the image.

✔ You also have the Color brush mode, which lets you smear the colors in an RGB image without harming the detail. Pretty nifty.

✔ The other brush modes — Hue, Saturation, and Luminosity — range from nearly useless to completely useless. Don't worry about them.

✔ Change the brush mode back to Normal to make the smudge tool function, er, normally.

✔ Depending on your computer system, Photoshop may slow down dramatically when you increase the Pressure setting above 80 or 90 percent, select a large brush size, or change the brush mode. And if you do all three at once, the program may run so lethargically that you may think you've crashed. Just go get a cup of coffee for a few minutes, and Photoshop should be finished when you get back.

✔ Select the Finger Painting check box to dip your brush into the foreground color before smudging. Photoshop applies a little dab of foreground color at the beginning of your drag and then begins to smear into the existing colors in the image as usual.

To temporarily turn on Finger Painting when the check box is deselected, press Alt as you drag with the smudge tool. If the Finger Painting check box is selected, Alt+drag to smudge in the normal fashion.

✔ The Sample Merged check box doesn't make any difference unless you're editing an image with layers, and even then it doesn't make much difference. Ignore it.

Color Plate 9-1 shows before and after shots of a few effects mixed together. I created the second image by selecting the Finger Painting check box, setting the Pressure slider to 90 percent, and changing the brush mode to Color. I dragged several times with the smudge tool, about half the time with the foreground color set to red and the other half with it set to yellow.

All Them Other Edit Tools

The remaining edit tools fall into a group that experts call "the other guys." Whereas you may pick up the smudge tool every third day or so, you'll be lucky if you select one of the other guys once a week. Even so, they can prove fantastically helpful — well, moderately helpful, anyway — if used properly. The upcoming sections contain my choice bits of wisdom for using the other guys.

Focusing from the hip

It's true that the smudge tool is a wonderful little device. But it's not always the right tool for the job. For example, let's say that you have a harsh transition between two colors. Maybe one of the shark's teeth looks a little jagged, or you want to soften the edge of a fin. Which of the following methods would you use to fix this problem?

✔ Smear the colors a bit with the smudge tool.

✔ Soften the transition between the colors using the blur tool.

I prepared you for that question by saying that the smudge tool isn't always the right tool and using words like "soften," so naturally you chose the second answer. (You did choose the second answer, didn't you?) But believe me, there will come a time when you run into this exact situation and your first reflex will be to reach for the smudge tool.

So let me try to drive the point home a bit with the aid of Figure 9-9. The figure starts off with the harshest of all possible color transitions, that between white and its arch enemy, black. You want to smear the colors together so they blend a little more harmoniously, so naturally you reach for the smudge tool. The problem with this method — as illustrated in the second example in the figure — is that you can't get a nice, smooth transition between the two colors no matter how hard you try. Even if you Shift+drag with the smudge tool, you get some inconsistent smudging. You also run the risk of smearing surrounding detail. All this happens because the smudge tool is designed as a free-form smearing device, not as an edge softener.

Meanwhile, an edge softener is sitting nearby waiting for you to snatch it up. If you drag the blur tool between the white and black shapes — whether you drag perfectly straight or wobble the cursor back and forth a bit — you get a softened edge like the one shown in the final example of Figure 9-9.

While I've got your attention, let me jot down a few other items about the focus tools:

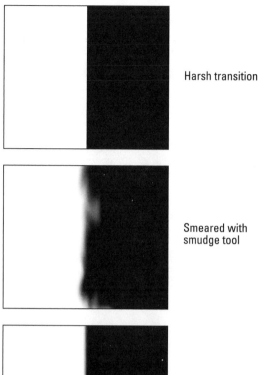

Harsh transition

Smeared with
smudge tool

Figure 9-9:
The parable
of the harsh
transition,
the smudge
tool, and the
blur tool.

Softened with
blur tool

✔ Just as the blur tool softens transitions, the sharpen tool firms the transitions back up.

✔ At least, that's what the sharpen tool is supposed to do. In practice, it tends to make an image overly grainy. Use this tool sparingly, and be sure to save your image before you experiment.

✔ You can adjust the impact of the blur and sharpen tools by changing the Pressure setting in the Focus Tools Options palette — which you get to by pressing Enter when the tool is selected or double-clicking on the tool icon in the toolbox. I like to set the Pressure to about 60 percent for the blur tool and 30 percent for the sharpen tool.

✔ When you work with the focus tools, you have access to the same brush modes as you do when using the smudge tool. The important ones are Darken, Lighten, and Color. Any of the three can help downplay the effects of the sharpen tool and make it more usable.

✔ If you want to adjust the focus of large areas of an image — or an entire image — use the commands under the Filter menu as described in Chapter 17. These commands work much more uniformly than the focus tools.

Dodge? Burn? Those are opposites?

Wondering why the dodge and burn tool icons look they way they do? It's because the dodge and burn tools have their roots in traditional stat camera techniques in which you shoot a photograph of another photograph to correct exposure problems. The dodge tool is supposed to look like a little paddle that you wave around to block off light, and the burn tool is a hand focusing the light. It may seem, therefore, that dodging would make the image darker and burning would make it lighter. But Photoshop is thinking in terms of negative film, where black is white, up is down, right is left, and Tweedle Dee is a Cornish game hen.

I must confess that, although I've been using Photoshop since I was in diapers, I still can't remember which tool lightens and which darkens without looking it up. To help both you and me remember, I offer the following:

✔ The dodge tool lightens images, just as a dodge ball lightens your body by about ten pounds when it tears off your head.

✔ The burn tool darkens images, just as a sunburn darkens your body and eventually turns it a kind of charbroiled color from melanoma.

If those little insights don't help you remember how the dodge and burn tools work, nothing will.

Generally, you adjust the performance of the dodge and burn tools just like the other edit tools and the paint tools — by changing the brush size, alternating the brush mode, and so on. (You can read more about brush sizes and brush modes in Chapter 8.) To get to the Brush size options, press F5 to display the Brushes palette. To get to the other tool options, found in the Toning Tools Options palette, double-click on the dodge or burn tool icon in the toolbox, or — if you like to do things the easy way — just press Enter.

A few of the options in the Toning Tools Options palette require some explanation:

✔ The Exposure slider bar indicates how much an area will be lightened or darkened. As always, lower the value to lessen the impact of the tool and raise the value to increase the impact.

✔ The pop-up menu in the upper-left corner of the palette contains just three options: Highlights, Midtones, and Shadows. The default setting is Midtones, which lightens or darkens medium colors in an image and leaves the very light and dark colors alone. Figure 9-10 shows the result of dragging all over the shark with the dodge tool while Midtones was the active brush mode.

Figure 9-10: By setting the brush mode to Midtones and dragging indiscriminately with the dodge tool, I lightened the shark without eliminating contrast.

✔ The Shadows brush mode ensures that the darkest colors are affected, while Highlights impacts the lightest colors. In Figure 9-11, I set the brush mode to Shadows and scribbled with the dodge tool. The payoff is a shark that looks like it ate the world's supply of glowworms. Even the darkest shadows radiate, making the image uniformly light.

✔ To darken an image with similar uniformity, select the burn tool and set the brush mode to Highlights.

Figure 9-11:
Using the dodge tool in combination with the Shadows brush mode makes the shark's darkest shadows tingle with light.

Version 4 offers a variation of the dodge and burn tools in the form of the Color Dodge and Color Burn brush modes, as explained in Chapter 8. When you use the regular dodge and burn tools, you simply lighten or darken your image. But when you use one of the painting tools with the Color Dodge or Color Burn brush modes, you can both lighten or darken and infuse the image with color. For example, if you want to lighten an image and give it a yellowish glow, paint with yellow and the Color Dodge brush mode.

Playing with the Color knob

The sponge tool is designed to be used on full-color images. Don't try using it on grayscale images because it doesn't do you any good. It's not that it doesn't work — it does — it just doesn't work correctly. On a grayscale image, the sponge tool either lightens or darkens pixels like a shoddy version of the dodge or burn tool.

When you work on a color image, the sponge tool increases or decreases saturation. Ever used the Color knob on your television? Turn the knob up, and the color leaps off the screen; turn it down, and the colors look gray. What you are doing is adjusting the TV's saturation. Increasing saturation makes the colors more vibrant; decreasing saturation makes the colors more drab. The sponge tool works in much the same way.

Here's how you use the sponge tool:

1. **Select the tool.**

   Press the O key until the sponge icon appears in the toolbox.

2. **Press Enter.**

   Photoshop displays the Toning Tools Options palette.

3. **Select the desired option from the pop-up menu in the upper-left corner of the palette.**

   Select Saturate to make the colors vibrant; select Desaturate to make the colors drab.

4. **Press a number key to change the Pressure value.**

   Or drag the slider bar in the palette. Either way, the setting affects the impact of the sponge tool.

5. **Drag with the tool inside a color image.**

   Watch those colors change.

The primary reason that the programmers provide the sponge tool is to desaturate colors that may get lost when you convert from RGB to CMYK. As I mention in Chapter 5, red, green, and blue can mix to form some very bright colors that cyan, magenta, yellow, and black can't express. So you can dab at the colors with the sponge tool to bring them more in line with the CMYK spectrum.

But I like to use the sponge tool for the exact opposite purpose — to make colors more saturated. Oh, sure, maybe you won't be able to print the colors correctly, but at least they'll be as bright as they can be. If dragging with the sponge tool set to Saturate doesn't have any effect on the colors in an image, it's because the colors are already as bright as they can be.

Chapter 10

Cleaning Up Goobers

*I*f you've ever had an image scanned to disk or CD, you know the story. You send out a lovely photograph that you've cherished all your life, and the scan comes back looking like someone stuck it inside the lint trap of a dryer. Big, gnarly hairs wiggle across the image. Little dust flecks seem to have reproduced like rabbits. And if you really hit the jackpot, you may even spy a few fingerprints on your image. It's enough to make you call up the service bureau and ask them whether they recently employed a shedding malamute that hasn't bathed in six weeks and has a penchant for jelly sandwiches.

Unfortunately, sarcasm doesn't get you anywhere. But the dust-busting tools discussed in this chapter can. With a keen eye and a little bit of elbow grease, you can scrub away those imperfections and make your image appear absolutely spotless.

Photoshop offers two different methods for dusting away the specks:

✔ The Dust & Scratches command automates the removal of image imperfections, but it can do more harm than good by getting rid of important detail as well.

✔ The rubber stamp tool lets you clone (copy) portions of an image to cover up blotches. The rubber stamp takes more time to use than the Dust & Scratches command and requires a considerable amount of clicking and dragging, but it also results in a better-looking picture.

This chapter explains the pros and cons of each method and throws in a few other ideas for spit-shining your images as well.

Using the Dust & Scratches Command

Ever own a really nice sports car, like a Porsche or a Jaguar? Me neither, but I've known folks who have, and they can be amazingly protective of their automobiles. Most Porsche/Jaguar owners would sooner vote for a Socialist than take their cars through one of those drive-through wash joints where big floppy pieces of blue plastic flog your car and take little bits of your paint job along with them. Automobile aficionados know that the only way to clean a car is to tenderly rub its surface with specially treated pieces of felt dipped in no-tears baby shampoo.

Although I might think that those car buffers are off their rockers, I wholeheartedly endorse this policy when it comes to cleaning images. That's why I'm not so fond of the Dust & Scratches filter — it's akin to sending your image through a car wash.

I should mention that the Dust & Scratches command is a *filter,* meaning that it automatically corrects an image by mixing up the pixels in some predefined manner. It works much like filters that change the focus of an image, discussed in Chapter 17.

But just because I may not approve of the Dust & Scratches command, that's no reason not to give you a crack at it. You're an adult. I'm not your keeper. Who knows, maybe the command will even come in useful. Maybe you need to clean up an image in a hurry for that last-minute space in the company newsletter, and the car wash solution is the only one you have time to try.

With that enthusiastic endorsement out of the way, it's high time I show you how to use the Dust & Scratches filter. The lab rat for today's outing is Figure 10-1. This figure demonstrates another variety of splatter that can plague images — old photo gunk. The lines, scratches, and dots in this image weren't introduced in the scanning process; they were a part of the original photo. Shot near the beginning of this century, this picture of Halley's comet has held up amazingly well over the years. I hope to look half as good when I'm its age.

Incidentally, if you're a fellow lover of things extraterrestrial, you can't go wrong with Digital Stock's "Space & Spaceflight" CD, which includes about as many views of the sun, moon, planets, and outlying nebula as a person could hope for.

To tidy up an image that presents similar symptoms, choose Filter➪Noise➪Dust & Scratches. Photoshop displays the strange and mysterious Dust & Scratches dialog box, which is pictured in all its glory in Figure 10-2 and explained in the next two sections.

Figure 10-1:
Halley's
comet as it
appeared in
1910, replete
with old
photo gunk.

If you select a portion of your image before you choose the Dust & Scratches command, the command affects just the selected area.

Preview cursor   Preview box

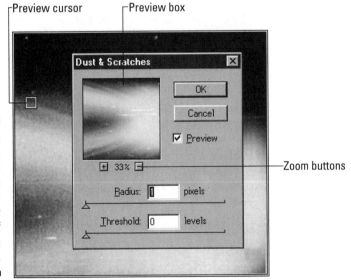

Zoom buttons

Figure 10-2:
The Dust &
Scratches
dialog box
provides a
hefty
supply of
previewing
options.

Previewing the filter effects

The makers of the Dust & Scratches dialog box know that it doesn't make a lick of sense, so they thoughtfully provide some preview options (all labeled in Figure 10-2) to enable you to see what happens when you make some otherwise meaningless adjustment. Here's how these preview options work:

- ✔ The preview box shows how your modifications look when applied to a tiny portion of the image.

- ✔ If you move the cursor outside the dialog box, it changes to a hollow square. Click on an area in the image to capture it inside the preview box.

- ✔ You can also scroll the contents of the preview box by dragging inside the box. Your cursor changes to a little hand.

- ✔ To magnify or reduce the contents of the preview box, click on the plus or minus zoom button.

- ✔ You can also access the standard magnifying glass cursor inside the preview box by pressing the Ctrl key (to zoom in) or the Alt key (to zoom out).

- ✔ As long as the Preview check box is selected, Photoshop previews your settings in the image window as well as in the preview box.

- ✔ You can even use the standard hand and zoom cursors inside the image window while the Dust & Scratches dialog box is open. Just press the spacebar to get the hand cursor or Ctrl or Alt to get the zoom cursors. This technique is a great way to preview an effect at two different zoom ratios, one inside the dialog box and one outside.

- ✔ If Photoshop seems to be slowing down too much as it tries to preview an effect in the image window, just click on the Preview check box to turn the function off.

I know, I know, you didn't want to know quite that much about previewing, but it will serve you well in the future. These same options are found in a few dialog boxes that I describe in Chapter 17 as well as a couple of others that you may decide to discover on your own (you Vasco da Gama, you).

Specifying the size of the speck

The Dust & Scratches dialog box (Filter⇨Noise⇨Dust & Scratches) offers just two options that affect the performance of the filter: the Radius and Threshold slider bars. The slider bars work as follows:

✔ Change the Radius value to indicate the size of the dust specks and the thickness of the hairs that you want to eliminate. In geometry, radius means half the width of a circle, so the Radius value is half the width of a dust speck. The minimum value is 1, meaning that the filter wipes out all specks and hairs up to 2 pixels thick.

✔ "Ah ha," you might think, "If I just crank up the Radius value as far as it goes (16 pixels), that should be enough to eliminate entire colonies of dust bunnies." Well, no. See, the Dust & Scratches filter doesn't really know a speck from a tiny bit of detail. So if you have it rub out 16-pixel radius dust globs, it also rubs out 16-pixel details such as Uncle Ralph's head. Figure 10-3 shows the effects of setting the Radius value to 1 on the left and 3 on the right. Notice how fuzzy the image became when I applied a 3-pixel radius? If you value my advice — I guess you value it to the tune of $19.99, anyway — you'll never set the radius value higher than 2.

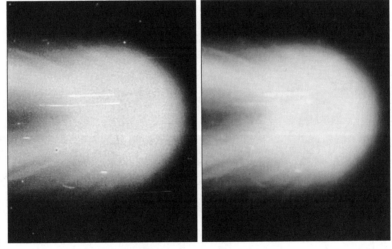

Figure 10-3:
The results of applying the Dust & Scratches filter with the Radius slider set to 1 pixel (left) and 3 (right).

✔ The Threshold value tells Photoshop how different the color of a dust speck has to be from the color of the surrounding image to be considered a bad seed. The Threshold slider works just like the RGB sliders in the Color palette (discussed in Chapter 5) — that is, it varies from 0 to 255.

✔ The default Threshold value of 0 tells Photoshop that dust and image need only be 0 color levels different from each other. Because all colors are at least 0 levels different, Photoshop ignores the Threshold value and considers only the Radius value. Both images in Figure 10-3 were filtered with a Threshold value of 0.

✔ By raising the Threshold value, you tell Photoshop to be more selective. If you set the value to 10, speck and image colors must vary by at least 10 levels before Photoshop covers up the speck, as in the first example of Figure 10-4. If you raise the Threshold to 20 — as in the second example — Photoshop disregards still more potential impurities. Notice that the two horizontal streaks in the second image remain intact, having been ruled out by the Threshold setting. (By the way, I set the Radius value to 3 in Figure 10-4 — something I earlier warned you against doing — in order to make the effects of the Threshold setting more noticeable.)

✔ If you set the Threshold value any higher than 100, the dust specks have to be white and the image black — or vice versa — to receive any attention. I don't recommend using values over 15.

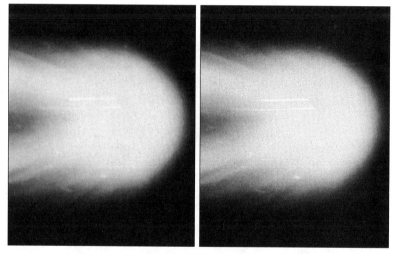

Figure 10-4:
With the Radius set to 3 pixels, I set the Threshold to 10 (left) and then to 20 (right).

In my long ramblings about the Radius and Threshold values, I neglected to mention one disconcerting fact. Even though the Dust & Scratches filter variously obliterated the detail in Figures 10-3 and 10-4, none of the images are completely free of spots and streaks. Admittedly, this old, moldy picture is a lot worse off than most of your images are likely to be, but the fact remains that the Dust & Scratches filter is an imperfect solution. Just like a cheap car wash, it gets rid of most of the dirt — but not all of it — and it takes away some of the paint and detailing along with it.

Spot Cleaning Your Image with TLC

If you're willing to expend a little extra energy and you can stand up to your friends when they call you compulsive, the tool of choice for cleaning up images is the rubber stamp. The fifth tool from the top on the left side of the toolbox, the rubber stamp lets you take a good portion of an image and paint it onto the bad portion. This miraculous process is called *cloning*.

You can also clone part of your image by copying and pasting it, as described in the section "Moving and Cloning Selections" at the end of Chapter 13. You should get familiar with both methods of cloning because both have their place in the retouching world.

Stamping out splatters

Want to see how the rubber stamp tool works? Try out these steps:

1. Select the rubber stamp tool and press Enter.

To select the rubber stamp from the keyboard, press the S key. Pressing the Enter key — or double-clicking on the rubber stamp tool icon in the toolbox — displays the Rubber Stamp Options palette, shown on the right side of Figure 10-5.

2. Make sure that Clone (Aligned) is chosen in the Option pop-up menu.

This option lets you clone from relative points in your image. You'll see what I mean in a sec.

3. Start dragging randomly inside your image.

Whoops, I bet you got an error message, didn't you? If I'm right, the message says something about — I can almost see it; it's becoming clearer — Alt+clicking to define a source! How do I know these things? Because I am psychic, that's how. Even from here in Boulder, Colorado, months before you'll read this, I can foresee the error messages in your future. Ah, really, it's nothing. Been able to do it since I was a kid.

Okay, I'm lying, I just got that message myself and I reckoned that you may get it, too. See, to use the rubber stamp, you have to tell Photoshop which portion of your image you want to clone before you begin cloning it. Photoshop isn't a mind reader, you know. I might be a mind reader, but Photoshop most certainly is not.

Now that you've learned this valuable lesson, grab a pen and put a big *X* through Step 3 so that you never make the same mistake again.

Rubber stamp

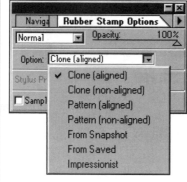

Figure 10-5:
The rubber
stamp and
its trusty
Options
palette,
partners in
cloning.

4. Alt+click on the portion of the image that you want to clone.

For example, to fix that big goober near the beginning of the lower tail of Halley's comet, I Alt+clicked at a location that appeared to contain similar gray values to the comet stuff that surrounds the goober, as demonstrated in Figure 10-6. The point is to pick a portion of your image that will blend in with areas around the blemish you want to eliminate.

When you Alt+click, the little upside-down triangle at the bottom of the rubber stamp cursor becomes white. Fascinating, huh?

According to Webster's, the word *goober* is derived from the Kongo word *gnuba,* which means peanut. And peanut (wink) is exactly what I mean (nudge, nudge).

5. Now click or drag on the offending blemish.

Actually, that mark on my comet looks more like a pimple than a peanut, doesn't it? To apply the digital zit cream, I clicked directly on the critter and purged it good. No muss, no fuss, the glitch is gone.

┌The dreaded cosmic goober

Alt+click with rubber stamp

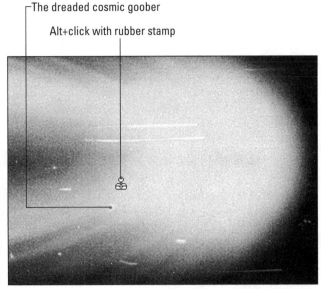

Figure 10-6:
Alt+click on
a good
portion of an
image to
establish
the cloning
source.

When you click or drag with the rubber stamp, Photoshop displays a cross cursor along with the stamp cursor, as shown in Figure 10-7. This cross represents the clone source, or the area that you're cloning from. As you move the mouse, the cross cursor also moves, providing a continual reference to the portion of your image that you're cloning. (Things work differently when you have an option other than Clone (Aligned) selected in the Rubber Stamp Options palette, however, as explained in the next section.)

Clone source   Rubber stamp cursor

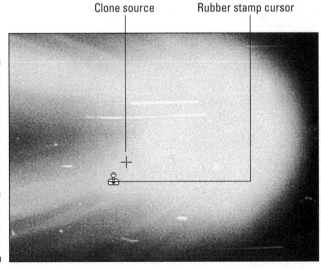

Figure 10-7:
When you
use the
rubber
stamp, a
small cross
follows you
to show you
what part of
the image
you're
cloning.

If the cloned area doesn't blend in well, just choose Edit⇨Undo (Ctrl+Z), Alt+click in the image with the rubber stamp to specify a better source for your cloning, and click or drag with the tool to test out a different clone. You may have to do this several times to get it just right.

Just for the sheer heck of it, Figure 10-8 shows the comet after I finished using the rubber stamp. Now isn't that way better than anything from Figures 10-3 and 10-4? And it took about 15 minutes. We can all afford 15 minutes, can't we?

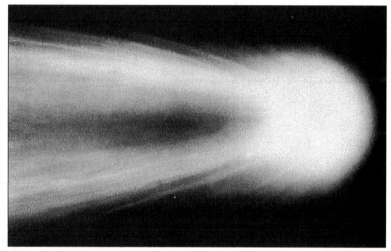

Figure 10-8: Halley's comet, all dressed up and nowhere to go for 76 years.

Performing more magic with the rubber stamp

If you never learned another thing about the rubber stamp tool, you'd be able to clean images quite easily after reading the preceding section. But the rubber stamp is an amazing tool with more facets and capabilities than any other Photoshop tool:

- ✔ To change the size or shape of the area that's cloned, change the brush size in the Brushes palette, just as you would for other painting or editing tools. (Press F5 to display the Brushes palette.) For more information about the Brushes palette, see Chapter 8.

- ✔ To make the clone more translucent or less translucent, use the Opacity slider in the Rubber Stamp Options palette. A setting of 100 makes your clone opaque. (To display the palette, press Enter or double-click on the rubber stamp tool in the toolbox.)

✔ To clean up a straight hair or scratch, Alt+click with the tool to specify the source for the cloning as you normally would. Then click at one end of the scratch and Shift+click at the other.

✔ If the first clone doesn't look exactly right but is pretty close, you may want to modify the clone slightly rather than redo it. Lower the Opacity setting in the Rubber Stamp Options palette by pressing a number key and then clone from a different position by again Alt+clicking and dragging. This allows you to mix multiple portions of an image together to get a more seamless blend.

✔ The blocky rubber stamp cursor that appears by default makes predicting the outcome of your clone difficult. To get a better idea of the size of your clone before you click, press Ctrl+K, Ctrl+3 to open up the Display & Cursors panel of the Preferences dialog box. (Or choose File➪Preferences➪Display & Cursors). Select the Brush Size radio button from the Painting Cursors area of the dialog box. Now your cursor reflects the size of your brush.

✔ Normally, the rubber stamp tool clones from a relative location. If you move your cursor to a different location, the clone source moves with you. But what if you want to clone multiple times from a single location? In this case, choose Clone (Non-Aligned) from the Option pop-up menu in the Rubber Stamp Options palette. Now you can Alt+click once to set the source and click and drag multiple times to duplicate that source.

✔ The other options in the Option pop-up menu enable you to paint with a pattern (the two Pattern options), revert the image (From Snapshot and From Saved), or paint a goofy effect (Impressionist). The From Snapshot and From Saved options are discussed in the next chapter. The other three options are too stupid to merit your attention.

✔ You can clone between images. What am I talking about? If you have two images open, you can Alt+click inside one image to specify the source and drag in the other image to clone. It's like painting one image onto another.

✔ Color Plate 10-1 shows an example of cloning between images. Starting with the two images on the left side of the figure (which I scaled to the same file size using Image➪Image Size, as discussed in Chapter 4), I Alt+clicked inside the top image and then dragged with the rubber stamp inside the bottom image. I cloned the woman's face and blouse using a large fuzzy brush and then switched to a smaller brush for the touch-ups. To match the skin tones in the forehead and the base of the nose, I cloned from the woman's cheeks at an Opacity setting of 50 percent. Pretty gruesome, huh?

✔ If your image contains layers, as discussed in Chapter 15, remember that the rubber stamp tool normally clones from the active layer only. If you select the Sample Merged check box in the Rubber Stamp Options palette, the rubber stamp reads the pixels in all visible layers to create the clone. When you then click or drag with the rubber stamp, Photoshop paints the clone onto the active layer.

✔ All the brush modes that apply to the painting tools apply to the rubber stamp as well. This means that you can achieve interesting special effects by selecting the Multiply, Screen, Overlay, Difference, or Color option from the pop-up menu in the upper-left corner of the Rubber Stamp Options palette. For more on brush modes, see the end of Chapter 8.

✔ Try cloning between two different images with a special brush mode in effect. For example, if you clone with the Multiply brush mode, you emblazon the first image onto the second. If you have half an hour to waste, play with the different modes and see what you can do.

Chapter 11

Turning Back the Digital Clock

• •

• •

*H*ere's how you know that you're a consummate computer nerd: When you snag your favorite sweater, say something highly objectionable to your spouse, or spill a well-known staining agent on your newly installed carpeting, your first reaction is not one of panic or regret. You merely think, "Undo."

Unfortunately, the real world provides no Undo command. After a horrible deed is done, it takes an obscenely disproportionate amount of fussing, explaining, or scrubbing to fix the transgression.

Not so in the magical world of personal computing. Edit⇨Undo is standard equipment with just about every Windows (and Macintosh) program out there. With one press of Ctrl+Z — the Undo command's keyboard equivalent — your previous operation disappears for good, leaving you one step backward in time.

But Photoshop doesn't stop there. You can revert specific portions of an image back to the way they looked when you last saved the image to disk. You can also take a picture of an image and later revert to that. This chapter explains all the Photoshop methods for regaining the past so that you can edit worry-free, safe in the knowledge that nearly everything you do can be undone.

Nuking the Last Operation

The more you work with Photoshop, the more reflexive your actions become. Certainly, this means that you can do work more quickly, but it also means that you are likely to make more mistakes. Reflexive, after all, is a close cousin to thoughtless. And when you don't think, you can wander into some pretty nasty situations.

Doing the Undo

The Undo command ensures that you aren't punished for working reflexively. To get a sense of just how wonderful this command can be, try out these steps:

1. **Open an image.**

   If you already have an image open, good for you.

2. **Select the paintbrush tool and drag across the image.**

   Draw a mustache or something. Just make sure to draw a single brush stroke and no more.

3. **Take a break.**

   You've worked hard, you deserve it. Watch TV for your daily allowance of six hours. Take up macramé. Enlist in the armed forces. The point is, no matter how long you're away, Photoshop remembers the last operation you performed (as long as you don't have a power outage or some similar computing disaster).

4. **Choose Edit➪Undo.**

   Actually, the name of the command should be Undo Paintbrush. The name of the Undo command changes to tell you what action you're about to undo.

   You can also choose the Undo command by pressing Ctrl+Z. Either way, your brush stroke is gone.

After you choose the Undo command, the command changes to the Redo command. For example, if you choose Undo after completing Step 4, the command name is Redo Paintbrush. If you choose the Redo Paintbrush command, your brush stroke comes back and the Redo Paintbrush command becomes the Undo Paintbrush command again. In other words, you can undo an action, and then redo it, and then undo it, and then redo it, and so on, until you make up your mind or collapse from exhaustion, whichever comes first.

The Undo command works even after you choose File⇨Print. This means that you can adjust an image, print it to see how it looks, and undo the adjustment if you don't like it. Choosing File⇨Page Setup — or any other command except Print — wipes out your chance to undo that adjustment, though.

Undo limitations

Although the Undo command is certainly a powerful tool, bear in mind that it does have some limitations. I'd hate to see you go hog-wild on an image and then discover that your changes are set in stone. So here are a few guidelines to stash away in the back of your brain:

- You can't undo the Print command. Print involves marking up real pieces of paper, and the Undo command is powerless in the real world. Instead, Undo just ignores Print, as you saw in the preceding steps.

- File⇨Save and File⇨Save As are beyond the reach of the Undo command. After the Save command finishes, the image is saved, and the previous version of the image is gone. (The Save As command leaves the previous version of the image intact, so you need never worry when choosing it.)

- Not only can you not undo Save or Save As, these commands render the Undo command null and void. After the Save operation completes, the Undo command appears dimmed, meaning that you can't choose it. The operation you performed before choosing Save is now permanent (doubly so, because the changes are saved to disk).

- You can't undo the Exit command. There's a surprise. Also, when you relaunch Photoshop, it has no idea what you did during the previous session, so you can't undo the last changes you made before quitting.

- You also can't undo changing a foreground or background color, adjusting a setting using one of the commands under the File⇨Preferences submenu, hiding or displaying palettes, changing a palette setting, or selecting a tool. Like the Print command, these operations are ignored by Undo, thus enabling you to undo the previous "significant" operation.

- You may think that Photoshop treats File⇨Page Setup like one of the File⇨Preferences commands because you're just adjusting printing preferences. But Photoshop remembers your changes inside the Page Setup dialog box and lets you undo them. So don't choose Page Setup before Print if you want to undo a brush stroke or other operation after printing the image.

The Amazing Powers of the Eraser

If you want to undo the cumulative effects of several operations, the eraser is your tool. Immediately to the left of the pencil in the toolbox, the eraser lets you erase in a couple of ways:

- ✔ If you drag with the eraser in an image that contains only one layer, the tool paints in the background color, which is typically white. I suppose that you can call this process erasing, but it's really just painting in a different color. Who needs it?

- ✔ If your image contains more than one layer (layers are discussed in Chapter 15), the eraser works a little differently and becomes a lot more useful. If you drag the eraser on the background layer, the eraser paints in the background color, as usual. But on any other layer, the pixels you scrub with the eraser become transparent, revealing pixels on underlying layers. This assumes that the Preserve Transparency check box is turned off in the Layers palette. If this check box is turned on, the eraser paints in the background color.

- ✔ If you Alt+drag with the tool, you reveal the image as it appeared when you last saved it to disk. If your image has layers, your drag affects the active layer only. This is another useful function (and one which is explained in the very next section).

Erasing to the last-saved version

On the off chance that you're not clear on what it means to reveal an image to its saved appearance, the following steps give you an opportunity to try it out for yourself. In these steps, you paint a halo around the central subject of an image without harming the subject itself. First, you color outside the lines and then you clean it up with the eraser.

1. **Open an image.**

   For these steps, open something with a strong central subject, like a person or an animal. You can't go wrong with a fish like the one in Figure 11-1.

2. **Set the foreground color to white.**

   Just press D to get the default colors — black for the foreground and white for the background — and then press X to switch them.

Figure 11-1:
This lingcod
stands out
proudly
from his
surroundings.

3. **Trace the central subject with the airbrush tool.**

Don't worry about getting white all over the central subject. In Figure 11-2, for example, I've made a complete mess of things. There's no way to be careful with the airbrush — it sprays all over the place.

Figure 11-2:
Using the
airbrush, I
traced
sloppily
around the
lingcod.

4. Select the eraser tool.

To select the tool from the keyboard, press the E key.

5. Alt+click anywhere inside the image.

This may sound like a weird step, but Photoshop has to reload the original image from disk before it can erase to it. By Alt+clicking, you tell Photoshop to get its act in gear.

You don't absolutely have to Alt+click, but if you just start Alt+dragging, you'll most likely have to wait out a lengthy delay. Photoshop may even ignore your drag entirely.

6. Alt+drag to erase inside the central subject.

After Photoshop finishes loading the image — your hard disk stops making noises and/or the little hard drive light stops flashing — Alt+drag inside the central subject (in my case, the lingcod).

Getting to the image shown in Figure 11-3 required that I perform Step 6 with some care and effort. I wanted to erase inside the subject only and leave the white airbrush paint intact in the background. Creating similar effects may take many strokes and many undos to get it just right, but the practice is good for you. Just don't forget to press that Alt key every time you erase — teaches you patience and all that.

Figure 11-3:
The lingcod glows eagerly as he emerges from his nuclear chamber.

Here are some more things to know about erasing to the last-saved version of your image:

✔ If you're erasing a multiple-layer image, the eraser tool erases changes to the active layer only.

✔ You can also select a portion of your image, as explained in the next chapter, and revert just that portion to the last saved version using the Edit➪Fill command. For details, see the section "Select your stuffing" in Chapter 14.

✔ Your first thought on finishing the preceding steps might be, "If Alt+dragging is so useful, why don't those bozo programmers make it the default setting?" I can't answer that question — and, really, don't call them bozos; they're sensitive — but I can tell you how to change things so that the eraser tool erases to the last-saved version of the image by default.

First, display the Eraser Options palette, shown in Figure 11-4. (Either double-click on the eraser tool icon in the toolbox or, if the eraser tool is selected, press Enter.) Then select the Erase to Saved check box in the lower-right corner of the palette. Dragging with the eraser now reveals the saved image and Alt+dragging paints in the background color. This means that in Step 5, you can now simply click inside the image to load it from disk, and in Step 6 you can drag without ever once pressing the Alt key. Much more acceptable, yes?

Figure 11-4:
Select the
Erase to
Saved
check box
to make
using the
eraser
easier.

Adjusting your eraser

Though there is only one eraser tool in the toolbox, Photoshop actually provides four kinds of erasers. To switch erasers, select an option from the pop-up menu in the upper-left corner of the Eraser Options palette.

You can also switch from one kind of eraser to the next from the keyboard by pressing the E key. The first press of E just selects whichever eraser you last used. Press E again to switch to the next eraser in the list. Press E a third time to get the next eraser, and so on.

Three erasers are named after painting tools — Paintbrush, Airbrush, and Pencil — and work exactly like these tools, down to the inclusion of the Wet Edges check box for the paintbrush option. This means that you can change the brush size in the Brushes panel and adjust the Opacity setting to partially reveal the saved image or, in a layered image, make pixels only partially transparent. (For a refresher on changing the brush size and opacity, review Chapter 8.)

The fourth option, Block, changes the eraser to the square, hard-edged, fixed-size eraser featured in Photoshop 2.5. The options in the Brush Size palette don't affect the block eraser, nor do the Opacity slider bar or any of the other settings in the Eraser Options palette except Erase to Saved. The block eraser can be useful when you want to completely erase general areas, but you probably won't take it up very often.

Why won't the eraser work?

Just as the Save command messes up the undo process, a few operations prevent the eraser tool from revealing the saved image. The feature only works if the image on-screen and the one saved on disk share the same file size — that is, they each contain exactly the same number of pixels. Any operation that changes the size of the on-screen image throws a monkey wrench into the works.

The following operations prevent you from revealing with the eraser:

- ✔ Trimming the image with the crop tool.
- ✔ Applying the Image Size command with the Resample Image check box selected. (As long as Resample Image is unchecked, you can change the dimension or resolution without causing problems.)
- ✔ Using the Canvas Size command.
- ✔ Applying any of the commands under the Image➪Rotate Canvas submenu (except 180°) to the entire image.

To avoid problems, be sure that you like what you've done to an image before you initiate any of the above operations. Then save the image immediately after the operation completes. This way, you can erase back to the saved image without any complications.

Abandoning Edits En Masse

Sometimes you make small mistakes, and sometimes you make big ones. If, after several minutes of messing about, you decide that you hate all your edits and want to return the entire image to its original saved appearance so that you can just start over again, choose File⇨Revert. Photoshop displays an alert box to make sure that you didn't choose the wrong command; after all, you've been all thumbs today. If you click on the Revert button or press Enter, the program reloads the image from disk and throws away all your changes.

Don't feel bad. I use the Revert command once a day at least. It's a great way to test out changes and then throw them away when they're no good.

You can't undo File⇨Revert, so make sure that you really want to do it before you click on the Revert button.

Capturing the Moment

Most of the time, the Undo command and eraser provide you with all the flexibility and forgiveness you need. But what if you need just a little more? Suppose that you like the way an image looks now, but you may still need access to the saved version, so you don't want to save over it. How do you make it possible to revert to the current on-screen image without saving over the version on disk?

The Take Snapshot command is the answer. Choosing Edit⇨Take Snapshot saves to memory a copy of the image as it currently appears. You can then restore portions of the snapshot later in the game using the rubber stamp tool.

To set the rubber stamp to erase to the snapshot, double-click on the rubber stamp icon in the toolbox. Select the From Snapshot option from the Option pop-up menu in the Rubber Stamp Options palette, as in Figure 11-5. Then click or drag with the rubber stamp on the portions of your image that you want to restore to the snapshot version.

Figure 11-5: The From Snapshot option gives you another way to turn back the clock.

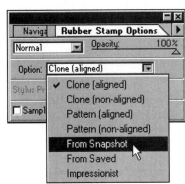

And now for a few other tidbits on this subject.

- ✔ If your image has layers, Take Snapshot stores only the contents of the active layer. That means that you can use the rubber stamp to revert to the saved version of that layer only. If you choose Edit⇨Take Merged Snapshot instead, you can use the rubber stamp on any layer to erase to the visible image. In other words, the rubber stamp "sees" all the layers that are visible. (For more on layers, see Chapter 15.)

- ✔ The Option pop-up menu in the Rubber Stamp Options palette also provides a From Saved option that lets you revert to the saved image, a duplication of the eraser tool's capability. This option doesn't serve much of a function because the eraser tool is equally capable.

- ✔ If you select a portion of your image, as explained in Chapter 12, you can revert only that selection to the snapshot version by using the Edit⇨Fill command. For more on that juicy topic, see the section "Select your stuffing" in Chapter 14.

Don't confuse the Take Snapshot command with the Save A Copy command. Both commands save a copy of your image. But when you use the Save A Copy command, you can't use the eraser or rubber stamp to revert to the saved version. If you want to be able to bring back portions of your saved image using the eraser or rubber stamp, you have to use Edit⇨Take Snapshot or Edit⇨Take Merged Snapshot.

Also, snapshot copies are only temporary. Photoshop is capable of storing only one snapshot for each image. The next time you choose the Take Snapshot or Take Merged Snapshot command, the current snapshot of that image is replaced by the new one.

Part IV
Select before You Correct

By Rich Tennant

"...AND THROUGH IMAGE EDITING TECHNOLOGY, WE'RE ABLE TO RECREATE THE AWESOME SPECTACLE KNOWN AS TYRANNOSAURUS GWEN."

In this part . . .

The first time children arm themselves with crayons and coloring books, they all do the same thing: They scribble. Few children have sufficient coordination to color tidily and, frankly, I doubt that they see much point in it. But there's always one adult who says, "Darling, try to color inside the lines."

It's tough to unlearn a lesson that's ingrained into every one of us at such a trusting age, but the truth is, carefully coloring inside the lines is and always has been a counter-intuitive and nonartistic operation. It defeats expressionism and prevents you from seeing the larger picture.

"This may be so," you might argue, "but what if I'm trying to perform a delicate adjustment to a complex image? I can't just start scribbling all over the place." Ah, but there's where you're wrong. That's exactly what you can do. See, any time you want to constrain an effect to a small area of your image, you should first select it. After you've done that, Photoshop automatically ensures that the larger image remains intact, no matter how sloppy your motor skills.

As you might expect, selecting is the topic of Chapters 12 through 14. Here you find out how to select an element in your image, how to modify the selection if you don't get it exactly right the first time, and how to color selections.

So the next time you see some kids coloring inside the lines, you'll know what to tell them. "Hey you kids, don't you know that tidy people never prosper? Break off the tips of those crayons and start scribbling!"

Chapter 12

The Great Pixel Roundup (Yee Ha)

*I*f you're an old ranch hand, you may find it helpful to think of the pixels in your image as a bunch of cows. A pixel may not have any horns and it rarely moos, but it's a cow all the same. Consider these amazing similarities:

✔ Both pixels and cows travel in herds. Come on, when's the last time you saw one pixel out on its own?

✔ They're both dumb as dirt. And obstinate to boot.

✔ They both eat alfalfa. (Okay, that's a lie. I was just trying to see if you were paying attention.)

✔ Neither of them lays eggs.

✔ And — here's the absolute clincher — you round them both up by using a lasso.

The only difference between pixels and cows, in fact, is in the vernacular. When you lasso a cow or two on the lone prairie, it's called ropin'. When you lasso a mess of pixels, it's called selectin', as in, "'N case you're lookin' for us, Ma, me 'n' Tex'll be out back selectin' pixels."

I'm allowed ta make fun of Westerners 'cause I am one. My great grandpappy owned a farm in Kansas, my grandpappy worked on a ranch in New Mexikee, my pappy once took us campin' in Wyomin', 'n' I've even been on a horse once or twice. Don't know nothin' 'bout you sissy Easterners and Southerners, but I kin make fun of Westerners till the pixels come home.

Dang, how about that dialect? Anyway, after you select the desired pixels, you can do things to them. You can move them, duplicate them, and apply all kinds of alterations that I describe in future chapters. Selecting lets you grab hold of some detail or other and edit it independently of other portions of your image. It's a way of isolating pixels with the intent to manipulate them, just as you might isolate a few cows and milk them, brand them, or just tip them over.

This chapter and Chapter 13 discuss methods for selecting portions of an image. With a little practice, you can rustle pixels better than most hands rope dogies, and that's no bull.

Learning the Ropes

Photoshop 4 provides several selection tools, all labeled in Figure 12-1. These tools include the lasso, the new polygon lasso, four so-called marquee tools, and an automatic color-selector known as the magic wand. Here's how they work:

✔ Drag inside the image with the lasso to select free-form areas. The shape of the selection conforms to the shape of your drag.

✔ Use the polygon lasso tool, which shares a flyout menu with the regular lasso, to draw polygon selections — that is, selections made up of straight sides. In Photoshop 3, you Alt+clicked with the regular lasso tool to draw polygons. You can still use that technique in Photoshop 4, but you also have the option of using the dedicated polygon lasso tool.

✔ The rectangular marquee tool lets you select a rectangular area. Just drag from one corner of the area you want to select to the other. The outline drawn with the tool looks like a border of moving dots — which is how *marquee* managed its way into the tool name.

✔ This use of the term *marquee* has been around for several years now. I suppose somebody thought that the moving dots looked like a movie marquee, but whatever the reason, the term stuck. Computer folks even use it as a verb, as in "Marquee that area over there, won't you Brenda?" "No, I will not, Sam. You can darn well marquee your own areas." These computer discussions can get pretty heated.

✔ The elliptical marquee draws oval selections. The word *ellipse,* incidentally, is what mathematicians say when they're talking about ovals. In fact, I'd just call it the *ovoid marquee tool,* but I'm afraid that you'd think I was talking about a home pregnancy test.

Elliptical marquee
Single row
Single column
Rectangular marquee

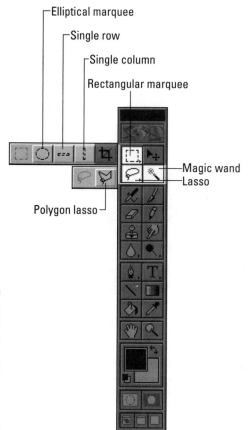

Magic wand
Lasso
Polygon lasso

Figure 12-1:
Use these
tools to
select the
portion of
your image
you want
to edit.

✔ The single-column and single-row marquee tools select one solitary column or row of pixels in your image. Both these tools fall under the limited-use category. In Photoshop 3, the single-row and single-column marquee options resided in the Marquee Tools Options palette. They still have a summer home there, but in PhotoShop 4 you can also reach those marquee options at their toolbox address.

✔ The magic wand selects areas of continuous color. For example, if you want to select the sky without selecting the clouds, you just click in the sky. At least, that's the way it's supposed to work, but you never know. The magic wand isn't always as magic as you may think.

Getting to the Tools

As explained in Chapter 2, the arrow in the lower-right corner of the marquee and lasso tool icons in the toolbox indicates that a flyout menu of hidden tools lurks beneath each icon.

To switch between the tools on the flyout menus, you can Alt+click on whichever tool icon happens to be visible in the toolbox at the time. You can also select tools using these keyboard shortcuts:

✔ Press the M key to access the rectangular and elliptical marquee tools. If the rectangular marquee tool is active, pressing M changes it to the elliptical marquee tool, and vice versa.

✔ Press L to get the lasso tools. As with the marquee tools, the same shortcut also switches you between the two lasso tools: If the regular lasso is active, pressing L brings up the polygon lasso.

✔ Press W to get the magic wand. The tool is more unpredictable than magic, making W — for Wacky Wand — a logical keyboard equivalent.

Throwing Lassos

Both of the lasso tools are so easy to use, your newborn could master them. If you don't have a newborn, I guess that you are going to have to muddle through on your own.

Using the regular lasso

I have only one instruction for using the lasso: Trace around the portion of the image that you want to select with the tool. That's it. In Figure 12-2, for example, I dragged around the mushroom to select it independently of its surroundings. As the figure shows, Photoshop displays a dotted outline around the selected area after you release the mouse button. This outline represents the exact path of your drag. (If you release before completing the shape — that is, before meeting up with the point at which you began dragging — Photoshop simply connects the beginning and ending points with a straight line. So you won't hurt anything if you release too early.)

I was careful to draw the outline just right in Figure 12-2. There's no trick to it; I've just had plenty of practice. If your outlines aren't quite so accurate, however, don't sweat it. There are plenty of ways to modify the outline after you draw it, as I explain in Chapter 13.

Lasso cursor ¬   ┌Selection outline

Figure 12-2:
I selected
the
mushroom
by dragging
around it
with the
lasso.

Drawing straight-sided selections

Consider the image shown in Figure 12-3. Suppose that you want to select that cube-with-a-ball thing in the center of the image. You can drag around it with the lasso tool, but a better option is to use the polygon lasso, which makes it easy to create selections with straight sides.

Figure 12-3 shows a close-up view of one of the many cool and unusual images in the Digital Stock "Cyberstock" image collection, by the way.

To select an object in the aforementioned manner, click with the polygon lasso to set the beginning of the first line in the selection. Then move the mouse cursor to the point where you want the line to end, and click again. Keep clicking to create new line segments. To complete the selection, you have two options. If you double-click, Photoshop draws a segment between the spot you double-click and the first point in your selection. You can also move the cursor over the first point in your selection until you see a little circle next to the polygon lasso cursor. Then simply click to close the selection.

Now, if you paid particular attention to the image in Figure 12-3, you may have noticed that part of the selection is curved. "Hey," you ask, "what up with that? I thought the polygon lasso created straight-sided selections." Well, the answer is that you can switch to the regular lasso in midselection to create a curved segment. Just press and hold down the Alt key and drag to draw your curved line. When you release the Alt key, the tool reverts back to the polygon lasso.

Marquee   Polygon lasso cursor

Figure 12-3:
The new
polygon
lasso tool is
helpful for
creating
straight-
sided
selections.

You can also press Alt while drawing a selection with the regular lasso to access the polygon lasso. Just press Alt and click to set the endpoints of your straight-sided segments, as you normally do with the polygon lasso. To start another curved segment, just drag. You can keep the Alt key down or not — it doesn't matter. But be sure that the mouse button is down any time you press or release the Alt key, or Photoshop will complete the selection outline.

The very clever in the audience may realize that because of this Alt+click thing, you really only need to make friends with one or the other of the lasso tools. The one time when you might really need to switch back and forth between tools is when modifying an existing selection outline, as explained in the next chapter. When you have an existing selection outline, the Alt key subtracts from the selection in Version 4. So you can't use Alt to switch between lassos in that instance.

Exploring your lasso options

Whether you use the regular lasso or the polygon lasso, you can modify the performance of the tool via the two check boxes in the Lasso Options palette. (The palette's called the Polygon Lasso Options palette if you're using the polygon lasso.) To display the palette, double-click on the tool icon in the toolbox or press Enter while the tool is selected.

Though small in number, the options for the lasso tools are some tough little hombres:

- First off, both options — Feather and Anti-aliased — affect future selection outlines drawn with the lasso tool. If you want to modify an outline that you've already drawn, you have to choose a command under the Select menu. Because these commands affect outlines drawn with any tool, I describe them in the next chapter.

- Normally, selections drawn with the lasso tools have soft, natural-looking edges. As I mention in Chapter 8, this softening is called *antialiasing*. To turn the softening off, click on the Anti-aliased check box in the palette to get rid of the check mark. From now on, outlines drawn with the tool will have jagged edges.

- Figure 12-4 shows two lassoed selections moved to reveal the white background in the image. In the left example, the Anti-aliased check box was turned off; in the right example, the option was turned on. The edges of the left example are jagged; those of the right example are soft. (The next chapter explains all the ways to move selections. But if you want to try moving a selection now, just drag it with the move tool, which is the top-right tool in the toolbox. Or Ctrl+drag with any other tool but the pen or hand tool.)

Antialiasing off   Antialiasing on

Figure 12-4: The difference between dragging a jagged (left) and anti-aliased (right) selection.

Jagged edges   Soft edges

✔ Most of the time, you want to leave the Anti-aliased check box turned on. Just turn it off when you want to select precise, hard-edged areas. (Which may be never. Who knows?)

✔ Enter a value into the Feather option box to make the outline fuzzy. The value determines the radius of the fuzziness in pixels. If you enter a value of 3, for example, Photoshop extends the fuzzy region 3 pixels up, 3 pixels to the left, 3 pixels down, and 3 pixels to the right. As demonstrated in the first example of Figure 12-5, that's a lot of fuzz. A higher value results in a more fuzzy selection outline, as witnessed in the right example, which sports a Feather value of 10.

✔ Anytime one of the lasso tools is active, you can highlight the Feather value by pressing Enter. Then just enter a new value and press Enter again to apply it. You don't even have to move your mouse. That's what I call slick shootin'.

Feather 3 pixels   Feather 10 pixels

Figure 12-5:
A bigger Feather value means more fuzzy fungus.

Selecting Rectangles, Squares, Ellipses, and Circles

If you want to create a selection that's rectangular or elliptical, you use — guess what — the rectangular and elliptical marquee tools.

The rectangular and elliptical marquee tools are so easy to use that they make the lasso look complicated. You just drag from one corner to the opposite corner and release the mouse button. (Okay, ovals don't have corners, so you have to use your imagination a little bit.) The dotted marquee follows the movements of your cursor on-screen, keeping you apprised of the selection outline in progress.

But Photoshop has never been one to provide you with only one way to use a tool — or, in this case, two tools. For example, you can also use these tools to select perfect squares or circles. The program's cup of flexibility forever runneth over, and the marquee tools are no exception.

Grabbing a square or circle

Every so often, you may feel the urge to apply some puritanical constraints to your selection outlines. Enough of this random width and height business — you want perfect squares and circles. Lucky for you, Photoshop obliges these fussbudget impulses by letting you constrain shapes drawn with the marquee tool:

- ✔ To draw a perfect square, press the Shift key after you begin dragging with the rectangular marquee tool. To draw a perfect circle, press Shift after you begin dragging with the elliptical marquee tool.

- ✔ Drawing squares and circles is a little trickier than you might expect. For the best results, you should first begin dragging; then press and hold Shift, drag to the desired location and release the mouse button, and finally release Shift. In other words, press Shift after you start the drag and hold it until after you complete the drag.

- ✔ If you press Shift before dragging, you run the risk of adding to the previously selected area, as I describe in lucky Chapter 13. Here's the deal: If a portion of your image was selected before you started Shift+dragging, Photoshop sees to it that that area remains selected and selects the marqueed area as well. Meanwhile, the shape of the marquee is not constrained to a square or a circle. Befuddling, huh? If this happens to you, press Ctrl+Z to undo the selection and try again, this time taking care to press Shift during — not before — your drag.

The marquee tools can come in handy not only for selecting part of your image, but for creating geometric shapes as well. For example, if you want to draw a rectangle, create a marquee with the rectangular marquee tool. Then choose Edit⇨Stroke to *stroke* the marquee with the foreground color — in other words, to paint a line along the marquee. For more on the Stroke command, see "Your Image Needs Strokes, Too," in Chapter 14.

Getting even more control over selections

Are you crazed for control? Do your tyrannical desires know no bounds? If so, you probably aren't appeased by drawing a square or a circle. What you want is to apply even more stringent constraints.

For example, say that you're the sort of pixel-oppressor who wants to select a rectangular or oval area that is exactly twice as wide as it is tall. With your marquee tool selected, press Enter to display the Marquee Options palette. Then choose Constrained Aspect Ratio from the Style pop-up menu, as shown in Figure 12-6. The Width and Height option boxes then come to life, letting you specify an aspect ratio, which is a precise proportion between the wideness and tallness of a marquee. To make the marquee twice as wide as it is tall, enter 2 as the Width value. Then press Tab to highlight the Height value and enter 1. The deed is done.

But that's not all. You can also set up the marquee to select a row or column of pixels that is a single pixel tall or wide. To do this, select the Single Row or Single Column icon from the marquee flyout menu in the toolbox or just select the tool option from the Shape pop-up menu in the upper-left corner of the

Figure 12-6: Select Constrained Aspect Ratio (top) and enter Width and Height values (bottom) to make future marquees conform to rigid proportions.

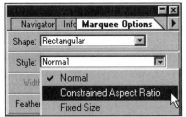

Marquee Options palette. Then click to create the marquee. If you select Single Row, the marquee is 1 pixel tall and extends across the entire width of your image; if you select Single Column, the marquee is 1 pixel wide and as tall as your image. After you click to create the marquee, you can drag it to reposition it if necessary.

Finally, to constrain the marquee to an exact size, select Fixed Size from the Style pop-up menu. Then enter the exact dimensions of your desired marquee into the Width and Height option boxes. The values are always measured in pixels. It's very unlikely that you may ever want to do this — even if you live to be 103 — but I didn't want you to think that I neglected to explain one of these silly options for no good reason.

One last item submitted for your approval: Like the Lasso Options palette discussed earlier in this chapter, the Marquee Options palette sports Anti-aliased and Feather options, which respectively soften the selection outline and make it blurry. However, the Anti-aliased check box is dimmed when you use the rectangular, single column, and single row marquee tools. Perpendicular edges never need softening because perpendicular edges can't be jagged. Antialiasing, therefore, would be a waste of time.

Drawing from the center out

As I mentioned earlier, you draw a rectangle or oval from corner to opposite corner. But you can also draw a marquee from the center outward. To do this, begin dragging with either marquee tool and then press Alt.

If you decide midway into your drag that you don't want to draw the shape from the center outward, just release the Alt key and continue dragging. What was once the center of the marquee now becomes a corner.

To draw a square or circle from the center outward, press both Shift and Alt after you begin dragging with the appropriate marquee tool. (If you press Shift and Alt before you begin dragging, you select the intersection of two selections, as explained in Chapter 13.)

Wielding the Wand

The magic wand is even easier to use than the marquee tools. (Pretty soon, things will get so easy that you won't need me at all.) But it's also the most difficult selection tool to understand and predict. To use the tool, you just click inside an image. Photoshop then selects the area of continuous color that surrounds the cursor.

'Scuze me while I click the sky

Figure 12-7 provides an example of how the magic wand works. In the first image, I clicked with the magic wand tool in the sky above the fake dinosaur. Photoshop automatically selected the entire continuous area of sky. In the second example, I made the selection more apparent by pressing Ctrl+Backspace, which filled the selection with the background color, white. I also got rid of the selection outline by deselecting the area. (Don't worry, I explain deleting and deselecting in full, rich detail in future chapters.)

Notice that the wand selects only uninterrupted areas of color. The patch of sky below the creature's tail, for example, remains intact. Also, the selection bit slightly into the edges of the dinosaur. Very small pieces along the top of the plastic behemoth were removed when I pressed Ctrl+Backspace.

The next section explains how to modify the magic wand's performance to select more or fewer pixels. The section after that offers an alternative to try when you can't get the magic wand to select the stuff you want to select.

Teaching the wand tolerance

You can modify the performance of the magic wand by double-clicking on the wand icon in the toolbox or pressing Enter with the tool selected. Either way, the Magic Wand Options palette appears, offering three options — Anti-aliased, Sample Merged, and Tolerance.

I covered Anti-aliased earlier in this chapter, in the section "Exploring your lasso options," so I'm not going to beat that poor horse anymore. Sample Merged only comes into play when your image contains more than one layer, as discussed in Chapter 15. When Sample Merged is turned off, the magic wand selects colors on the active layer only. If you want the magic wand to select colors from all visible layers, turn the option on.

That leaves the Tolerance value, which has the most sway over the performance of the magic wand. It tells Photoshop which colors to select and which not to select. A lower Tolerance value instructs the wand to select fewer colors; a higher value instructs it to select more colors.

Color Plate 12-1 shows what I mean. Each row of images demonstrates the effect of a different Tolerance value, starting with the default value of 32 at the top and working up to 180 at the bottom. In each case, I clicked at the same location, just to the right of the big giraffe's schnoz. The left image in each row shows the selection outline created when I clicked; the right image shows what happened when I filled the selection with white and then deselected the selection.

Figure 12-7: Look what happens when I click in the sky above T-Rex with the magic wand (top) and fill the selection with white.

In the color plate, a Tolerance value of 32 selected too little sky; a value of 180 selected all the sky but also got some huge chunks of giraffe face and rolling foothill. A value of 90 appears to be just right.

The problem is, finding the best Tolerance setting is a completely random exercise in the futile art of trial and error. Like changes to any tool setting, changes to the Tolerance value have no effect on the current selection. You have to click with the magic wand to try out each and every new value. In fact, here's the typical approach:

1. **Click with the magic wand tool.**

   The point at which you click marks the base color — the one Photoshop uses to judge which other colors it should select.

2. **Express displeasure with the results.**

   Gnash your teeth for good measure.

3. **Press Enter.**

   Pressing Enter while the magic wand is active displays the Magic Wand Options palette — if it's not already visible — and highlights the Tolerance value.

4. **Enter a new Tolerance value and press Enter.**

   Enter a higher value to select more colors next time around; enter a lower value to select fewer colors.

5. **Choose Select⇨None or press Ctrl+D.**

   Photoshop deselects the previous selection.

6. **Repeat Steps 1 through 5 until you get it right.**

Believe me, even longtime Photoshop hacks like me who've been using the software since Copernicus discovered that the Earth orbits the sun go through this ritual every time they use the magic wand tool. What can I say? It's a useful little tool, but it requires some experimenting.

Selecting with the Better Magic Wand

Photoshop provides an even better magic wand in the form of the Color Range command, which is found under the Select menu. This command lets you select multiple areas of color at a time, even if they aren't continuous. Also, you can adjust the equivalent of the Tolerance setting and see its effect on the selection before you apply the command. The Color Range command is a little complex, but it makes the magic wand look like dog meat.

If you were to investigate the Color Range command and its accompanying dialog box on your own, you might mistake it for one of the most complicated Photoshop functions. But deep down inside, it's a pussycat. You just have to know which options to use and which to ignore.

Strolling through the Color Range

Because we're venturing into some pretty unfriendly territory, I'm going to step you through the Color Range command. Just look where I tell you to look and avert your eyes from the scary stuff, and you won't go wrong.

1. **Select the eyedropper tool.**

   You select the eyedropper by pressing the I key.

2. **Click on a spot inside the area you want to select.**

   Use the eyedropper as if it were the magic wand tool. Nothing becomes selected, of course, but you change the foreground color. The Color Range command uses the foreground color as the base color, just as the magic wand uses the color on which you click as the base color.

3. **Choose Select⇨Color Range.**

   The Color Range dialog box shown in Figure 12-8 appears. I've taken the liberty of dimming all the options that aren't important.

Figure 12-8:
The slider bar, the selection preview, and the OK and Cancel buttons are the only important elements of this dialog box.

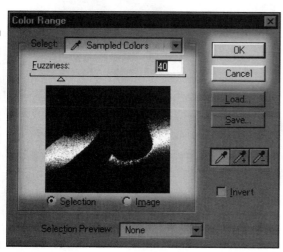

The selection preview box shows your selection in black and white. The white areas are selected, the black areas are not selected, and the gray areas are blurred selection edges (just as if you had feathered them).

In case you're wondering what that big black blob is in the middle of Figure 12-8, it represents the giraffe image shown in Color Plate 12-2. Before choosing the Color Range command, I clicked to the right of the big giraffe's snout.

4. Change the Fuzziness value from 1 to 200 to adjust the tolerance.

As with the magic wand's Tolerance setting, higher Fuzziness values select more colors, lower values select fewer colors. As you change the value, the selection preview box shows you how the new Fuzziness setting affects the selection. In Figure 12-9, you can see how the selected area — in white — grows as I increase the Fuzziness value.

5. Click on the OK button when you finish.

Or press Enter. Photoshop selects the area displayed as white in the selection preview.

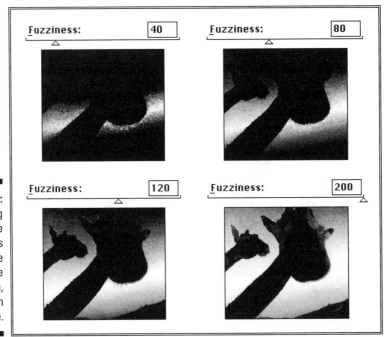

Figure 12-9: Increasing the Fuzziness value spreads the selection, shown in white.

The left example in Color Plate 12-2 shows the result of applying the Color Range command with a maximum Fuzziness value of 200 to the giraffe image. I then pressed Ctrl+Backspace to fill the selection with white and deselected the image to arrive at the right example. The Color Range command selected colors on both sides of the giraffe, even though I lifted the base color from the right half of the sky.

The Color Range dialog box in Version 4 offers an Invert check box, which does the same thing as the Select⇨Inverse command. It selects everything that's currently not selected and deselects everything that's selected. In other words, it selects the exact opposite of what's currently selected. For more on the Select⇨Inverse command, see the section "Swapping what's selected for what's not" in Chapter 13.

If you choose the Color Range command when a portion of your image is selected, the command selects colors only if they fall inside the current selection. Colors outside the selection are ignored. Therefore, unless you specifically want to isolate part of your image to create a precise selection, be sure to press Ctrl+D to deselect the image before choosing Select⇨Color Range. Doing so makes the entire image accessible to the command.

Broadening your color base

Despite the Color Range command's prowess, I wouldn't call Color Plate 12-2 an unqualified success. A lot of blue remains in the second example that the magic wand managed to pick up in Color Plate 12-1.

The fact is, the magic wand and Color Range commands evaluate colors differently (which is why their color-sensing options — Tolerance and Fuzziness — have different names). The wand uses the Tolerance value to decide whether colors are similar to the base color and then selects them. The Color Range command selects all occurrences of the base color in an image and then feathers the selection according to the Fuzziness value. So the magic wand creates definite selection outlines with antialiased edges; the Color Range command creates more nebulous ones with blurry edges.

But there's more to the Color Range command, Horatio, than is dreamt of in your philosophy. Unlike the magic wand, the Color Range command lets you specify more than one base color. After choosing Select⇨Color Range, move the cursor outside the Color Range dialog box and over the image. The cursor changes to the eyedropper, allowing you to change the base color if you want. Press and hold the Shift key, and you see a small plus sign appear next to the eyedropper. Click with this cursor to add a second base color. Continue to Shift+click to add a third base color, fourth, fifth, and so on. Add as many as you like.

In Color Plate 12-3, I specified three base colors. I set the first one before choosing Select⇨Color Range by clicking to the right of the giraffe nose with the eyedropper tool, just as in Color Plate 12-2. I set the other two by Shift+clicking in the image while inside the Color Range dialog box, once above the giraffe's ear and once below its neck (as the cursors in the color plate indicate).

Adding base colors increased the size of the selected area. To make the selection outline less blurry, I lowered the Fuzziness value to 60. The first image in Color Plate 12-3 shows the resulting selection outline; the second image shows what happened when I filled the selection with white and then deselected the selection. Even though the background is now completely white, the giraffes still blend in naturally, an effect that you can't easily achieve with the magic wand.

It is possible to add too many base colors. As a result, you may select portions of your image that you don't want to select. If this happens, you can delete base colors from inside the Color Range dialog box by Alt+clicking on the image. When the Alt key is pressed, a little minus sign appears next to the eyedropper cursor.

If adding and deleting base colors starts to get confusing, you can reset the selection in the Color Range dialog box by clicking on the image without pressing Shift or Alt. This returns you to a single base color.

Chapter 13

More Fun with Selections

*I*n the old days, image-editing programs expected perfection from their users. If you didn't get a selection outline right the first time, too bad. You had to start over and try again.

Photoshop broke this heartless trend by expanding its range of selection options. In other words, it got smarter so that you and I can be dumber. Like all the world's best computer programs, Photoshop knows that human beings are a pretty fallible lot and need all the help they can get.

So Photoshop lets you modify a selection outline after you draw it. You can select additional pixels or trim the selection down to a smaller area. You can even smooth out sharp corners, expand a selection to include all similar colors, or swap the selected and deselected portions of the image. All things considered, Photoshop is about the most flexible selector there ever was.

This chapter explains how to modify an existing selection and also touches on more techniques that you can use with the selection tools discussed in Chapter 12. It also tells you how to move and clone selections and explores a wealth of commands under the Select menu that you probably haven't even looked at yet. By the end of this chapter, you'll have a clearer understanding of selection outlines than any other kid on the playground (unless he or she reads this chapter, too).

The Wonders of Deselection

Before I plow into all that whiz-bang, awesome stuff that Photoshop lets you do to a selection outline, I need to touch on selection's exact opposite, deselection. Though this may seem at face value to be a ridiculously boneheaded topic — one that hardly merits space in a scholarly tome like *Photoshop 4 For Windows For Dummies* — deselecting is actually an integral step in the selection process.

Suppose, for example, that you select one part of your image. Then you change your mind and decide to select a different portion instead. Before you can select that new area, you have to deselect the old one. You can deselect an existing selection outline in several ways:

- ✔ Click anywhere in the image with one of the lasso or marquee tools.

- ✔ To get rid of an existing selection and create a new one at the same time, just drag or click to create the new selection as you normally would. Photoshop automatically deselects the old selection when you create a new one.

- ✔ Click inside the selection with the magic wand. (If you click outside the selection, you not only deselect the selection, you create a new selection.)

- ✔ Choose Select⇨None or press Ctrl+D (for deselect).

You can regain a selection outline right after deselecting it by pressing Ctrl+Z. That's right, the Undo command even keeps track of selections.

Selecting Everything

When no part of an image is selected, the entire image is up for grabs. You can edit any part of it using the paint or edit tools or any of about a billion commands. But you can also make the entire image available for edits by choosing Select⇨All (Ctrl+A) to select everything.

Beginning to see the mystery here? If you can edit any part of the image by deselecting it, why choose Select⇨All, which also lets you edit everything? Because some operations require a selection, that's why. In fact, if you want to apply any of the following operations to your image in its entirety, you must first press Ctrl+A:

- ✔ Clone an image by Alt+dragging it with the move tool, as discussed later in this chapter.

- ✔ Cut, copy, or paste an image using any of the commands under the Edit menu (discussed in Chapter 15).

> ✔ Apply Edit⇨Stroke (explored in Chapter 14) on the Background layer of an image (as explained in Chapter 15).
>
> ✔ Apply the Layer⇨Free Transform command or any of the commands under the Layer⇨Transform submenu on the Background layer of an image. (The Transform commands are sniffed out in Chapter 20.)

Unless you're doing one of these things, you need never worry about Select⇨All. A deselected image usually serves just as well.

Selective Arithmetic

I almost never like the first selection outline I create. Whether I draw it with a lasso or marquee tool, the magic wand, or the Color Range command, I usually have some problem with the selection. I didn't quite get the hair selected right, or that finger is still clipped off. Whatever the problem, I can remedy it by adding to the selection outline or subtracting from it. And so can you.

The last section of Chapter 12 ("Broadening your color base") explains how you can Shift+click on an image while inside the Color Range dialog box to add base colors and Alt+click to delete base colors. These two keys — Shift and Alt — are the universal add and subtract selection modifiers throughout Photoshop.

For those readers who upgraded to Version 4 from an earlier version of Photoshop, I repeat: The keyboard shortcut for subtracting from a selection is now the Alt key, not the Ctrl key as in previous versions. The Ctrl key now accesses the move tool temporarily when another tool is selected.

Adding and subtracting from a selection

To add an area to the current selection, Shift+drag with a lasso or marquee tool. Or Shift+click with the magic wand. It doesn't matter which tool you used to select the image previously, nor does it matter whether you Shift+click inside the selection or outside of it.

For example, in the obligatory person-holding-up-the-Tower-of-Pisa photo in Figure 13-1, I first selected the tower by dragging around it with the lasso tool, as shown in the left example. To add the woman to the selection, I Shift+dragged around her, creating the selection outline shown in the right example.

To remove an area from a selection, Alt+drag with a lasso or marquee tool or Alt+click with the magic wand. To deselect the gap between the woman's legs in Figure 13-1, for example, I could Alt+drag with the lasso tool. To deselect the area under the right arm (her left arm), I could Alt+click with the magic wand.

Figure 13-1:
First, I selected the tower (left) and then I Shift+dragged around the woman to select her, too (right).

Here are a few more addition and subtraction items to keep in mind:

- ✔ When you're adding to a selection, a little plus sign appears next to your cursor. When you're subtracting from the selection, a little minus sign appears. And when you're selecting the intersection of two existing selections (as explained next), a little multiply sign appears. See, your math teacher was right — knowing arithmetic comes in handy in all kinds of situations.

- ✔ You can also use the Shift and Alt keys in conjunction with the Color Range command. Shift+choose Select⇨Color Range to add to the selected area; Alt+choose the command to subtract from the selection.

The intersection of selection and selection

If you press the Shift and Alt keys together while clicking with the magic wand or dragging with a lasso or marquee tool, you select the intersection of the previous selection and the newest one. (Like that made any sense, right?) Take a look at Figure 13-2. I first dragged around the black rectangle. Then I Shift+Alt+dragged around the gray rectangle. Photoshop then selected all portions of the second marquee that fell inside the first marquee and deselected everything else, leaving me with the selection shown in the right half of the figure. That's an *intersection*.

Figure 13-2:
I marqueed the black rectangle and Shift+Alt+marqueed the gray rectangle (left). Photoshop then selected the intersection of the two marquees (right).

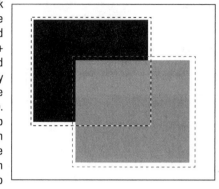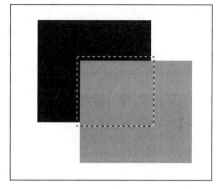

Try selecting an area with the lasso or one of the marquee tools and then Shift+Alt+clicking inside it with the magic wand. Or click with the magic wand and then Shift+Alt+drag with one of the other selection tools. Either technique lets you limit the area of colors selected with the magic wand tool.

As I discussed earlier in this chapter, if a portion of your image was selected using the Color Range command, you can Shift+choose or Alt+choose the command again to add to or subtract from the selection. If you don't press a key when choosing Select⇨Color Range, Photoshop selects an area inside the current selection. In other words, Photoshop already creates an intersection, so you don't gain anything by pressing both Alt and Shift when choosing this command.

Avoiding keyboard collisions

In Chapter 12, I discuss a variety of ways to use the lasso and marquee tools while pressing keys. Pressing Alt while using one of the lasso tools, you may recall, temporarily accesses the other lasso tool. Pressing Shift while using a marquee tool results in perfect squares and circles.

But what happens when you start combining all these add, subtract, and intersect shortcut keys with the ones discussed in the previous chapter? The following list answers your most burning questions:

✔ To add a square or circular area to an existing selection, start by Shift+dragging with the appropriate marquee tool. You get an unconstrained rectangle or oval, just as if the Shift key weren't down. Then midway into the drag — here's the catch — release the Shift key and then press it again, all the while keeping the mouse button down. The shape snaps to a square or circle with the second press of Shift. Keep the Shift key down until after you release the mouse button. Bet you didn't see that one coming.

✔ Pressing Alt to temporarily access the polygon lasso when the regular lasso is active causes trouble when you have an existing selection, because pressing Alt in that scenario sets you up to subtract from the selection. So if you want to add or subtract a straight-sided selection, use the polygon lasso — don't try to Alt+click with the regular lasso.

✔ The same advice goes if you want to find the intersection of a selection and a straight-sided shape.

Automatic Selection Discombobulators

Shift+dragging, Alt+dragging, and all those other wondrous techniques that I just finished describing — and, possibly, you just finished reading about — are wildly helpful when it comes to selecting complex details. But they aren't the only selection modifications you can make. Photoshop offers a handful of automatic functions that reshape selection outlines, blur them, and otherwise mess them up.

All the commands discussed in the next few sections — Grow, Similar, Inverse, Feather, and so on — reside under the Select menu. I don't discuss every command under the Select menu, just the ones you need to know. But you can take it from me, the commands I don't mention are just so much wasted space.

Extending the magic wand

Two commands, Grow and Similar, are extensions of the magic wand tool. The Grow command expands the size of the selection to include still more continuous colors. For example, if clicking with the magic wand doesn't select all the colors you want it to, you can either increase the Tolerance value inside the Magic Wand Options palette and reclick with the tool or just choose Select➪Grow to incorporate even more colors. It's kind of a clunky method, especially now that the Grow command doesn't have a keyboard shortcut, as it did in earlier versions of Photoshop (Ctrl+G now groups layers). I prefer to Shift+click with the wand tool, but every once in a while the Grow command works like you'd expect. (You can use the Grow command with selections made with tools other than the magic wand, by the way.)

The Similar command selects all colors that are similar to the selected colors regardless of whether they're interrupted by other colors or not. In other words, Similar selects all the continuous colors that Grow selects, as well as all similarly colored pixels throughout the image.

Both Grow and Similar judge color similarity exactly like the magic wand tool does — that is, according to the Tolerance value in the Magic Wand Options palette. So if you increase the Tolerance value, the commands select more colors; if you decrease the value, the commands select fewer colors. For example, if you want to select all colors throughout the image that are exactly identical to the ones you've selected so far, enter 0 into the Tolerance option box and choose Select⇨Similar.

Swapping what's selected for what's not

Sometimes it's easier to select the stuff you don't want to select and then tell Photoshop to select the deselected stuff and deselect what's selected. This technique is called *inversing a selection,* and you do it by choosing Select⇨Inverse or pressing Ctrl+Shift+I.

For example, suppose that you want to select the clock tower shown on the left side of Figure 13-3. A typical work of baroque madness, this building has more spikes and little twisty bits than a porcupine. Therefore, selecting it would prove a nightmare.

Selecting the sky, on the other hand, is quite easy. By clicking and Shift+clicking a couple of times with the magic wand tool (set to the default Tolerance of 32), I was able to select the entire sky in a matter of 2 or 3 seconds. Then when I chose Select⇨Inverse, I inversed the selection so that the building became selected and the sky became deselected. To better show off the selection, I filled it with white, as shown in the right example in the figure.

Making the selection fuzzy around the edges

The preceding chapter explains how you can blur the edges of a selection created with the lasso or marquee tools by increasing the Feather value in the corresponding Options palette. But more often than not, you want to leave the Feather value set to 0 and apply your feathering after you finish drawing the outline.

To feather an existing selection, choose Select⇨Feather or press Ctrl+Shift+D. A dinky dialog box with a single option box appears on-screen. Enter the amount of fuzziness, in pixels, that you want to apply to the selection and press Enter. The selection outline probably won't change very much, but you see a distinct blurring effect when you edit the selection.

Figure 13-3:
This building
(left) is too
darn ornate
to select
easily, but
it's a snap to
select the
sky and then
inverse the
selection.
Filling the
selection
with white
shows how
accurate the
selection is
(right).

You can use feathering to make an image appear to fade into view. For example, take a look at the kid-in-a-basket image shown on the left side of Figure 13-4. I selected the elliptical marquee tool and encircled the little duffer. Then I chose Select⇨Inverse to select the background instead. Next I chose Select⇨Feather, entered a value of 8 pixels, and pressed Enter. Finally, I pressed Ctrl+Backspace to fill the selection with white. The result is the locket with fuzzy edges shown on the right side of Figure 13-4. Isn't he just adorable?

Border, Smooth, and the rest

The remaining selection outline modifiers, all found in the Select⇨Modify submenu, aren't quite as useful, but they come in handy every now and then:

- ✔ The Border command selects an area around the edge of the selection. You tell Photoshop the width, in pixels, of the border you want to select. This command is probably the least useful command of the bunch. If you want to color the outline of a selection, it's easier to use Edit⇨Stroke, as described in Chapter 14.

- ✔ Select⇨Modify⇨Smooth rounds off the corners of a selection outline. If the selection is very irregular and you want to straighten out the twists and turns, use this command. Photoshop asks you to enter a value from 1 to 16 to tell it how far it can move any point in the outline. Enter **2** or **3** to be safe.

Figure 13-4:
A tiny tot trapped in a basket (left) receives a classic feathering treatment (right).

✔ If you want to increase the size of a selection a few pixels outward, choose Select⇨Modify⇨Expand and then enter the number of pixels. The maximum value is 16 pixels; if you want to expand the outline farther, you have to choose Expand a second time.

✔ Select⇨Modify⇨Contract is the opposite of the Expand command. This command shrinks the selected area by 1 to 16 pixels all the way around.

Moving and Cloning Selections

Before bidding a fond farewell to Chapter 13, I want to quickly touch on the two most common things you can do with a selection: Move it and clone it.

Moving and cloning work differently in Version 4 — very differently — thanks to the addition of the new move tool, which is the one in the upper-right corner of the toolbox. Here's the lowdown:

✔ To move a selection, grab the move tool (press V to select the tool from the keyboard) and drag the selection. A little pair of scissors appears by your cursor to show that you're about to remove the selection from its current home. When you move the selection, the area where the selection used to be is filled with the background color, as illustrated in Figure 13-5.

Figure 13-5:
After
selecting
the
Washington
Monument
(top), I
dragged it to
a more
convenient
location
(bottom),
leaving a
gaping hole
in the
Capitol
skyline.

✔ You can temporarily access the move tool by pressing Ctrl when any tool but the hand or pen tool is selected.

✔ To nudge a selection one pixel, press one of the arrow keys while the move tool is selected. Or press Ctrl and an arrow key when any tool but the pen or hand tool is selected. The up arrow nudges the selection one pixel up; the right pixel nudges it to the right, and so on, just like you'd think. To nudge a selection 10 pixels, press Shift along with an arrow key while the move tool is selected.

✔ To clone and move a selection, Alt+drag with the move tool or Ctrl+Alt+drag with any other tool but the hand or pen tool. Your cursor changes into two arrowheads — your reminder that you're creating a clone of your selection.

✔ To clone and nudge, select the move tool and then press Alt and one of the arrow keys. Or, when any other tool but the hand or pen tool is selected, press Ctrl and Alt as you press the arrow keys. Press Shift and Alt with an arrow key to clone the selection and move it 10 pixels.

✔ To move a selection outline without moving the image inside it, select a lasso or marquee tool. Then just drag the selection outline or nudge it with the arrow keys. This is a great way to reposition a selection outline without disturbing so much as a single pixel in the image.

✔ You can move and clone selections and selection outlines between images just as you would within a single image. Just drag the selection or selection outline from its current window into the other image window. For more on this topic, see Chapter 15.

✔ Yet another way to move a selection is to use the Layer⇨Free Transform command, discussed in Chapter 20, in the section "Stretching the Face This Way and That." Free Transform enables you to move, resize, rotate, and distort your image by manipulating a special selection marquee. To move the selection, just drag inside the marquee. To discover how to perform other Free Transform tricks, see the aforementioned section in Chapter 20.

✔ When you're moving or cloning a selection, those animated dots that parade around the outline — called marching ants in some quarters — can be downright distracting. Sure, the ants permit you to see the boundaries of your selection, but sometimes you need to see how the edges of the selection blend in with their new surroundings. To do this, choose View⇨Hide Edges or press Ctrl+H.

✔ To bring back the marching ants, press Ctrl+H again.

✔ If you want to see more than an outline of your selection as you move it about, press and hold inside the selection for a full second and then start dragging. This slight pause tells Photoshop to display the selection in full detail as you move it. Your movements may appear a little jerkier because Photoshop has to work a lot harder to display the image in motion, but if you need to see exactly what's going on, this is the only way to go.

Chapter 14
Coloring inside the Lines

· ·

In This Chapter

▶ Painting and editing inside a selection outline

▶ Using the paint bucket tool

▶ Filling from the keyboard

▶ Using the Fill command

▶ Reverting a selection

▶ Creating gradients

▶ Applying different types of gradients

▶ Stroking a selection

· ·

*E*ver spray-painted with a stencil? In case you've never engaged in this riveting pastime, let me explain how it works:

1. **Hold the stencil up to the surface you want to paint.**

2. **Spray recklessly.**

When you take the stencil away, you discover a painted image that matches the shape of the stencil. It's the epitome of a no-brainer.

In Photoshop, a selection outline works the same way. Just as a stencil isolates the area affected by the spray paint, a selection outline isolates the area affected by a paint or edit tool. You can also fill a selection outline with color or trace an outline around it.

Sounds easy, doesn't it? Like an unremarkable bit of information that virtually flings itself at the attention of the most casual observer. Like something you could have figured out on your own, for example, and saved $19.99. Well, whatever it sounds like, I intend to walk you through every nuance of painting, filling, and tracing selections. I reckon that after spending two chapters creating and manipulating selection outlines, it's high time you found out what to do with them. (The selection outlines, that is, not the chapters. You already know what to do with the chapters — tear them out and use them to line the parrot cage.)

Put Down Newspaper Before You Paint

If some portion of an image is selected, Photoshop treats all deselected areas as protected. You can use any paint or edit tool inside the selection without worrying about harming areas outside the selection.

Fix your gaze upon Figure 14-1. This jar-in-a-nook has a certain austere beauty about it — it's just the sort of prop that would feel right at home in a hoity-toity kitchen of the idle rich. But imagine that you are consumed with a desire to muck it up. Specifically, you want to paint inside the jar without harming the background. To this end, you would do the following:

1. **Select the jar.**

   This is the only step that takes any work. You might start out by selecting the body of the jar with the elliptical marquee tool. If you have problems getting the marquee exactly on the jar — it's hard to know where to start dragging so that it comes out right — just make sure that the marquee is approximately the right size, select one of the marquee or lasso tools and then use the arrow keys to nudge the outline into position. After you select the body to your satisfaction, you might Shift+drag with the lasso tool to incorporate the neck of the jar into the selection as well.

2. **Make any modifications you deem necessary.**

   In this case, you may want to blur the selection outline a tad using Select⇨Feather, as explained in Chapter 13. If your selection outline isn't dead on, the Feather command helps to fudge the difference a little.

Figure 14-1:
A jar-in-a-nook is a terrible thing to leave unmolested.

3. Choose <u>V</u>iew⇨Hide <u>E</u>dges or press Ctrl+H.

This step is extremely important. By hiding the selection outline, you can see how your edits affect the image without those distracting marching ants getting in your way.

4. Paint and edit away.

Feel free to use any tool you want. You can paint with the paintbrush, airbrush, or pencil; edit with the smudge, focus, or toning tools; clone with the rubber stamp; or reveal the saved image with the eraser — all with the assurance that the area outside the selection will remain as safeguarded from your changes as the driven snow (or whatever the saying is).

While editing away, be sure not to press Ctrl+D or click with one of the selection tools. Because the selection outline is hidden, you won't notice any difference when you deselect the image. If you do inadvertently deselect, press Ctrl+Z right away. If you wait until after you apply a brush stroke, Ctrl+Z undoes the stroke but not the selection outline.

In Figure 14-2, I painted inside my selected jar using a single tool — the air-brush — with a single brush size and only two colors, black and white. As a result, I was able to transform the jar into a kind of marble. Looks mighty keen, and there's not so much as a drop of paint outside the lines.

Figure 14-2:
I painted inside the selected jar with the airbrush. (You can't see the selection outline because it's hidden.)

This stenciling feature is so all-fired handy that I almost always select an area before applying a paint or edit tool. The fact is, the selection tools are easier to control than the painting or editing tools, so you may as well take advantage of them.

Dribbling Paint from a Bucket

Photoshop lets you fill a selection with the foreground color, the background color, or a gradual blend of colors called a *gradient.* You can even fill a selection with the saved version of the image or a snapshot.

But before I explain any of these eye-popping options, I want to cover the paint bucket tool, which is part selection tool and part fill tool. The second tool from the bottom on the right side of the toolbox (it looks like a tilted bucket of paint), the paint bucket tool lets you fill an area of continuous color by clicking on the area.

In Figure 14-3, for example, I set the foreground to white and clicked with the paint bucket tool on the row of broccoli in the jar. Photoshop fills the broccoli with white, turning it into the rough facsimile of cauliflower.

Paint bucket

Figure 14-3:
The paint bucket fills a continuous area of color with a different color.

To adjust the performance of the paint bucket, press Enter to open the Paint Bucket Options palette, also shown in Figure 14-3. As with the magic wand, the Tolerance value determines how many pixels in your image are affected by the paint bucket. The only difference is that the paint bucket applies color instead of selecting pixels. You can also select the Anti-aliased check box to soften the edges of the filled area. (In Figure 14-3, the Tolerance value was 32 and Anti-aliased was turned on, as it is by default.)

The problem with the paint bucket tool is that it's hard to get the Tolerance value just right. You usually end up choosing Undo several times and resetting the Tolerance value until you find the value that colors the pixels you want to color and no more. Overall, I consider the paint bucket a poor tool for filling areas in Photoshop. If you select an area in your image using the magic wand, discussed in Chapter 12, and then fill the area with color — as described in the next sections — you not only produce the same effect as with the paint bucket, you have more alternatives at your disposal.

If you decide to ignore my advice and take up the paint bucket at your earliest opportunity, you can select the tool quickly by pressing the K key. You know, for bucKet.

Applying Color to Selection Innards

Now that I've expressed my opinion regarding the paint bucket — ick, yuk, stay away — it's time to move on to the essential methods for filling a selection outline in Photoshop:

✔ To fill a selection with the foreground color, press Alt+Backspace.

✔ To fill a selection with the background color, press Ctrl+Backspace.

✔ In earlier versions of Photoshop, you could press Delete to fill a selection with the background color. You can still use that method in Version 4 *if* the selection exists on the background layer *and* hasn't been moved. Otherwise, pressing Delete gets rid of the selected area instead of filling it with the background color. So that you don't have to worry about the possibility of destroying your selection instead of filling it, get in the habit of always using Ctrl+Backspace instead of Delete to fill a selection.

✔ When you're working on a layer and want to fill the opaque part of a selection with the foreground color while leaving the rest of the selection transparent, press Shift+Alt+Backspace. Press Ctrl+Shift+Backspace to fill the opaque area with the background color. (And if all this makes no sense at all, read Chapter 15, which explains layers and transparency.)

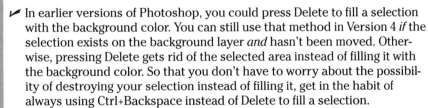

✔ Choose <u>E</u>dit➪Fi<u>l</u>l to display the Fill dialog box, which lets you fill the selection with translucent color or with the saved image or snapshot.

✔ Drag with the gradient tool to create a gradient (blend) between two or more colors.

Two of these options — <u>E</u>dit➪Fi<u>l</u>l and the gradient tool — require more discussion than I have devoted to them so far, which is why the rest of this chapter is so filled to the gills with text.

Fill, I Command You!

Choose <u>E</u>dit➪Fi<u>l</u>l to display the Fill dialog box, shown in Figure 14-4. The Use pop-up menu lets you specify the color or stored image with which you want to fill the selection; the Blending options let you mix the filled colors with the colors already inside the selection. All these options are discussed in more detail in the upcoming paragraphs.

You can also display the Fill dialog box by pressing Shift+Backspace.

Select your stuffing

The most important part of the Fill dialog box is the Use pop-up menu. Here you select the stuff you want to use to fill the selection. The options are as follows:

✔ The Foreground Color option fills the selection with the foreground color, and the Background Color option fills it with the background color. I can see by your expression that you're not surprised by this news.

Figure 14-4: Specify how you want to fill a selection by using the options in the Fill dialog box.

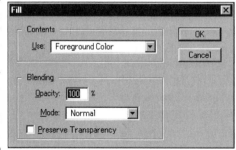

↙ The next option, Pattern, fills a selection with a repeating pattern. To use this option, you must first define the pattern by selecting a rectangular area and choosing Edit➪Define Pattern. If no pattern has been defined, the Pattern option is dimmed. As I state in Chapter 10 when discussing the rubber stamp and will also state now, the Pattern option doesn't serve much of a practical purpose.

↙ Choose the Saved option to fill the selection with the saved version of that portion of the image. Using this option is just like reverting a selected area (as discussed in Chapter 11), except that Photoshop decided to stick it in this out-of-the-way place where no one would think to look for it. This is a great feature, and you'll use it often.

↙ Similarly, the Snapshot option lets you change the selection to the way it looked when you chose Edit➪Take Snapshot. For more about the Take Snapshot command, see Chapter 11.

↙ The last three options — Black, 50% Gray, and White — fill the selection with black, medium gray, or white. What's the point? Not much. If the foreground and background colors are set to blue and orange and you don't want to change them, I suppose that you might find these options useful. And pigs might fly. You just never know.

How not to mix colors

You can enter a value into the Opacity option box of the Fill dialog box to mix the fill color or saved image with the present colors in the selection. You can also mix the fill and the selected color using the options in the Mode pop-up menu, which include Multiply, Screen, Difference, and all those other wacky brush modes from Chapter 8 (and Color Plate 8-2).

Notice that I said you *can* do these things, not that you should. The truth is, you don't want to use the Fill dialog box's Blending options to mix fills with selections. Why? Because the Fill dialog box doesn't let you preview the effects of the Blending options. Even seasoned professionals have trouble predicting the exact repercussions of Opacity settings and brush modes, and it's likely that you will, too. And if you don't like what you get, you have to undo the operation and choose Edit➪Fill all over again.

The better way to mix fills with selections is to copy the selection to a new layer, fill it, and experiment with the Opacity slider and mode options in the Layers palette. Naturally, you have no idea what I'm talking about if you haven't read the supremely insightful Chapter 15. Until then, take my valuable advice and be content to ignore the Opacity and Mode options in the Blending area at the bottom of the Fill dialog box.

The Preserve Transparency check box comes into play when you're working on a layer other than the background layer, as discussed in Chapter 15. If the check box is turned on, only the opaque pixels in a selection are filled when you apply the Fill command — the transparent areas remain transparent. If the check box is turned off, the entire selection is filled. The option is dimmed if the Preserve Transparency option in the Layers palette is turned on.

The Ever-Changing Color Sea

The third tool from the bottom on the right side of the toolbox, the gradient tool, lets you fill a selection with a fountain of colors that starts with one color and ends with another. By default, the two colors are the foreground color and background color.

But Photoshop 4 can do more than create simple two-color blends. You can now create custom gradients that blend as many as 32 colors and vary from opaque to transparent throughout the blend. The gradient tool has gotten a lot more powerful — and a lot more complex — in Version 4, which is why I've broken down the necessary information into the easily swallowed chunks of text that follow.

Checking out the gradient tool

The following steps provide one of those in-depth introductions to the gradient tool that folks find so helpful nowadays:

1. **Select some portion of your image.**

   In Figure 14-5, I selected the jar again. I love that jar. It's so pristine, it just begs for me to mess it up.

   If you don't select a portion of your image before using the gradient tool, Photoshop fills the entire image with the gradient. (Or, if you're working on a layer, as discussed in the next chapter, the gradient fills the entire layer.)

2. **Select the gradient tool.**

   To do it quickly, just press the G key.

3. **Select the Foreground to Background option from the Gradient pop-up menu in the Gradient Tool Options palette.**

   To display the palette, press Enter. The Foreground to Background option is the default setting. It creates a gradient that begins with the foreground color and ends with the background color.

4. **Set the foreground and background colors the way you want them.**

   This step is up to you. You can stick with black and white or select new colors with the eyedropper tool or Color palette. For the purposes of Figure 14-5, I just set my colors to the defaults, black and white.

5. **Begin dragging at the point where you want to set the foreground color.**

   In Figure 14-5, I began my drag at the bottom of the jar.

6. **Release where you want to position the background color.**

   I released at the top of the jar. The result is a black-to-white gradation.

If you Shift+drag with the gradient tool, Photoshop constrains the direction of your drag to a horizontal, vertical, or 45-degree diagonal angle.

Gradient tool

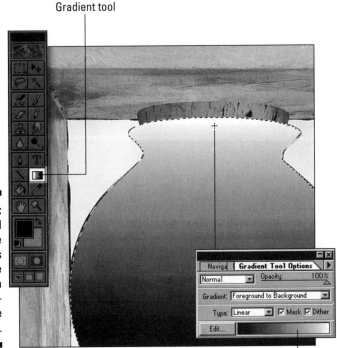

Figure 14-5:
I replaced the vegetables inside the jar with a black-to-white gradient.

Gradient preview

Changing the way of the gradient

You can muck around with the performance of the gradient tool by double-clicking on its toolbox icon or pressing Enter to display the Gradient Tool Options palette shown in Figure 14-5.

Like the Opacity settings and brush modes available inside the Fill dialog box, the Opacity and brush mode options inside the Gradient Tool Options palette are best ignored. If you want to mix a gradation with the existing colors in a selection, create the gradation on a layer and select options inside the Layers palette, as discussed in Chapter 15.

Choosing between linear and radial

Number one on the Important Option Hit Parade is the Type pop-up menu. This wonderful little control lets you choose between two basic kinds of gradients, Linear or Radial:

- The Linear option creates a gradient in which colors blend in a straight line, as in the left examples in Figure 14-6.

- If you select Radial, the colors blend in concentric circles, from the center outward, as in the two examples on the right side of the figure.

- Note that in every example in Figure 14-6, the foreground color is white and the background color is black. You almost always want to set the lighter color to the foreground color when using the Radial option, because this creates a glowing effect. If the foreground color is darker than its background compatriot, the gradation looks like a bottomless pit.

- Next to the Type pop-up menu are two check boxes, Mask and Dither. The Dither check box is easy: When turned on, it helps eliminate a problem known as *banding,* in which you can see distinct bands of color in a printed gradient (that's a bad thing in 9 out of 10 households). Leave the check box turned on unless you're feeling especially contrary and want to create a banding effect.

- The Mask check box is a little more complicated. Here's the scoop: Gradients can include areas that are partially or fully transparent. In other words, they fade from a solid color to a more transparent color. When the Mask check box is turned off, Photoshop creates the gradient using all opaque colors, ignoring the transparency information.

  The best way to get a grip on what the Mask check box does is to try a little experiment. First, turn on the check box and press D to get the default foreground and background colors. Now choose the Transparent Stripes option from the Gradient pop-up menu and draw a gradient. You get a fill pattern that consists of a series of black and transparent stripes. Next, draw a gradient with the Mask check box turned off. You now get a series of solid black and white stripes. In most cases, you don't need to bother with the check box — just leave it turned on.

Linear

Radial

Foreground to background

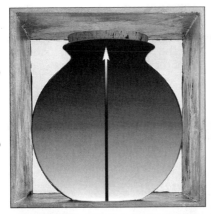

Figure 14-6:
Our jar filled
with two
different
gradient
types —
Linear (left)
and Radial
(right) — as
well as two
different
styles (top
and bottom).

Foreground to transparent

✔ If you upgraded from an earlier version of Photoshop, you may be wondering what happened to the Midpoint and Radial Offset sliders that used to live in the Gradient Tool Options palette. In Version 4, you adjust the offset and midpoint using the midpoint markers in the Gradient Editor dialog box, explained in the upcoming section "Becoming a gradient wizard."

Selecting your colors

The Gradient pop-up menu lets you change the way colors blend inside the gradation and select from a variety of prefab gradients:

✔ Normally, Foreground to Background is selected. This option does just what it sounds like it does, blending between the foreground and background colors, as in the two top examples in Figure 14-6.

✔ If you select one of the Transparent options, the gradient tool blends the foreground color into the original colors in the selection. Both bottom examples in Figure 14-6 were created with the Foreground to Transparent option selected.

✔ The remaining options in the Gradient pop-up menu create a variety of factory-made gradients, some involving just a few colors and others blending a whole rainbow of colors.

When you select a gradient from the pop-up menu, Photoshop displays it in the gradient preview at the bottom of the Gradient Tool Options palette, as labeled in Figure 14-5.

If none of the existing gradients suits your taste, you can create your own custom gradient, as I did in Color Plate 14-1. The next section explains the ins and outs of building your own gradients.

Becoming a gradient wizard

You can design your own custom gradient by editing an existing gradient or starting an entirely new gradient from scratch. To do either, display the Gradient Tool Options palette by double-clicking on the gradient tool icon in the toolbox or pressing Enter with the tool selected. Then click on the Edit button at the bottom of the Gradient Tool Options palette. The Gradient Editor dialog box, shown in Figure 14-7, appears. Uh-oh. Looks like you've ventured too far into geek space, doesn't it?

The Gradient Editor dialog box is a bit complex, and chances are you won't use it much. But I don't want you to feel as though you didn't get the full value for your $19.99, so the following list gives you a brief introduction to the dialog box:

✔ The scrolling list at the top of the dialog box lists all the prefab gradients — the same ones in the Gradient pop-up menu in the Gradient Tool Options palette. Select the gradient you want to edit from this list. Then click on Duplicate to create a copy of the gradient and give it a new name. Now you can edit that gradient without worrying about wrecking the original.

✔ To create a new gradient that isn't based on an existing gradient, click on the New button.

✔ The two radio buttons, Color and Transparency, let you adjust, uh, the color and transparency of the gradient. When the Color button is selected, the fade bar (labeled in Figure 14-7) shows the gradient colors. You can then add, change, or delete colors from the gradient, as explained in the next section.

✔ When the Transparency button is turned on, you can change the transparency of your gradient, as explained in the upcoming (and appropriately named) section "Changing the transparency." The fade bar displays the opaque colors in the gradient in black and the transparent areas in white. Gray areas represent colors that are partially transparent.

Color stop   Midpoint marker   Fade bar

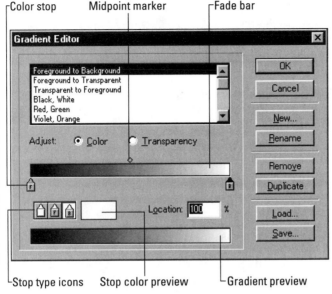

Figure 14-7:
The new
Gradient
Editor
gives you
complete
control
over your
gradients.

Stop type icons   Stop color preview   Gradient preview

✔ The little house-shaped boxes underneath the fade bar are called color stops when the Color button is selected and transparency stops when the Transparency button is selected. You use these stops to change the colors and transparency of the gradient, as explained in the upcoming two sections.

✔ The preview bar at the bottom of the dialog box displays both the colors and transparent areas of your gradient. Transparent areas are represented by a gray-and-white checkerboard pattern.

✔ The Save button saves your gradient to a different location on disk. You don't need to save the gradient using this button unless you want to store your gradient in some spot other than where the rest of the gradients are located, however. After you edit a gradient and click on OK, the gradient is automatically added to the Gradient pop-up list in the Gradient Tool Options palette.

✔ To remove a gradient from the list, select the gradient in the Gradient Editor dialog box and click on the Remove button.

Changing, adding, and deleting colors

To change one of the colors in the gradient, first check to see whether the "roof" on that color's color stop is black. The black roof indicates the active color stop — the one that is to be affected by your changes. If the roof isn't black, click on the color stop to make it active.

After you activate the color stop, you can make one of three choices. Click on the leftmost stop type icon (labeled in Figure 14-7) to change the color to the one showing in the stop color preview box (also labeled in Figure 14-7). To change the color in the color preview box, you can either click on a color in your image, in the Color palette, or in the fade bar.

If you click on the F or B stop type icons, you change the color marked by the color stop to the foreground or background color, respectively. Keep in mind that if you change the foreground or background color, the color in the gradient changes automatically, too. The change doesn't affect any gradients you've already drawn, but does affect any future gradients you create.

Here's some more stuff you need to know about playing with the colors in your gradient:

✔ To add a color to the gradient, select a stop type icon and then click just below the fade bar at the point where you want the color to appear. You get a new color stop icon representing the color.

✔ To remove a color from the gradient, drag its color stop down away from the fade bar.

✔ If you drag a color stop to the right or left, you can change the position of the color in the gradient. Suppose that you have a gradient that fades from black to white. If you want more black and less white, drag the black color stop toward the white stop.

✔ The little diamonds on the top of the fade bar represent the midpoint between two colors. Using the example of a black-to-white gradient again, the midpoint marks the spot at which the gradient contains equal amounts of black and white. To move a midpoint, just drag the diamond.

✔ The Location option box shows the placement of the active color stop or midpoint marker. If you want to be terribly precise, you can enter a value into the Location box to position a color stop or midpoint marker instead of dragging the icons.

When a color stop is active, a value of 0 (zero) represents the very beginning of the gradient; 100 represents the very end. Midpoint values are always relative to the two color stops on either side of the midpoint. A value of 50 percent places the midpoint an equal distance from both color stops. For reasons unknown, the minimum and maximum Midpoint values are 13 and 87 percent. Just thought you might like to store that useless bit of information in your memory banks.

Changing the transparency

Hold on to your stomach — now we're really veering into the land of the propeller heads. Photoshop 4 lets you adjust the amount of transparency in a gradient. You can make a portion of the gradient fully opaque, completely transparent, or somewhere in between the two.

Suppose that you want to create a gradient that starts out white, gradually fades to completely transparent, and then becomes completely white again. In other words, you want to create a variation of the effect shown back in the bottom half of Figure 14-6. Here's how to create such a gradient:

1. **First, make white the foreground color.**

2. **Inside the Gradient Editor dialog box, choose the Foreground to Transparent gradient from the scrolling list.**

   The gradient you want to create is similar to one that already exists, so you may as well save yourself the trouble of starting from scratch.

3. **Click on Duplicate and give your new gradient a name.**

   Photoshop creates a copy of the Foreground to Transparent gradient for you to muck up.

4. **Click on the Transparency radio button.**

   The fade bar now shows your gradient in terms of transparent and opaque areas. Black represents opaque areas; white represents transparent areas; gray areas represent everything in between. The preview bar at the bottom of the dialog box shows you the opaque areas in their actual colors and transparent areas in a gray and white checkerboard pattern.

   When you have the Transparency button selected, the color stops become transparency stops, enabling you to change the opacity of different portions of your gradient. The midpoint marker represents the spot at which the gradient is 50 percent white and 50 percent transparent.

5. **Click on the rightmost transparency stop.**

   In this example, the rightmost stop represents the completely transparent end of the gradient.

6. **Change the value in the Opacity option box to 100.**

   (The Opacity option box replaces the stop type icons and the stop color preview box when you have the Transparency radio button selected.) You now have a gradient that fades from fully opaque white to . . . fully opaque white. Wow, that's exciting, huh?

   It's tempting to press Enter after you change the option box value, but don't — pressing Enter closes the dialog box. The value you enter into the option box takes effect without any press of the Enter key. To switch to another option box, press Tab.

7. **Click in the middle of the fade bar to create a new transparency stop.**

   By default, each new stop you create is 100 percent opaque.

8. Change the value in the Opacity option box to 0 (zero).

You now have a gradient that starts out fully opaque, becomes transparent in the middle, and becomes opaque again at the end. Apply it to an image to get a better idea of what you just created. Heady stuff, eh?

You can also add as many transparency stops as you want and set different Opacity values for each. To move a transparency stop, just drag it right or left; to delete a stop, drag it off the bar. To move a midpoint, drag it right or left.

The Mask check box in the Gradient Tool Options palette determines whether transparency settings are ignored or not when you apply a gradient. If the check box is turned off, your gradient is completely opaque. For example, if you turn off the check box when applying the gradient created by the preceding steps, you get a completely white gradient instead of one that fades from white to transparent and back again.

Your Image Needs Strokes, Too

The last item on today's agenda is Edit⇨Stroke, a command that traces borders around a selection. When you choose this command, Photoshop displays the Stroke dialog box shown in Figure 14-8. Enter the thickness of the border you want into the Width option box. This value is measured in pixels.

In Figure 14-9, for example, I traced a 16-pixel wide black border around the jar. (This is the maximum Width value, incidentally.) Then I swapped the foreground and background colors, chose Edit⇨Stroke again, and entered 8 into the Width option box. The result is a white border inside a black border. Slick, huh? (Oh, come on, say it is, even if it's just to make me feel better.)

Figure 14-8:
Use the Stroke dialog box to draw a border around a selection.

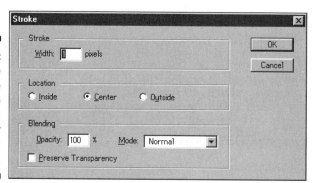

Figure 14-9:
The classic double-border effect, so in demand at today's finer jar emporiums.

How the border rides the track

The Location options in the Stroke dialog box determine how the border rides the selection outline. The border can cruise around fully inside or fully outside the selection or it can sit astride (centered on) the selection. Why might you want to change this setting? Well, take another look at Figure 14-9. Suppose that instead of the white border flanked on either side by black, which I created using the Center option, I want the two borders to sit beside each other. If I select the Inside option, the white border appears inside the selection and the black border inside that, as in the first example of Figure 14-10. If I select Outside, the white border traces the outside of the jar and the black border extends even farther out, as in the figure's second example.

Actually, I don't recommend selecting the Outside option. It has a nasty habit of flattening off the edges of curves, as you can see along the sides of the jar in the second image in Figure 14-10. For the best results, stick with Inside or Center.

Figure 14-10:
Variations
on the
borders
from our last
figure using
the Inside
(left) and
Outside
(right)
options.

Mix your stroke after you press Enter

Like the Blending and Opacity options in other dialog boxes, the ones in the Stroke dialog box don't provide you with a preview of how the effect will look when applied to your image. So if you want to play with the blend modes or opacity of your stroke, ignore the options in the dialog box. Instead, create a new layer (as explained in Chapter 15) and do your selecting and stroking on that layer. You can then adjust the blend mode and opacity via the Layers option palette, also discussed in Chapter 15.

On the off chance that you're curious about the Preserve Transparency check box, it affects only images with layers. If you don't have any layers going, don't worry about it. (Again, layers are explained in Chapter 15.) Even if your image does contain layers, don't worry about this option. It just ensures that the transparent portions of layers remain transparent.

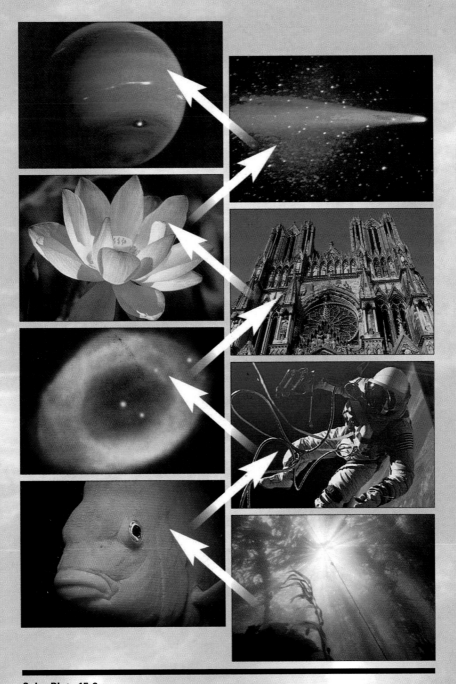

Color Plate 15-2:
The eight images I used to create Color Plate 15-1. The arrows show the layering order of the images, from the kelp (lower right) at the bottom of the heap to the planet Neptune (upper left) at the top.

Normal, 100% Opacity

50% Opacity

Fish: Multiply; Cathedral: Screen

Difference

Color Plate 15-3:
After positioning the cathedral on one layer, the fish on a layer beneath it, and the kelp in the Background layer (top left), I experimented with various Opacity settings and modes. First I changed the Opacity of both layers to 50 percent (top right). Then I returned the Opacity to 100 percent and applied the Multiply mode to the fish and the Screen mode to the cathedral (bottom left). Finally, I applied the Difference mode to both layers (bottom right).

Overlay

Fish: Soft Light; Cathedral: Hard Light

Color

Luminosity

Color Plate 15-4:
Continuing from Color Plate 15-3, I applied the Overlay mode to both fish and cathedral (top left). Then I applied Soft Light to the fish and Hard Light to the cathedral (top right). Finally, I tried out the Color (bottom left) and Luminosity (bottom right) modes on both layers.

Color Plate 16-1:
Photoshop lets you create some wild type effects that are either difficult or impossible to produce in other programs. Some examples include double outline type (top), text with soft drop shadows (middle), and translucent text (bottom).

Color Plate 17-1:
Starting with the original inset image, I selected the dark portions of the image with Select➪Color Range, applied the Add Noise filter with an Amount value of 100 and the Gaussian option selected, and then followed things up with the Motion Blur filter. The only difference between the top and bottom images was the setting of the Monochromatic check box in the Add Noise dialog box. In the top image, it was turned off; in the bottom image, it was on.

Color Plate 18-1:
Don't be surprised if you open up a scanned image and find it looking like the one on the left. The image isn't beyond redemption, it just needs some color correction. In fact, I was able to correct the colors using the Levels and Variations commands in about ten minutes (right).

Color Plate 18-2:
The results of adding blue (left) and yellow (right) to the image using Image➪Adjust➪Variations. Colors that have little or no blue or yellow in them — such as the reds in the bows and the greens in the packages and apples — remain virtually unaffected.

Color Plate 18-3:
Here I used the Levels command to correct the colors in a muted image. For reference, the histogram and Input Levels options from the Levels dialog box are inset with each step. Starting with the uncorrected Photo CD scan (top left), I adjusted the black slider triangle (top right), the white triangle (bottom left), and the gamma point (bottom right) to create a sound image with excellent color depth.

Original

More Blue

More Blue

More Magenta

More Magenta

More Blue

Part V

So, You Say You're Serious about Image Editing

The 5th Wave — By Rich Tennant

"Of course graphics are important to your project, Eddy, but I think it would've been better to scan a _picture_ of your worm collection."

In this part . . .

One of the great legacies of Walt Disney — the man, not the company — was his insistence that animation take full advantage of its unreal medium. He and his staff perfected techniques, camera angles, and character movements that would have proven impossible had the studio been working with live actors and sets. Ironically, these very unreal techniques produced the effect of heightened realism, in which backgrounds shifted on multiple planes, cameras swooped and glided without regard for terrain, and characters moved more gracefully and far more expressively than their human counterparts.

Simply put, Walt figured that there was no point in creating cartoons if all you intended to do was slavishly adhere to the dictates of real life. The same argument can be made for digital image editing. What's the point of going to all the trouble of scanning an image to disk and opening it up in Photoshop if you're not going to take it beyond the boundaries of real life in the process? In a word, none. In a few more words, if you're going to use Photoshop, then there's no reason not to make every image you create more real than reality.

Chapters 15 through 18 show you how. Here you'll discover how to mix images to create breathtaking visual collages, add type to your images, automatically correct the focus of images, stamp images in metal and create other special effects, and bring out brilliant colors that you never knew were there. In other words, you discover how to turn your images into something much better than they were before.

Chapter 15
Layers upon Layers upon Layers

● ●

● ●

*I*nsofar as "high art" is concerned, the heyday for surrealism was 60 to 70 years ago. But the problem with guys like Max Ernst, René Magritte, and even Salvador Dalí was that they never got around to learning how to use Photoshop. Oh, sure, Ernst and Magritte were long dead by the time Photoshop debuted, and Dalí may have had better things to do in his final days than learn a new piece of software. But still, think of what they could have done. A paintbrush is great, but it pales when compared to Photoshop as a means for merging photo-realistic images to create flat-out impossible visual scenarios.

Color Plate 15-1 shows what I mean. No matter how hard you work at it, you can never assemble these elements in a photo shoot. It's just so darn difficult to squeeze a giant fish, the Reims Cathedral in France, and the planet Neptune into the same room together. If you had talent streaming like fire-hydrant jets out your ears, you might be able to paint the image, but most of us would have thrown in the towel at the prospect of re-creating a High Gothic cathedral façade that took a team of thirteenth-century masters 65 years to carve.

But we live in a sparkling modern age, filled with more dazzling masterworks of automation than we know what to do with. Thanks to one such masterwork — I speak here of Photoshop, naturally — I was able to throw together Color Plate 15-1 in a couple of hours. Altogether, the composition comprises eight separate images, but required not so much as a single stroke of a painting or editing tool. I simply selected the images, combined them, blended them together, and erased a few stray pixels that weren't doing the final study in surrealism a lick of good.

Because it can be difficult to distinguish every one of the eight images, Color Plate 15-2 shows each one on its own. The arrows indicate the order in which the images are stacked on top of each other. For example, the underwater kelp jungle in the bottom-right corner of Color Plate 15-2 lies at the bottom of the composition in Color Plate 15-1; the photo of Neptune in the upper-left corner of the second color plate rests at the top of the composition. The image appears as if I cut out a picture of the kelp and pasted it onto a page, cut out the fish and pasted it on the kelp, cut out the astronaut and pasted him in front of the fish, and so on.

Some images are blended together using the same brush modes I discuss in Chapter 8. For example

- ✔ Remember the Multiply mode, the one that darkens colors as if they were painted on top of each other with watercolors? I used Multiply to blend the nebula — the image just below the flower in Color Plate 15-2 — with the fish to create the black eye effect in Color Plate 15-1.

- ✔ The spray coming out of the fish's mouth is the comet from the upper-right corner of Color Plate 15-2. I blended the two using the Screen mode.

- ✔ I blended the Reims Cathedral and Neptune with the images behind them using modes I haven't discussed yet. Respectively, these modes are Luminosity and Hard Light. I explain more about them in the section "Playing around with blend modes," near the end of this chapter.

This is the point at which you ask, "Yeah, yeah, yeah, but how in the world do I pull off something like this?" Well, wouldn't you know it, that's what this chapter is all about. I tell you how to get different images into the same document, how to assign them to separate layers, and how to mix them together using modes and the eraser tool. And remarkably, it's all a lot easier than you may think.

Pasting Images Together

Suppose that you want to paste the fish image from the bottom of Color Plate 15-2 into the neighboring kelp image, as in Figure 15-1. How do you go about it? Here's one approach:

1. **Open the fish image and select the fish.**

2. **Press Ctrl+C.**

Ctrl+C is the time-honored keyboard shortcut for the Edit⇨Copy command, which places a copy of your selection onto the Clipboard. The *Clipboard* is a temporary storage area for image data. Any previous occupant of the Clipboard — sent there via Edit⇨Copy or its close cousin, Edit⇨Cut — is displaced by the fish.

3. **Open the kelp image.**

4. **Press Ctrl+V.**

That's the shortcut for the Edit⇨Paste command, which dumps the current contents of the Clipboard into your image. Consider fish and kelp combined into one. The original fish image remains intact, because the fish you pasted into the kelp was merely a copy.

Figure 15-1: The kelp image before (left) and after (right) pasting the fish image.

But these steps aren't the only way to combine images. You also have these options at your disposal:

✔ To cut a selection from one image and paste it into another, choose Edit⇨Cut and then Edit⇨Paste. The selection is removed entirely from the first image and planted in the second.

✔ You can clone a selection between images by dragging it with the move tool or Ctrl+dragging it with any tool except the hand or pen tool.

✔ This method of cloning between images is known in the computer world as *dragging and dropping,* by the way.

🖊 To transfer an entire image to another image window, choose Select➪All (Ctrl+A) before dragging or using the Cut or Copy commands.

🖊 For a weird but occasionally useful trick, use Edit➪Paste Into to paste an image inside an existing selection, as described in the upcoming section "Filling a selection with a selection."

When you use the Paste command, Photoshop places the pasted image on a new layer. When you drag and drop a selection from one image to another, Photoshop places the selection on a new layer as well. For more on working with layers, start reading at the section "Excuse Me, but What's a Layer?" and keep going to the end of the chapter.

When you use the move tool to move or clone a selection within the same image, Photoshop creates a *floating selection,* which has special properties similar to those offered by layers. For the lowdown on that topic, see the section "Exploring floating selections," which happens to come next.

Exploring floating selections

As I just mentioned, when you move or clone a selection using the move tool, Photoshop creates what's known as a *floating selection.* A floating selection hovers over the surface of an image, as if it lives on its own independent plane. This means that you can move the selection by dragging it or by pressing an arrow key without leaving a hole in the underlying image. Here are a few other things you can do with a floating selection:

🖊 Delete part of a floating selection by Alt+dragging around it with a lasso or marquee tool or Alt+clicking with the magic wand. The part you Alt+drag around or Alt+click disappears entirely.

🖊 You can blend the floating image with the underlying image using the Opacity slider and blend modes pop-up menu in the Layers palette, which I discuss a little later in this chapter. Or press any number key (1 through 0) to change the opacity in 10 percent increments. For example, press 1 to change the opacity to 10 percent. You can also enter a more specific value — say 23 percent — by simply typing the number quickly on the keyboard. (A selection tool must be active for this trick to work.)

🖊 Fill the floating selection using the Backspace key tricks discussed in Chapter 14.

In Photoshop 3, you could turn a selection into a floating selection by choosing the Float command (or pressing Ctrl+J). Although the Float command is gone in Photoshop 4, you can still float a selection — albeit in a rather roundabout way. With the move tool selected, press Alt+↑ to clone the selection and move it one pixel north. Then press the down arrow once to move the clone back into its original position. You now have a clone that floats above the surface of the original.

Setting a floater down

If you defloat the selection, it becomes part of the underlying image. The selection may remain selected, but you can't mix it with the underlying image and you can't move it without leaving a background-colored hole. The following operations defloat a selection:

- ✔ Shift+dragging in the image with a lasso or marquee tool or Shift+clicking with the magic wand. When you add to the selection outline, you defloat the selection.

- ✔ Applying painting tools, filters, and other editing commands, including Edit⇨Stroke.

- ✔ Cloning the selection by Alt+dragging it with the move tool (or Ctrl+Alt+ dragging with another tool). Alt+dragging defloats the original; only the clone remains floating.

- ✔ Choosing Layer⇨Defloat or pressing Ctrl+E.

- ✔ Deselecting the selection by clicking with the lasso or marquee tool, pressing Ctrl+D, or by selecting a different portion of the image.

- ✔ Selecting a different layer in the Layers palette.

- ✔ Quitting the program.

Of course, one day you may have to perform one of these operations. Just make sure that you don't defloat the selection until you finish moving it around and otherwise adjusting it. The only way to preserve a floating selection forever is to assign it to its own layer, as described next.

Turning a selection into a layer

If you want a floating selection to retain its floating properties no matter what editing actions you take, you can turn it into a layer. Discussed in the second half of this chapter, layers are in essence permanent floating selections.

To turn a floating selection into a layer, press Ctrl+Shift+J and name the layer in the resulting dialog box. Or, to create the layer without displaying the dialog box, just click on the new layer icon in the Layers palette (labeled in the upcoming Figure 15-4). Photoshop gives your layer a name like Layer 1. You can also convert a floating selection to a layer by simply double-clicking on the Floating Selection item in the Layers palette. Alt+double-click to bypass the layer name dialog box.

To send a regular (non-floating) selection to its own layer, choose Layer⇨New⇨Layer Via Cut or press Ctrl+Shift+J. Either way, the selection is removed from its original location and placed on the new layer. If you want to keep the selection intact in its original home and place a copy on the new layer, choose Layer⇨New⇨Layer Via Copy or press Ctrl+J to create your layer. To name the layer as you create it, press Alt as you choose the command.

When you turn a selection into a layer, the selection outline disappears. Not to worry; this is perfectly normal. Because the image sits on a layer by itself, you no longer need a selection outline to isolate it. If you apply a filter, for example, it affects the active layer only; none of the other layers are touched.

Filling a selection with a selection

The Edit➪Paste Into command lets you insert an image into an existing selection outline. For example, I wanted to paste the fish behind some of the vegetation in the neighboring kelp image so that the fish would appear to be intertwined with his environment. In the first example of Figure 15-2, I selected an area inside the kelp stalks and feathered the selection by choosing Select➪Feather, as discussed in Chapter 13. Then I chose Paste Into (Ctrl+Shift+V) to create the fish-inside-the-kelp shown in the second example. (Note that I've hidden the selection outlines in the second example so that you can better see the transitions between fish and stalks.)

Photoshop pastes the selection to a new layer. You can then move and blend the pasted image just as if it were a floating selection. It's just that the pasted image is invisible outside the boundaries of the previous selection outline.

You can also paste into the deselected area of an image by pressing the Alt key as you choose Edit➪Paste Into. If I had done this with the image in Figure 15-2, for example, the fish would show through the exact opposite areas of the kelp bed as he does now.

Figure 15-2:
After selecting an area of kelp (left), I chose the Paste Into command to introduce the fish to his new kelpy home (right).

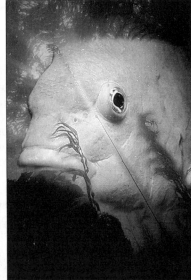

Resizing an Image to Match Its New Home

When you bring two images together, you always have to deal with the issue of relative size. For example, the fish that I've been having so much fun with is too large for its surroundings. Here's how to ensure that the two images you want to combine are sized correctly:

1. **Magnify the two images to the exact same zoom factor.**

   In order to see them side by side, a zoom ratio of 50 percent or smaller will probably be necessary.

2. **If either of the two images appears disproportionately large, scale it down using Image⇨Image Size.**

   In this case, you don't care at all about the dimensions or resolution of the image; all you care about is the file size — that is, the number of pixels comprising the image. If the image you want to copy or drag (Fish) is too large, scale it down just enough to fit inside the destination image. If the destination image (Kelp) is too large, reduce it as desired. Keep Ctrl+Z ready in case you accidentally go too far. (See Chapter 4 for more information about the Image Size command.)

   Be careful not to over-reduce! Remember that you're throwing away pixels and therefore sacrificing detail. If you go too far, you can always restore the original by choosing File⇨Revert, as discussed in Chapter 11.

3. **Combine the two images.**

   Copy and paste, drag and drop, or punt on fourth down.

4. **Position the image vaguely where you want it.**

   For my part, I stuck the fish in the upper-right corner.

5. **Choose Layer⇨Transform⇨Scale.**

   This command lets you fine-tune the relative size of the imported image with respect to its new home. A marquee with four corner handles surrounds the image.

6. **Drag a corner handle to scale the image.**

   Shift+drag a handle to scale the image proportionally. The first example in Figure 15-3 catches me in the act. After you release the handle, Photoshop previews how the resized image will look. Don't worry that the preview is a little choppy; the scaled image will be smooth.

   Don't scale the image up; only scale it down. Otherwise, Photoshop has to make up pixels, which is most assuredly not one of the program's better capabilities.

Figure 15-3:
Use the
Scale
command to
refine the
image size.

7. **Move your cursor inside the marquee and double-click.**

When you have resized the image as desired — you can drag the corner handles all you want — move your cursor inside the marquee. Double-click or press Enter to accept the image's new size and tell Photoshop to work its magic. The resized image will appear perfectly smooth.

If the scaled image looks choppy after you double-click, you probably have a preference set wrong. Choose File➪Preferences➪General or press Ctrl+K and then select the Bicubic option from the Interpolation pop-up menu.

If you decide that you don't want to scale the image before you double-click or press Enter, press Esc to get rid of the marquee. If you already have double-clicked or pressed Enter, you can restore the image to its original size by pressing Ctrl+Z.

Excuse Me, but What's a Layer?

So far in this book, I've made about a bazillion references to layers. By now, you're probably getting fairly annoyed, wondering when the heck I'm going to explain just what the term means.

Well, here's a little analogy to get things rolling. Imagine that you have three sheets of acetate — you know, like folks used to slide into overhead projectors to bore audiences before the days of multimedia presentations. Anyway, on one sheet you draw a picture of a fish. On another, you draw a fishbowl. And on the third, you draw the table on which the fishbowl sits. When you stack all the sheets on top of each other, the images blend together to create a seamless view of a fish in his happy home.

Layers in Photoshop work just like that. You can keep different elements of your image on separate layers and then combine the layers to create a composite image. You can rearrange layers, add and delete layers, blend them together using different opacity values and blend modes, and do all sorts of other impressive things.

Another advantage of using layers is that you can edit or paint on one layer without affecting the other layers. That means that you can safely apply commands or painting tools to one portion of your image without worrying about messing up the rest of the image — and without having to bother selecting the element you want to edit.

Although layers were introduced in Photoshop 3, they play a much bigger role in Version 4. Photoshop now automatically creates a new layer any time you paste a selection using the Paste command. Also, the old Float command, which used to turn a selection into a floating selection, is gone. If you press Ctrl+J, the old keyboard shortcut for floating a selection, Photoshop sends the selection to a new layer, as discussed earlier in this chapter. (I present a workaround to this change earlier in this chapter in the section "Exploring floating selections.")

You aren't restricted to the layers that Photoshop creates automatically, however. You can create as many new layers as your computer's memory allows. In the case of the image shown in Color Plate 15-1, I kept kelp, fish, astronaut, nebula, cathedral, flower, comet, and Neptune on separate layers. Though they may appear to blend together along the edges, they are in fact as distinct as peas in a pod.

Photoshop 4 also lets you create a special kind of layer called an *adjustment layer*. An adjustment layer allows you to play with the color-correction commands discussed in Chapter 18 without permanently affecting any of your image layers. For more on that juicy topic, see Chapter 18.

Finding your way around the Layers palette

The Layers palette, shown in Figure 15-4, is Grand Central Station for managing layers. To display the palette, choose Window⇨Show Layers or just press F7.

Display layer

Blend mode

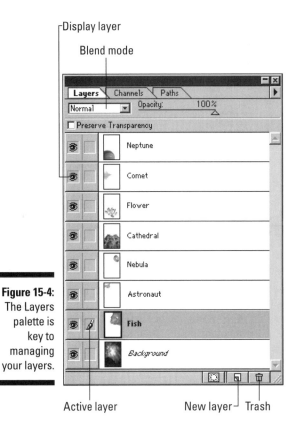

Figure 15-4:
The Layers
palette is
key to
managing
your layers.

Active layer   New layer Trash

Here's what you need to know to navigate the Layers palette:

- The Background layer is the bottom layer in the image. Every image has a Background layer.

- The order of the layers in the Layers palette represents their order in the image. The top layer in the palette is the top layer in your image, and so on.

- You can edit only one layer at a time — the active layer. The active layer is the one that's highlighted in the Layers palette and has a little paintbrush icon to the left of the layer name. To make another layer active, just click on its name.

- Press Alt+] (right bracket) to move up one layer; press Alt+[(left bracket) to activate the next layer down. Press Shift+Alt+] to move to the very top layer; press Shift+Alt+[to move to the Background layer. (If you upgraded from Version 3, note that the old shortcuts for moving through layers, Ctrl+] and Ctrl+[, now change the order of the active layer, as discussed in the following section "Moving and manipulating layers.")

✔ An eyeball icon next to a layer name means that the layer is visible. To hide the layer, click on the eyeball. To display the layer, click on the eyeball column to bring the eyeball back.

✔ To hide all layers but one, Alt+click on the eyeball in front of the name of the layer you want to see. Alt+click again to redisplay all the layers.

✔ If you hide the Background layer, you see a checkerboard pattern surrounding your images. The checkerboard represents the transparent areas of the visible layers.

✔ To find out how to use the blend mode pop-up menu and the Opacity slider at the top of the palette, read the upcoming section "Tending Your Many Splendid Blends" three times fast.

✔ To create a new, blank layer, click on the new layer icon at the bottom of the palette (labeled in Figure 15-4). To create a duplicate of an existing layer, drag the layer to the new layer icon.

When you create a layer in the manner mentioned in the above paragraph, Photoshop gives the layer a name like Layer 1, Layer 2, and so on. If you want to name the layer, double-click on the layer name in the Layers palette and enter a name in the Layer Options dialog box that appears.

✔ Alternatively, you can create the layer by choosing the New Layer or Duplicate Layer command from the Layers palette menu (click on the right-pointing arrow at the top of the palette). If you use this method of creating a layer, Photoshop prompts you to give the layer a name.

✔ If you create a floating selection, it appears in the Layers palette with the name Floating Selection (oddly enough). To turn the selection into its own layer, click on the new layer icon or press Ctrl+Shift+J.

✔ When the Layers palette contains a Floating Selection, clicking on another layer name defloats the selection.

✔ To delete a layer, drag it to the Trash icon. Keep in mind that you're throwing away the layer along with the image on it.

✔ In Chapter 14, I mention that you can paint inside a selection outline to paint just the selection and leave the surrounding areas untouched. But when you send a selection to a layer, the selection outline disappears, so how do you just paint inside the image on a layer? For example, maybe I want to paint stripes on my fish without going outside the lines. The solution is to select the Preserve Transparency check box near the top of the Layers palette. The transparent areas around the fish stay transparent, allowing you to paint only inside the opaque and translucent fishy bits.

✔ For a quick way to turn the Preserve Transparency check box on and off, just press the forward slash key (/).

✔ Just in case you ever want to re-create that selection outline around the elements on a layer, though, Photoshop gives you an easy way to do it. Just Ctrl+click on the layer name in the Layers palette.

Moving and manipulating layers

Layers are flexible things — you can move them, group them together, shuffle their order, and otherwise rearrange them as though they were a deck of playing cards. Here's a look at some of the more common layer-manipulation moves you might need to make:

- ✔ To move an image on a layer, drag it with the move tool or Ctrl+drag with any other tool except the hand or pen tool. To move the layer in 1-pixel increments, press an arrow key with the move tool selected or press Ctrl plus an arrow key with any tool but the hand or pen. To move the layer in 10-pixel increments, press Shift as you press the arrow key.

- ✔ Turn on the Pixel Doubling check box in the Move Tool Options palette (press Enter with the move tool selected to display the palette). This option speeds up on-screen previews when you drag layers. The drawback is that Photoshop displays only every other pixel, making the preview a little blotchy.

- ✔ To link an active layer to another layer, click in the second column of the layers palette — just to the left of the layer name — next to the layer that's not active. A little link icon appears in the column. Now you can move, scale, and rotate both layers at once. To remove the link, click on the link icon.

- ✔ Can't figure out what layer holds the element you want to edit? With the move tool selected, press Alt as you right-click on the element. Or Ctrl+Alt+right-click with any tool but the hand or pen tool. Photoshop automatically activates the appropriate layer.

- ✔ After you get a few layers going, you can move one in front of or behind another by dragging it up or down in the list of layers in the Layers palette. A heavy black line shows where the layer will be inserted.

- ✔ Another way to rearrange layers is to use the commands in the Layer⇨Arrange submenu. Click on the layer that you want to move in the Layers palette. Then choose Layer⇨Arrange⇨Bring to Front (Ctrl+]) to make the layer the topmost layer; Bring Forward (Ctrl+Shift+]) to move the layer one level up; Send Backward (Ctrl+Shift+[) to move the layer one level down; and Send to Back (Ctrl+[) to move the layer to just above the Background layer.

- ✔ You can copy an entire layer to another image by selecting the layer in the Layers palette and dragging and dropping the layer to the new image. The layer is dropped at the spot where you release the mouse button and resides one layer above the active layer in the new image.

- ✔ You can even change the placement of a floating selection by dragging the Floating Selection item up or down in the list.

Flattening and merging layers

Sadly, layers aren't all fun and games. To put it bluntly, they come at a steep price and require some concerted management skills. First, if an image contains layers, saving it in any other format other than the Photoshop format (as discussed in Chapter 6) merges all the layers into one. The Photoshop format is the only format that preserves layers. Second, layers can really slow Photoshop down. To keep running at peak efficiency, it's best to juggle as few layers as possible at a time.

If you want to save your image for use in a different program but you're not willing to sacrifice your layers just yet, you can save the composition to a different file and flatten it — that is, smush all the layers together. To do this, choose File⇨Save a Copy. The familiar Save dialog box appears on-screen, but it includes an additional Flatten Image check box. No need to turn on Flatten Image; just select TIFF, JPEG, or some other option from the Save As pop-up menu, and Photoshop selects Flatten Image for you. Then name the image and press Enter. Photoshop saves the flattened image to a different file; the layers in the on-screen image remain intact. Even the name on the title bar remains unaffected, meaning that the next time you press Ctrl+S, Photoshop saves to the original file in the Photoshop format, not the Save a Copy file in the new format.

But useful as that is, you're still going to want to merge layers every so often to keep your image manageable. Otherwise, operations slow to a snail's pace, and that's an insult to the snail. Slow is hardly the word. Watching your arm hair grow is action-packed compared with working in a ten-layer Photoshop image. We're talking slow like a potted plant here, and a dead potted plant at that. So here are your merging options:

- ✔ To merge several layers into one, hide all layers except the ones you want to merge. In other words, eyeball icons should appear in front of the layers you want to merge. Hide the eyeball if you don't want to merge the layer. Then choose Merge Visible from the Layers palette menu (by dragging from that right-pointing arrowhead in the upper-right corner of the palette) or from the regular Layer menu at the top of the Photoshop window. Or, even simpler, press Ctrl+Shift+E.

- ✔ You can merge one layer into the layer below it by choosing Layer⇨Merge Down or pressing Ctrl+E. You can also choose the Merge Down command from the Layers palette menu.

- ✔ If you want to flatten the entire image and get rid of all the layers, choose the Flatten Image command from the palette menu or from the Layer menu. You can undo the command right after you choose it, and you can revert to a saved version of the image that contains layers, but otherwise your layers are gone for good.

Tending Your Many Splendid Blends

Being able to segregate different portions of your image onto separate layers is a great way to edit one part of your image without harming another. But as image editing goes, this aspect of layers isn't terribly exciting. The real fun begins when you start playing around with different options that Photoshop gives you for blending all your various image layers together.

Fooling with layer opacity

One neat trick to try with a layer is to make it partially translucent using the Opacity slider in the Layers palette. In Figure 15-5, for example, I made the fish partially translucent by setting the Opacity to 70 percent. In the second example, I made him even more ghostly by lowering the Opacity to 30 percent. Whether the image is on its own layer or just temporarily floating, you can use the Opacity slider bar in the Layers palette to achieve this sort of effect.

Opacity: 70%   Opacity: 30%

Figure 15-5: Hey, kids, it's Phantom Phish, the exciting translucent character whose mer-chandising will clutter markdown shelves any day now.

To change the Opacity setting for a layer or floating selection from the key-board, make sure that a selection tool — marquee, lasso, wand, move, crop, or type — is selected and press a number key. Press 9 for 90 percent, 8 for 80 percent, and so on, down to 1 for 10 percent. To return to 100 percent, press 0. You can also enter more specific Opacity values — such as 72 — from the keyboard.

To see Phantom Phish in color, turn to Color Plate 15-3. In the top-left example, both the fish and cathedral are positioned on their own layers, and both layers are fully opaque. In the top-right image, I changed the Opacity for both layers to 50 percent. Sends a chill down your spine, doesn't it?

Keep in mind that the Opacity setting only applies to floating selections and layers. You can't change the Opacity of the Background layer, Kelp, because nothing lies behind it. You'd be looking though the kelp into the empty void of digital space, a truly scary prospect. The same is true for the blend modes discussed in the next section.

Playing around with blend modes

The options in the blend mode pop-up menu in the top-left corner of the Layers palette correspond exactly to the brush modes in the Options palette, discussed in Chapter 8. You have Multiply, Screen, Overlay, and the rest of the gang. These options aren't called brush modes when they're applied to floating selections or layers because no brush is involved. You can call them overlay modes or blend modes; some folks call them calculations. But just plain modes is fine, too.

✔ Multiply burns the floating image into the images behind it, darkening all colors where they mix. Screen is just the opposite, lightening the colors where they mix.

✔ I love descriptions like that, because they make no sense. Pure wonderful computer gibberish. If you want sense, take a look at the bottom-left example in Color Plate 15-3. I applied Multiply to the fish and Screen to the cathedral. Imagine this: The kelp background is a poster on a wall. The fish is printed on a piece of transparent film and tacked in front of the kelp. The cathedral is a slide loaded in a projector and shined onto the poster. This is precisely how Multiply and Screen work.

✔ The Difference mode has no real-world analogy. It creates a photo negative — or inversion — of the blended images according to their colors. Where one of the images is black, no inversion takes place. Where the images are light, you find lots of inversion. In the bottom right example of Color Plate 15-3, for example, the cathedral looks normal at its base because the kelp beneath it is black. The center of the kelp is white, however, so the fish's face changes from yellow to its opposite, blue, and the top of the cathedral changes from light brown to deep violet.

✔ Overlay, Soft Light, and Hard Light are very similar options. Overlay multiplies the dark colors and screens the light ones, as witnessed by the fish and cathedral in the top-left example of Color Plate 15-4. Soft Light — applied to the fish in the top-right example in the color plate — produces a more subtle effect. Hard Light is more dramatic than Soft Light or Overlay. You can still see the base of the cathedral in the top-right image in Color Plate 15-4 even though it overlaps the black area of the kelp. Meanwhile, the base of the Overlay cathedral is swallowed up in the murk.

✔ Like Multiply and Screen, the Color and Luminosity modes produce exactly opposite effects. The Color mode blends the color of the layer with the detail from the underlying images. Luminosity keeps the detail from the layer and mixes it with the colors of the underlying images.

✔ In the bottom-left image in Color Plate 15-4, for example, Color is applied to both fish and cathedral. The colors from the fish are bright; those of the cathedral are muted. But you can see each stalk of kelp clearly because Color doesn't obscure detail.

✔ In the bottom-right image, I applied the Luminosity mode to fish and façade. Now you can clearly see the fish pores and the cathedral carvings, but the color comes from the kelp.

✔ For some other interesting effects, experiment with the Color Dodge, Color Burn, and Exclusion modes, new to Photoshop 4. Suppose that you have two layers, a background layer and Layer 1. Color Dodge lightens the pixels in the background layer and infuses them with colors from Layer 1. Color Burn darkens the pixels and infuses them with color. Exclusion works similarly to Difference; it turns all black pixels white, all white pixels black, and all medium colors gray.

✔ You can skip the other blend modes — Dissolve, Lighten, Darken, Hue, and Saturation. They range from boring to duller than dull, and they rarely come in handy.

Two other blend modes — Behind and Clear — pop up when you have a floating selection on a layer. Few experienced users know what the heck these do, but because I'm such a swell guy, I'll tell you.

✔ The Behind mode slips the floater behind the nonfloating pixels in the layer, much like the fish-in-the-kelp image in Figure 15-2.

✔ If you select Clear, Photoshop turns the floating selection into a floating hole in the layer. You can move the hole around to see through different parts. And you don't do any damage to the image unless you defloat the selection. If you decide not to carve a hole in the layer, just select a different mode or delete the floater.

Just so you know, you can mix a translucent Opacity setting with a blend mode. But you can't select more than one blend mode at a time. It would be fun to combine Luminosity with Multiply, for example — you know, to apply detail that only darkens — but you just can't do it. Oh well.

Erasing holes in layers

If a layer has a lot of weird little flecks in it or some other distracting gook, you can simply erase it away with the eraser tool. When you work on a layer, the eraser tool erases transparent holes in the layer, assuming the Erase to Saved check box in the Eraser Options palette is not turned on. If Erase to Saved is turned on, you can Alt+drag with the eraser to make holes in the layer. Also, the Preserve Transparency check box must be deselected in the Layers palette. If the check box is turned on, the eraser paints in the background color.

Figure 15-6 shows examples of erasing parts of the fish layer. In the first example, I erased around the outside of the fish; in the second example, I erased inside the fish. In both cases, the eraser was set to the Airbrush mode, ensuring soft, subtle transitions between the opaque pixels in the layer and the transparent ones.

Figure 15-6:
Two ways to erase a fish layer, around the outside (left) and inside (right).

Creating an image like Color Plate 15-1

Assuming that you've read through the first part of this chapter and now have some vague idea about how layers work, take another look at Color Plate 15-1 just to make sure that everything gels. Here's the lowdown on each of the layers, starting at the bottom and working our way up:

- The kelp was the base image — the one that I dropped the others into — so it served as the Background layer.

- I reduced the fish using Layer⇨Transform⇨Scale and erased some of the gook around its edges. The blend mode was Normal and the Opacity was 100 percent.

- ✔ In the original astronaut image, the astronaut is missing his right arm and parts of his left hand and leg. So I erased these areas away to create a soft transition. I also tinted the image yellow using the Variations command (discussed in Chapter 18). As with the fish, the blend mode was Normal and the Opacity was 100 percent.

- ✔ I rotated the nebula 90 degrees counterclockwise by choosing Image⇨ Rotate Canvas⇨90° CCW. Then I scaled it to fit the fish's eye and assigned the Multiply mode to it. I erased the center of the nebula to reveal the white of the fish's eye. The Opacity setting was 100 percent.

- ✔ I shrunk the height of the cathedral, increasing the appearance of perspective. Then I applied the Luminosity mode with the usual Opacity of 100 percent. I erased the tops of the towers slightly so that they merged with the fish.

- ✔ Not much happened to the flower. I changed the Opacity to 80 percent, but the overlay mode is Normal.

- ✔ All those little white sparkles come from the comet. I applied the Screen mode to it so that it lightened the image and used an Opacity of 100 percent. Then I erased the tip of the comet to fit it in the fish's mouth. That's Halley's comet again, by the way, but this time it's a 1986 version.

- ✔ Good old Neptune. I reduced this planet to little more than a circle of color by positioning it in the lower-left corner and applying the Hard Light mode to it. The Opacity remained set to 100 percent. I love the way those deep blue columns show through from the cathedral.

Keep in mind that I selected every one of the images before dragging and dropping it inside the composition, so none of the black, blue, or multicolored backgrounds from the original images shown in Color Plate 15-2 were included.

Naturally, I didn't create the image in exactly this order. I'm not that organized, and I might suggest that the artistic process doesn't benefit from such organization. The idea is to just experiment, experiment, experiment until you get what you want. Hopefully, this chapter has paved the way a little, but you can expect to still be in for a lot of pleasant and amazing surprises.

Chapter 16
Digital Graffiti

• •

In This Chapter

▶ Using the new, improved type tool

▶ Entering and editing text in the Type Tool dialog box

▶ Cutting and pasting text

▶ Assigning formatting attributes

▶ Creating outline type

▶ Adding drop shadows

▶ Making your text translucent

▶ Kerning text

• •

C hapters 12, 13, and 14 — known collectively as Part IV — lead you on a merry tour of the various tools and commands for selecting a part of your image. But those chapters skip one other type of selection outline you can create in Photoshop, and you'll never guess what it is. Not in a million years. Give up? The answer is text. That's right, Photoshop lets you build a selection outline out of numbers, vowels, consonants, and any other character you can tap in from your keyboard.

Check out Figure 16-1 if you're having trouble believing me. In the top example, I created two lines of text using the type mask tool, which is a variation of the old type tool from earlier versions of Photoshop. Notice that dotted outlines surround the letters, showing that they're selected. The letters are filled with the foreground color, black. As with any selection outline, I can fill the text with a different color, stroke it, or even paint inside it, as demonstrated in the bottom example of the figure.

The Photoshop approach to text makes it an ideal program for subjecting large letters to special effects. On the other hand, you shouldn't mistake Photoshop for a word processor. After text is on the page, you can't select and edit it with the type tool as you can in other programs. So don't attempt to use Photoshop to create large chunks of text or even medium-sized chunks of text; instead, use a desktop publishing program like PageMaker.

Figure 16-1: Text created with the type mask tool is just a bunch of selection outlines stamped into the shapes of recognizable letters.

To make sure that you understand the gist of the message I seek to convey, take this little quiz.

Photoshop is great for creating text that is:

A. Large.

B. Enormous.

C. Gargantuan.

D. All of the above, only bigger.

The great thing about this quiz is that there are no wrong answers. Everyone's a winner, except you folks who went and wrote in your own answers like "Miserably small and peculiar-looking" or "Itsy-bitsier than a single-celled organism." As long as you understand that the bigger your text, the better it looks, you're mentally prepared to create text in Photoshop.

Two, Two, Two Types of Text

Photoshop 4 provides two tools for creating text: the standard type tool, whose toolbox icon looks like a big letter T; and the new type mask tool, which resides on the same flyout menu as the regular type tool and is represented in the toolbox by a dotted outline of the letter T. To select the type tool that's visible in the toolbox, press T. Press T again to select the other type tool. Isn't it great when icons and keyboard shortcuts make so much sense?

Here's the lowdown on the type tools:

- ✔ The standard-issue type tool creates foreground-colored text on a new layer. (Layers are explained in excruciating detail in the preceding chapter.) As with any other element on a layer, you can paint, edit, and otherwise abuse the text without worrying about touching the underlying image. You can make the text more or less translucent by playing with the Opacity slider in the Layers palette, and you can blend the text with the underlying layers using the blend modes pop-up menu. And, perhaps most important, you can replace or update your text as needed without affecting the rest of the image.

- ✔ The new type mask tool creates your text as a selection outline. You can manipulate, edit, paint, and otherwise play with the selection outline as you would any other selection outline. And because the type mask tool works like any other selection tool, you can use it to add to or subtract from an existing selection outline, as described in Chapter 13. (Shift+click with the tool to add character-shaped outlines to the existing selection; Alt+click to subtract character-shaped outlines from the existing selection; and Shift+Alt+click to find the intersection between the text selection and the existing selection.)

So, which tool do you use when? It depends upon what sort of effect you're trying to create. If you want opaque type, obviously, use the regular type tool. If, on the other hand, you want to create character outlines such as those shown in the top example in Color Plate 16-1, use the type mask tool and then simply stroke the selection outline using Edit⇨Stroke. If you want to soften the edges of your letters — for example, to create a fuzzy shadow behind your letters, as in the middle example in the color plate — you can use the type mask tool and soften the selection outline using Select⇨Feather. (I give the how-tos for creating both these examples later in this chapter.)

The truth is, though, that you can create both of these effects using the regular type tool, too. It just involves a few more steps and a slightly different approach. Similarly, if you want to create opaque type in the foreground color, you can just as easily use the type mask tool and then fill the selection outline by using Alt+Backspace.

In other words, either tool can get you where you want to go. So just remember that the basic difference between the two tools is that one creates foreground-colored type on a new layer; the other simply gives you a selection outline in the shape of your characters. Pick the tool that gives you the quickest route to the effect you're trying to achieve.

The biggest disadvantage of the type mask tool is that when you deselect the text selection, the text becomes permanently fused to the underlying image, making editing difficult. But you can get around this problem by creating a new layer before you click with the type mask tool. Now any text effects you create exist on their own layer.

Putting Your Words On-Screen

To type out a few letters in Photoshop, select either of the type tools and click inside the image. It doesn't really matter where you click, by the way. Photoshop positions your text at the spot you click, but you can always move the text after you create it. (However, if a selection outline is active and you click inside it with the type mask tool, Photoshop simply deselects the current selection. You need to click again to create your text.)

Rather than responding with a little blinking cursor or some other subtle doohickey that you may have come to expect from working in other programs, Photoshop goes all out and displays the Type Tool dialog box shown in Figure 16-2. This dialog box is where you enter your text, format it, and otherwise get it ready for its debut inside the image window.

Actually, when you first click with the type tool, Photoshop may display a message telling you that it's building some kind of font list. This just means that Photoshop is trying to load all the typefaces available to your system into memory. Just wait the message out. It goes away soon enough, and the dialog box appears in all its glory.

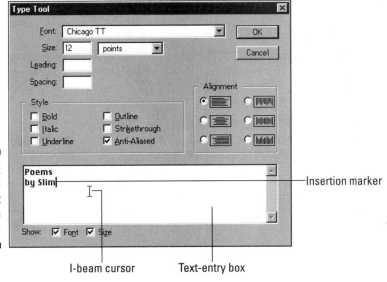

Figure 16-2:
To create
text, enter it
into this
dialog box.

I-beam cursor   Text-entry box

Typing what must be typed

When you first enter the Type Tool dialog box, the text-entry box — labeled in
Figure 16-2 — is active. Here's where you enter the text that you want to add to
your image. If this is the first time you've entered text in Photoshop, a little
vertical line called an *insertion marker* blinks away next to the left side of the
box. If you've entered text before, the previous text appears highlighted, thus
allowing you to edit the text or enter new text. You can do a number of things
inside the text-entry box:

✔ Start typing away to create the text you want to add to your image. If any
existing text in the box was highlighted, Photoshop replaces it with the
new text.

✔ After entering your text, you may find that you've made a mistake or two.
To delete a letter, click in front of it and press the Delete key. To add text,
click at the point where you want to insert it and enter the new text from
the keyboard.

✔ When you move the cursor inside the text-entry box, it changes to an
I-beam, as labeled in Figure 16-2. To replace text, drag over it with the
cursor to highlight it and then start whacking those keys. To delete more
than one letter, highlight the letters and press Delete.

✔ You can highlight a whole word by double-clicking on it. To highlight
multiple words, hold the mouse button down on the second click and drag.

✔ Press the arrow keys to move the insertion marker one letter to the left or
right or one line up or down. Press Shift with an arrow key to select letters
and lines.

✔ To move the insertion marker one whole word in a given direction, press Ctrl along with the left or right arrow key. Ctrl+Shift+left arrow or right arrow selects whole words.

✔ Photoshop automatically wraps words to the next line when it reaches the right boundary of the text-entry box. But it places all words on a single line in the image unless you insert a paragraph return by pressing the Enter key. In Figure 16-2, for example, I typed **Poems**, Enter, **by Slim**.

✔ If the text is too long to fit entirely inside the text-entry box, you can use the scroll bar to see hidden text above or below the visible text.

When inside the Type Tool dialog box, you can access the Cut, Copy, Paste, and Undo commands under the Edit menu. These commands enable you to move text around and undo mistakes. For example, to move some letters from one place to another, follow these steps:

1. **Highlight the text you want to move.**

   Drag over the text with the I-beam cursor, double-click to select words, or use the arrow keys as I described a moment ago.

2. **Press Ctrl+X.**

   Photoshop removes the text and puts it in a special location in your computer's memory called the Clipboard.

   Ctrl+X, by the way, is the universal keyboard shortcut for the Edit⇨Cut command. You can't access the command from the Edit menu while inside the Type Tool dialog box, but the keyboard shortcut works just fine.

3. **Click at the point where you want to move the text.**

   Your click repositions the insertion marker.

4. **Press Ctrl+V.**

   Ctrl+V is the shortcut for the Edit⇨Paste command. Photoshop retrieves the text from the Clipboard and inserts it at the desired spot.

If you want to duplicate a word, you can highlight it, choose Edit⇨Copy (Ctrl+C), reposition the insertion marker, and choose Paste. You can also undo the last edit by choosing Edit⇨Undo or by pressing Ctrl+Z.

Changing how the type looks

The remaining options inside the Type Tool dialog box determine how your text looks. These options control the typeface, the type size, the amount of space between lines, and all that other rigmarole. When all these characteristics get together in the same room, they're usually called *formatting attributes*. You can, of course, make additional enhancements to the appearance of your text after you return to the image window, but the formatting options let you set up the fundamental stuff.

In Photoshop, all text in the text-entry box is formatted the same. For example, you can't highlight a single word and assign it a different typeface than you assign to its neighbors. Therefore, the following formatting options affect each and every character in the text-entry box equally and without prejudice:

✔ Select a typeface and type style from the Font pop-up menu. Assuming that you installed Photoshop correctly — as I tell you to in Appendix A — type styles such as bold and italic appear in their own submenus. But if they don't, no biggie. Just select a typeface from the pop-up menu and set the style using the check boxes above the text-entry box.

✔ In order to successfully use PostScript fonts in Photoshop, you must be using ATM (that's Adobe Type Manager, not Automatic Teller Machine or Arbitrary Toaster Molester). If your text comes up smooth and beautiful, not to worry. If your text is so jagged that it looks like you drew it on an Etch a Sketch — as in the case of Bad type in Figure 16-3 — something's wrong. Either use a different font or consult with your local computer know-it-all to figure out the problem.

Figure 16-3:
If your text looks smooth (top), super. If not (bottom), try a different font or ask someone smart for help.

Good type
Bad type

✔ Enter the size of the text into the Size option box. The Size value is measured in points (one point equals $1/72$ inch or pixels, depending on the setting in the pop-up menu to the right of the option box.

✔ The size of a point on-screen depends on the Resolution setting in the Image Size dialog box (discussed back in Chapter 4). If the Resolution value is 400 ppi, a 36-point letter is 200 pixels tall. If the Resolution is only 72 ppi, that same type is only 36 pixels tall. Talk about confusing! To remain sane, I always set the pop-up menu to pixels, because a pixel is a pixel the world around.

✔ To hop from one option box to another, press Tab. Pressing Tab jumps your cursor from the text-entry area to the Font pop-up menu, from the

Size option box to the Size pop-up menu, and so on. To go backward, press Shift+Tab.

✔ The Leading value controls the amount of space between lines of type. It's called leading (pronounced *ledding*) because back in the old days — we're talking anywhere from the 1600s to the 1950s — printers used to stick pieces of lead between lines of type. Of course, Photoshop doesn't do anything like that, but old terms die hard.

✔ If you don't enter a Leading value, Photoshop assigns spacing equal to 120 percent of the Size value. If you do enter a value, I recommend that it be equal to at least 90 percent of the Size value to keep the lines from overlapping. In Figure 16-4, for example, the Size value was 144 pixels and the Leading value was 130 pixels.

Figure 16-4: Here's how the Size (dark gray) and Leading (light gray) values are measured.

✔ A positive Spacing value adds space between each letter of text. A negative Spacing value tightens the space between letters. No Spacing value — or a value of 0 — just spaces the letters normally.

✔ Like the Size value, both the Leading and Spacing values are measured in points or pixels, depending on the pop-up menu setting.

✔ Select one or more Style check boxes to assign different type styles. Bold makes the text thicker; Italic makes it slanted or cursive; Underline — well, you know what that does.

✔ Don't select the Outline or Strikethrough styles. They produce unspeakably ugly results that will inspire your family to disinherit you, your friends to alienate you, and your business associates to bar you from all future staff parties and reindeer games. I tell you some better ways to outline text later in this chapter.

✔ Always select the Anti-aliased check box. If you turn it off, your text has tiny jagged edges, and you don't want that. (This check box doesn't cure big, huge jags created by the font problems I mentioned earlier.)

✔ Select an Alignment option to determine whether multiple lines of text are aligned by their left edges, right edges, or centers. Don't select any of the options along the right side of the dialog box. They create vertical text, which is just as ugly as the Outline and Strikethough styles I warned you away from a moment ago.

Previewing a few formatting attributes

The two check boxes underneath the text-entry box — Font and Size — control how text looks inside the dialog box. If you turn the options on, Photoshop displays the text using the actual font and size you selected. If you turn the option off, Photoshop displays the text using a generic font and size. Note that you have to select the pixels option in the Size pop-up menu to get a true reflection of your text size.

The effects of the Leading, Spacing, Anti-aliased, and Alignment settings are not reflected in the text-entry box, regardless of which check box you select.

Bringing text and image together

To instruct Photoshop to create your text, click on the OK button or press the Enter key on the numeric keypad. If you press the other Enter key, you run the risk of wiping out the letters in the text-entry box because that Enter key adds a paragraph return. (Okay, a few of you may have noticed that the Enter key does activate the OK button when you're editing the Size, Leading, or Spacing values, but it's best to get in the habit of pressing Enter on the numeric keyboard just to be safe.)

Photoshop then creates your text in the image window. If you notice a misspelled word or some other typographical gaffe, don't attempt to drag over the text with a type tool and edit it. Instead, press Ctrl+Z to undo things and then click again with the type tool to revisit the Type Tool dialog box. Photoshop displays your previous settings and even retains the text in the text-entry area. You're right back at the spot you last left off.

If you created text with the type mask tool and you notice an incorrect character at the end or beginning of a word, you can Alt+drag around the blooper with the lasso tool to eliminate the character from the selection outline. For example, if you typed *Bye* when you meant to type *by,* you can Alt+drag around the *e.* You probably won't find yourself in this particular pickle very often, but it's nice to know all the possible ways to clean up your messes, don't you think?

Declaring Open Season on Type

If you've created your type and it's sitting there selected inside your image, you can do all kinds of things with it, including the following:

- ✔ You can move the text around. If you created your text with the regular type tool, select the move tool and then drag the text or press the arrow keys to move the text, as you would any other element on a layer. (Press Ctrl to drag or nudge the text with any of the other tools except the hand or pen tool.)

- ✔ To move a text selection outline created with the type mask tool, drag with the type mask tool or one of the other selection tools. Or press the arrow keys to nudge the selection outline this way or that.

  To move or clone the text selection itself, use the same techniques you use to move or clone any other selection (see Chapter 13 for a refresher). Drag with the move tool to move the text; Alt+drag to clone the text. Ctrl+drag and Ctrl+Alt+drag with any other tool but the hand or pen.

  In other words, selections that you create with the type mask tool work just like any other selection.

- ✔ You can paint inside the text as demonstrated back in Figure 16-1. After you paint inside the letters, you can use the edit tools to smear the colors, blur them, lighten them, and so on.

- ✔ You can fill the text with the foreground color by pressing Alt+Backspace. To fill the text with the background color, press Ctrl+Backspace. To fill the text with a blend of colors, just drag across the text with the gradient tool. It just couldn't be easier.

- ✔ You can apply a border around your type by choosing Edit⇨Stroke.

- ✔ Before you fill or stroke a selection outline, be sure that your text is positioned where you want it. You can't move the stroked text after you create it without leaving a hole in your image. Ditto with any other painting or editing commands you apply to a text selection outline.

- ✔ Remember that if you created the text with the regular type tool, the text exists on its own layer. If the Preserve Transparency option in the Layers palette is selected, you can't paint or apply editing commands outside the confines of your text. If you want to alter the appearance of the background on the text layer, deselect the check box. (For example, if you want to apply a stroke around the outside edges of your character, you need to deselect the check box.)

✔ To delete text that was created with the regular type tool, just drag the text layer to the trash icon in the Layers palette (for help, see Chapter 15). Or just click on the layer name and then click on the trash icon. If you want to delete text that was created with the type mask tool — and you didn't take my advice to create that text on its own layer — you may be able to choose File⇨Revert, discussed in Chapter 11, to bring your image back to its pre-text appearance.

Every one of these techniques can achieve some truly remarkable effects. Just to show you what I mean, I provide some step-by-step examples that show you how to create outline type and text with shadows, as I promised earlier. I also show you how to create translucent type. For full-color demonstrations of these techniques, see Color Plate 16-1.

Tracing outlines around your letters

Off we go. Today's first set of steps tells you how to create genuine outline type, like the stuff shown in Figure 16-5 and the top example in Color Plate 16-1. You can see through the interiors of the letters and you can make the borders as thick as you please. What more could you ask from life?

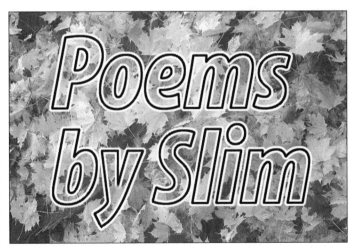

Figure 16-5:
Outline type created the right way.

1. Create a new layer.

You don't have to put your text on its own layer, but doing so makes it simpler to edit the text later on if necessary. To create a layer, click on the new layer icon in the Layers palette, as discussed in Chapter 15.

2. **Use the type mask tool to create your text.**

Click with the tool, type away into the text-entry area, format to your heart's content, and click on OK. Then move the text selection outline into the desired position by dragging it or nudging it with the arrow keys.

3. **Set the foreground color to white.**

You can do this quickly by pressing D to get the default colors and then X to swap them.

4. **Make sure that the Preserve Transparency check box in the Layers palette is deselected.**

In the next step, you apply a stroke to the center of your selection outline (that is, with half the stroke appearing on the inside of the outline and half appearing on the outside). If you don't deselect the Preserve Transparency check box, Photoshop doesn't let you paint outside the selection outline.

5. **Choose Edit⇨Stroke, select the Center radio button, and enter 12 as the Width value.**

After making your selections in the Stroke dialog box, press Enter. You now have a 12-pixel thick, white outline around your type.

6. **Make black or some other dark color the foreground color.**

To create the top example in Color Plate 16-1, I changed the foreground color to red.

7. **Choose Edit⇨Stroke and enter 4 as the Width value.**

Then press Enter. Congratulations, you have now arrived at the effect shown in Figure 16-5 and the top of Color Plate 16-1. If you created your text on a layer, as I heartily recommended back in Step 1, you can use the move tool to reposition the text if needed. (Be sure to press Ctrl+D to deselect the text first.) You can also play with the blend modes and Opacity slider in the Layers palette to change how the text blends with the underlying image.

Adding shadows behind your letters

In these steps, you create letters with shadows, as shown in Figure 16-6 and the second example in Color Plate 16-1. These kinds of shadows are commonly called *drop shadows* because they don't extend away from the letters; instead, they merely rest behind the letters.

1. **Create a new layer.**

Always a good step when creating text with the type mask tool.

2. **Create and format your text using the type mask tool.**

Blah de blah de blah. (In other words, do what needs to be done, Bucko.)

3. Position the outline where you want the text shadow to appear.

Put the outline a little down and to the right of where you want the foreground text.

4. Choose Select⇨Feather.

The Feather command softens the selection outline to give your shadow a fuzzy, shadowlike effect. Use a fairly high Feather value, such as 10. Press Enter to exit the Feather dialog box.

5. Set the foreground color to black.

To do it quickly, press D.

6. Press Alt+Backspace.

Photoshop fills the selection with black.

7. Click with the type mask tool again.

Up pops the Type Tool dialog box again. You want to use the same text as before, so don't change anything. Just click on OK.

8. Use the arrow keys to position the selection outline with respect to the shadow.

Position the outline above and to the left of the shadow.

9. Change the foreground color to white.

Press X to get there quickly.

10. Press Alt+Backspace.

Photoshop fills the selection with white.

11. **Change the foreground color to medium gray or some other medium color.**

    In Color Plate 16-1, I used purple. This color is for the soft shading inside the letters.

12. **Paint a couple of streaks across the letters with the airbrush tool.**

    If it helps to hide the marching ants around the letters, press Ctrl+H. You now have something resembling the image shown in Figure 16-6 and in the middle of Color Plate 16-1.

Turning your letters into ghosts of their former selves

This last set of steps explains how to create translucent letters, which are just the ticket for creating ghosted or tinted text, as shown in Figure 16-7 and the third example in Color Plate 16-1. You might think that this effect would be rather difficult, but in truth, it's way easier than the previous techniques.

1. **Start with a light background.**

   I lightened my leaves a little to achieve Figure 16-7. (I explain how to adjust the colors in your image in Chapter 18.)

2. **Change your foreground color to something dark.**

   In Figure 16-7, I used black, one of your darker colors. In Color Plate 16-1, I opted for dark orange.

3. **Select the regular type tool and create your text.**

   Photoshop creates type in the background color and places it on a new layer.

4. **Drag or nudge the text into position using the move tool.**

5. **Press a number key.**

   When you're working with a layer, pressing a number key changes the opacity of the layer. Higher numbers make the selection more opaque; lower numbers make it more transparent. Chapter 15 explains all of this in more detail, but for now, just press the number keys until you get the effect you want. (You can also drag the Opacity slider in the Layers palette, if you prefer.)

6. **Deselect the Preserve Transparency check box in the Layers palette.**

   This allows you to paint the areas around the letters on the text layer, which you do two steps from now.

Figure 16-7:
Translucent
text is the
picture of
subtlety and
good taste,
especially
when you're
creating the
title for a
book of
cowboy
poetry like
this one.

7. **Select the airbrush tool and set the brush mode to Behind.**

   Press A to get the airbrush, press Enter to open the Airbrush options palette, and select the Behind mode from the brush mode pop-up menu in the palette. The Behind mode lets you paint behind the existing elements on a layer, which you do one step from now.

8. **Set the foreground color to white and take a couple of swipes at the background with the airbrush.**

   Ooh, isn't that pretty. I can't decide whether it looks more like the title for a wedding invitation, a soap opera, or a wake, but it sure is pretty.

Keep in mind that you can apply any of the techniques in the preceding three sets of steps to any layer as well as to text created with the type tools.

Moving and Deleting Characters

I would be remiss in my duties if I failed to pass along one last tip before I tuck in this chapter and tell the bedbugs not to bite. After you exit the Type Tool dialog box, Photoshop lets you manually adjust the amount of space between letters. This kind of letter spacing adjustment is sometimes called *kerning* by folks who have enough time on their hands to go around inventing new and weird-sounding words.

You can only kern characters in text that exists on its own layer. In other words, if you used the type mask tool to create your text and you didn't create that text on a new layer, as I advise earlier in this chapter, you're stuck. Moving the characters leaves a background-colored hole in your image. So does deleting the characters.

If your text does exist on its own layer, kerning is a cinch. First, select the characters you want to kern with the lasso tool. Shift+drag to add additional characters to the selection. Then Ctrl+drag the letters (pressing Ctrl activates the move tool, which enables you to drag the text). Alternatively, you can press Ctrl and press the arrow keys to move the characters in 1-pixel increments. Press Shift as you press the arrow keys to nudge the selected characters in 10-pixel jumps.

If you want to delete characters instead of moving them, use the lasso tool to select the characters to be terminated and just press Delete. Those characters vanish in a puff of electronic smoke. Remember that you only want to delete characters in this way when they exist on an independent layer — otherwise, you end up cutting holes in your image.

Chapter 17

Forays into Filters

*I*f you're a photographer or you've taken a photography course or two, you know how photographic filters work. They refine or refract light to modify the image as it comes into the camera. A daylight filter strains some of the blue out of the image; a polarization lens eliminates reflected light; a fish-eye lens refracts peripheral imagery into the photo.

But real-life filters present a couple of problems. First, they're a nuisance. They take up a ton of room in your camera bag, they generally bang around and get scratched, and you never know when you're going to contract a sudden case of butterfingers and drop a lens on a marble floor. Second, you have to decide which filter you want to use while shooting the photo. Not only is it difficult to experiment through a viewfinder, whatever decision you ultimately make is permanent. If you go with a fish-eye lens, you can't go back and "undistort" the image later.

The Photoshop filters are another story entirely:

✔ All filters reside under a single menu (called Filter, surprisingly enough).

✔ You can immediately undo a filter if you don't like the results.

✔ You can preview the outcome of the most common filters.

✔ You can apply several filters in a row and even go back and revisit a single filter multiple times.

✔ Most Photoshop filters have no real-world counterparts, which means that you can modify images in ways that simply aren't possible inside a camera.

If you're a photographer, you may want to forego a few of your camera's filters and take up Photoshop filters instead. Granted, you may still want to use corrective lenses to adjust color and keep out reflected light, but avoid any special-effects filter that makes the image look like more than what your eyes can see. Such filters merely limit the range of effects you can apply later inside Photoshop.

If you aren't a photographer, filters open up a whole new range of opportunities that no other Photoshop function quite matches. They apply changes automatically, so there's no advantage to being an artist (although an artistic vision certainly comes in handy). Filters can make poor images look better and good images look fantastic. And you can use them to introduce special effects, such as camera movement and relief textures. Frankly, filters turn Photoshop into a lean, mean, photo-munching machine. In a good way, of course.

Photoshop 4 brings you 48 new filters, for a whopping total of 90 filters altogether. (The new effects formerly were available as a stand-alone product, Adobe Gallery Effects.) This chapter doesn't even start to cover all the Photoshop filters, just those that you're likely to use on a regular basis. To see some of the others in action, check out Chapter 20, "Ten Amusing Ways to Mess Up a Loved One's Face."

A Few Fast Filter Facts

Before I launch into explanations of Photoshop filters, I want to share a few introductory facts:

✔ If some portion of your image is selected, the filter affects the selection and leaves the rest of the image unmodified. If no portion of the image is selected, the filter affects the entire image.

✔ To create smooth transitions between filtered and unfiltered areas in an image, blur the selection outline by choosing Select⇨Feather, as discussed in Chapter 13.

✔ After you apply a filter, you can reapply it in the very same manner by choosing the first command in the Filter menu or by pressing Ctrl+F.

✔ Some filters display a dialog box so that you can control how the filter is applied. If the last filter was one of these, press Ctrl+Alt+F to redisplay the dialog box and apply the filter again using different settings.

✔ The section "Previewing the filter effects" in Chapter 10 explains how to use the preview options and other controls inside filter dialog boxes.

✔ To undo the last filter, press Ctrl+Z. Unlike a canceled filter, the undone filter remains at the top of the Filter menu, so you can later apply it by pressing Ctrl+F.

✔ Some filters take a few seconds or even minutes to apply. You can cancel such a filter in progress by pressing Esc. The name of the previous filter remains at the top of the Filter menu, so you can't press Ctrl+F to apply a canceled filter.

✔ Before applying two or more filters in a row, save your image just to be safe. You can restore the saved image if you don't like the results.

✔ In Photoshop 3, you could blend a filtered image with the unfiltered original by taking advantage of the Float command. The Float command is gone in Photoshop 4, as I discuss in Chapter 15. But Version 4 offers the Fade command, which is designed specifically for blending a filtered image with its unmolested twin. If you choose Filter⇨Fade or press Ctrl+Shift+F immediately after applying a filter, the dialog box shown in Figure 17-1 appears, enabling you to play with the Opacity and blend mode of the filtered image. This command enables you to create all sorts of variations on a filter, as illustrated in Figure 17-2.

✔ Remember, you have to apply the Fade command *immediately* after you apply the filter. If you choose another command or apply a painting or editing tool to the image, you can't use the Fade command.

Figure 17-1:
The new
Fade
command
lets you
blend a
filtered
image with
the
unfiltered
original.

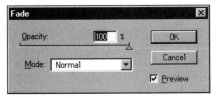

Figure 17-2:
A dapper gentleman takes on a new look after I apply the Fresco filter once. Applying the Fade command with a 60 percent Opacity setting and with the Darken blend mode creates variations on the effect.

Original Fresco

Opacity 60% Opacity 60%, darken

How to Fortify Those Wishy-Washy Details

No matter how you acquired an image or how good it looked before you scanned it, chances are better than even that it appears a little out of focus on-screen. Not necessarily blurry, but a bit soft.

The image in Figure 17-3, from which I captured a subject for Figure 17-2, is an exaggerated example. Snapped around the time Stonehenge was built — well, around the time of the Magna Carta, then — this photo has suffered the cruel scourges of time. It probably wasn't that sharply focused in the first place, but lo these many years later, it looks so soft you'd swear that it was sculpted out of Jell-O.

The solutions to softness are the four commands under the Filter⇨Sharpen submenu. The following sections explain how these filters work and when — if ever — to apply them.

Figure 17-3:
Antique
images
such as this
one are
notoriously
soft on
focus.

The single-shot sharpeners

The first three sharpening filters — Sharpen, Sharpen Edges, and Sharpen More — are what I call single-shot filters. You choose them, and they do their work without complex dialog boxes or other means of digital interrogation. These filters, with their straightforward names, are a breeze to use.

Unfortunately, when it comes to Photoshop, you get back what you put in — mentally, that is. In other words, if you don't have to work at it, it's liable to deliver rather mediocre results. As demonstrated in Figure 17-4, all three of these Sharpen filters sharpen, but none satisfactorily remedies the image's focus problems.

Figure 17-4 shows the results of applying each of the three single-shot sharpeners to a detail from the image. In each case, I applied the filter once — as shown in the middle row — and then a second time — as shown in the last row. For the record, here's what each of the filters do:

Sharpen   Sharpen more   Sharpen Edges

Figure 17-4: The effects of applying each of the single-shot sharpeners are shockingly shabby.

✔ Filter➪Sharpen➪Sharpen enhances the focus of the image very slightly. If the photo is already well focused but needs a little extra fortification to make it perfect, the Sharpen filter does the trick. Otherwise, forget it.

✔ The Sharpen More filter enhances focus more dramatically. Although it's easily the most useful of the three single-shooters, it's still fairly crude. For example, the center image in Figure 17-4 is not sharp enough, while the bottom image is so sharp that little flecks — called *artifacts* — are starting to form in the woman's dress. Boo, hiss.

✔ The Sharpen Edges filter is a complete waste of time. It sharpens the so-called edges of an image without sharpening any of the neutral areas in between. In the figure, for example, the filter sharpens the outline of the guy's face but ignores the interior of his jacket. The result is an inconsistent effect that eventually frays the edges and leaves nonedges looking goopy by comparison.

As you may have gathered by now, I'm not a big fan of these filters. Still, you may want to go ahead and apply Sharpen or Sharpen More to an image to see whether it does the trick or not. If a single-shot sharpener turns out to be all you need, great. If not, undo the effect (press Ctrl+Z) and try out the Unsharp Mask command, explained next. It's a little scarier, but it works like a dream.

Unsharp Mask: The filter with a weird name

If the Photoshop programmers had been in charge of naming Superman, they would have called him "Average Guy from Krypton." Rather than describing what the guy does, the programmers describe his origins. I say this because that's exactly what they did with Filter⇨Sharpen⇨Unsharp Mask. Rather than calling the filter "Supersharpen," which would have made a modicum of sense and may have even encouraged a few novices to give it a try, they named it after a 40-year-old stat camera technique that a few professionals in lab coats pretend to understand in order to impress members of the opposite sex.

So forget Unsharp Mask and just think "Supersharpen." To use the "Supersharpen" command, choose Filter⇨Sharpen⇨Unsharp Mask. The "Supersharpen" dialog box appears, as shown in Figure 17-5.

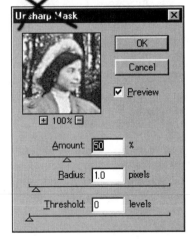

Figure 17-5: Experts agree that the Unsharp Mask dialog box really should be called the Supersharpen dialog box.

Inside the "Supersharpen" dialog box

Like the Dust & Scratches dialog box that I discuss in Chapter 10, the one from Figure 17-5 allows you to preview what happens when you change the values in the three option boxes. You can preview the filter both inside the dialog box and in the main image window. If you can't quite remember how these previewing functions work, skim through the "Previewing the filter effects" section of Chapter 10.

From the people who brought you the uncola nut ...

For those of you who are the least bit interested, an unsharp mask is not a fuzzy disguise that you wear on Halloween. Here's how it used to work: A negative version of an image was shot out of focus — hence, the "unsharp" part. The negative was then used to mask off portions of the original image, much like a stencil. Believe it or not, this soft mask sharpened the edges of the original without significantly sharpening the graininess — just the ticket for Figure 17-3.

Any technique that makes this little sense must have been an accident, and unsharp masking was no exception. It was developed to prevent alignment problems; the sharpening effect was pure coincidence.

To sharpen an image, use the three slider bars like so:

- ✔ Change the Amount value from 1 to 500 percent to change the amount of sharpening. This may strike you as obvious, but just to be sure, higher Amount values produce more sharpening.

- ✔ Adjust the Radius value to specify the width of the edges you want to sharpen. If the image is generally in good shape, use a Radius of 0.5. If the edges are soft and syrupy, like the ones in Figure 17-3, use a Radius of 1.0. And if the edges are almost nonexistent, go with 2.0. Generally speaking, you won't want to go any lower than 0.5 or any higher than 2.0 (though 250.0 is the maximum).

- ✔ You don't have to enter **1.0** or **2.0** into the Radius option box. A simple 1 or 2 will suffice. It's just that you can enter $1/10$ values — such as 1.1 and 1.9 — if you're in a particularly precise mood.

- ✔ As with the Threshold option in the Dust & Scratches dialog box, the Unsharp Mask Threshold option determines how different two neighboring pixels must be to be considered an edge. (See Chapter 10 for a review of this concept.) The default value of 0 tells Photoshop to sharpen everything. By raising the value, you tell Photoshop not to sharpen low-contrast pixels.

- ✔ This idea is great, but the implementation by Photoshop leaves something to be desired. The filter creates an abrupt transition between sharpened and ignored pixels, resulting in an unrealistic effect. Therefore, I recommend that you leave Threshold set to 0.

Some sharpening scenarios

Figure 17-6 demonstrates the effects of several different Amount and Radius values on the same detail to which I applied the piddly little Sharpen More command in Figure 17-4. Throughout Figure 17-6, the Threshold value is 0.

Figure 17-6 is organized into two rows. To create the images in the top row, I started with an Amount value of 200 percent and a Radius of 0.5. Then I halved the Amount value and doubled the Radius in each of the next two images. Though the effect is similar from one image to the next, you can see that the right image has thicker edges than the left image. (The differences are subtle; you may have to look closely.)

Figure 17-6:
The effect of a whole bunch of Amount and Radius values on detail from an ancient photo.

200%, 0.5   100%, 1.0   50%, 2.0

500%, 0.5   250%, 1.0   125%, 2.0

The bottom row of the figure features more pronounced sharpening effects. Again, I started with one set of Amount and Radius values — 500 percent and 0.5 — and progressively halved the Amount and doubled the Radius. Notice that not only are the edges in the right image thicker, but the left image contains more artifacts (those little flecks in the jacket and hat).

After experimenting with a few different settings — hey, you don't have to know what you're doing to experiment — I decided that my favorite setting was an Amount of 250 percent and a Radius of 1.0. The final image sharpened with these settings is shown in Figure 17-7. Not bad for an image as old as the pharaohs.

Figure 17-7:
The image
from Figure
17-3
sharpened
with an
Amount
value of 250
percent and
a Radius
value of 1.0.

Myopia Adds Depth

If you want to make a portion of your image blurry instead of sharp, you can apply one of the commands under the Filter⇨Blur menu. Right off the bat, you quick thinkers are thinking to yourselves, "Blurry? Why would I want my image to be blurry?" This is a classic problem. You're thinking of blurry as the opposite of sharp. But blurry and sharp can go hand in hand inside the same image. The sharp details are in the foreground, and the blurry stuff goes in the background.

Take Figure 17-8, for example. In this image, I selected and blurred the background. The scene becomes a little more intimate, as if the background were far, far away. It also has the effect of making the foreground characters seem more in focus than ever.

To make the effect complete, I selected the lower-right corner of the image, which represents the ground coming toward us. I feathered the selection (using Select⇨Feather set to a value of 30) and then blurred it. The result is a gradual blurring effect, as if the ground were becoming progressively out of focus as it extends beyond our field of vision.

Figure 17-8:
Blurring the
background
as well as a
small tip
of the
foreground
(bottom
right) brings
the family
up close
and
personal.

For the most part, then, blurring is a special effect. Unlike sharpening, which has the effect of correcting the focus, blurring heightens reality by exaggerating the depth of an image. In other words, you never have to blur an image — and you probably won't do it nearly as frequently as you sharpen — but it's a lot of fun.

Choosing your blur

The first two commands under the Filter⇨Blur submenu — Blur and Blur More — are the Dumb and Dumber of the blur filters. Like their Sharpen and Sharpen More counterparts, they produce predefined effects that never seem to be quite what you're looking for.

The "Superblur" command — the one that offers the powers you need to get the job done right — is Filter⇨Blur⇨Gaussian Blur. The filter is named after Karl Friedrich Gauss, a dusty old German mathematician who's even older than the photograph from Figure 17-3. But just think "Superblur" — or, as Mr. Gauss would have put it, "Ueberblur."

When you choose Filter⇨Blur⇨Gaussian Blur, Photoshop displays the dialog box shown in Figure 17-9. The Radius value determines the number of pixels that get mixed together at a time. You can go as high as 250.0, but any value over 10.0 enters the realm of the legally blind. In Figure 17-8, I blurred the background with a Radius value of 4.0 and the lower-right patch of ground with a Radius of 2.0.

Figure 17-9:
Specify the
exact
amount of
blur you
want in the
Ueberblur
dialog box,
a.k.a. the
Gaussian
Blur dialog
box.

Creating motion and puzzle pieces

The Filter➪Blur submenu contains three additional filters — Motion Blur, Radial Blur, and Smart Blur — all of which are exclusively special-effects filters. The Motion Blur filter makes an image appear to move in a straight line; the Radial Blur filter can be used to either move the selection in a circle or zoom it outward toward the viewer.

The Smart Blur option, new to Photoshop 4, finds the edges in your image and then blurs only between the edges — it's as if Photoshop is carving your image up into puzzle pieces and then blurring each piece. If you apply the effect in heavy doses, the result is an image that resembles a watercolor painting and isn't too far removed from the effect created by the Filter➪Artistic➪Watercolor filter.

Of the three filters, Motion Blur is the filter you're more likely to use. First, the dialog box offers the standard previewing options, making this filter accessible and predictable. Second, it's much easier to use. Finally, when compared with Radial Blur, it takes a lot less time to use; Radial Blur is one of the slowest Photoshop filters.

When you choose Filter➪Blur➪Motion Blur, Photoshop displays the dialog box in Figure 17-10. The filter smears pixels at a specified angle and over a specified distance. Enter the angle and distance into the appropriately named option boxes. You can also drag the spoke inside the circle on the right side of the dialog box to change the Angle value.

Figure 17-10:
The Motion
Blur filter
wiggles
pixels back
and forth to
create the
illusion of
movement.

By way of example, Figure 17-11 shows a couple of discrete applications of the Motion Blur filter. To blur the boy, I selected him, feathered the selection, and applied the Motion Blur filter with an Angle value of 90 degrees — straight up and down — and a Distance of 30 pixels. To blur his sister's arm — the one nearest her beaming brother — I used an Angle of 45 degrees and a Distance of 6 pixels. As you can see, Distance values over 20 smear the image into oblivion; smaller Distance values create subtle movement effects.

Figure 17-11:
Two unlikely
applications
of the
Motion Blur
filter.

Filter Potpourri

The Filter⇨Sharpen and Filter⇨Blur submenus contain the filters you use most often. In fact, if you like, you can blow off the rest of the chapter without being much the poorer for it. But if you have five minutes or so to spare, I'd like to show you a few other interesting commands scattered throughout the Filter menu.

Giving your images that gritty, streetwise look

For starters, you have the Add Noise command. Not to be confused with the as-yet uncompleted Adenoids filter, Add Noise randomizes the colors of selected pixels. The result is a layer of grit that gives smooth images a textured appearance.

Choose Filter⇨Noise⇨Add Noise to display the Add Noise dialog box shown in Figure 17-12. Here's how to use the options found therein:

✔ Drag the Amount slider triangle or enter a value between 1 and 999 to control how noisy the image gets. Low values — such as the default value 32 or lower — permit a small amount of noise; high values permit more. Anything over 100 pretty much wipes out the original image.

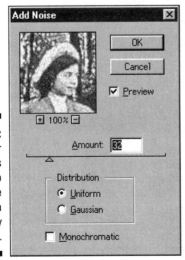

Figure 17-12: This filter adds "noise" to your image to give it a gritty texture.

✔ Select a Distribution radio button to control the color of noise. The Uniform option colors pixels with random variations on the shades it finds in the original image; the Gaussian option — which should be labeled High Contrast — colors pixels with more exaggerated light and dark shades. Therefore, Gaussian produces a noisier effect, about twice as noisy as Uniform. For example, an Amount value of 32 combined with Gaussian produces a similar visual effect to an Amount value of 64 combined with Uniform.

✔ The Monochromatic check box adds grayscale noise to full-color images. When the option is turned off, Photoshop adds all colors of noise. (The option has no effect on grayscale images except to shift the pixels around a little.)

To rough up the dark areas in the mom and son detail shown on the left side of Figure 17-13, I used Select⇨Color Range to select the dark areas in the image and then applied the Add Noise filter. By changing the Amount value to 100 and selecting Gaussian, I arrived at the effect shown in the middle example in the figure. To achieve the right-hand image, I applied Filter⇨Blur⇨Motion Blur with an Angle value of 45 degrees and a Distance of 6 pixels. Photoshop creates an etched metal effect that suits these two characters to a T.

Original	Add Noise	Motion Blur

Figure 17-13: I selected the dark portions of the image on the left and applied the Add Noise filter (middle) followed by Motion Blur (right).

Color Plate 17-1 shows the same Add Noise and Motion Blur effect applied to the dark portions of a full-color image. But there's a slight twist. In the top image, I applied the Add Noise filter with the Monochromatic check box turned off; in the bottom image, the check box is turned on. As a result, the top image contains color streaks, and the bottom image contains black-and-white streaks. I prefer the black-and-white streaks for this particular image — they give it a more rustic look — but you, of course, are free to do as you see fit.

Stamping your image in metal

Another intriguing and sometimes useful filter is Emboss. This filter makes your image appear as if it were stamped in metal. The edges in the image appear in relief, and the other areas turn gray.

When you choose Filter⇨Stylize⇨Emboss, Photoshop displays the dialog box shown in Figure 17-14. You enter the angle of the light shining on the metal into the Angle option box. The Height value determines the height of the edges, and the Amount value determines the amount of contrast between blacks and whites.

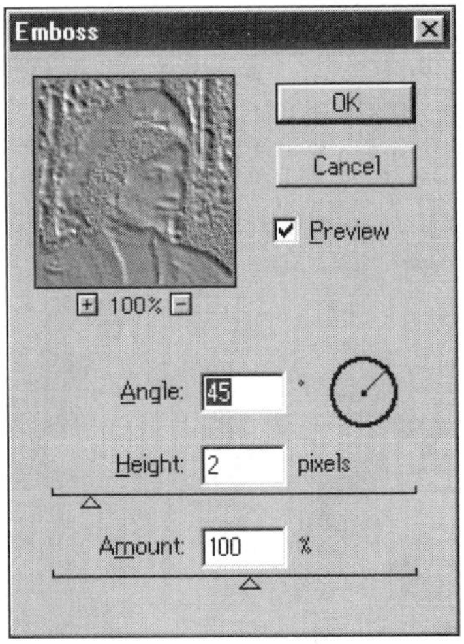

Figure 17-14:
Use the
Emboss
filter to
stamp
images into
sheets of
metal
(figuratively,
of course).

I'm breezing over these options because they aren't the most useful gang in the world. In fact, they can be big time wasters. From personal experience, I can tell you

  ✔ How you set the Angle value doesn't matter. Feel free to drag the spoke on the circle around until you get what you want, but don't expect big differences between one angle and another.

  ✔ Set the Height value to 1 or 2. Any value over 2 has a habit of impairing detail.

  ✔ Okay, the Amount value is useful. Enter 50 percent for a very subtle effect, 100 percent for a medium Emboss effect, and 200 percent for added drama. You can go as high as 500, but higher values make the contrast between blacks and whites too abrupt (in my humble opinion).

TIP

Like Add Noise, Emboss isn't the kind of filter you go around applying to an entire image. I mean, after you've done it once or twice, it gets a little old. Rather, you want to apply it to selected areas.

In the first example of Figure 17-15, I selected the dark areas in the mother/son image and applied the Emboss filter with an Angle of 45 degrees, a Height of 2, and an Amount of 200 percent. In the middle example, I blurred the selection using the Gaussian Blur filter set to a Radius of 2 pixels. Then I applied Unsharp Mask with an Amount of 500 percent and a Radius of 2 pixels, arriving at the thrilling mottled metal effect on the far right.

| Emboss | Gaussian Blur | Unsharp Mask |

Figure 17-15: After selecting the dark portions of the image, I embossed it (left), blurred it (middle), and sharpened it (right), creating a soft relief.

TECHNICAL STUFF

Sharpening the blur

After you read about Figure 17-15, your reaction may be one of, "Whoa, hold up a minute here. First you blur and then you sharpen? What kind of crazy logic is that?" Well, pretty sound logic, actually.

After I applied Gaussian Blur, the image turned overly gray, as you can see in the second example in the figure. Luckily, one of the properties of Unsharp Mask is that it increases the amount of contrast between dark and light pixels. So to bring the blacks and whites back from the dead,

I set the Radius value inside the Unsharp Mask dialog box to the exact value I had used inside the Gaussian Blur dialog box — that is, 2.0. Using this value ensured that Unsharp Mask was able to correctly locate the blurred edges and boost their contrast.

If you can figure it out, it's a great technique. If not, you can use the Auto Levels or Levels command to change the contrast, as I describe in the next chapter.

Merging colors in flaky images

The last two filters I cover in this chapter — Facet and Median — average the colors of neighboring pixels to create areas of flat color. Both throw away detail, but they're great for smoothing out the imperfections in old, cruddy images such as the one that keeps popping up in this chapter.

Filter➪Pixelate➪Facet is a single-shot command that roams the image looking for areas of similarly colored pixels and then assigns the entire area a single color. In Figure 17-16, I started with the elder daughter from way back in Figure 17-3, before she was sharpened. In the middle example, I applied Filter➪Pixelate➪Facet. See how the image is now divided up into a bunch of globby areas of color? To make the image more clear, I applied the Unsharp Mask filter to the right-hand example, using an Amount value of 250 percent and a Radius value of 0.5.

Original	Facet	Unsharp Mask

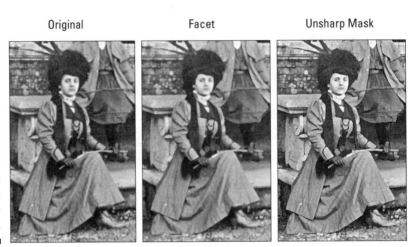

Figure 17-16: Starting with the original image (left), I applied the Facet filter (middle) and then reinforced the edges with Unsharp Mask (right).

Filter➪Noise➪Median averages the colors of so many neighboring pixels. To tell Photoshop the "so many" part, choose the Median command and enter a value from 1 to 16 into the Radius option box.

Figure 17-17 shows the result of applying various Radius values to the elder daughter. The top row shows the effects of the Median command; the bottom row shows what happened when I applied Unsharp Mask to each image. Notice how higher values melt away more of the image's detail. A Radius value of 3 makes the image gooey indeed; any higher value is pure silliness.

Radius: 1   Radius: 2   Radius: 3

Figure 17-17:
I applied the
Median filter
at three
different
Radius
settings (top
row) and
then
sharpened
the results
(bottom
row).

Median

Unsharp Mask

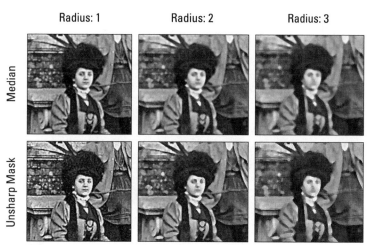

You can use Facet and Median to blur background images, just as I did earlier with Gaussian Blur. Or you can combine them with the Add Noise and Emboss filters to create special effects.

Keep in mind that the real beauty of these more specialized filters is in combining them and applying them to small, selected portions of your image.

Chapter 18

Drawing Color from a Dreary Wasteland

. . . .

. . . .

*H*ere's a common scenario for you: You get some pictures or slides back from the photo developer — I'm talking regular photos here, not the digital kind — and one of them catches your eye. The color is great, the composition is fantastic, everyone's smiling; it ranks among the best pictures you've ever shot. It's not 100 percent perfect, but you figure you can fix the few glitches inside Photoshop.

A few days later — after you've had the photo scanned to Photo CD — you open the image inside Photoshop, and your heart sinks to the pit of your stomach. The image is dark, colorless, and generally a big, fat disappointment. That little picture on the cover of the CD jacket looks better than this murky mess on-screen.

In a perfect world, this would never happen. The service bureau that scanned the image would have corrected the colors so that they would look the way they did in your photo. But in practice, even the best service bureaus let a few duds fall through the cracks, and some don't bother with color-correction at all. It's a pickle.

Take Color Plate 18-1, for example. The original slide looked something like the example on the right, but when I opened the image in Photoshop, it appeared as shown on the left. Sure, it's an old slide — that's me in the striped shirt, so you know that a couple of years have passed — and the composition leaves something to be desired. (I have a fake tree growing out of my shoulder and my sister seems to be balancing a flower-adorned globe on her head.) But, come on, it didn't look this bad. I mean, are we auditioning for the remake of *20,000 Leagues Under the Sea* here or what?

If you run into a similar problem, never fear — you have cause to be optimistic. The colors may not look like much now, but chances are better than even that you have enough colors to get by. Though it may be hard to believe, your image very likely contains a few million colors; it's just that they're all squished toward the dark end of the spectrum. Your job is to bring these colors back to life.

Want proof? The image on the right side of Color Plate 18-1 isn't a different scan, it's just a color-corrected version of its neighbor on the left. In fact, I revived the color using only two commands — Levels and Variations. I didn't touch a painting or editing tool, I didn't draw a selection outline, I didn't do anything to add colors to the image. I merely took the existing colors and stretched them across the spectrum.

Photoshop offers several color-correction commands, but you only need three of these — at the most — to get the job done. In this chapter, I show you how these miracle commands work and encourage you to ignore the rest. I also explain how to use Version 4's new adjustment layers, which let you do some of your color correcting on an independent layer, providing you with extra flexibility and safety.

The Color-Correction Connection

The Photoshop color-correction commands are located in one central spot, under the Image⇨Adjust submenu. Of these commands, only three should be of the least concern to you at this stage in your mastery of Photoshop: Levels, Auto Levels, and Variations.

Your friends Auto Levels, Levels, and Variations

Choose Image⇨Adjust⇨Auto Levels or press Ctrl+Shift+L to automatically correct the contrast of an image. For example, Figure 18-1 shows a typically low-contrast image composed entirely of cheerless grays. The inset squares show the lightest and darkest colors in the image as well as some sample shades in between. If I apply the Auto Levels command, Photoshop automatically makes the lightest gray white and the darkest gray black and stretches out the colors in between. Figure 18-2 shows the result.

Figure 18-1: What a dismal scene: Come to this gas station and get your tank filled with depression. The grim reaper will change your oil.

Figure 18-2: The Auto Levels command brings out some strong blacks and whites, but the grays remain dark and dreary.

Unfortunately, Auto Levels doesn't always do the trick. Figure 18-2, for example, contains strong blacks and whites, but the grays appear overly dark (as witnessed by the shades in the inset squares). The solution is Image➪Adjust➪Levels, which you can access from the keyboard by pressing Ctrl+L. The Levels command takes some getting used to, but it lets you adjust the darkest and lightest colors as well as the medium gray. (I explain the command in detail later in this chapter, in the section "Leveling the Contrast Field.") Figure 18-3 shows the Gulf station running in tip-top condition, thanks to the Levels command. See how much clearer the details in the cars now appear?

Figure 18-3:
A nice, even transition of grays makes a day at the gas station seem like a walk through the park.

Unlike Auto Levels and Levels, which serve grayscale and color images equally well, Image➪Adjust➪Variations is specifically designed to correct full-color images. (You can use the command on grayscale images, but it merely duplicates some of the options inside the Levels dialog box.) You can increase or decrease the intensity of colors or tint the image to remove a color cast. For example, if an image is too yellow, you can add blue to it, as in the first example in Color Plate 18-2. If the image is too blue, add yellow, as in the second example. In both cases, Variations preserves non-blue and non-yellow colors. Throughout, for example, the Christmas tree remains true to its natural color of pink.

Upcoming sections explain how to use Levels, Auto Levels, and Variations in detail. But just for the record, here's the general approach to take when color correcting an image in Photoshop:

1. **Apply the Auto Levels command.**

   Regardless of whether you're editing a grayscale or color image, this is a good first step.

   If you like what you see, you can skip all the other steps. If you think some more tweaking might be in order, proceed to Step 2.

2. **Apply the Levels command.**

   Use this command to change the contrast of the image and to lighten or darken the medium colors.

   If you're editing a grayscale image, this command is the end of the line. If your full-color image looks a little drab, however, keep correcting.

3. **Choose the Variations command and select the Saturation radio button.**

   The options inside the Variations dialog box let you boost the intensity of colors in an image, as discussed in the section "Variations on a Color Scheme," in this chapter.

   If the colors now look the way you want, press Enter and get on with your life. Continue only if you want to tint the image with a certain color or remove a color cast.

4. **Still inside the Variations dialog box, select the Midtones radio button and adjust the colors in the image.**

   The section "It sure feels good to remove that color cast" at the end of this chapter tells all.

The other color correctors (boo, hiss)

The other color-correction commands in the Image⇨Adjust submenu range from useful but very complex to simple but completely inept. Just in case you're chock full of curiosity, here's the rundown:

- ✔ The Curves command is even more capable than the Levels command, allowing you to change every one of the possible 16 million colors to a different color. Unfortunately, this feature is also very difficult to use.

- ✔ The Brightness/Contrast command is utterly and completely worthless. I'm serious. If you've never used it, don't start. If you have used it, stop — you're hurting your images.

- ✔ Color Balance is another loser. You keep thinking that it's going to produce some kind of useful results, but it never does. Worthless and irritating — what a combination.

- ✔ Hue/Saturation is good, but not great. It lets you change the color, intensity, and lightness of an image using three slider bars. However, the Variations dialog box provides these same controls and does a better job.

✔ Desaturate is just the thing for draining the color from a selected area and leaving it black and white. But if you want to convert an entire image to grayscale, see the "The road to grayscale" section in Chapter 6.

✔ The Replace Color command is a combination of Select⇨Color Range and the Hue/Saturation command. What's the point?

✔ The Selective Colors command lets you modify a range of colors using CMYK slider bars. Not a terrible command, but not a particularly useful one either.

✔ The other commands on the Adjust menu — Invert, Equalize, Threshold, and Posterize — are typically used for creating special effects. Invert, for example, makes all white pixels black and all black pixels white, creating a photo-negative effect. Fun to play with, but not the sort of tool you can use to brighten up a dingy gas station.

Leveling the Contrast Field

Not one image in this book — except the gloomy-looking Figure 18-1 — has escaped a thorough going-over with the Levels command. I consider this command to be one of the most essential functions inside Photoshop. In fact, if an image displays any of the following symptoms, you can correct it with Levels:

✔ The image is murky, without strong lights and darks, like the one in Figure 18-1.

✔ The image is too light.

✔ The image is too dark.

✔ The image is gaining weight, losing hair, and developing bags under its eyes.

Whoops, that last item sneaked in by mistake. If an image gains weight, loses hair, and develops baggy eyes, you have to send it on a three-week cruise of the Caribbean.

Leveling on a layer

Photoshop 4 offers a new feature to use in conjunction with the Levels command (and, in a roundabout way, the Auto Levels command): adjustment layers. Adjustment layers are just like the layers discussed in Chapter 15, except that you use them expressly to apply color-correction commands.

At any rate, adjustment layers offer several advantages:

- ✔ The color-correction affects all the underlying layers in the image. If you don't use an adjustment layer, the color-correction affects the active layer only.

- ✔ You can create as many different adjustment layers as you want. So if you want a few layers to use one set of color-correction settings and the rest of the image to use another set, you just create two different adjustment layers.

- ✔ Because the color-correction "exists" on its own layer, you can experiment freely without fear of damaging the image. If at some point you decide that you don't like the effects of the color-correction, you can edit the adjustment layer or just delete it entirely and start fresh.

- ✔ You can blend the adjustment layer with the other layers using the Opacity and blend mode controls in the Layers palette, just as you can with any layer. This feature gives you even more control over how your image appears.

To create an adjustment layer, do the following:

1. In the Layers palette, click on the top layer you want to color correct.

When you create an adjustment layer, Photoshop places it directly on top of the active layer in the Layers palette. The adjustment affects the layer or layers underneath, depending on what setting you choose in the New Adjustment Layer dialog box in Step 2.

If you select a portion of your image before creating the adjustment layer, the color-correction affects the selected area across all underlying layers.

2. Choose Layer⇨New⇨Adjustment Layer or Ctrl+click on the new layer icon at the bottom of the Layers palette.

The dialog box shown in Figure 18-4 appears. Here's a field guide to your options: If you want to give your adjustment layer a specific name, enter the name into the top option box. The Type pop-up menu lists all the different color-correction commands you can select — the only one you need to worry about is Levels, which is selected by default.

Although the Auto Levels command isn't available in the Type pop-up menu, you can apply the Auto Levels command on an adjustment layer by choosing the Levels option from the pop-up menu. The option leads you to the Levels dialog box, which has an Auto button that works just like the Auto Levels command.

Skip the Opacity and Mode pop-up menus; if you want, you can change these settings later, in the Layers palette. Skip the Group with Previous Layer check box, too.

Figure 18-4:
The New Adjustment Layer dialog box enables you to do your color correcting on an independent layer.

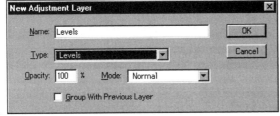

3. Press Enter.

Photoshop adds the adjustment layer to the Layers palette and displays the Levels dialog box, which is explained in the next section.

Remember that an adjustment layer works just like any other layer in the Layers palette. You can vary the effects of the adjustment by playing with the Opacity slider and blend modes, you can move the layer up or down in the layers palette to affect different layers, and you can merge the layer with an underlying layer to permanently fuse the color-correction to the image. (You can't, however, merge an adjustment layer with another adjustment layer.)

If you ever want to change the color-correction settings for an adjustment layer, just double-click on the adjustment layer name in the Layers palette. Photoshop redisplays the Levels dialog box, where you can modify the settings. To delete the adjustment layer, drag it to the trash icon in the Layers palette.

You can flip back and forth between a view of your corrected image and your uncorrected image by simply clicking on the eyeball icon next to the adjustment layer name in the Layers palette. When the eyeball is present, the layer is visible, showing you the color-corrected image. When the eyeball is hidden, so is the layer, giving you a "before" view of your image.

Making friends with the Levels dialog box

To apply the Levels command, you can either create a new adjustment layer, as described in the preceding section, or choose Image⇨Adjust⇨Levels or press Ctrl+L. If you choose the command from the Image menu or press the keyboard shortcut, the color-correction is applied directly to the image and affects the active layer only.

Either way, the dialog box shown in Figure 18-5 appears. Luckily, you don't need to address all the options that inhabit this dialog box. So before you break into a cold sweat, shriek at the top of your lungs, or do whatever it is you do when you see terrifying sights like Figure 18-5, let me try to distinguish the important options in this dialog box from the stuff you won't use in a month of Sundays:

✔ The options in the Channel pop-up menu let you adjust one color channel in a full-color image independently of the others. These options are helpful if you know what you're doing, but not terribly important.

Histogram

Figure 18-5:
The complicated-looking Levels dialog box contains a lot of options that you don't need to worry about.

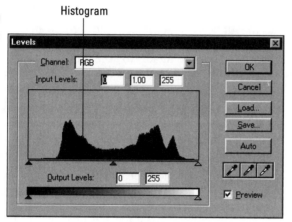

✔ The three Input Levels option boxes control the settings of the darkest, medium, and lightest pixels in your image, in that order. These options are important, which is why I cover them thoroughly in the next section.

✔ That black birthmark in the middle of the dialog box is called a *histogram*. It shows you how the colors in your image are currently distributed. It also rates the Seal of Importance.

✔ The slider bar beneath the histogram provides three triangles, one each for the darkest, medium, and lightest pixels in your image. These triangles are the most important options of all.

✔ The Output Levels option boxes and the accompanying slider bar let you make the darkest colors lighter and the lightest colors darker, which is usually the exact opposite of what you want to do. Mark these options Not Particularly Important.

✔ The OK and Cancel buttons are as important as always. One applies your changes, the other doesn't. No news here.

✔ Press the Alt key to change the Cancel button to a Reset button. Click on the button while pressing Alt to reset the settings to the way they were when you entered the dialog box. Very helpful.

✔ Click on the Save button to save the settings in this dialog box to disk. Click on the Load button to later load and reapply them. Unless you're color correcting about 20 images in a row, all of which require exactly the same treatment, these buttons are about as important to your health and well-being as lava lamps. Ignore them.

✔ Click on the Auto button to automatically change the darkest pixels to black and the lightest ones to white, exactly as if you had chosen Image➪Adjust➪Auto Levels. The only time you need to use this button is when you want to apply the Auto Levels command on an adjustment layer, as discussed earlier. Otherwise, just choose the command from the Image➪Adjust menu or press Ctrl+Shift+L and save yourself some work.

✔ When you press the Alt key, the Auto button changes to an Options button. I only tell you about this feature because I'm afraid that you may notice it for yourself when you press the Alt key to access the Reset button. But whether you notice it or not, the Options button is totally unimportant. And if you do notice it, don't muck with the settings that become available to you when you click on the button.

✔ The three eyedropper icons let you click on colors in your image to make them black, medium gray, or white. If I were you, I'd steer clear of these icons except to stamp them Not Important, Ditto, and Doubly So.

✔ The Preview check box lets you view the effect of your edits inside the image window. It's very important that you turn this option on.

Figure 18-6 shows the Levels dialog box as it appears after you strip it down to its most important components. As you can see, the Input Levels options — which include the three option boxes, the histogram, and the slider bar — represent the core of the Levels command. The other options are just icing on the cake.

Figure 18-6: When you strip the Levels dialog box of its excessive regalia, it becomes far less daunting.

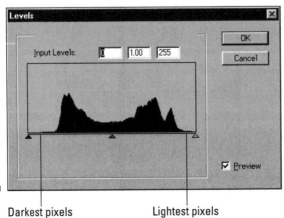

Darkest pixels   Lightest pixels

Brightness and contrast as they should be

The histogram in Figure 18-6 is a graph of the color in the uncorrected image in Figure 18-7. (I didn't even choose the Auto Levels command.) The graph is organized from darkest colors on the left to lightest colors on the right. The peaks and valleys in the histogram show the color distribution. If the darkest colors were black, the histogram would start on the far left edge of the slider bar. If the lightest colors were white, it would continue to the far right edge. But as it is, the left and right edges taper off into flatlands. This means that the darkest and lightest pixels in the image are not as dark or light as they could be.

Figure 18-7: Though they lived in a time when Photoshop was not available, these uncorrected characters still managed to find something to smile about.

If some of that information went a little over your head, not to worry. Some folks understand graphs, while other folks think that they're in a board meeting and start to nod off the second they see anything resembling a graph. Either way, remember that the histogram is provided for your reference only. All that matters is how you adjust the slider triangles underneath the histogram:

✔ To make the darkest pixels black, drag the left slider triangle to the right so that it rests directly under the beginning of the first hill in the histogram. Figure 18-8 shows the dragged triangle and its effect on the image.

✔ To make the lightest pixels white, drag the right-hand triangle to the left so that it lines up directly under the end of the last hill in the histogram, as in Figure 18-9.

Figure 18-8:
Dragging the first triangle affects the darkest pixels in the image.

Figure 18-9:
The image lightens up when I drag the white triangle to the left.

✔ If you already chose the Auto Levels command or the Auto button in the Levels dialog box, you most likely won't have to change either the left or right slider because Photoshop has already done this automatically. (You may want to adjust the sliders slightly, but that's up to you.) Instead, just concentrate on positioning the middle slider, described next.

✔ The most important triangle is the middle one. Called the *gamma point* — just in case you get stuck in an elevator with the guys from R&D and find yourself scraping for something to talk about — this triangle lets you change the brightness of the medium colors in your image. Drag to the right to make the medium colors darker. But more likely, you want to drag to the left to make the medium colors lighter, as demonstrated in Figure 18-10.

The values in the three option boxes above the histogram update as you drag the slider triangles. The left and right values are measured in color levels. Just like the values in the Color palette — where you define colors (see Chapter 5) — 0 is black and 255 is white. So if the left value is 45, as it is in Figures 18-8 through 18-10, any pixel that is colored with a level of 45 or darker becomes black. The gamma value — the middle one — is measured as a ratio . . . er, forget it, it doesn't make any sense and it matters even less. The point is, a value of more than 1 lightens the medium colors; a value less than 1 darkens them.

Figure 18-10:
Dragging the middle triangle brings out the detail in an image.

The old stock photo featured in Figures 18-7 through 18-10 is a wonderful example of a work of art that takes on new meaning the more you look at it. Three of the subjects are proudly displaying unlighted tobacco products, the fourth guy is using a paper cup for a megaphone, and all four have feathers in their caps (figure that one out). Meanwhile, you can see their shadows on the wall in back of them. Call me picky, but it sort of ruins the illusion that they might be outdoors enjoying a chilly sporting event.

If you want to see the effect of the Levels command on a full-color image, you need look no further than Color Plate 18-3. Nestled in this quiet corner of the book is a homemade Italian gate. Starting with the uncorrected image in the upper-left corner, I adjusted each of the slider triangles, eventually arriving at the much superior color balance shown in the lower-right image. It just goes to show you, Levels is bound to do any image good.

If you notice a loss of color in your image after you apply the Levels command, don't worry. You can get that color back by using the Variations command, discussed in the next section.

Variations on a Color Scheme

One negative effect of the Levels command is that it can weaken some of the colors, particularly if you lighten the medium colors by dragging the gamma point in the Levels dialog box to the left. To bring the colors back to their original intensity, call on Image⇨Adjust⇨Variations.

The Variations command can also cure color casts, in which one color is particularly prominent in the image. A photograph shot outdoors, for example, may be overly blue; one shot in an X-rated motel room may be a shade heavy in the reds. Whatever color predominates your image, the Variations command can tone it down with elegance and ease.

Turning plain old color into Technicolor

To bolster the intensity of colors in your image — for what it's worth, color intensity is called *saturation* in image-editing vernacular — follow these pleasant steps:

1. **Choose Image⇨Adjust⇨Variations.**

   The enormous Variations dialog box erupts onto your screen, filled with about a million small previews of your image.

2. **Select the Saturation radio button in the upper-right corner of the dialog box.**

   Most of the small preview images disappear. Only five remain, as shown in Figure 18-11. The three previews in the middle of the dialog box represent different color intensities. The top two previews show the image as it appeared before you chose the Variations command and how it looks now, subject to the changes in the Variations dialog box.

3. **Drag the slider triangle in the upper-right corner to the left, toward Fine.**

   This slider controls the extent of the changes made inside the Variations dialog box. If you drag the triangle toward Coarse, the changes become more drastic; drag it toward Fine, and they become more gradual. The setting is reflected inside the left and right previews in the middle of the dialog box, which become more subtle.

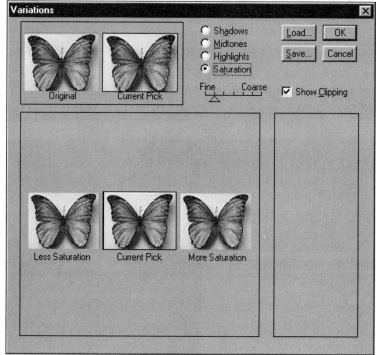

Figure 18-11:
Click on the
More
Saturation
preview to
boost the
intensity of
the colors in
an image.

Because color intensity is a very sensitive function inside Photoshop, it's best to set the slider to one of the first two notches so that you can make gentle, incremental changes.

4. To increase color intensity, click on the preview labeled More Saturation.

Clicking once increases the intensity by a gradual amount, owing to the slider bar setting. To add more intensity, click again. Each time you click, the Current Pick previews — one in the middle and one at the top — update to reflect your latest change.

If inconsistently colored pixels begin to emerge, Photoshop is telling you that these colors are outside of the CMYK color range and will not print. Don't worry about it until the weird pixels take over a third or more of your image. (If you don't care whether the colors will print correctly or not, turn off the Show Clipping check box to view the pixels normally.)

If at any time you want to reset the Current Pick preview to the original image, just click on the preview labeled Original in the upper-left corner of the dialog box.

5. When you're satisfied with the increased color intensity, press Enter.

Photoshop applies your settings to the original image, just as they were shown in the Current Pick preview. No surprises with this dialog box.

Changes you make via the Variations dialog box affect the active layer only. Unfortunately, you can't apply the Variations command using an adjustment layer as you can the Levels and Auto Levels commands.

Color Plate 18-4 shows the difference between a butterfly whose splendor I completely destroyed using the Levels command and that same butterfly restored to its original luster and brilliance via the Variations command. To achieve this radical transformation, I set the slider bar inside the Variations dialog box to the second notch over from the left and clicked on the More Saturation preview a total of six times.

It sure feels good to remove that color cast

Images are like people in that they hate to wear casts. When your image is encumbered by a color cast, it becomes uncomfortable and downright crotchety. Take the first image in Color Plate 18-5, for example. To the inexperienced eye, this image may appear happy and at peace with itself. But in truth, its life is a living heck, made miserable by a decidedly yellow color cast.

To remove the color cast once and for all, revisit the Variations command:

1. **Choose Image⟹Adjust⟹Variations.**

   The Variations dialog box takes over your screen.

2. **Select the Midtones radio button in the upper-right corner of the dialog box.**

   This option lets you edit the medium colors in your image. (You can also edit the dark or light colors by selecting Shadows or Highlights, but these options produce extremely subtle effects and have little impact on your image.)

   After you select Midtones, the central portion of the dialog box fills with seven previews, as shown in Figure 18-12. These previews let you shift the colors in the image toward a primary color — green, yellow, red, magenta, blue, or cyan. As usual, the Current Pick preview in the center of the cluster updates to show the most recent corrections applied to the image.

   The three previews along the right edge of the Variations dialog box let you lighten and darken the image. But because they're less capable than the gamma point control in the Levels dialog box, you can feel free to ignore them.

3. **Click on one of the More previews to shift the colors in the image toward that color.**

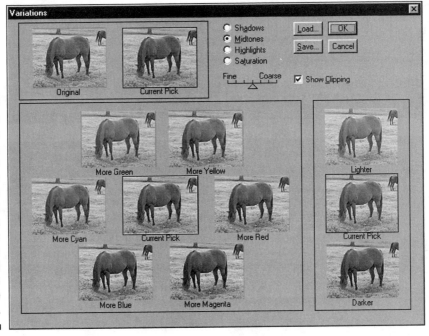

Figure 18-12:
Click on the More Blue preview to add blue and remove yellow in an image. Click on More Magenta to add magenta and remove green.

First, identify the color cast. Then click on the preview opposite to that color. In the case of the horse image from Color Plate 18-5, the cast is clearly yellow and, to a lesser extent, green. To eliminate the yellow cast, I clicked on More Blue. To eliminate the green cast, I clicked on More Magenta.

Remember Color Plate 5-3, which shows that yellow ink filters out blue light and magenta ink filters out green light? This means that yellow and blue are direct opposites, as are magenta and green. Such opposite colors are termed *complementary*. I'm not sure why. I guess it's like a marriage of opposites in which each spouse complements the other. If they don't kill each other first, of course.

4. **If you go too far toward one color, just click on the opposite color to step backward.**

In Color Plate 18-5, for example, I clicked on the More Blue preview twice, clicked on More Magenta twice, and then clicked on More Blue again. But after some concerted soul searching, I decided that I had gone too far. The resulting image — shown in the bottom-right corner of the color plate — was too blue and too magenta. So I clicked on the More Yellow button to remove the last application of blue and clicked on More Green to remove the last application of magenta. The bottom-left example in the color plate shows the result.

As when you adjust color saturation, you can vary the impact of the previews on the image by dragging the slider triangle toward Fine or Coarse. The images in Color Plate 18-5 were all created with the triangle set right in the center, as it is by default.

If your image has more than one layer, your color-cast manipulations affect the active layer only.

Part VI
The Part of Tens

In this part . . .

Some say that there's magic in the number three. Bears, pigs, Musketeers, and Stooges regularly cavort about in groups of three. But I say that the real magic is in tens. The Ten Commandments, the ten amendments that make up The Bill of Rights, and the ten ingredients in a Big Mac — if you count both all-beef patties and the three sesame seed buns — are items that we can count on the ten fingers of our hands (or the ten toes of our feet when we're at the beach). Top ten lists abound in newspapers, magazines, books, and late-night TV shows. And I say, why buck a trend? If everyone else is doing it, I for one am happy to mindlessly follow along.

But then I thought, "What ho, if there's magic in threes and in tens, why not do both?" So that's what I did. This part contains three chapters, each of which contains ten factoids. Ten great shortcuts that you'll want to assign to memory, ten great ways to wreak havoc on a loved one's face, and ten things you can do with your image after you finish messing it up in Photoshop.

As if that's not enough, the last chapter of this book — Chapter 21 — is divisible not only by 3, but also by the lucky number 7. We are talking major number magic at work here, the kind of stuff that numerologists, fortune tellers, and lottery fanatics would give their eyeteeth for. And it only cost you $19.99, a number whose only claim to fame is that it's slightly cheaper than $20.

Chapter 19

Ten Tricky Techniques to Assign to Memory

Some guy named Odell Shepard said, "Memory is what makes you wonder what you've forgotten." I don't know anything about this Odell fellow — he was just lucky enough to get picked up by one of those books of quotations that are supposed to make you sound like a halfway-intelligent human being without really trying. Not having met Odell — Odie, I call him — I can only hazard the guess that he was talking about that feeling you get — usually, when you're in bed, trying to sleep, or when you're on the way home from work and it's too late to turn back — that you've forgotten something that's pretty much going to send your life spinning into a state of absolute chaos. In fact, I believe that feeling is known as the Odie Syndrome.

Well, I can't help you with every aspect of your life, but I can help you with Photoshop. Say, for example, that you wake up at 2 a.m. one morning with the dread suspicion that you've forgotten an important Photoshop shortcut. Normally, of course, your life would be forfeit. You'd just have to give up on your technological pursuits and take up beet farming. But thanks to this chapter, people like you can again live happy and productive lives because all of the most important Photoshop shortcuts are contained in these pages. A few minutes of reading, and order is restored.

Displaying and Hiding the Toolbox and Palettes

Tab

I'm ashamed to admit this, but there was a time when I wanted to view an image on-screen all by itself, without the toolbox. I had no idea how to do it. I even called the Photoshop product manager and asked him how to do it. He told me it was impossible.

Naturally, he was wrong. It was possible then, and it's possible now. Just press the Tab key. The toolbox, the status bar, and all the palettes disappear, leaving just you and the image. To bring the toolbox, status bar, and palettes back, press Tab again. To make the toolbox, status bar, and palettes flash crazily on-screen and off, press Tab over and over again until your finger gets numb. I'm not sure why you'd want to do this, but I like to spell out all the options.

If you want to hide the palettes but keep the toolbox and status bar visible, by the way, press Shift+Tab. Press Shift+Tab again to bring the palettes back.

If you have a dialog box open or an option in a palette is active (highlighted), Tab and Shift+Tab take you to the next option box or move you back one option box, respectively. But after you close the dialog box or press Enter to apply the palette option, Tab and Shift+Tab control your palettes and toolbox once again.

F5, F6, F7, F8

Press F5 to hide or display the Brushes palette, F6 to hide or display the Color palette, and F7 to hide or display the Layers palette. To display the Navigator palette, press F8, which brings up the Info palette. Then click on the Navigator palette tab. Press F8 twice to hide the palette.

Changing the Way a Tool Works

Enter

After selecting a tool in the toolbox, press Enter to bring up the Options palette for that tool. If the palette contains an option box, the value inside the option box becomes highlighted, allowing you to change it.

Scrolling and Zooming

Spacebar

Press the spacebar to temporarily access the hand tool. As long as the spacebar is down, the hand tool is available. Spacebar-drag to scroll the image.

Ctrl+spacebar, Alt+spacebar

To get to the zoom in cursor, press both Ctrl and spacebar. Pressing Alt+spacebar gets you the zoom out cursor. This means that you can magnify the image at any time by Ctrl+spacebar+clicking. To zoom out, Alt+spacebar+ click. You can also Ctrl+spacebar+drag to marquee an area and magnify it so that it takes up the entire image window.

Ctrl++ (plus), Ctrl+– (minus)

Another way to magnify or reduce the image is to press Ctrl++(plus) to zoom in or Ctrl+–(minus) to zoom out.

Double-click on the hand icon

To zoom the image so that you can see the whole thing on your monitor, double-click on the hand tool icon in the toolbox. Or press Ctrl+0 (zero).

Double-click on the zoom icon

To restore the image to the 100 percent (Actual Pixels) zoom factor, double-click on the zoom tool icon or press Ctrl+Alt+0 (zero).

Shift+Enter

When you change the zoom factor using the magnification box in the lower-left corner of the image window, press Shift+Enter instead of Enter after you enter a new zoom value. That way, the option box remains active after Photoshop zooms your image. If you need to further magnify or reduce your image, just enter a new zoom value from the keyboard. When you have the image at the magnification you want, press Enter to finalize things.

This trick also works when you're using the magnification box in the Navigator palette.

Changing the Brush Size

Left bracket ([ )

Press [(left bracket) to reduce the brush size to the next smallest one in the brushes palette. If you're using the smallest fuzzy brush, pressing [selects the largest smooth one.

Right bracket (])

Press] (right bracket) to select the next brush size up. If you're using the largest smooth brush, pressing] selects the smallest fuzzy one.

Shift+[, Shift+]

Shift+[(left bracket) selects the first brush size in the Brushes palette, which is the single-pixel brush. Shift+] (right bracket) selects the last brush size. By default, this is the 100-pixel fuzzy brush, but if you've created some custom brushes of your own, Photoshop selects the last one in the Brushes palette.

Changing Opacity

1, . . . , 9, 0

To change the Opacity setting for a selected painting or editing tool, just press a number key — 1 equals 10 percent Opacity, 9 equals 90, and 0 equals 100 percent. You can also enter more specific values — 89, for example — from the keyboard. (You need to press the two number keys in fairly rapid succession for this technique to work.)

If a selection tool or the move tool is active, pressing a number key changes the opacity of the active layer or floating selection.

Creating Straight Lines

Shift+click

To create a straight line with any of the painting or editing tools, click at one end of the line and Shift+click at the other. Photoshop connects the two points with a straight line.

Click with polygon lasso, Alt+click with regular lasso

The new polygon lasso creates straight-sided selections; you just click to set the first point in your selection and keep clicking to create additional points.

When working with the regular lasso tool, you can temporarily switch to the polygon lasso by Alt+clicking. Alt+click to set the first point in the selection and keep Alt+clicking until you finish drawing the desired outline.

However, don't use this approach when you want to add or subtract from an existing selection marquee. When you have an active selection marquee, pressing Alt subtracts from the selection instead of switching you between lasso tools. So use the polygon tool to add or subtract straight-sided areas from a selection.

Adding to and Subtracting from Selection Outlines

Shift+drag, Shift+click

To select an additional area of your image without deselecting the part that is currently selected, Shift+drag around the new area with a lasso or marquee tool or Shift+click with the magic wand. You can also Shift+choose Select⇨Color Range.

Alt+drag, Alt+click

To deselect an area of the selection, Alt+drag around it with a lasso or marquee tool or Alt+click with the magic wand. You can also Alt+choose the Select⇨ Color Range command.

Shift+Alt+drag, Shift+Alt+click

To retain the intersection of the existing selection and the new outline you draw with a lasso or marquee tool, Shift+Alt+drag with the tool. To retain an area of continuous color inside a selection, Shift+Alt+click with the magic wand.

Moving, Nudging, and Cloning

Ctrl key

In Photoshop 4, you use the move tool to move selections and layers. To temporarily access the move tool when any tool except the pen or hand tool is active, press and hold Ctrl.

Arrow key

To nudge a selection one pixel, press one of the arrow keys with the move tool selected. Or press Ctrl and an arrow key with any tool except the hand or pen tool.

Shift+arrow key

To nudge a selection 10 pixels, select the move tool and press Shift with an arrow key. Or select any tool but the pen or hand tool and press Ctrl+Shift with an arrow key.

Alt+dragging, Alt+arrow key, Shift+Alt+arrow key

To clone a selection and move the clone, Alt+drag the selection with the move tool. You can also press Alt with an arrow key to clone a selection and nudge it one pixel or press Shift+Alt+arrow key to clone and nudge 10 pixels.

When any other tool but the hand or pen tool is selected, you can accomplish the same cloning feats by pressing and holding the Ctrl key with the other keys. (Pressing Ctrl temporarily accesses the move tool, remember?)

Drag with a selection tool

To move a selection outline without moving anything inside the selection, just drag it with a marquee tool, lasso tool, or the magic wand. You can also press the arrow key or Shift+arrow key to nudge the selection outline in 1-pixel and 10-pixel increments, respectively.

Filling a Selection

Ctrl+Backspace

To fill a selection with the background color, press Ctrl+Backspace. If the selection is nonfloating and exists on the Background layer, you can also press Delete to accomplish the same thing. However, if the selection is on a layer or is floating on the Background layer, pressing Delete wipes out the selection instead of filling it. So it's a good idea to always press Ctrl+Backspace instead of Delete to fill your selections.

Alt+Backspace

To fill any selection — floating or not — with the foreground color, press Alt+Backspace.

Shift+Backspace

Press Shift+Backspace to bring up the Fill dialog box, which lets you fill a selection with all kinds of stuff, including the saved version of that portion of the image.

Making, Switching, and Selecting Layers

Ctrl+J, Ctrl+Shift+J

To clone a selection and place the clone on a new layer, press Ctrl+J. To move a nonfloating selection and place the selection on a new layer, press Ctrl+Shift+J.

Click on new layer icon, Ctrl+Shift+J

To assign a floating selection to its own layer, click on the new layer icon in the Layers palette or press Ctrl+Shift+J.

Alt+[, Alt+]

To activate the layer below the one that is currently active, press Alt+[(left bracket). To activate the next layer up, press Alt+] (right bracket).

Alt+right-click, Ctrl+Alt+right-click

To activate the layer belonging to a certain image, Alt+right-click on that image with the move tool. Or Ctrl+Alt+right-click with any other tool except the pen or hand tool.

Ctrl+click on layer name

To generate a selection outline from the contents of a layer, Ctrl+click on the layer name in the Layers palette. You can use any tool to do the job.

So Many Shortcuts, So Little Time

The preceding tips don't address all of the many Photoshop shortcuts. For some additional time-savers, be sure to check out the Cheat Sheet at the front of this book.

Chapter 20

Ten Amusing Ways to Mess Up a Loved One's Face

. . . .

In This Chapter

▶ Pinching the face inward

▶ Bending the face outward

▶ Twisting the face around a taffy pull

▶ Melting the face into a heap of goo

▶ Giving the face a bath

▶ Stretching the face this way and that

▶ Applying the nuclear sunburn effect

▶ Applying the I-don't-know-what-it-is effect

▶ Stamping the face in a marble haze

▶ Effecting a total molecular breakdown

▶ Framing the face with a shadow or vignette

. . . .

*N*ormally, we're all pretty fond of our loved ones. Friends and family members make life a real treat 364 days of the year. But on that one day when the loved one gets kind of pesky — or two days during leap years — it's nice to have Photoshop within easy reach.

Mad at your boyfriend for going on that trip to Paris with a childhood sweetheart? Just scan his face and while away the hours modifying it in a way he won't soon forget. Peeved at your sister for snagging all of Aunt Rowena's multimillion-dollar inheritance? Open Sis in Photoshop and distort her as you please. No need to get angry. Just warp your loved one's face, print it out, and send it off to your local newspaper or tack it up on neighborhood telephone poles.

This chapter — considered by many as an essential step toward utter Photoshop fulfillment — supplies an assortment of delightful recipes for making a digital mess of the one you love. Build understanding, facilitate dialog, and establish bonds that will last a lifetime by mucking up the kissers of those near and dear to your heart.

If I could, I would make a show of solidarity by applying these techniques to a loved one of my own. Alas, I am one of those rare people who has never experienced anger or resentment in my life. I read about these feelings once in *Boy's Life,* but that was as close as I've come.

So instead, I'll take a stab at the absolute strangers shown in Figure 20-1. As I understand it, both women were actresses, captured in the moment of auditioning for a commercial. Though the line of dialog was the same — "Goodness, don't tell me my toilet bowl cleanser isn't working!" — the two women took opposite artistic approaches. Obviously, neither of them was cast in the part, but in tribute to their stirring performances, I'm going to trod heavily upon them in the following sections.

If you're the kind who's a stickler for detail, you may have noticed that the introductory list to this chapter actually includes 11 items, while the headline promises only 10. Please don't let this fact upset your equilibrium — just think of this chapter as a buy-ten-get-one-free sort of deal. Where else are you going to get that kind of value for your money?

Figure 20-1:
Two faces that cry out, "Muck me up in Photoshop!"

Pinching the Face Inward

Here's how to get the effect applied to the surprised character in Figure 20-2:

1. **Select the face with the elliptical marquee tool.**

   You can use some other tool, but an oval selection outline produces the best results. No need to be very precise; an approximate selection is entirely adequate.

2. **Feather the selection.**

   Choose Select➪Feather, enter **6** or thereabouts as the Feather Radius value, and press Enter. This step ensures a smooth transition between the distorted and undistorted areas.

3. **Choose Filter➪Distort➪Pinch.**

   The Pinch dialog box appears, allowing you to collapse the selected image toward its center.

4. **Enter** 50 **as the Amount value and press Enter.**

   The face pinches slightly, as shown in the first example in Figure 20-2. This is a dangerous step in the process because the face may actually look better. Typically, the forehead, jaw, and chin grow, while the nose shrinks — all ingredients that might be misconstrued as indications of beauty. So whatever you do, don't stop now.

Figure 20-2:
Pinch the face once (left) and then pinch again (right).

5. **Press Ctrl+F to reapply the filter.**

The second example in the figure shows the result. Now we're looking at some extreme distortion.

You may be wondering why I didn't just tell you to raise the value in Step 4 rather than applying the filter twice. After all, the Pinch dialog box accepts values as high as 100. However, thanks to the way the filter works, it's better to apply it multiple times using a low value than once with a high value.

Bending the Face Outward

The opposite of the Pinch filter, Filter➪Distort➪Spherize, bends the face outward, as shown in Figure 20-3. Here's how to create a similar effect:

1. **Select the face with the elliptical marquee tool.**

Make your selection just as instructed in the preceding steps.

2. **Feather the selection.**

Again, you're just doing the same thing you did before.

3. **Choose Filter➪Distort➪Spherize.**

Now this part is different. The Spherize filter brings up the Spherize dialog box, which reflects the image on the back of a spoon so that it curves outward. (Remember staring sleepily at your spoon before diving into the Lucky Charms or Count Chocula? Even in those remote years, the Spherize filter was at work.)

4. **Enter 100 and press Enter.**

Unlike the Pinch filter, Spherize works just fine at the maximum setting. (Better algorithm, don't you know.) The first example in Figure 20-3 shows the nose-expanding, chin-contracting results.

5. **Select a different area inside the first selection.**

One swipe of the Spherize filter is never enough, but you can't apply the filter twice to the same area without losing detail. The eyes may start sliding off the face, for example. So select an area inside the first selection to do more damage. (Shift+Alt+drag with the elliptical marquee tool to get the job done.)

6. **Feather the selection.**

Choose Select➪Feather or press Ctrl+Shift+D and press Enter. Whatever value you use the first time does well the second time around.

Figure 20-3:
Bend the
face once
(left) and
then select
a different
area and
bend it
outward
some more
(right).

7. Press Ctrl+F to reapply the Spherize filter.

Ooh, isn't that nice? The second example in Figure 20-3 shows what happened to my image. A couple of swipes more, and I bet we can see right up her nostrils.

Twisting the Face around a Taffy Pull

To twist a face so that it looks like it's being put through a blender — as demonstrated in Figure 20-4 — follow these steps:

1. Select the face with the rectangular marquee tool.

For this effect, a rectangular selection outline works best.

2. Choose Filter⇨Distort⇨Twirl.

The Twirl dialog box lets you do the twisting.

3. Enter an <u>A</u>ngle value between 100 and 200 and press Enter.

The first example in Figure 20-4 shows the effect of a 100-degree twist; the second example shows a 200-degree twist. Any value over 200 eliminates too much detail for our purposes. Negative values between –100 and –200 are also acceptable.

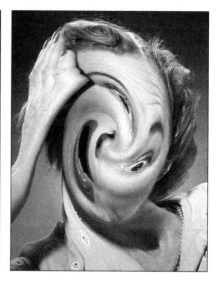

Figure 20-4:
The Twirl
filter applied
at 100
degrees
(left) and 200
degrees
(right).

4. Sharpen the image.

The Twirl filter tends to blur the detail. To make it sharp again, choose Filter⇨Sharpen⇨Unsharp Mask. Enter an Amount value of 50 percent, a Radius of between 0.5 and 1.0, and press Enter.

Melting the Face into a Heap of Goo

No matter how long you use Photoshop, you are likely to never come up with this technique without at least some help. It's just too weird. But even so, it results in the awesome melted face effect shown in Figure 20-5. Don't try to understand it, just do it.

1. Press Ctrl+D.

Ctrl+D deselects everything in your image. You have to apply the technique I outline here to the entire image, so you can't have any active selection outlines.

2. Choose Filter⇨Distort⇨Polar Coordinates.

The Polar Coordinates dialog box appears, giving you the power to turn an image inside out. Not a trick for the squeamish.

3. Select the Polar to Rectangular radio button and press Enter.

The first image in Figure 20-5 shows the result. It's hard to see what's going on, but there's some good stuff there.

Figure 20-5:
A face
subjected to
the Polar
Coordinates
filter (left)
and then
flipped and
offset (right).

4. **Choose Image⇨Rotate Canvas⇨Flip Vertical.**

   The image turns upside down, which makes it a little more recognizable.

5. **Press the Alt key and press and hold on the page preview box in the bottom-left corner of the window.**

   You remember the file size box — from Chapter 3, right? It's that thing that says 379K/379K or 1.8M/3.6M or whatever. When you Alt+click on it, you see the dimensions of your image.

6. **Write down the Width value (in pixels) and then divide that value by 2.**

   My image is 360 pixels wide; 360 divided by 2 is 180.

7. **Choose Filter⇨Other⇨Offset.**

   Up comes the Offset dialog box, which moves the pixels in an image around. An incredibly obscure feature, Offset is useful only for the occasional special effect.

8. **Enter your special divided-by-2 value into the Horizontal option box.**

   I entered 180.

9. **Select the Wrap Around radio button and press Enter.**

   That's it; you're done. By offsetting the image half its width and wrapping the excess around to the other side of the image, you center the image inside the window, as shown in the second image in Figure 20-5.

Giving the Face a Bath

If you're only slightly piqued at your loved one, you may want to make the face appear under water, as shown in Figure 20-6. Here's how to submerge the image:

1. Select the image any which way you want.

No special constraints this time.

2. Choose Filter⇨Distort⇨Ripple.

I bet you're beginning to think that all the great face-mucking features are under the Filter⇨Distort submenu. As it turns out, Ripple is the last one that is.

3. Select Medium from the <u>S</u>ize pop-up menu in the Ripple dialog box.

The Small option isn't enough, and the Large option is too much. As with the baby bear in the famous story — I believe Snow White and the three little pigs is the one — Medium is just right.

4. Enter any old <u>A</u>mount value you want and press Enter.

In Figure 20-6, I applied an Amount value of 300 to the first image and 999 — the maximum setting — to the second image.

Figure 20-6: What happens when you apply the Ripple filter with an Amount value of 300 (left) and 999 (right).

Stretching the Face This Way and That

Why don't you and I take a break from the commands under the Filter⇨Distort submenu and try out some manual distortion techniques? Figure 20-7 shows how you can distort an image using the new Photoshop 4 Transform and Free Transform commands. The following steps tell you what the figure leaves out.

1. Select something.

Again, select what you want. I can't make all the decisions for you. But you have to select something or you can't access the command I'm about to instruct you to use. If you want to apply the command to your entire image, press Ctrl+A or choose Select⇨All.

2. Press Ctrl+H.

Photoshop hides the selection outline. Otherwise, the outline just gets in your way.

3. Choose Layer⇨Free Transform or press Ctrl+T.

The Free Transform command surrounds the selection with a marquee and displays square handles on the sides and at the corners. With the Free Transform marquee, you can resize, rotate, skew, distort, and apply perspective effects to your selection.

To scale (resize) the selection, drag any handle. Shift+drag to scale proportionately, and Alt+drag to scale symmetrically around the center of the selection. To rotate the selection, move the cursor outside the marquee until you see a curved, double-headed arrow, and then drag. To move the selection, drag inside the marquee.

But to really have some fun, use the following techniques: Ctrl+drag any handle to distort the image freely. Ctrl+Shift+drag a side handle to skew the image. And Ctrl+Shift+Alt+drag a corner handle to apply perspective effects.

Be patient when working with the Transform command — Photoshop sometimes takes a while to generate the effects of your drags. If you don't like the outcome of a drag, just press Ctrl+Z to undo it.

4. When you've distorted the image to your satisfaction, press Enter.

Figure 20-7 shows two lovely effects created by tugging this way and that on my crying woman. In the left example, I skewed and distorted the image, giving Miss Crocodile Tears shoulders that a linebacker would envy. In the right example, I Ctrl+Shift+Alt+dragged to create an infant-looking-up-from-a-crib view.

The Layer⇨Transform submenu contains individual commands for distorting, skewing, scaling, rotating, and adding perspective to the image. When you choose one of these Tranform commands, you get the transform marquee as you do when using Free Transform. Just drag the handles to apply the effect — no Alt, Ctrl, Shift key combinations required. If you want to apply a different effect, you have to choose the desired effect from the L̲ayer⊅Transform submenu. I usually prefer the Free Transform command — it's one-stop-shopping for transforming.

You can choose the Flip Horizontal and Flip Vertical commands, also found in the Transform submenu, when you are in the process of transforming your image using the Free Transform command.

Figure 20-7: The Free Transform command lets you bend, pull, rotate, and otherwise stretch a selection in whatever way you please.

Applying the Nuclear Sunburn Effect

Phew, that's enough of that manual stuff. You're entitled to automation, and automation is exactly what you're going to get. This next effect takes a different approach. Rather than moving the pixels around, the Nuclear Sunburn effect relies on commands that change the pixels' colors. As you can see in Figure 20-8, the face becomes lighted with a kind of eerie luminescence.

1. **Select your image.**

   Make your selection as detailed or as imprecise as you like.

2. **Choose Fil̲ter⊅Stylize⊅Solarize.**

Sounds like an exciting command, huh? Actually, by itself, Solarize is pretty dull. It makes the black pixels black, the medium pixels medium, and the white pixels black again. Big whoop. But have no fear, we're going to spruce things up a little.

3. Choose Image⇨Adjust⇨Auto Levels.

Photoshop lightens the gray pixels and makes them white, as shown in the first example in Figure 20-8. The areas that were previously either dark or light are now dark; the medium areas are now light.

Figure 20-8: Choose the Solarize filter and the Auto Levels command (left) and then press Ctrl+I.

4. Choose Image⇨Adjust⇨Invert or just press Ctrl+I.

This command inverts the image, turning the black pixels white and the white pixels black, as in a photo negative (kind of like a simplified version of the Difference mode). The finished result is shown in the second example of Figure 20-8.

Applying the I-Don't-Know-What-It-Is Effect

I really don't know what to make of this effect. Each time I look at it, a metaphor flashes into my head and then I lose it. It's like a face riddled with protozoa or some kind of crazy, impossible X-ray. "The Face under the Electron Microscope" — maybe that's it. Well, whatever it is, you can check it out in Figure 20-9.

1. **Select your image.**

   What a fresh step for you.

2. **Choose Filter⇨Stylize⇨Find Edges.**

   The left example in Figure 20-9 shows how the Find Edges filter traces the contours of the selected face. Moderately cool, but not killer.

Figure 20-9: The Find Edges filter on its own (left) and after sharpening the image to its utmost limit (right).

3. **Press Ctrl+Z to undo the effect.**

   We can do better than that.

4. **Choose Filter⇨Sharpen⇨Unsharp Mask.**

   If you can bring out some additional edges, you give the Find Edges command more to work with. And nothing brings out the edges like Unsharp Mask.

5. **Enter the maximum Amount value, 500 percent, and the very high Radius value of 10.**

   Such a high Radius value takes you into the realm of special-effects sharpening. It really sharpens the holy heck out of the image.

6. **Press Enter.**

   That caps off the Unsharp Mask filter.

7. **Choose Filter⇨Stylize⇨Find Edges.**

   The result appears in the second example in Figure 20-9. Now that's what I call killer. I don't know what else to call it, of course, so I guess killer will have to do.

Stamping the Face in a Marble Haze

Again, this is a fairly weak name for a wonderful effect. The following steps alternatively lighten and darken the image utilizing a cloud pattern that ends up looking a lot like marble, as you can see in Figure 20-10.

1. **Select your image.**

   Yeah, yeah, yeah.

2. **Choose Filter⇨Render⇨Difference Clouds.**

   Of the two Clouds filters, this one is the more exciting. It blends Photoshop-generated clouds with the selected image using the Difference mode. The first example in Figure 20-10 shows the result of this single-shot filter.

Figure 20-10: The result of choosing the Difference Clouds command once (left) and five times (right).

3. **Press Ctrl+F to reapply the Difference Clouds filter.**

   Photoshop blends the clouds with the image. Things are getting more mottled.

4. **Repeat Step 3 three times.**

   That's right. Press Ctrl+F, Ctrl+F, and yet another Ctrl+F.

5. **Choose Image⇨Adjust⇨Auto Levels.**

   Looking a little dark? Auto Levels brings the colors back to life.

6. **Apply the Unsharp Mask filter.**

An Amount value of 50 percent and a Radius of 0.5 should bring back some of the detail. The second example of Figure 20-10 shows how the face now appears emblazoned on a dense, marble wall. At least, that's what the image looks like to me. Feel free to draw your own conclusions.

Effecting a Total Molecular Breakdown

This technique reduces your image to a bunch of colored shapes and then blends them with the original image to form something truly other-worldly, as shown in Figure 20-11.

1. **Select your image.**

Admit it, you'd miss this step if it weren't here. You've seen it so many times, it seems like an old friend.

2. **Choose Filter➪Pixelate➪Crystallize, enter** 30, **and press Enter.**

Nice words, Pixelate and Crystallize, but what do they mean? Like most of the commands under the Filter➪Pixelate submenu, Crystallize subdivides the image into blocks of color. In this case, the blocks resemble little particles of stained glass, as in the first example in Figure 20-11.

Figure 20-11: After applying the Crystallize command to my image, I used the Fade command to mix the new image with the original using the Difference mode (right).

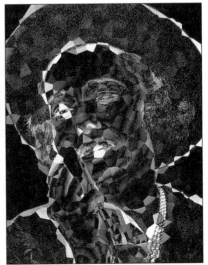

3. **Choose Filter⇨Fade.**

   The Fade command, new to Version 4, lets you mix the filter effect with the unfiltered original by using the same blending modes and Opacity slider you find in the Layers palette.

4. **Choose the Difference option from the Mode pop-up menu and press Enter.**

   Photoshop uses the stained-glass pattern to invert the face.

5. **Press Ctrl+L and use the options in the Levels dialog box to lighten the image.**

   As things stand now, the image is way too dark to print. I lightened the image on the right side of Figure 20-11 by setting the three Input Levels values to 0, 2.30, and 170 respectively. Press Enter to apply the changes.

6. **Apply the Unsharp Mask filter.**

   I used an Amount value of 100 percent and a Radius of 0.5, but I encourage you to sharpen according to your personal tastes.

Framing the Goofy Pose

Sometimes, you're lucky enough to dig up a photograph of your unruly loved one that's embarrassing all on its own — no special effects required. In that case, all you need to do is add a little finishing touch, such as the drop shadow or vignette effect shown in Figure 20-12.

In Photoshop 4, the new Actions palette contains prerecorded macros (sets of commands) that apply the effects shown in Figure 20-12. Here's how to create the drop shadow effect using the Actions palette:

1. **Save your image.**

   After you apply the effect, you won't be able to use Edit⇨Undo if you don't like the results. Photoshop actually applies a series of commands to generate the effect, and Edit⇨Undo only reverses the last command in the chain, which doesn't get you back to your original image. But if you save your image before you apply the effect, you can use File⇨Revert to return to your original image if necessary.

2. **Choose Window⇨Show Actions to display the Actions palette.**

3. **Click on the Drop Shadow (full image) item.**

   Photoshop sets about applying a drop shadow to your image.

4. When you see a dialog box, press Enter.

As Photoshop applies the drop shadow effect, two dialog boxes are presented enabling you to alter the effect a little. Just press Enter to accept the default settings. Photoshop creates the shadow and places it on a separate layer.

To create a rectangular vignette, as shown in the right-hand example in Figure 20-12, follow the same steps, only choose the Vignette (full image) item in the Actions palette. This time, Photoshop doesn't present you with any dialog boxes, so you can skip Step 3. Again, the effect appears on its own layer.

I applied the drop shadow and the vignette effects in Figure 20-12 to the same original image. As you can see from the figure, the drop shadow effect enlarges your overall image size a little — Photoshop adds the shadow around the outside of your original image. But the vignette effect eats away at your image, because the vignette is applied from the edges of the image inward. If you want more control over how your vignette is applied, you may prefer the method I explain in Chapter 13, in the section "Making the selection all fuzzy around the edges."

Figure 20-12: You can easily create a drop shadow or vignette effect using the Actions palette in Photoshop 4.

Well, that should do it. If you don't have the anger worked out of your system by now, I suggest counseling. Or better yet, you kids kiss and make up. That's what my wife and I always do. (Oh, dang, there goes my *Boy's Life* story!)

Chapter 21

Ten Things to Do with Your Photoshop Masterpiece

*A*fter you finish creating your image in Photoshop, you may experience a hint of letdown. I mean, now that you're done with the image, what do you do with it? You can't just sit there and look at it on your screen for the rest of your life.

Well, that is an option, I suppose, but certainly not your only option. Photoshop is one of the key programs used by graphics professionals, and only a few of said professionals create images just to sit around and stare at them all day. More often, these images have specific purposes and are used in very specific ways.

This chapter examines a few options. Some of them cost money, and some involve the use of other programs that I don't explain in this book. All of the following options provide food for future thought.

Printing and Dispersing

Just about everyone who has a computer also owns a printer. Assuming that you do too, make sure that the image fits onto a sheet of paper and print it out (refer back to Chapter 7 if you need help). Then you can photocopy the image and hand it out to everyone you know or stick it in an envelope and mail it to your grandmother. Digital images are a welcomed gift any time during the year.

Framing Your Work of Art

Okay, the preceding option was obvious. This one isn't, and it's expensive to boot. If you've created just about the best-looking image you could possibly imagine, you can actually print it out and frame it. The image needs to have a resolution of at least 150 ppi, and you probably want it to be fairly large to justify the expense (although many classic works of art are only a few inches tall). And, of course, the image should be full color, RGB.

When the image is ready to go, call around to a few service bureaus in your neck of the woods and find one that can print to a dye-sublimation printer. A dye-sub printer creates images that look just like photographs — no little dots, like you see in newspaper photos, just smooth colors. You can't reproduce from dye-sub prints, but they look great. (Professionals use them for proofing to make sure that the colors in the printed image look the way they want.)

A dye-sub printout will probably cost you around $20. But provided the image looks good, the results can be fantastic.

When you go to get the image framed, make sure to ask for UV-protected glass, which also runs around $20 to $30. Dye-sub prints can fade when exposed to direct or even indirect light, so hang the piece away from a window.

Placing the Image into PageMaker or QuarkXPress

Adobe PageMaker and QuarkXPress are two popular page-layout programs. They allow you to combine text and graphics to create multipage documents such as newsletters, reports, catalogs, and even books. This book, for example, was laid out in PageMaker; the color plates were laid out in XPress.

If you want to use a Photoshop image in one of these programs, save it in the TIFF format with LZW compression. Then import the file from disk into PageMaker by choosing the Place command (Ctrl+D), found under the File menu, or into XPress using the Get Picture command (Ctrl+E), also found under the File menu. (Both commands are found inside the respective programs, not inside Photoshop.)

You can change the dimensions of the image, move it on the printed page, run text around it, and print the final pages, all inside PageMaker or XPress. So unless you want to further modify the image, you have no reason to return to Photoshop. However, if you have a low-end printer, it's best to scale the image to the final desired size inside Photoshop rather than in your page-layout program. Otherwise, the image may take a long time to print.

Whatever you do, don't copy the image in Photoshop and paste it into PageMaker or XPress. When you copy the image, it is sent to the Windows Clipboard, which converts the image to the Windows Metafile format. Trust me, you won't be happy with the results of the conversion.

Placing the Image into Illustrator, FreeHand, or CorelDRAW

Adobe Illustrator, MacroMedia FreeHand, and CorelDRAW are graphics programs like Photoshop, but instead of enabling you to edit images, they let you create smooth-line artwork. Information graphics, maps, architectural plans, general artwork, and single-page documents such as flyers are all projects ideally suited to Illustrator, FreeHand, and CorelDRAW.

All three programs let you import images. In the case of Illustrator, save your Photoshop image in the Photoshop EPS format. Then import it from disk by choosing the Place Art command inside Illustrator. For FreeHand, go ahead and save the image as a TIFF file. Then choose the Place command (Ctrl+Shift+D) from inside FreeHand. To import an image into CorelDRAW, you can use either the TIFF or Photoshop EPS format. Place the image into your CorelDRAW document by using the File⇨Import command (Ctrl+I) inside CorelDRAW.

After placing the image, you can combine it with smooth-line artwork or integrate it into a single-page document. The IDG Books Worldwide, Inc., production staff used FreeHand to label Figure 2-1 and the other figures that required labels in this book. It's not possible to label the figures inside Photoshop — which is where they all originated — because small text in Photoshop is jagged and illegible. PageMaker, meanwhile, is great for creating long text documents but not so good at handling little bits of text here and there.

Here's how labeled figures such as Figure 2-1 got onto their respective pages:

1. **I saved the image in the TIFF format.**

   Then I copied the TIFF file to disk and sent it to IDG Books Worldwide, Inc., in Indiana.

2. **A member of the IDG crackerjack production staff placed the images into FreeHand.**

   A production artist then created all the labels and saved the FreeHand document in the EPS format. EPS is the best format for smooth-line artwork and high-resolution text. It also retains the image.

3. **Inside PageMaker, another production artist imported the FreeHand EPS graphic.**

   The layout artist then positioned the EPS graphic and ran the text around it, as you see the page now.

4. **The final PageMaker document was saved to disk and shipped to the commercial printer.**

   The printer printed the pages and reproduced the pages onto the paper you're reading now.

How's that for a start-to-finish examination of how this process works? And just in case you thought I was spilling out some trade secrets, just about every publisher creates books this way these days. It's a desktop world.

Pasting the Image into Persuasion or PowerPoint

Adobe Persuasion and Microsoft PowerPoint are a couple of popular presentation programs used for creating slides and on-screen presentations for board meetings, product demonstrations, and kiosks. Photoshop is a great tool for creating backgrounds for these presentations or refining head shots that may appear on the slides.

Because Persuasion and PowerPoint do most of their work on-screen, it's perfectly acceptable to transfer the image from Photoshop via the Clipboard. While inside Photoshop, just select the portion of the image you want to use, copy it by pressing Ctrl+C, switch to Persuasion or PowerPoint, and paste the selection by pressing Ctrl+V.

However, this recommendation holds only if you're creating an on-screen presentation or plan to print the presentation on a non-PostScript printer. If you want to print overheads on a color PostScript printer, don't use the Clipboard to place the images into your presentation program. Instead, import the image into PowerPoint as a TIFF file and into Persuasion as a Photoshop EPS file.

As you can in PageMaker, you can move the image around, change the dimensions, and wrap text around it. If you plan on displaying the presentation on-screen, you want to give some thought to the file size of the image. For example, if you intend for the image to serve as a background for a presentation that takes up an entire 13-inch monitor, the image should be 640 pixels wide by 480 pixels tall. A good size for a head shot may be 300 pixels tall by 200 pixels wide. Experiment to find the file sizes that work best for you.

Making a Desktop Pattern in Windows 95

You know that pattern that appears in the background behind all the icons on your Windows 95 desktop? You can create your own custom background using Photoshop.

Here's what you do:

1. Create your image.

If you want a single image to fill your entire screen, make the image the same size as the Desktop Area setting in the Windows Desktop Properties dialog box. To check the setting, right-click anywhere on the desktop, choose the Properties command to display the Display Properties dialog box, and then click on the Settings tab. If the setting is 640 by 480, for example, make your image 640 pixels wide by 480 pixels tall. Set the image resolution to 72 ppi.

2. Save your image in the BMP format.

When you save the image, be sure to deselect the RLE Encoding option.

3. Right-click anywhere on the Windows 95 desktop to display the Desktop Properties dialog box.

That's assuming that you don't already have the dialog box open from Step 1.

4. Click on the Background tab.

5. Click on the Browse button in the Wallpaper section of the dialog box.

Windows displays a dialog box showing all your drives, directories, and files.

6. Select your image in the dialog box and press Enter.

You should see your image name selected in the Wallpaper drop-down menu.

7. Choose a Display option.

If you choose the Tile radio button, your image is repeated across the screen. If you choose the Center button, the image is centered on the screen.

8. Click on Apply.

Windows applies your new wallpaper to your screen without closing the Display Properties dialog box. If you don't like what you see, you can change the Display option or choose another image to use as your wallpaper (wallpaper images must be in the BMP format). You can also play with the settings on the Appearance tab to change the color of the labels under your desktop icons so that they coordinate with the new wallpaper.

9. Press Enter to close the dialog box.

Turn Your Face into a Mouse Pad

Now that more and more folks are acquiring the ability to produce digital images, copy shops such as Kinko's are offering a plethora of products on which you can print your image. You can get your favorite Photoshop image transferred onto a mouse pad, coffee cup, T-shirt, calendar, and a whole bunch of other items that are guaranteed to be a big hit come holiday gift-giving season. What employee wouldn't love to receive a mouse pad with your smiling face on it, after all? Check with your copy shop for information on any image size, resolution, or file format requirements you need to follow when preparing your image.

Engaging in Tag-Team Editing

Just because you're an electronic artist doesn't mean that you have to work alone. If you want to give another artist or a friend a whack at one of your images, copy it to disk and mail it off. Then have the associate/friend mail the disk back when he or she is done. Or just send the file back and forth using e-mail, if you're hooked into the Internet or some other online service that offers e-mail.

You didn't have nearly this range of give-and-take editing options back in the days before computers. I mean, you can keep trading images for years. It's like a long-distance chess game — whoever comes up with the craziest editing trick wins.

Posting the Image over the Internet or an Online Service

Both the CompuServe and America Online electronic information services have Photoshop forums, and subscribers can connect to either service using a modem. You can then upload images to the forums to make them available to other subscribers. You have to pay for the time it takes to upload the image — and so does the person who downloads the image — so keep the images fairly small and save them in the JPEG or CompuServe GIF format.

If you happen to have your own Web page — or know someone who does — you can also add your image to the page, thereby making it available to Web surfers worldwide. As discussed in Chapter 6, you can use JPEG or the CompuServe GIF format to post images on the Web.

Just in case you haven't gotten enough of me through the course of reading this book, by the way, you can check out my Web page at the following URL: `www.DekeMC.com`. It offers some Photoshop tips and tricks along with a bunch of other stuff, including lots of shameless self-promotion. But hey, what's the point of having a Web page if you can't brag a little, right?

Adding It to Your Private Collection

No one says that you have to produce artwork for public consumption. I do plenty of stuff just for my own amusement and edification. What you see in the book, for example, represents about half of what I came up with; the other images are working files, experiments, or just too hideous for publication.

So share the stuff you're proud of, keep the random experiments to yourself, and try to learn from your inevitable mistakes. Oh, yeah, and don't beat the computer when it crashes.

Appendix A
How to Install Photoshop

● ●

*P*rograms like Photoshop don't magically appear on your hard drive. You have to go out and get them, bring them home, and install them by unwrapping and inserting disks. I know, such manual activities should be illegal in a computer-run economy like ours — I, for one, was led to believe that the 1990s would be a time when servo-robots catered to my every whim, so that the atrophy of my body would allow me to evolve into a floating brain — but, sadly, these things still require a lot of driving about, signing checks, ripping apart cellophane, and other laborious tasks. *Quel bummerre,* as the French say.

Now, of course, I could just tell you, "If you haven't yet installed Photoshop, read the Getting Started manual included with the program." But you didn't pay $19.99 of your hard-earned cash along with a nickel that you found on the street for me to tell you that. So without any further ado — I just love to say "ado," don't you? — here's how to install Photoshop.

Putting Photoshop on Your Hard Disk

To put Photoshop on your hard disk, just follow these steps:

1. **Insert the Photoshop application CD into your CD-ROM drive.**

   Or, if you're installing from floppy disk, insert the disk labeled *Installer—Disk 1* into your floppy disk drive.

   If you're running Windows 95 or Windows NT and are installing from the CD, a startup screen appears automatically. Choose the Install Adobe Photoshop option and skip to Step 3.

2. **Run the Setup program.**

   If you're using Windows 3.1 or installing from floppy disk, you need to start the Photoshop Setup program "manually." To do this, you activate a file called Setup.exe.

   If you're installing from floppy disk, use Explorer (Windows 95 or NT 4.0) or File Manager (Windows 3.1) to open the disk and then double-click on the Setup.exe file. If you're installing from CD, open the CD, open the disk 1 folder, and then double-click on the Setup.exe file.

3. Click the Next button or press Alt+N.

4. State your name, company, and serial number.

That is, type the information requested by the setup program. You can find the serial number on the registration card for your copy of Photoshop.

5. Click on Next and then click on Yes.

This step tells Photoshop that you spelled your name and company name right in Step 4.

6. Select the Custom Install option and click on Next.

A list of check boxes becomes available.

7. Select the following check boxes:

❑ Program Files

❑ ICC Profiles

❑ Filter Files

❑ Duotone Files

If you have tons of free space on your hard drive, you can install the Sample Files, too. But the components listed above are the essential ones. In fact, you can probably do without the Duotone Files also, if you're really pressed for disk space.

8. Verify the Destination Directory.

Beneath the component check boxes discussed in Step 7, you see the name of the drive and directory where the installer plans to put Photoshop. If you want to put the program elsewhere, click on the Browse button and choose a different drive or directory. Chances are, though, that the choice the installer made for you is fine.

9. Click on Next or press Alt+N.

10. Choose a program folder and click on Next.

If you want all your Adobe programs to appear in one program folder, go with the Adobe option, which is selected by default.

11. Confirm your choices.

After you complete Step 10, the installer gives you a rundown of the installation options you selected. If you want to change anything, click on the Back button. If everything looks okay, click on Next to begin the installation.

If you're installing from CD, you can take a break while the installer does its thing. If you're installing from floppy disk, don't wander off; you need to feed the various program disks into your floppy disk drive when the installer prompts you to do so.

12. **Register your program or not.**

If you have a modem and want to register your copy of Photoshop online, click on the Finish button. Otherwise, click on the check box labeled "Yes, I want to register electronically" to remove the check mark from the box. Then click on Finish.

13. **Click on OK.**

The installer may need to restart your system to finish its job. Close any open programs and then give the installer the go-ahead.

If the installer program complains that you don't have enough space on your hard disk to hold Photoshop, there's only one solution: Quit the installer and delete some stuff from your hard disk. I can't tell you what to delete — I can't quite see your computer from this angle — so you'll have to decide for yourself. Or ask the advice of friends who have more experience than you, and see whether they can help out. Keep in mind that you need some empty hard drive space over and above what Photoshop demands for installation because working in the program consumes some drive space as well.

What's This QuickTime Thing?

If you want to view the introductory movies provided on the companion CD included with Photoshop, you need to install QuickTime and Acrobat Reader, which are both included on the Photoshop application CD. However, I recommend that you skip this option because QuickTime can cause headaches for some PC video cards.

Installing Adobe Type Manager

In addition to installing Photoshop, you may also want to install Adobe Type Manager (ATM). Version 3.02 is included ATM is crucial for working with Type 1 PostScript fonts in Photoshop. Unfortunately, Version 3.02 doesn't work with Windows NT, so this option applies only to Windows 95 and Windows 3.1 users.

To install ATM, open the Photoshop application CD (using File Manager or Explorer), open the ATM302 folder, and then double-click on the Install.exe file. Then follow the on-screen prompts to complete the installation.

Appendix B
Photo Credits

··

*T*he following pages list every figure and color plate that features a photograph (or partial photograph) and the collection or photographer from which the photograph comes. My sincere thanks to the generous folks who contributed photos for inclusion in this book.

Figures	*Photographer/Product*	*Company*
Figure 1-1 (frame)	Signature Series #4, "The Painted Table"	PhotoDisc
Figure 1-2 (text)	Kent Knudson, Signature Series #2, "Urban Perspectives"	PhotoDisc
Figure 1-2 (eyes & mouth)	Vol. 11, "Retro Americana"	PhotoDisc
Figures 1-3 through 1-6	Vol. 11, "Retro Americana"	PhotoDisc
Figure 1-7	Vol. 13, "Italian Fine Art, Prints, & Photographs"	PhotoDisc
Figures 2-2, 2-3 (flower)	"Natural World"	Digital Stock
Figure 3-2	"Southern California"	Digital Stock
Figure 3-3	"Active Lifestyles 2"	Digital Stock
Figures 3-4, 3-5	"Children & Teens"	Digital Stock
Figure 3-6	"Active Lifestyles 2"	Digital Stock
Figure 3-8	"Southern California"	Digital Stock
Figure 4-1	"Children & Teens"	Digital Stock
Figures 4-3, 4-4, 4-5	Frederick Shussler, Signature Series #3, "Children of the World"	PhotoDisc
Figures 5-2, 5-6, 7-5, Color Plates 5-1, 7-1	"Indigenous Peoples"	Digital Stock
Color Plates 5-1, 7-1 (background)	"Natural Textures"	Digital Stock
Color Plates 5-2, 5-3 (background)	"Conceptual Backgrounds"	Digital Stock

Figures	Photographer/Product	Company
Figure 5-3	"Natural World"	Digital Stock
Figure 7-2	"Space Exploration"	Digital Stock
Color Plates 8-1, 8-2 (background)	"Conceptual Backgrounds"	Digital Stock
Figure 8-9	Robert Yin, "Undersea Textures"	Digital Stock
Figures 9-1, 9-2, 9-3	"Space Exploration"	Digital Stock
Figures 9-5, 9-6, 9-7, 9-10, 9-11, and Color Plate 9-1	"Undersea Life"	Digital Stock
Color Plate 9-1 (background)	"Urban Textures"	Digital Stock
Figures 10-1 through 10-4; 10-6 through 10-8	"Space & Spaceflight"	Digital Stock
Color Plate 10-1	"Indigenous Peoples"	Digital Stock
Color Plate 10-1 (background)	"Urban Textures"	Digital Stock
Figures 11-1, 11-2, 11-3	"Undersea Life"	Digital Stock
Figures 12-2, 12-4, 12-5	Eric Wunrow, "Sampler One"	ColorBytes
Figure 12-3	"Cyberstock"	Digital Stock
Figure 12-7	"Animals"	Digital Stock
Figures 12-8, 12-9, Color Plates 12-1, 12-2, 12-3	"Animals"	Digital Stock
Color Plate 12-1 (background)	"Urban Textures"	Digital Stock
Color Plates 12-2, 12-3 (background)	"Conceptual Backgrounds"	Digital Stock
Figure 13-1	"Buildings & Structures"	Digital Stock
Figure 13-3	"Buildings & Structures"	Digital Stock
Figure 13-4	Frederick Shussler, Signature Series #3, "Children of the World"	PhotoDisc
Figure 13-5	"Skylines of North America"	Digital Stock
Figures 14-1, 14-2, 14-3, 14-5, 14-6, 14-9, 14-10, Color Plate 14-1	Signature Series #4, "The Painted Table"	PhotoDisc
Color Plate 14-1 (background)	"Conceptual Backgrounds"	Digital Stock

Figures	Photographer/Product	Company
Figures 15-1, 15-2, 15-3, 15-5, 15-6	"Undersea Life"	Digital Stock
Color Plate 15-1 through 15-4 (fish and kelp)	"Undersea Life"	Digital Stock
Color Plates 15-1 through 15-4 (cathedral)	"Buildings & Structures"	Digital Stock
Color Plates 15-1 and 15-2 (Neptune, comet, astronaut, and nebula)	"Space & Spaceflight"	Digital Stock
Color Plates 15-1, 15-2 (lily)	"Flowers"	Digital Stock
Color Plates 15-1, 15-2 (background)	"Antistock"	Digital Stock
Color Plates 15-3, 15-4 (background)	"Natural Textures"	Digital Stock
Figures 16-1, 16-5, 16-6, 16-7 (leaves)	Hans Wiesenhofer, Signature Series #1, "Colors"	PhotoDisc
Color Plate 16-1 (trees)	Hans Wiesenhofer, Signature Series #1, "Colors"	PhotoDisc
Color Plate 16-1 (background)	"Natural Textures"	Digital Stock
Figures 17-2 through 17-17	Vol. 13, "Italian Fine Art, Prints, & Photographs"	PhotoDisc
Color Plate 17-1	"Western Scenics"	Digital Stock
Color Plate 17-1 (background)	"Tranquility"	Digital Stock
Figures 18-1, 18-2, 18-3	Vol. 11, "Retro Americana"	PhotoDisc
Figures 18-7 through 18-10	Vol. 11, "Retro Americana"	PhotoDisc
Color Plates 18-1, 18-2	Daniel McFarland	
Color Plates 18-1, 18-2 (background)	"Conceptual Backgrounds"	Digital Stock
Color Plate 18-3	Denise McClelland	
Color Plate 18-3 (background)	"Antistock"	Digital Stock
Figure 18-11, Color Plate 18-4	"Animals"	Digital Stock

Figures	*Photographer/Product*	*Company*
Figure 18-12, Color Plate 18-5	"Animals"	Digital Stock
Color Plates 18-4, 18-5 (background)	"Conceptual Backgrounds"	Digital Stock
Figures 20-1 through 20-12	Vol. 11, "Retro Americana"	PhotoDisc

Index

(continued)

(continued)

• W •

12 Free Photo CD Scans. . .

Not All Photo CD Scans Are Equal

Quality, excellent service and support… just a few of the reasons Photoshop users, artists, designers, photographers, and publishers from around the United States choose PALMER'S for their Photo CD scanning. Your image is taken seriously whether you need one scan or thousands.

Introduce yourself to the PALMER'S difference. We'll scan 12 negatives or slides for free* (a $36 value) with an order of $36 (12 Repro scans) or more. That's it! You'll find PALMER'S is America's premier Photo CD service.

PALMER'S

MOUNTAIN VIEW
650 Castro Street
415 969 1950
415 969 1956 *fax*

SACRAMENTO
2313 C Street
916 441 3305
916 441 1157 *fax*

SMART SOLUTIONS
800 735 1950
pcd@palmers.com

Yes!
I Want 12 Free!

Name

Company

Address

City

State/Zip

How did you hear about us?

Title

Telephone

Fax

Business Type

Scans Per Month

*This offer is good for **35mm film** and **one time only**, although pass it along to your friends.
(does not include disc and offer subject to change)

IDG

7/29/96

The Internet For Macs® For Dummies,® 2nd Edition	by Charles Seiter	ISBN: 1-56884-371-2	$19.99 USA/$26.99 Canada
The Internet For Macs® For Dummies® Starter Kit	by Charles Seiter	ISBN: 1-56884-244-9	$29.99 USA/$39.99 Canada
The Internet For Macs® For Dummies® Starter Kit Bestseller Edition	by Charles Seiter	ISBN: 1-56884-245-7	$39.99 USA/$54.99 Canada
The Internet For Windows® For Dummies® Starter Kit	by John R. Levine & Margaret Levine Young	ISBN: 1-56884-237-6	$34.99 USA/$44.99 Canada
The Internet For Windows® For Dummies® Starter Kit, Bestseller Edition	by John R. Levine & Margaret Levine Young	ISBN: 1-56884-246-5	$39.99 USA/$54.99 Canada

MACINTOSH

Mac® Programming For Dummies®	by Dan Parks Sydow	ISBN: 1-56884-173-6	$19.95 USA/$26.95 Canada
Macintosh® System 7.5 For Dummies®	by Bob LeVitus	ISBN: 1-56884-197-3	$19.95 USA/$26.95 Canada
MORE Macs® For Dummies®	by David Pogue	ISBN: 1-56884-087-X	$19.95 USA/$26.95 Canada
PageMaker 5 For Macs® For Dummies®	by Galen Gruman & Deke McClelland	ISBN: 1-56884-178-7	$19.95 USA/$26.95 Canada
QuarkXPress 3.3 For Dummies®	by Galen Gruman & Barbara Assadi	ISBN: 1-56884-217-1	$19.99 USA/$26.99 Canada
Upgrading and Fixing Macs® For Dummies®	by Kearney Rietmann & Frank Higgins	ISBN: 1-56884-189-2	$19.95 USA/$26.95 Canada

MULTIMEDIA

Multimedia & CD-ROMs For Dummies,® 2nd Edition	by Andy Rathbone	ISBN: 1-56884-907-9	$19.99 USA/$26.99 Canada
Multimedia & CD-ROMs For Dummies,® Interactive Multimedia Value Pack, 2nd Edition	by Andy Rathbone	ISBN: 1-56884-909-5	$29.99 USA/$39.99 Canada

OPERATING SYSTEMS:

DOS

MORE DOS For Dummies®	by Dan Gookin	ISBN: 1-56884-046-2	$19.95 USA/$26.95 Canada
OS/2® Warp For Dummies,® 2nd Edition	by Andy Rathbone	ISBN: 1-56884-205-8	$19.99 USA/$26.99 Canada

UNIX

MORE UNIX® For Dummies®	by John R. Levine & Margaret Levine Young	ISBN: 1-56884-361-5	$19.99 USA/$26.99 Canada
UNIX® For Dummies®	by John R. Levine & Margaret Levine Young	ISBN: 1-878058-58-4	$19.95 USA/$26.95 Canada

WINDOWS

MORE Windows® For Dummies,® 2nd Edition	by Andy Rathbone	ISBN: 1-56884-048-9	$19.95 USA/$26.95 Canada
Windows® 95 For Dummies®	by Andy Rathbone	ISBN: 1-56884-240-6	$19.99 USA/$26.99 Canada

PCS/HARDWARE

Illustrated Computer Dictionary For Dummies,® 2nd Edition	by Dan Gookin & Wallace Wang	ISBN: 1-56884-218-X	$12.95 USA/$16.95 Canada
Upgrading and Fixing PCs For Dummies,® 2nd Edition	by Andy Rathbone	ISBN: 1-56884-903-6	$19.99 USA/$26.99 Canada

PRESENTATION/AUTOCAD

AutoCAD For Dummies®	by Bud Smith	ISBN: 1-56884-191-4	$19.95 USA/$26.95 Canada
PowerPoint 4 For Windows® For Dummies®	by Doug Lowe	ISBN: 1-56884-161-2	$16.99 USA/$22.99 Canada

PROGRAMMING

Borland C++ For Dummies®	by Michael Hyman	ISBN: 1-56884-162-0	$19.95 USA/$26.95 Canada
C For Dummies,® Volume 1	by Dan Gookin	ISBN: 1-878058-78-9	$19.95 USA/$26.95 Canada
C++ For Dummies®	by Stephen R. Davis	ISBN: 1-56884-163-9	$19.95 USA/$26.95 Canada
Delphi Programming For Dummies®	by Neil Rubenking	ISBN: 1-56884-200-7	$19.99 USA/$26.99 Canada
Mac® Programming For Dummies®	by Dan Parks Sydow	ISBN: 1-56884-173-6	$19.95 USA/$26.95 Canada
PowerBuilder 4 Programming For Dummies®	by Ted Coombs & Jason Coombs	ISBN: 1-56884-325-9	$19.99 USA/$26.99 Canada
QBasic Programming For Dummies®	by Douglas Hergert	ISBN: 1-56884-093-4	$19.95 USA/$26.95 Canada
Visual Basic 3 For Dummies®	by Wallace Wang	ISBN: 1-56884-076-4	$19.95 USA/$26.95 Canada
Visual Basic "X" For Dummies®	by Wallace Wang	ISBN: 1-56884-230-9	$19.99 USA/$26.99 Canada
Visual C++ 2 For Dummies®	by Michael Hyman & Bob Arnson	ISBN: 1-56884-328-3	$19.99 USA/$26.99 Canada
Windows® 95 Programming For Dummies®	by S. Randy Davis	ISBN: 1-56884-327-5	$19.99 USA/$26.99 Canada

SPREADSHEET

1-2-3 For Dummies®	by Greg Harvey	ISBN: 1-878058-60-6	$16.95 USA/$22.95 Canada
1-2-3 For Windows® 5 For Dummies,® 2nd Edition	by John Walkenbach	ISBN: 1-56884-216-3	$16.95 USA/$22.95 Canada
Excel 5 For Macs® For Dummies®	by Greg Harvey	ISBN: 1-56884-186-8	$19.95 USA/$26.95 Canada
Excel For Dummies,® 2nd Edition	by Greg Harvey	ISBN: 1-56884-050-0	$16.95 USA/$22.95 Canada
MORE 1-2-3 For DOS For Dummies®	by John Weingarten	ISBN: 1-56884-224-4	$19.99 USA/$26.99 Canada
MORE Excel 5 For Windows® For Dummies®	by Greg Harvey	ISBN: 1-56884-207-4	$19.95 USA/$26.95 Canada
Quattro Pro 6 For Windows® For Dummies®	by John Walkenbach	ISBN: 1-56884-174-4	$19.95 USA/$26.95 Canada
Quattro Pro For DOS For Dummies®	by John Walkenbach	ISBN: 1-56884-023-3	$16.95 USA/$22.95 Canada

UTILITIES

Norton Utilities 8 For Dummies®	by Beth Slick	ISBN: 1-56884-166-3	$19.95 USA/$26.95 Canada

VCRS/CAMCORDERS

VCRs & Camcorders For Dummies™	by Gordon McComb & Andy Rathbone	ISBN: 1-56884-229-5	$14.99 USA/$20.99 Canada

WORD PROCESSING

Ami Pro For Dummies®	by Jim Meade	ISBN: 1-56884-049-7	$19.95 USA/$26.95 Canada
MORE Word For Windows® 6 For Dummies®	by Doug Lowe	ISBN: 1-56884-165-5	$19.95 USA/$26.95 Canada
MORE WordPerfect® 6 For Windows® For Dummies®	by Margaret Levine Young & David C. Kay	ISBN: 1-56884-206-6	$19.95 USA/$26.95 Canada
MORE WordPerfect® 6 For DOS For Dummies®	by Wallace Wang, edited by Dan Gookin	ISBN: 1-56884-047-0	$19.95 USA/$26.95 Canada
Word 6 For Macs® For Dummies®	by Dan Gookin	ISBN: 1-56884-190-6	$19.95 USA/$26.95 Canada
Word For Windows® 6 For Dummies®	by Dan Gookin	ISBN: 1-56884-075-6	$16.95 USA/$22.95 Canada
Word For Windows® For Dummies®	by Dan Gookin & Ray Werner	ISBN: 1-878058-86-X	$16.95 USA/$22.95 Canada
WordPerfect® 6 For DOS For Dummies®	by Dan Gookin	ISBN: 1-878058-77-0	$16.95 USA/$22.95 Canada
WordPerfect® 6.1 For Windows® For Dummies,® 2nd Edition	by Margaret Levine Young & David Kay	ISBN: 1-56884-243-0	$16.95 USA/$22.95 Canada
WordPerfect® For Dummies®	by Dan Gookin	ISBN: 1-878058-52-5	$16.95 USA/$22.95 Canada

For scholastic requests & educational orders please call Educational Sales at 1. 800. 434. 2086

FOR MORE INFO OR TO ORDER, PLEASE CALL ▶ 800. 762. 2974

For volume discounts & special orders please call Corporate Sales, at 415. 655. 3000

Fun, Fast, & Cheap!™

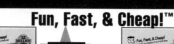

7/29/9

NEW!

The Internet For Macs® For Dummies® Quick Reference
by Charles Seiter

ISBN:1-56884-967-2
$9.99 USA/$12.99 Canada

NEW!

Windows® 95 For Dummies® Quick Reference
by Greg Harvey

ISBN: 1-56884-964-8
$9.99 USA/$12.99 Canada

SUPER STAR

Photoshop 3 For Macs® For Dummies® Quick Reference
by Deke McClelland

ISBN: 1-56884-968-0
$9.99 USA/$12.99 Canada

SUPER STAR

WordPerfect® For DOS For Dummies® Quick Reference
by Greg Harvey

ISBN: 1-56884-009-8
$8.95 USA/$12.95 Canada

Title	Author	ISBN	Price
DATABASE			
Access 2 For Dummies® Quick Reference	by Stuart J. Stuple	ISBN: 1-56884-167-1	$8.95 USA/$11.95 Canada
dBASE 5 For DOS For Dummies® Quick Reference	by Barrie Sosinsky	ISBN: 1-56884-954-0	$9.99 USA/$12.99 Canada
dBASE 5 For Windows® For Dummies® Quick Reference	by Stuart J. Stuple	ISBN: 1-56884-953-2	$9.99 USA/$12.99 Canada
Paradox 5 For Windows® For Dummies® Quick Reference	by Scott Palmer	ISBN: 1-56884-960-5	$9.99 USA/$12.99 Canada
DESKTOP PUBLISHING/ILLUSTRATION/GRAPHICS			
CorelDRAW! 5 For Dummies® Quick Reference	by Raymond E. Werner	ISBN: 1-56884-952-4	$9.99 USA/$12.99 Canada
Harvard Graphics For Windows® For Dummies® Quick Reference	by Raymond E. Werner	ISBN: 1-56884-962-1	$9.99 USA/$12.99 Canada
Photoshop 3 For Macs® For Dummies® Quick Reference	by Deke McClelland	ISBN: 1-56884-968-0	$9.99 USA/$12.99 Canada
FINANCE/PERSONAL FINANCE			
Quicken 4 For Windows® For Dummies® Quick Reference	by Stephen L. Nelson	ISBN: 1-56884-950-8	$9.95 USA/$12.95 Canada
GROUPWARE/INTEGRATED			
Microsoft® Office 4 For Windows® For Dummies® Quick Reference	by Doug Lowe	ISBN: 1-56884-958-3	$9.99 USA/$12.99 Canada
Microsoft® Works 3 For Windows® For Dummies® Quick Reference	by Michael Partington	ISBN: 1-56884-959-1	$9.99 USA/$12.99 Canada
INTERNET/COMMUNICATIONS/NETWORKING			
The Internet For Dummies® Quick Reference	by John R. Levine & Margaret Levine Young	ISBN: 1-56884-168-X	$8.95 USA/$11.95 Canada
MACINTOSH			
Macintosh® System 7.5 For Dummies® Quick Reference	by Stuart J. Stuple	ISBN: 1-56884-956-7	$9.99 USA/$12.99 Canada
OPERATING SYSTEMS:			
DOS			
DOS For Dummies® Quick Reference	by Greg Harvey	ISBN: 1-56884-007-1	$8.95 USA/$11.95 Canada
UNIX			
UNIX® For Dummies® Quick Reference	by John R. Levine & Margaret Levine Young	ISBN: 1-56884-094-2	$8.95 USA/$11.95 Canada
WINDOWS			
Windows® 3.1 For Dummies® Quick Reference, 2nd Edition	by Greg Harvey	ISBN: 1-56884-951-6	$8.95 USA/$11.95 Canada
PCs/HARDWARE			
Memory Management For Dummies® Quick Reference	by Doug Lowe	ISBN: 1-56884-362-3	$9.99 USA/$12.99 Canada
PRESENTATION/AUTOCAD			
AutoCAD For Dummies® Quick Reference	by Ellen Finkelstein	ISBN: 1-56884-198-1	$9.95 USA/$12.95 Canada
SPREADSHEET			
1-2-3 For Dummies® Quick Reference	by John Walkenbach	ISBN: 1-56884-027-6	$8.95 USA/$11.95 Canada
1-2-3 For Windows® 5 For Dummies® Quick Reference	by John Walkenbach	ISBN: 1-56884-957-5	$9.99 USA/$12.95 Canada
Excel For Windows® For Dummies® Quick Reference, 2nd Edition	by John Walkenbach	ISBN: 1-56884-096-9	$8.95 USA/$11.95 Canada
Quattro Pro 6 For Windows® For Dummies® Quick Reference	by Stuart J. Stuple	ISBN: 1-56884-172-8	$9.95 USA/$12.95 Canada
WORD PROCESSING			
Word For Windows® 6 For Dummies® Quick Reference	by George Lynch	ISBN: 1-56884-095-0	$8.95 USA/$11.95 Canada
Word For Windows® For Dummies® Quick Reference	by George Lynch	ISBN: 1-56884-029-2	$8.95 USA/$11.95 Canada
WordPerfect® 6.1 For Windows® For Dummies® Quick Reference, 2nd Edition	by Greg Harvey	ISBN: 1-56884-966-4	$9.99 USA/$12.99/Canada

DUMMIES PRESS™ PROGRAMMING BOOKS

7/29/96

COMPUTER BOOK SERIES FROM IDG

For Dummies who want to program...

Delphi Programming For Dummies®
by Neil Rubenking
ISBN: 1-56884-200-7
$19.99 USA/$26.99 Canada

Access Programming For Dummies®
by Rob Krumm
ISBN: 1-56884-091-8
$19.95 USA/$26.95 Canada

TCP/IP For Dummies®
by Marshall Wilensky & Candace Leiden
ISBN: 1-56884-241-4
$19.99 USA/$26.99 Canada

HTML For Dummies®
by Ed Tittel & Carl de Cordova
ISBN: 1-56884-330-5
$29.99 USA/$39.99 Canada

Windows® 95 Programming For Dummies®
by S. Randy Davis
ISBN: 1-56884-327-5
$19.99 USA/$26.99 Canada

Mac® Programming For Dummies®
by Dan Parks Sydow
ISBN: 1-56884-173-6
$19.95 USA/$26.95 Canada

PowerBuilder 4 Programming For Dummies®
by Ted Coombs & Jason Coombs
ISBN: 1-56884-325-9
$19.99 USA/$26.99 Canada

Visual Basic 3 For Dummies®
by Wallace Wang
ISBN: 1-56884-076-4
$19.95 USA/$26.95 Canada
Covers version 3.

ISDN For Dummies®
by David Angell
ISBN: 1-56884-331-3
$19.99 USA/$26.99 Canada

Visual C++ "2" For Dummies®
by Michael Hyman & Bob Arnson
ISBN: 1-56884-328-3
$19.99 USA/$26.99 Canada

Borland C++ For Dummies®
by Michael Hyman
ISBN: 1-56884-162-0
$19.95 USA/$26.95 Canada

C For Dummies, Volume I
by Dan Gookin
ISBN: 1-878058-78-9
$19.95 USA/$26.95 Canada

C++ For Dummies®
by Stephen R. Davis
ISBN: 1-56884-163-9
$19.95 USA/$26.95 Canada

QBasic Programming For Dummies®
by Douglas Hergert
ISBN: 1-56884-093-4
$19.95 USA/$26.95 Canada

dBase 5 For Windows® Programming For Dummies®
by Ted Coombs & Jason Coombs
ISBN: 1-56884-215-5
$19.99 USA/$26.99 Canada

Windows is a registered trademark of Microsoft Corporation. Mac is a registered trademark of Apple Computer. Dummies Press, the "...For Dummies Book Series" logo, and the IDG Books Worldwide logos are trademarks, and ----For Dummies, ... For Dummies and the "...For Dummies Computer Book Series" logo are registered trademarks under exclusive license to IDG Books Worldwide, Inc., from International Data Group, Inc.

For scholastic requests & educational orders please call Educational Sales at 1. 800. 434. 2086

FOR MORE INFO OR TO ORDER, PLEASE CALL ▶ 800. 762. 2974

For volume discounts & special orders please call Corporate Sales, at 415. 655. 3000

P C P R E S S

IDG
BOOKS
WORLDWIDE

7/29/96

"A lot easier to use than the book Excel gives you!"

Lisa Schmeckpeper, New Berlin, WI, on PC World Excel 5 For Windows Handbook

**Official Hayes Modem
Communications
Companion**
by Caroline M. Halliday

ISBN: 1-56884-072-1
$29.95 USA/$39.95 Canada
Includes software.

**1,001 Komputer Answers
from Kim Komando**
by Kim Komando

ISBN: 1-56884-460-3
$29.99 USA/$39.99 Canada
Includes software.

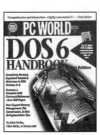

**PC World DOS 6
Handbook, 2nd Edition**
*by John Socha, Clint Hicks, &
Devra Hall*

ISBN: 1-878058-79-7
$34.95 USA/$44.95 Canada
Includes software.

**PC World Word
For Windows® 6 Handbook**
*by Brent Heslop
& David Angell*

ISBN: 1-56884-054-3
$34.95 USA/$44.95 Canada
Includes software.

**PC World Microsoft®
Access 2 Bible,
2nd Edition**
*by Cary N. Prague
& Michael R. Irwin*

ISBN: 1-56884-086-1
$39.95 USA/$52.95 Canada
Includes software.

**PC World Excel 5
For Windows® Handbook,
2nd Edition**
*by John Walkenbach
& Dave Maguiness*

ISBN: 1-56884-056-X
$34.95 USA/$44.95 Canada
Includes software.

**PC World WordPerfect® 6
Handbook**
by Greg Harvey

ISBN: 1-878058-80-0
$34.95 USA/$44.95 Canada
Includes software.

**QuarkXPress
For Windows® Designer
Handbook**
*by Barbara Assadi
& Galen Gruman*

ISBN: 1-878058-45-2
$29.95 USA/$39.95 Canada

**Official XTree
Companion, 3rd Edition**
by Beth Slick

ISBN: 1-878058-57-6
$19.95 USA/$26.95 Canada

**PC World DOS 6
Command Reference
and Problem Solver**
*by John Socha
& Devra Hall*

ISBN: 1-56884-055-1
$24.95 USA/$32.95 Canada

**Client/Server
Strategies™: A Survival
Guide for Corporate
Reengineers**
by David Vaskevitch

ISBN: 1-56884-064-0
$29.95 USA/$39.95 Canada

**"*PC World Word
For Windows 6
Handbook* is very
easy to follow with
lots of 'hands on'
examples. The
'Task at a Glance'
is very helpful!"**

Jacqueline Martens, Tacoma, WA

**"Thanks for publish-
ing this book! It's
the best money I've
spent this year!"**

*Robert D. Templeton,
Ft. Worth, TX, on MORE
Windows 3.1 SECRETS*

For scholastic requests & educational orders please
call Educational Sales at 1. 800. 434. 2086

FOR MORE INFO OR TO ORDER, PLEASE CALL ▶ 800. 762. 2974

For volume discounts & special orders please call
Corporate Sales, at 415. 655. 3000

Macworld® Mac® & Power Mac SECRETS™, 2nd Edition
by David Pogue & Joseph Schorr

This is the definitive Mac reference for those who want to become power users! Includes three disks with 9MB of software!

WINNERS 1994-95
TECHNICAL PUBLICATIONS AND ART COMPETITIONS OF THE SOCIETY FOR TECHNICAL COMMUNICATION

ISBN: 1-56884-175-2
$39.95 USA/$54.95 Canada

Includes 3 disks chock full of software.

NEWBRIDGE BOOK CLUB SELECTION

Macworld® Mac® FAQs™
by David Pogue

Written by the hottest Macintosh author around, David Pogue, *Macworld Mac FAQs* gives users the ultimate Mac reference. Hundreds of Mac questions and answers side-by-side, right at your fingertips, and organized into six easy-to-reference sections with lots of sidebars and diagrams.

ISBN: 1-56884-480-8
$19.99 USA/$26.99 Canada

Macworld® System 7.5 Bible, 3rd Edition
by Lon Poole

ISBN: 1-56884-098-5
$29.95 USA/$39.95 Canada

NATIONAL BESTSELLER!

Macworld® ClarisWorks 3.0 Companion, 3rd Edition
by Steven A. Schwartz

ISBN: 1-56884-481-6
$24.99 USA/$34.99 Canada

NATIONAL BESTSELLER!

Macworld® Complete Mac® Handbook Plus Interactive CD, 3rd Edition
by Jim Heid

BMUG SPRING 1995 CHOICE PRODUCT

ISBN: 1-56884-192-2
$39.95 USA/$54.95 Canada

Includes an interactive CD-ROM.

NEWBRIDGE BOOK CLUB SELECTION

Macworld® Ultimate Mac® CD-ROM
by Jim Heid

ISBN: 1-56884-477-8
$19.99 USA/$26.99 Canada

CD-ROM includes version 2.0 of QuickTime, and over 65 MB of the best shareware, freeware, fonts, sounds, and more!

Macworld® Networking Bible, 2nd Edition
by Dave Kosiur & Joel M. Snyder

ISBN: 1-56884-194-9
$29.95 USA/$39.95 Canada

Macworld® Photoshop 3 Bible, 2nd Edition
by Deke McClelland

ISBN: 1-56884-158-2
$39.95 USA/$54.95 Canada

Includes stunning CD-ROM with add-ons, digitized photos and more.

WINNERS 1994-95
TECHNICAL PUBLICATIONS AND ART COMPETITIONS OF THE SOCIETY FOR TECHNICAL COMMUNICATION

NEW!

Macworld® Photoshop 2.5 Bible
by Deke McClelland

ISBN: 1-56884-022-5
$29.95 USA/$39.95 Canada

NATIONAL BESTSELLER!

Macworld® FreeHand 4 Bible
by Deke McClelland

ISBN: 1-56884-170-1
$29.95 USA/$39.95 Canada

Macworld® Illustrator 5.0/5.5 Bible
by Ted Alspach

ISBN: 1-56884-097-7
$39.95 USA/$54.95 Canada

Includes CD-ROM with QuickTime tutorials.

Mac is a registered trademark of Apple Computer. Macworld is a registered trademark of International Data Group, Inc. ----SECRETS, and ----FAQs are trademarks under exclusive license to IDG Books Worldwide, Inc., from International Data Group, Inc.

For scholastic requests & educational orders please call Educational Sales at 1. 800. 434. 2086

FOR MORE INFO OR TO ORDER, PLEASE CALL ▶ **800. 762. 2974**

For volume discounts & special orders please call Corporate Sales, at 415. 655. 3000

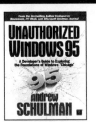

IDG BOOKS WORLDWIDE™

Order Center: **(800) 762-2974** *(8 a.m.–6 p.m., EST, weekdays)*

Quantity	ISBN	Title	Price	Total

Shipping & Handling Charges

	Description	First book	Each additional book	Total
Domestic	Normal	$4.50	$1.50	$
	Two Day Air	$8.50	$2.50	$
	Overnight	$18.00	$3.00	$
International	Surface	$8.00	$8.00	$
	Airmail	$16.00	$16.00	$
	DHL Air	$17.00	$17.00	$

*For large quantities call for shipping & handling charges.
**Prices are subject to change without notice.

Ship to:

Name _____

Company _____

Address _____

City/State/Zip _____

Daytime Phone _____

Payment: ☐ Check to IDG Books Worldwide (US Funds Only)

☐ VISA   ☐ MasterCard   ☐ American Express

Card # _____ Expires _____

Signature _____

Subtotal _____

CA residents add
applicable sales tax _____

IN, MA, and MD
residents add
5% sales tax _____

IL residents add
6.25% sales tax _____

RI residents add
7% sales tax _____

TX residents add
8.25% sales tax _____

Shipping _____

Total _____

Please send this order form to:

IDG Books Worldwide, Inc.
Attn: Order Entry Dept.
7260 Shadeland Station, Suite 100
Indianapolis, IN 46256

Allow up to 3 weeks for delivery.
Thank you!

IDG BOOKS WORLDWIDE REGISTRATION CARD

Visit our Web site at http://www.idgbooks.com

ISBN Number: 0-7645-0102-X

Title of this book: **Photoshop® 4 For Windows® For Dummies®**

My overall rating of this book: ❑ Very good [1] ❑ Good [2] ❑ Satisfactory [3] ❑ Fair [4] ❑ Poor [5]

How I first heard about this book:

❑ Found in bookstore; name: [6]

❑ Advertisement: [8]

❑ Word of mouth; heard about book from friend, co-worker, etc.: [10]

❑ Book review: [7]

❑ Catalog: [9]

❑ Other: [11]

What I liked most about this book:

What I would change, add, delete, etc., in future editions of this book:

Other comments:

Number of computer books I purchase in a year: ❑ 1 [12] ❑ 2-5 [13] ❑ 6-10 [14] ❑ More than 10 [15]

I would characterize my computer skills as: ❑ Beginner [16] ❑ Intermediate [17] ❑ Advanced [18] ❑ Professional [19]

I use ❑ DOS [20] ❑ Windows [21] ❑ OS/2 [22] ❑ Unix [23] ❑ Macintosh [24] ❑ Other: [25]_____

(please specify)

I would be interested in new books on the following subjects:

(please check all that apply, and use the spaces provided to identify specific software)

❑ Word processing: [26]

❑ Data bases: [28]

❑ File Utilities: [30]

❑ Networking: [32]

❑ Other: [34]

❑ Spreadsheets: [27]

❑ Desktop publishing: [29]

❑ Money management: [31]

❑ Programming languages: [33]

I use a PC at (please check all that apply): ❑ home [35] ❑ work [36] ❑ school [37] ❑ other: [38] _____

The disks I prefer to use are ❑ 5.25 [39] ❑ 3.5 [40] ❑ other: [41]_____

I have a CD ROM: ❑ yes [42] ❑ no [43]

I plan to buy or upgrade computer hardware this year: ❑ yes [44] ❑ no [45]

I plan to buy or upgrade computer software this year: ❑ yes [46] ❑ no [47]

Name: _____ Business title: [48] _____ Type of Business: [49] _____

Address (❑ home [50] ❑ work [51]/Company name: _____)

Street/Suite#

City [52]/State [53]/Zip code [54]: _____ Country [55]

❑ **I liked this book!** You may quote me by name in future
IDG Books Worldwide promotional materials.

My daytime phone number is _____

IDG BOOKS
WORLDWIDE
THE WORLD OF
COMPUTER
KNOWLEDGE®

❑ YES!

Please keep me informed about IDG Books Worldwide's World of Computer Knowledge. Send me your latest catalog.

BESTSELLING
BOOK SERIES
FROM IDG